Resurgent As

Advance Praise for *Resurgent Asia*

In this magisterial work, Deepak Nayyar discusses one of the most important socio-economic phenomena in human history - the (re-)rise of Asia since the 1950s. Based on a deep understanding of history, Nayyar provides a most profound analysis of this momentous event and a most thoughtful contemplation of the future of the region - and the world. His analysis is panoramic in scope but never loses sight of the diversity of the process and is always concerned with the welfare of real people. A singular achievement.

HA-JOON CHANG
University of Cambridge
Author of *Kicking Away the Ladder* and *Economics: The User's Guide*

The decades since the end of the Second World War have seen the remarkable resurgence of the role of Asia in the world economy after centuries of subordination to the West. In this book Deepak Nayyar provides a brilliant overview of this process and its historical antecedents, with a masterly deployment of the relevant statistics and a wealth of sharp analytical insights. The incisive policy perspectives and critiques highlight the lessons that subsequent latecomers to this process can draw. The succinct analysis of development outcomes in Asia, which could not have been imagined fifty years ago when Gunnar Myrdal published *Asian Drama*, is a fitting tribute to the memory of the great Swedish scholar. It will be a major reference for decades to come.

RONALD FINDLAY
Ragnar Nurkse Professor Emeritus of Economics, Columbia University

In this remarkable book, Deepak Nayyar analyses the economic rise of Asia over the past fifty years, which has restored its historic significance in the world economy to where it was in the mid-nineteenth century. The resurgence of Asia is surprising and puzzling for the global development community, as most Asian countries followed heterodox paths for their rejuvenation. In the 1960s, the East Asian Tigers adopted an export-promotion strategy, instead of the then fashionable import-substitution strategy, to witness an economic transformation described as a miracle. During the 1980s, other Asian economies adopted a pragmatic piecemeal approach, instead of the shock-therapy advocated by the prevalent neoliberal thinking, to make a transition from planned economies to market economies redefining the relationship between governments and markets. The book is a must read for anyone who wants to understand Asia's past, present and future, which could chart paths to prosperity in other parts of the developing world.

JUSTIN YIFU LIN
Dean and Professor, Institute of New Structural Economics,
Peking University, and former chief economist, the World Bank

This is a fascinating book which provides an incisive analysis of the dramatic changes in the economic fortunes of Asia during the last fifty years. It is conscious of history, informed by theory, and grounded in solid knowledge. The author unravels a success story that has defied the pessimism implicit in Gunnar Myrdal's *Asian Drama* and that has refused to be caught in paradigmatic straitjackets. Deepak Nayyar marshalls evidence with care, through the maze of diversity in a vast continent, to develop an understanding in a style that is engaging and accessible for readers. Lessons from experience are drawn for other countries, not to establish an 'Asian Model', but to signal diversity, complexity, experimentation and context-specificity, while highlighting real 'fundamentals' of development. This book is essential reading for anyone who wants to understand, and learn from, the rise of Asia. I would particularly recommend the book to African readers engaged in the search for a way forward after the blinding decades of neoliberalism.

THANDIKA MKANDAWIRE
Chair and Professor of African Development, London School of Economics

Deepak Nayyar's *Resurgent Asia* is an outstanding analysis of the development of the world's most dynamic economic region over the past five decades. In historical terms, it shows that the strong economic growth and increasing role of Asia in the world economy is in sharp contrast to the 'Great Divergence' generated by imperialism since the early nineteenth century. In sharp contrast with orthodox views, it argues that Asia's success was associated with a strategic rather than a passive integration into the world economy, in which sensible industrial policies implemented by effective governments played the critical role. It also presents an excellent view of diversity of development experiences in different sub-regions and countries, and a social pattern in which massive poverty reduction was accompanied by rising inequality within and among countries. It is a must read for development analysts and practitioners, but also for economic historians of the contemporary world.

JOSE ANTONIO OCAMPO
Member of the Board of the Central Bank of Colombia, Chair of the
United Nations' Committee for Development Policy and
Professor at Columbia University

Gunnar Myrdal was famously wrong in his economic prognosis for Asia. Asian growth miracles have come in waves since the end of the Second World War, with each wave largely a surprise to the rest of the world. Japan was first in the 1950s, followed by the Gang of Four (South Korea, Taiwan, Singapore, Hong Kong) in the 1960s and 1970s, Malaysia, Thailand, and Indonesia after the 1970s, China since the 1980s, Vietnam and India since the 1990s. Their experiences have often been analyzed through a lens that reflects the analyst's predilections instead of the reality on the ground. Deepak Nayyar's non-ideological, no-nonsense account avoids the common pitfalls and draws a comprehensive picture of the continent's economic development. It provides a unified interpretation informed by a broad theoretical perspective, while doing justice to the diversity of the Asian experience.

DANI RODRIK
Professor of International Political Economy, Harvard University

In an impressive, wide-ranging and penetrating account, this book records and analyses the Asian Drama of the last fifty years. Deepak Nayyar's ambitious and exciting book examines the remarkable transformation of the continent, from its marginal significance in the global economy to a situation where it accounts for almost a third of world output, and from abysmally low health, education and income levels, to a situation where human development is converging to levels achieved in developed countries and income levels are converging towards the world average. The author points to differences as well as similarities in political conditions and economic performance across countries in Asia, to recognize diversity and analyse success. The book explains why the twenty-first century might be termed 'the Asian century', following two centuries of underdevelopment which was largely due to structures and policies imposed by Western colonialism.

FRANCES STEWART
Emeritus Professor of Development Economics, University of Oxford

The last fifty years have constituted a significant historical time-marker for Asia. Countries ceased to be colonies of Europe or Japan and became independent nations. The economic basis of the transformative change since then is admirably analyzed in this book with lucid explanations and persuasive arguments. This would be comprehensible even to non-economists and other social scientists, such as sociologists, contemporary historians, commentators on politics, as well as general interested readers. What makes the book even more perceptive are the passing pointers to parallel concerns emanating from a variety of nationalisms affecting politics and democratic institutions, as also the imprint of change in social habits and cultural articulations.

ROMILA THAPAR
Professor Emeritus of History, Jawaharlal Nehru University

UNU World Institute for Development Economics Research (UNU-WIDER) was established by the United Nations University as its first research and training centre and started work in Helsinki, Finland, in 1985. The mandate of the institute is to undertake applied research and policy analysis on structural changes affecting developing and transitional economies, to provide a forum for the advocacy of policies leading to robust, equitable, and environmentally sustainable growth, and to promote capacity strengthening and training in the field of economic and social policymaking. Its work is carried out by staff researchers and visiting scholars in Helsinki and via networks of collaborating scholars and institutions around the world.

United Nations University World Institute for Development Economics Research
(UNU-WIDER)
Katajanokanlaituri 6B, 00160 Helsinki, Finland
www.wider.unu.edu

Resurgent Asia

Diversity In Development

DEEPAK NAYYAR

A study prepared by the United Nations University World Institute
for Development Economics Research (UNU-WIDER)

OXFORD
UNIVERSITY PRESS

OXFORD
UNIVERSITY PRESS

Great Clarendon Street, Oxford, OX2 6DP,
United Kingdom

Oxford University Press is a department of the University of Oxford.
It furthers the University's objective of excellence in research, scholarship,
and education by publishing worldwide. Oxford is a registered trade mark of
Oxford University Press in the UK and in certain other countries

Published in the United States of America by Oxford University Press
198 Madison Avenue, New York, NY 10016, United States of America

British Library Cataloguing in Publication Data
Data available

Library of Congress Control Number: 2019909293

ISBN 978-0-19-884951-3

DOI: 10.1093/oso/9780198849513.001.0001

Printed and bound in Great Britain by
Clays Ltd, Elcograf S.p.A.

Links to third party websites are provided by Oxford in good faith and
for information only. Oxford disclaims any responsibility for the materials
contained in any third party website referenced in this work.

For
Rohini, Dhiraj, and Gaurav

Foreword

Asian Drama: An Inquiry into the Poverty of Nations, Gunnar Myrdal's magnum opus, was published in 1968. It would be an understatement to say that Myrdal was negative about Asia and the region's development possibilities. However, the half-century since the publication of Asian Drama has seen the most astonishing social and economic transformation in Asia, a transformation that would have been difficult for Myrdal to envisage, let alone predict, at the time of authoring his tome. Thus, as I was taking over the directorship of UNU-WIDER, I was very excited to learn that Deepak Nayyar—a former Chair of the UNU-WIDER Advisory Board—was working on a study, in two volumes, to analyse the process of economic development and social progress in Asia since the publication of Asian Drama by Gunnar Myrdal.

Resurgent Asia: Diversity in Development provides a valuable complement to the comprehensive work Deepak and his project team—an esteemed group of economists and scholars—carried out in researching and producing the edited companion volume, *Asian Transformations: An Inquiry into the Development of Nations*. In this authored book, Deepak tells an engaging and fascinating story of progress and economic development in Asia, and contemplates what the future could hold for the region.

I would like to sincerely thank Deepak for what I can only describe as his labour, for no other word would be adequate. The phenomenal work and endless hours he has dedicated to this research has culminated in this very prolific academic inquiry for others to read, explore, ponder, and even enjoy.

UNU-WIDER gratefully acknowledges the support and financial contributions to its research programme by the governments of Finland, Sweden, in this case particularly the Swedish International Development Cooperation Agency – Sida, and the United Kingdom. Without this vital funding our research and policy advisory work would be impossible.

Kunal Sen
Director, UNU-WIDER

Helsinki
April 2019

Preface

At the outset, I would like to thank UNU-WIDER for their support, without which this study would not have been possible. I am particularly indebted to Finn Tarp, the then Director, for his acceptance of the idea and his commitment to what seemed an exceedingly difficult task at the time. Kunal Sen, the Director now, has been just as enthusiastic and supportive. Tony Addison, the Deputy Director, has been engaged with the study from the beginning and contributed with his perceptive and interesting ideas. I owe a special word of thanks to the staff at UNU-WIDER in Helsinki, who lent wonderful support for two years even though I lived in faraway New Delhi. Janis Vehmaan-Kreula, the project secretary, provided solid administrative support, with complete dedication, through the life cycle of this study and its companion volume. Lorraine Telfer-Taivainen, super efficient at whatever she does, helped in so many ways, with an initiative that is commendable and a response time that is incredible.

Let me turn the clock back fifty years, when I was a very young graduate student in Oxford, to record my intellectual debt to Paul Streeten, who was my supervisor and mentor as a doctoral student. He brought home to me the importance of questioning conventional wisdom and the significance of the heterodox or unorthodox in economics, particularly in thinking about development. This association exercised a profound influence on me in times to come and it was the beginning of our lifelong friendship. Given his close association with Gunnar Myrdal and *Asian Drama*, I had hoped to discuss this study with Paul in early 2018, soon after he turned 100, but by then he was too frail for such a conversation. Sadly, he passed away in early 2019. This book would have given him immense joy. Alas, it was not to be.

Such academic pursuits are always associated with an accumulation of intellectual debts to professional colleagues. For thoughtful questions, helpful comments, and constructive suggestions, I am deeply indebted to Ha-Joon Chang, Ronald Findlay, and Jose Antonio Ocampo, who read the entire manuscript from beginning to end as it was being written. For engaging questions and valuable comments, I am similarly indebted to Romila Thapar, the distinguished historian, who found the time and made the effort to read the whole manuscript, providing the reality-check that economists need. Gaurav Nayyar, from the next generation of economists, also read the entire manuscript, as it was being written, to ask perceptive questions and make valuable suggestions. For stimulating conversations, engaging discussion and innovative ideas, on some of the themes developed in this book, I would like to thank Joseph Stiglitz and Lance Taylor.

Some colleagues and friends—Amit Bhaduri, Prasenjit Duara, Padmanabha Gopinath, Sudipto Mundle, Anil Seal, Frances Stewart, and Peter Timmer—read a particular chapter that was of interest to them, to provide helpful comments. My discussion with contributors to the companion volume at different stages of the study, and in an informal brainstorming session during the second workshop of authors, at Shanghai in June 2018, to discuss the drafts of papers written for the companion volume, also provided valuable inputs for this study. I recall suggestions and ideas from Kaushik Basu, Amit Bhaduri, Prasenjit Duara, Rolph van der Hoeven, Ravi Kanbur, Mushtaq Khan, Justin Lin, Manuel Montes, Sudipto Mundle, Siddiqur Osmani, Frances Stewart, Finn Tarp, Peter Timmer, Rob Vos, Robert Wade and Guanghua Wan.

There were many who helped me in the research process. Rana Hasan and Gaurav Nayyar helped in my search for information and sources. Ananya Ghosh-Dastidar assisted with work on historical statistics. I am most grateful to Rajeev Malhotra, who worked as my principal assistant on the project with a strong commitment that is worthy of praise. He provided valuable assistance whenever, and in whatever form, it was needed. He also read several chapters and made useful suggestions. It was multi-tasking in every sense of the word. Given his own academic obligations, it was gracious of him to find the time for these tasks. I would especially like to thank my research assistant for this study, Atul Sanganeria, who was conscientious, meticulous, and efficient. The compiling of statistical information for this study, from diverse primary sources, was both painstaking and challenging. In this process, which was demanding in terms of both time and deadlines, his perseverance and patience were admirable. I would also like to thank K.K. Popli, who has been my secretary for more than three decades, for his superb support in everything he does. I owe him a debt of gratitude.

It is difficult for me to find the words to describe the fantastic support from my family over the past two years in which this study was my life. I recall conversations with my elder son, Dhiraj, about the nature of politics in India and elsewhere in the world, or even the best restaurants and travel destinations, just to unwind and getaway from thinking about the book. It was a particularly difficult period for my wife, Rohini, who was immobilized for much of the time, as a consequence of two accidents. Her patience and courage during this period of recovery and convalescence was an inspiration. In addition to her own health problems, she had to put up with an obsessive, sometimes difficult, man. Even so, she has waited patiently for my return from an emotional exile, sequestered in my study for almost twelve hours everyday, during the past six months. And she has been an incredible source of strength in the hours of frustration and moments of despair that are an integral part of the lives of authors. I hope that she will enjoy reading the book. It will be the first that she has not read while it was being written.

Deepak Nayyar

New Delhi
March 2019

Contents

List of figures

List of tables

Prologue

Gunnar Myrdal published his magnum opus, *Asian Drama: An Inquiry into the Poverty of Nations*, in 1968. At the time, I was a graduate student in economics at Oxford. It was a subject of conversation among students outside the classroom. It was brought up in questions at seminars about development. It led to animated discussion in the lively common room at Balliol College. It was also written about. The book made a splash. I walked across to Blackwell's next door and bought the three volumes, at twenty-five shillings (GB£1.25) each, for what was then a princely sum. And I read it, all 2300 pages, over the next six months. The primary motivation was that so much of the book was about India. But, in late 1968, after a tumultuous summer in Europe, it was also fashionable to be unfashionable in economics. Myrdal was critical of mainstream economics. It also coincided with the beginnings of change in my own thinking about development. Orthodox trade theory, which I had been immersed in, was no longer an exciting prospect. I had decided to work on India for my doctoral dissertation. Paul Streeten, who had had just returned to Oxford, agreed to supervise my research. Streeten and Myrdal were good friends who had worked closely with each other. It was sheer coincidence that I met Gunnar Myrdal at dinner in Paul Streeten's home. To be honest, I was overawed, for Myrdal had a reputation of being totally absorbed in his work, which was his life. But he was relaxed while chatting over dinner, to my relief not about India. He propounded a counter-intuitive thesis that one should expect young people to be conservative and to become more radical as they grow older. My intuitive belief, then, was the exact opposite. It was difficult to resist the temptation of getting into an argument. Fortunately, the wit and charm of Thomas Balogh, among the guests at dinner, came to my rescue.

Memories faded and life moved on. Even so, *Asian Drama* made a lasting impression, as it made me reflect on ideas in development and question conventional wisdom. It led me to revisit the book in bits-and-pieces from time to time. The three volumes that I bought in Oxford still adorn the bookshelves in my study. In September 2016, I was browsing through Appendix 3 on economic models, which was written by Paul Streeten who had been part of the Myrdal team. And it struck me that, in 2018, it will be fifty years since the book was published. Of course, the decades since then have witnessed a phenomenal economic transformation in Asia in a rapidly changing world. I thought that a study, which analyses the story of economic development in Asia, over this span of

Resurgent Asia: Diversity in Development. Deepak Nayyar, Oxford University Press (2019). © United Nations University World Institute for Development Economics Research. DOI: 10.1093/oso/9780198849513.001.0001

half a century, would be a wonderful idea. Further reflection led me to recognize that, for an individual scholar without any institutional support, this would be an exceedingly difficult task. It occurred to me that UNU-WIDER, located in the Nordic world, not far from Stockholm, with its focus on development would be the perfect institutional base for such a study. So I mentioned this adventurous idea to Finn Tarp, the then Director of WIDER. He said that he would think about it and explore possibilities. Barely two months later, he was in touch with me to say that WIDER would like to collaborate on such a study. It is how this book began life.

The motivation ran deeper than the coincidence in my study. The most obvious reason was that, over the past fifty years, Asia had experienced a profound transformation in terms of the economic progress of nations and living conditions of people, even if it had been uneven across countries and unequal among people. Yet, five decades ago, such change would have been thought of as imagination running wild. Indeed, at the time, the economic prospects of Asia were perceived as dim by most observers and analysts. In this sentiment, Myrdal and his associates were by no means alone in their pessimism about Asia. Of course, perfect foresight exists only as an abstraction in economic theory. But the benefit of hindsight does provide a good reason for an inquiry into the development of nations.

There was a second important reason. The story of economic change and social progress in Asia is part of a momentous ongoing shift in world economic history, which has interested me for some time (Nayyar, 2013). It is perhaps instructive to invoke a historical fact here. Until around 1750, Asia accounted for almost three-fifths of world population and world income, while China and India together accounted for about one-half of world population and world income. These two Asian giants also contributed 57 per cent of manufacturing production and an even larger proportion of manufactured exports in the world. The Industrial Revolution in Britain brought about a radical transformation of the situation over the next two centuries culminating in the decline and fall of Asia during the period from 1820 to 1950. The solitary exception was Japan after the Meiji Restoration in 1868. The second half of the twentieth century witnessed the beginnings of change once again. It began with the East Asian Tigers—South Korea, Taiwan, Hong Kong, and Singapore—in the early 1970s. Some Southeast Asian countries—Malaysia, Thailand, and Indonesia—followed in their footsteps in the late 1980s. China and India came next. Rapid economic growth, led by industrialization, has enabled Asia to narrow the gap. This needs to be explained and analysed.

The third reason was that, for far too long, the economic history of the world has been written largely in the West from an essentially European perspective. This motivated me to write *Catch Up*, which analysed the historical evolution of Asia, Africa, and Latin America in the world economy. Similarly, even in the post-colonial era, while there is a wealth of country-specific studies, studies spanning

Asia are rare. Myrdal's *Asian Drama*, too, was written from a European perspective, even if it was through a Nordic lens. It is, perhaps, time for such a study from an Asian perspective.

It needs to be said that *Asian Drama* is no more than a point of entry or reference for the study, which is not meant to be a sequel. It is hoped that that this work will have an identity of its own. Clearly, a study in three volumes was just not feasible. A stand-alone single book would have been an exceedingly difficult, if not impossible task, not only because its length would have become abominable but also because it could not have had the depth in particular domains that some readers might search for. After much deliberation, I chose the middle path of two volumes. The companion volume, *Asian Transformations: An Inquiry into the Development of Nations*, conceptualized and edited by me, comprises specialized in-depth studies by economists and social scientists who are among the best in their respective domains. It sets the stage with a focus on Gunnar Myrdal and *Asian Drama* in retrospect, which is followed by cross-country thematic studies, country studies and sub-region studies, analysing the past fifty years to reflect briefly on the next twenty-five years. It stands by itself as a study. Even so, while necessary, it might not suffice because it cannot provide a unified and integrated picture. The opening chapter by the editor, *inter alia*, presents a synthesis of themes and lessons that emerge, which is at best an overview. It is the *raison d'être* for this separate book by me, which seeks to provide a cohesive narrative and analysis of the Asian development experience. This also stands by itself as a study. Thus, the two books are best described as companion volumes that are complements rather than substitutes.

Gunnar Myrdal was a man of many parts. The word 'polymath' is an apt description, which might not suffice to describe a man who was a distinguished academic, policy practitioner, member of parliament, cabinet minister, international civil servant, political actor, public intellectual and concerned citizen. He is clearly a difficult act to follow. The enormity and diversity of Asia accentuates the problem. As if that were not enough, this study had to be completed in two years, compared with the luxury of ten years that Myrdal had. Even so, I mustered the courage, as our approaches have something in common, starting from the premise that economic problems cannot be studied in isolation but must be situated in their wider historical, social, and political context. For some time now, my own work has attempted to consider theory and policy in economics from a heterodox perspective, just as it has explored some intersections of economics and history, or economics and politics.

It was always an ambitious, if not daunting, task to write a book that spans such a diverse continent in space and five decades or more in time, to engage with so many contemporary debates in economics about development. Yet, I decided to take the plunge two years ago. The research turned out to be a journey in exploration and discovery. This book is the outcome. There is no such study yet. It is perhaps the first to address this vast theme on such a broad spectrum. It is about the big picture that is sketched with bold strokes on a wide canvas. And it is not about joining the little dots. It recognizes that there are different theoretical and ideological perspectives, often polar opposites, which invoke the Asian development experience in support of their hypothesis. This book is also written for scholars and readers, who wish to make up their own minds about what explains the story of development in Asia.

The object of this book is to analyse the phenomenal transformation of Asia, which would have been difficult to imagine, let alone predict, fifty years ago. In doing so, it provides an analytical narrative of this remarkable story of economic development, situated in historical perspective, and an economic analysis of the underlying factors, with a focus on critical issues in the process of, and outcomes in, development. The book considers differences in initial conditions, highlights turning points in economic performance, assesses how processes of change were managed or mismanaged, discusses the influence of development strategies and economic reforms, examines changes in engagement with the world economy, explores the role of governments and politics, and analyses the factors underlying successes, failures, or mixed-outcomes in development. There are also lessons that can be drawn from the Asian experience, which might help in thinking about its economic prospects, and suggest possibilities for countries elsewhere in the developing world. In this half century, the world has changed almost beyond recognition. Thus, the study also reflects, even if briefly, on how the next twenty-five years might unfold in Asia.

Given the size and the diversity of the Asian continent, the aggregate level is not always appropriate. Thus, the study disaggregates Asia into its four constituent sub-regions, and further into fourteen selected economies: China, South Korea, and Taiwan in East Asia; Indonesia, Malaysia, Philippines, Singapore, Thailand, and Vietnam in Southeast Asia; Bangladesh, India, Pakistan, and Sri Lanka in South Asia; and Turkey in West Asia. These countries, described as the Asian-14, account for more than four-fifths of the population and income of Asia. It needs to be said that West Asia is not considered in the same depth as the other sub-regions, partly because its oil-exporting economies are natural resource-based economies that are very different from the rest of Asia. Central Asia is not included in the study, essentially because its constituent countries were part of the erstwhile USSR for half the fifty-year-period. All the same, this coverage is far greater, as compared with *Asian Drama*, which sought to focus primarily on India, Pakistan, and Ceylon, the sub-region described as South Asia. It paid some attention to Burma and Indonesia, while Malaysia, Philippines, and Thailand were grouped together as the rest of Southeast Asia, with occasional references to Cambodia, Laos, and South Vietnam.

The structure of the book, a roadmap for the reader, is as follows. Chapter 1 provides a historical perspective on Asia in the world economy with a focus on the colonial era, and sketches a profile of the prevalent initial conditions in the early post-colonial era, to set the stage for the book. Chapter 2 outlines the broad contours of the story of development in Asia since then, disaggregated into its constituent sub-regions, situated in the wider context of the world economy, to sketch a picture of the transformation in terms of economic progress. Chapter 3 sets out an analytical narrative of the stunning economic growth in Asia, to develop a macroeconomic analysis of growth in the Asian-14. Chapter 4 discusses the process of structural change in Asian countries and their different paths to structural transformation, exploring the relationship with economic growth. Chapter 5 analyses openness and industrialization, which have been centre-stage in the economic transformation of Asia and have been the critical issues in the debates on development. Chapter 6 considers the crucial economic and political roles of governments in Asian development, by analysing the interaction between states and markets in the economic sphere, and exploring the relationship between governments and markets mediated through politics. Chapter 7 examines the unequal outcomes and emerging divergences during this era of rapid growth in Asia, associated with an uneven economic development across countries and an unequal distribution among people within countries. Chapter 8 discusses the evolution of the economic and political relationship between Asia and the world, in retrospect and prospect, to consider the economic implications of their engagement with each other for Asian development and the world economy. Chapter 9 concludes.

This book is the product of research in the academic sense of the word. But it is not written as a conventional academic monograph for specialists. It is accessible to a much wider readership. I am convinced that economics is, and should be, comprehensible to concerned readers who have an interest in the subject. In writing this book, I have attempted to simplify, to explain and to reach out to the reader. It should be of interest to economists, irrespective of their specialization. I also sincerely hope that it would interest scholars across disciplines in the social sciences, just as I hope that it might engage the policy practitioner and the concerned citizen.

In the quest to be reader-friendly, there are no copious footnotes about nuances or esoteric academic debates. There are endnotes which are optional for readers. The tables and graphs, often relating to long periods of time, are based on research from many primary sources. But the citation at the bottom of tables or graphs is short and simple. For research scholars, the details on statistical sources and notes on the compilation methods are set out in an Appendix. In the text, there is an occasional overload of information or a blizzard of numbers because the facts are important and are not widely known. Readers could, if they wish, be selective about statistics. The text is self-sufficient. And it is possible to read the book without studying the tables. The graphs, however, are worthy of attention for they sketch a picture or tell a story.

The essential objectives of this book are to enhance our understanding of development processes and outcomes in Asia over the past fifty years, draw out the analytical conclusions that contribute to contemporary debates on development, highlight some lessons from the Asian experience for countries elsewhere that are latecomers to development, and reflect briefly on Asia's prospects over the next twenty-five years. There are, inevitably, unexplored themes, unsettled issues and unanswered questions. Even so, this book is written in the hope that it will contribute to our understanding of, and stimulate further thinking on, the subject.

1

Historical perspective and initial conditions

This chapter sets the stage before the play begins. In doing so, it constitutes the starting point for an analysis of economic development in, and the dramatic transformation of, Asia over the past fifty years. It is divided into two parts. The first part, constituted by sections 1, 2, and 3, seeks to provide a historical perspective on the decline and fall of Asia in the world economy during the period from the early nineteenth century to the mid-twentieth century. Section 1 examines the sharp plunge in the share of Asia in world income, and compares levels of per capita income in Asia with those in other parts of the world, to trace the widening gap over time and outline the underlying differences in growth rates. Section 2 traces the progressive integration of Asia with the world economy, through trade, investment and migration, which led to a division of labour between Asia and Western Europe that was unequal in its consequences for development. Section 3 outlines the rapid decline in Asia's share of industrial production or manufacturing output in the world economy, to highlight the factors that led to its deindustrialization. The second part, constituted by sections 4, and 5 sets out the initial conditions that characterized Asian economies in the early post-colonial era, when it was the poorest continent in the world. Section 4 sketches a picture of the initial conditions in Asia, *circa* 1965, presenting evidence on selected demographic, social, and economic indicators, which epitomize its underdevelopment at the time. Section 5 discusses how these initial conditions might have been influenced, perhaps even shaped, by history and by the conjuncture at the end of the colonial era.

1. Asia in the world

A long-term historical perspective was largely missing from *Asian Drama* (Myrdal, 1968), which sought to focus on the early post-colonial era in an underdeveloped Asia. Its historical narrative began in the early twentieth century with a global perspective, to suggest that the First World War, the Russian Revolution which led to the rise of the Soviet Union, the Great Depression that was responsible for the economic crisis and conflict in the West, the emergence of Japanese colonialism in East Asia, and the Second World War which led

Resurgent Asia: Diversity in Development. Deepak Nayyar, Oxford University Press (2019). © United Nations University World Institute for Development Economics Research. DOI: 10.1093/oso/9780198849513.001.0001

to Japanese occupation of much of Southeast Asia, taken together, weakened European colonialism to strengthen nationalisms in Asian countries. The essential focus, however, was on the coming of independence and the transfer of power in the erstwhile colonies, in South Asian and Southeast Asian countries that were the object of study. This short digression into history was concerned more with the political implications than with the economic consequences of European colonialism in Asia.[1] It was a largely Western perspective, even if it was through a Nordic lens. It did not quite recognize that the observed backwardness and underdevelopment of Asia might have been a consequence of colonialism, or that Asia and Europe might have been similar in terms of their levels of development in the mid-eighteenth century. Obviously, this historical perspective was not long enough to recognize the overwhelming significance of Asia in the world economy during the first half of the second millennium. Such a long-term historical perspective about Asia and the world economy spanning the second millennium is provided by Findlay (2019).[2] However, the focus of the discussion that follows is on the period from 1820, when the decline and fall of Asia in the world economy began, to 1962, when it reached its nadir.

1.1 Shares in world income and population

The significance of Asia in the world economy is reflected in the changes in its share of income and population in the world. Such an exercise is possible as there are studies by Angus Maddison that provide estimates of long-term changes in world population and world income, dis-aggregated by regions and country-groups, for selected benchmark years.[3] The Maddison estimates of gross domestic product (GDP) are in 1990 international (Geary–Khamis) dollars, in purchasing power parity (PPP) terms, which are used to evaluate output. These calculations are based on a specific method of defining international prices so as to facilitate cross-country comparisons over time.[4] Although these estimates are subject to criticism in the academic literature on economic history,[5] this is about the only source of historical statistics which is widely used. Even so, it is important to recognize these limitations and use other sources wherever possible to provide confirmation.

In the year 1000, Asia accounted for 66 per cent of world population and 68 per cent of world income. Even 500 years ago, in 1500, it accounted for about 62 per cent of both world population and world income. In both years, China and India, taken together, accounted for 50 per cent of world population and world income. The beginnings of change are discernible over the next three centuries. By 1820, the share of Asia in world population returned to 66 per cent but its share of world income dropped to 57 per cent. Yet, China and India together accounted for almost 50 per cent of world income even in 1820 (Nayyar, 2013).

Table 1.1 presents evidence on the share of 'The West' and 'The Rest' in world population and world GDP for selected benchmark years from 1820 to 1962. It needs to be said that these estimates starting from 1820 are far more robust, in terms of their statistical foundations, than the estimates for earlier years cited above, which are indicative numbers rather than precise statistics. Between 1820 and 1962, the share of 'The West' in world income almost doubled from 37 per cent to 73 per cent, and the share of 'The Rest' more than halved from 63 per cent to 27 per cent, of which the share of Asia plummeted from 57 per cent to 15 per cent. This transformation started around 1820. It was discernible by 1870,

Table 1.1 Shares of the West and the Rest in world population and world GDP: 1820–1962

World population

	1820	1870	1900	1913	1940	1950	1962
THE WEST	25.6	32.2	35.8	36.8	35.2	33.0	30.9
Western Europe	12.8	14.7	14.9	14.6	12.8	12.1	10.6
Western Offshoots	1.1	3.6	5.5	6.2	6.7	7.0	7.0
Eastern Europe	3.5	4.2	4.5	4.4	4.1	3.5	3.2
Former USSR	5.3	7.0	8.0	8.7	8.5	7.1	7.1
Japan	3.0	2.7	2.8	2.9	3.2	3.3	3.1
THE REST	74.4	67.8	64.2	63.2	64.8	67.0	69.1
Latin America	2.1	3.2	4.1	4.5	5.7	6.5	7.3
Africa	7.1	7.1	7.0	7.0	8.4	9.0	9.5
Asia (of which)	65.2	57.6	53.0	51.7	50.7	51.5	52.2
China	36.6	28.1	25.6	24.4	22.6	21.6	21.2
India	20.1	19.8	18.2	16.9	16.8	14.2	14.5
Indonesia	2.6	3.0	2.3	1.9	1.7	1.5	1.1

World GDP

	1820	1870	1900	1913	1940	1950	1962
THE WEST	36.9	57.4	67.4	70.4	71.0	72.9	73.4
Western Europe	22.9	33.0	34.2	33.0	29.7	26.2	27.2
Western Offshoots	1.9	10.0	17.6	21.3	23.2	30.7	27.6
Eastern Europe	3.6	4.5	5.2	4.9	4.1	3.5	3.6
Former USSR	5.4	7.5	7.8	8.5	9.3	9.6	10.0
Japan	3.0	2.3	2.6	2.6	4.7	3.0	5.0
THE REST	63.1	42.6	32.6	29.6	29.0	27.1	26.6
Latin America	2.2	2.5	3.6	4.4	5.6	7.8	8.1
Africa	4.5	4.1	3.4	2.9	3.5	3.8	3.5
Asia (of which)	56.5	36.1	25.6	22.3	19.9	15.6	14.9
China	33.0	17.1	11.1	8.8	6.4	4.6	4.0
India	16.1	12.2	8.6	7.5	5.9	4.2	3.8
Indonesia	1.6	1.7	1.6	1.7	1.9	1.2	1.1

Source: Author's calculations from Maddison Online Database, see Appendix.

when the share of 'The West' in world income rose to 57 per cent, and the share of 'The Rest' fell to 43 per cent, while the share of Asia dropped to 36 per cent. The dramatic decline and fall in the relative importance of Asia occurred in just 140 years, which was a short span of time in world history. It was the Asia that Gunnar Myrdal studied in the early 1960s.

These striking changes in shares of world income are broadly consistent with evidence from other sources. Bairoch (1981 and 1983) estimates GNP in selected benchmark years from 1750 to 1950 for two country-groups in the world economy: Asia, Africa, and Latin America; and Europe, North America, and Japan. These estimates are in 1960 US dollars and prices, in PPP terms, adjusted for differences in the purchasing power of currencies. The share of Asia, Africa, and Latin America in world GNP was 69.1 per cent in 1830 and 57.4 per cent in 1860 (somewhat higher than the Maddison estimates of 63.1 per cent in 1820 and 42.6 per cent in 1870). This share dropped sharply to 38.3 per cent in 1900 and 33.5 per cent in 1913 (closer to the Maddison estimates of 32.6 per cent in 1900 and 29.6 per cent in 1913). It was 30.2 per cent in 1928 and 27.5 per cent in 1950 (almost the same as the Maddison estimates of 29 per cent in 1940 and 27.1 per cent in 1950). It would seem that the Bairoch estimates of these shares of 'The Rest' in world income are higher than the corresponding Maddison estimates, particularly during the nineteenth century, but the rise of 'The West' and the decline of 'The Rest' are just as clear (Nayyar, 2013).

In view of the pronounced decline of Asia, it may be misleading to consider 'The Rest' as an aggregate. Figure 1.1a separates Asia, Africa, and Latin America in terms of their shares of world population and world GDP during the period 1820 to 1962. It shows the sharp increase in the asymmetry between Asia's share of world population and world GDP over time, as the former declined slowly while the latter dropped sharply so that the gap between the two shares jumped from a modest 9 percentage points in 1820 to a massive 37 percentage points in 1962.[6] For Africa, the shares in world population and GDP were relatively stable, although the latter was consistently lower. For Latin America, the shares in world population and world GDP were symmetrical throughout and both proportions rose significantly over the period so that the gap between the two shares was minimal while its share in world GDP more than trebled. Indeed, it would seem that Latin America was the success story among 'The Rest' in this era.[7] In sharp contrast, Asia was a story of dismal failure, which was concentrated in the two Asian giants. Between 1820 and 1962, taken together, the share of China and India in world GDP plummeted from 49 per cent to 8 per cent, while their share in world population fell from 57 per cent to 36 per cent. This rapid increase in the asymmetry between their shares in world population and world GDP, from 8 percentage points to 28 percentage points, is clearly depicted in Figure 1.1b. It also shows that for Indonesia—Asia's third largest country—shares in world GDP and population, though small, were broadly symmetrical.

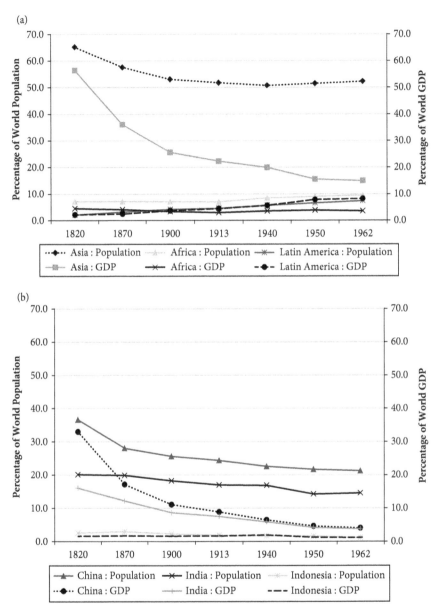

Figure 1.1a Shares of Asia, Africa and Latin America in world GDP and population: 1820–1962, Figure 1.1b Shares of China, India and Indonesia in world GDP and population: 1820–1962

Source: Table 1.1.

1.2 Divergence in per capita incomes

It is most difficult to compare levels of per capita income across countries and regions in the world economy during the first 750 years of the second millennium. The available estimates are at best rough approximations. The Maddison estimates of GDP per capita, in 1990 international (Geary–Khamis) dollars, show that levels of income per capita were about the same across the world 1000 years ago and not significantly different even 500 years ago. Thus, it is no surprise that shares in world population and world income were roughly symmetrical for regions and country-groups (Nayyar, 2013). Average life expectation at birth was also similar everywhere in the world (Maddison, 2001). But this situation changed in the centuries that followed.

The Maddison statistics show that the ratio of income per capita in Asia to that in Western Europe was 1.11 in 1000, 0.74 in 1500, 0.65 in 1600, and 0.58 in 1700. Of course, the comparison often made is that between Western Europe and Asia in the mid-eighteenth century. There are two contesting views. Landes (1969) argues that Western Europe was already rich in comparison with other parts of the world even before the Industrial Revolution, which was attributable to centuries of slow capital accumulation, the appropriation of resources from outside Europe and substantial technological progress. Kuznets (1971) endorsed this view, indirectly, by suggesting that per capita income levels in less developed parts of the world in 1965 were much lower than in Western Europe before industrialization. This hypothesis was supported by Maddison (1983). Such analysis is the basis of the view that, *circa* 1750, income per capita in Western Europe was roughly twice that in Asia. In contrast, Bairoch (1981) shows that, in 1750, the average standard of living as measured by GNP per capita, in the now industrialized countries was slightly lower than that in countries he describes as the Third World.

It is almost impossible to resolve this debate one way or the other, since different assumptions about growth rates and different adjustment factors can and do produce very different results.[8] There is, however, research beyond statistics on income per capita. It suggests that, in the mid-eighteenth century, levels of development in Europe and Asia were broadly similar in terms of demography, technology, and institutions.[9]

Table 1.2 compares GDP per capita in Western Europe and Western Offshoots (United States, Canada, Australia, and New Zealand), taken together, with GDP per capita in other regions and countries of the world during this period that spanned just over 140 years. It reveals a rapidly widening gap, far more pronounced in Asia than elsewhere, which has been described as the 'Great Divergence'. Between 1820 and 1962, as a proportion of GDP per capita in what is now the industrialized world, in approximate terms, GDP per capita in Latin America dropped from three-fifths to one-third, in Africa from one-third to one-eighth and in Asia from one-half to one-tenth. This divergence was significantly less in

Table 1.2 Divergence in GDP per capita between Western Europe–Western Offshoots and rest of the world: 1820–1962

GDP per capita ratios

	1820	1870	1900	1913	1940	1950	1962
Western Europe and Western Offshoots	100	100	100	100	100	100	100
Eastern Europe	57.2	45.8	45.1	42.5	36.9	33.6	35.8
Former USSR	57.6	46.1	38.8	37.3	40.2	45.2	45.7
Japan	56.0	36.1	37.0	34.8	53.9	30.5	52.7
Latin America	57.8	33.1	34.9	37.5	36.2	39.9	35.7
Africa	35.1	24.5	18.8	16.0	15.2	14.1	11.8
Asia (of which)	48.3	26.6	19.1	16.5	14.4	10.1	9.2
China	50.2	25.9	17.1	13.8	10.5	7.1	6.1
India	44.6	26.1	18.8	16.9	12.9	9.8	8.4
Indonesia	51.2	28.3	22.1	21.9	21.8	12.8	11.4

Source: Author's calculations from Maddison Online Database, see Appendix.

Japan and the former USSR. Latin America experienced the divergence only until 1870 and fared much better thereafter. The divergence in Africa was uninterrupted but somewhat less. Asia was the disaster story. Its GDP per capita, compared with that of Western Europe and Western Offshoots, dropped from 48 per cent to 9 per cent. Much of this collapse was attributable to its three largest economies, particularly its two giants, as the same proportions dropped from 50 per cent to 6 per cent in China, from 45 per cent to 8 per cent in India, and from 51 per cent to 11 per cent in Indonesia. The Bairoch (1981) estimates of GNP per capita, for selected benchmark years from 1800 to 1950, reveal a similar striking divergence between 'The West' and 'The Rest', to provide confirmation, although these do not provide any separate estimates for Asia (Nayyar, 2013).

1.3 Disparities in growth rates

Over time, for regions, country-groups or countries, differences in their GDP growth rates underlie their changing shares in world GDP, while differences in their GDP per capita growth rates underlie divergences in their per capita incomes. Table 1.3 presents evidence on growth rates in GDP and GDP per capita for the periods 1820–1870, 1870–1913, 1913–1950 and 1950–1962. These growth rates are based on the Maddison estimates of GDP and GDP per capita, in 1990 international (Geary–Khamis) dollars, in the selected benchmark years.

The dramatic decline in the share of Asia in world income from 1820 to 1950 was attributable to its much slower GDP growth as compared with every other part of the world. The problem was even more acute for China and India.

Table 1.3 Growth rates in the world economy by regions: 1820–1962 (per cent per annum)

GDP

	1820–1870	1870–1913	1913–1950	1950–1962
THE WEST				
Western Europe	1.68	2.12	1.19	4.93
Western Offshoots	4.31	3.92	2.83	3.66
Eastern Europe	1.41	2.33	0.86	4.89
Former USSR	1.61	2.40	2.15	5.00
Japan	0.41	2.44	2.21	9.10
THE REST				
Latin America	1.22	3.52	3.39	4.98
Africa	0.75	1.32	2.56	3.87
Asia (of which)	0.04	0.98	0.84	4.23
China	−0.37	0.56	0.04	3.41
India	0.38	0.97	0.23	3.71
Indonesia	1.1	1.75	0.77	3.76

GDP per Capita

	1820–1870	1870–1913	1913–1950	1950–1962
THE WEST				
Western Europe	0.99	1.34	0.76	4.18
Western Offshoots	1.41	1.81	1.56	1.82
Eastern Europe	0.63	1.39	0.60	3.65
Former USSR	0.63	1.06	1.76	3.19
Japan	0.19	1.48	0.88	7.89
THE REST				
Latin America	−0.04	1.86	1.41	2.14
Africa	0.35	0.57	0.90	1.55
Asia (of which)	−0.11	0.43	−0.08	2.26
China	−0.25	0.10	−0.56	1.73
India	0.00	0.54	−0.22	1.70
Indonesia	−0.11	0.83	−0.17	2.15

Source: Author's calculations from Maddison Online Database, see Appendix.

The marked revival of growth in Asia and its three giants in the early post-colonial era, 1950–1962, slowed down but did not stop this decline in shares. In contrast, the rise in the share of Latin America in world GDP from 1870 to 1962 was attributable to its GDP growth rates, which were higher than everywhere in the world except Western Offshoots during 1870–1913 and Japan during 1950–1962. The share of Africa in world GDP was broadly maintained during 1820–1870, dipped in 1870–1913, but recovered during 1913–1950 to remain there during 1950–1962, on account of its respectable GDP growth, except in the second period. For Western Europe, its GDP growth rate, compared with others, accounts for the increase in its share of world GDP during 1820–1870, the stability in its share during 1870–1913, a decrease in its share during 1913–1950, and some recovery during 1950–1962. For Western Offshoots, much higher GDP growth rates than elsewhere in the world, attributable largely to the United States, account for the continuous increase in their share of world GDP throughout the period 1820–1950 with a modest decline during 1950–1962 as growth elsewhere also gathered pace.

The divergences in incomes per capita over time reflect differences in GDP per capita growth rates. The widening gap experienced by Asia was attributable to GDP per capita growth rates that were negative over long periods, 1820–1870 and 1913–1950, and barely positive at 0.4 per cent per annum during 1870–1913, when these growth rates were much higher almost everywhere. China, India, and Indonesia fared even worse. It was the power of compound growth rates over 130 years that led to the striking divergence in incomes per capita, driven mostly by faster growth elsewhere but partly by an absolute decline, albeit small, in Asia. The respectable GDP per capita growth rates in Asia during the early post-colonial era, 1950–1962, slowed down this divergence but could not reverse it. For Western Europe, GDP per capita growth rates were in the range 0.8–1.3 per cent per annum (but much higher at 4 per cent per annum during 1950–1962), and for Western Offshoots in the range 1.4–1.8 per cent per annum, which were modest by contemporary standards. It is just that these growth rates were significantly lower elsewhere during 1820–1870. However, during 1870–1913 and 1913–1950, these growth rates were higher in Latin America and comparable in Japan, but distinctly lower in Africa.[10] It is worth noting the phenomenal spurt in growth of GDP per capita in Japan, during 1950–1962, at almost 8 per cent per annum, which was perhaps a sign of times to come.

2. Integration with the world economy

Asia and Africa have been engaged with the world economy for at least a millennium if not longer. So has South America since the discovery of the New World. The nature and degree of this engagement may have changed over time through different epochs of globalization. The focus here is on Asia and its economic integration with the world, through trade, investment, and migration across borders, during the period from the early nineteenth to the early twentieth century.

The integration of Asia with the world economy through international trade increased steadily in these 100 years to reach its zenith during 1870–1914. The belief that this expansion in international trade was attributable to trade liberalization is misleading if not wrong. In fact, free trade was imposed on Asia as imperialism prised open markets through gunboat diplomacy or colonial dominance. In 1842, China signed a treaty with Britain which opened its markets to trade and capped tariffs at 5 per cent. In the 1840s, free trade was imposed on India by Britain and on Indonesia by the Netherlands. In 1858, Japan signed the Shimoda-Harris treaties, persuaded by the American gunboats of Commodore Perry to switch from autarchy to free trade. Korea followed the same path through its forced opening and then annexation by Japan.[11]

Latin America was different. The unequal treaties signed in the early 1800s, before independence, expired in the 1870s, after which tariff levels in Latin America were the highest in the world, leading to rapid industrialization and economic growth (Clemens and Williamson, 2002). Asia was just the opposite. In the late nineteenth and early twentieth centuries, India, China, and Indonesia practiced free trade, as much as Britain and the Netherlands, with average tariff levels that were close to negligible in the range of 3–5 per cent (Nayyar, 2006). In contrast, tariff levels in Germany, Japan, and France were significantly higher at around 12–18 per cent, whereas tariff levels in the United States were much higher at 40–50 per cent.[12]

During the period 1870–1914, a large proportion of this international trade consisted of inter-sectoral trade, exchanging primary commodities for manufactured goods. The leading trading nation in this era, Britain exported manufactures to, and imported primary commodities from Asia (Foreman-Peck, 1983).[13] Much the same was true of northwest Europe. North America exported primary commodities for some time but, by 1914, rapid industrialization there also turned the United States into a net exporter of manufactures (Findlay and O'Rourke, 2007). The international division of labour implicit in this pattern of trade was aptly described as the 'Great Specialization' (Robertson, 1938). This specialization was proactively shaped by colonialism and imperialism through the development of mines and plantations.[14]

The geographical spread and economic significance of international investment in this era matched that of international trade. But evidence on Asia alone is not available. The gross value of the stock of foreign capital in Asia, Africa, and Latin America, at current prices, increased from $5.3 billion in 1870 to $11.3 billion in 1900 and $22.7 billion in 1914 (Maddison, 1989, p. 30). This was the equivalent of 32 per cent of the GDP of fifteen selected countries in Asia and Latin America in 1900, which were the major destinations for investment from abroad (Nayyar, 2013). It has also been estimated that in 1914 total foreign investment in the world economy was $44 billion, of which $30 billion was portfolio investment while $14 billion was direct investment (Dunning, 1983). In terms of destination, it was distributed as follows: $14 billion in Europe (32 per cent), $10.5 billion in the United States (24 per cent), $8.5 billion in Latin America (19 per cent) and $11 billion in Asia and Africa (25 per cent). In terms of origin, it was far more concentrated: $19 billion from Britain (43 per cent), $9 billion from France (21 per cent), $6 billion from Germany (13.5 per cent), $5.5 billion from Belgium (12.5 per cent), and $4.5 billion from the United States (10 per cent). Thus, in

1914, 44 per cent of foreign investment was in Asia, Africa, and Latin America but 90 per cent of it came from Europe (UNCTAD, 1994, p. 158).

Around the same time, in 1913, the primary sector accounted for 55 per cent of long-term investments in the world, transport, trade, and distribution accounted for 30 per cent, while manufacturing accounted for only 10 per cent and much of that was concentrated in the United States or Europe (Dunning, 1983). It would seem that during the late nineteenth and early twentieth centuries, Asia, Africa, and Latin America, were integrated into the world economy as sources of primary commodities through international investment in mines and plantations, supported by connectivity from the hinterland to ports, in an international division of labour shaped through trade and driven by imperialism.

This process of economic integration extended to international migration. The abolition of slavery in the British Empire was followed by the movement of indentured labour which was yet another form of servitude. Starting around the mid-1830s, for a period of fifty years, about 50 million people left India and China to work as indentured labour on mines, plantations, and construction in the Americas, the Caribbean, southern Africa, Southeast Asia, and other distant lands (Tinker, 1974 and Lewis, 1978). This was probably close to 10 per cent of the total population of India and China *circa* 1880 (Nayyar, 2002b). The destinations were mostly British, Dutch, French, and German colonies. But the United States and Latin America were important destinations where indentured labour also came from Japan. This was followed by a somewhat different form of international migration from Asia associated with colonialism, during the periods 1900–1914 and 1919–1938, as white-collar workers (many among whom worked for British colonial governments) and people engaged in trade and commerce (who were not available in local populations) moved, particularly from India, to countries in Africa, the Middle East, and Southeast Asia that were part of the British Empire.

The migration of people from India and China as indentured labour for mines and plantations, together with the movement of capital from European countries, sought to exploit natural resources or climatic conditions in Southeast Asia, southern Africa, and the Caribbean. In this process, contrary to the dominant construct in orthodox trade theory, international movements of capital and labour were complements and not substitutes (Nayyar, 1998). Similarly, the migration of white-collar workers and traders from India to other countries in the British colonial empire where these skills did not exist, or were scarce, served important needs of colonialism. In either case, international migration was critical in the evolution of the world economy from the 1830s to the 1930s (Nayyar, 2013).

In retrospect, it is clear that this era witnessed a progressive integration of Asia into the world economy, as 1870 was a turning point in the shift from colonialism to imperialism. The process may have gathered momentum in the 'Age of Empire' from 1870 to 1914 (Hobsbawm, 1987), but it evolved over a period that spanned more than a century (Findlay and O'Rourke, 2007). It was driven by the economic and political interests of Western Europe. It also coincided with the decline and fall of Asia. This evolution of the international economic order led to a profound change in the balance of economic and political power in the world. It was attributable to three developments. The first was the Industrial Revolution in Britain in the late eighteenth century, which spread to Western Europe, even if slowly, during the first half of the nineteenth century. The second was the transformation of colonialism driven by economic interests into imperialism driven by political quests for empires, which reinforced each other. The third was the revolution in transport and communication in the mid-nineteenth century, manifest in the railway, the steamship, and the telegraph, which dismantled barriers in distance and time. These three developments, which overlapped in time, transformed the world economy by creating patterns of specialization in production, associated with a division of labour through trade and investment, reinforced by the politics of imperialism.

3. Deindustrialization of Asia

The share of Asia in world population and world income was overwhelmingly large until 1500. These shares diminished over the next 300 years, but were still substantial in 1820. Similarly, the significance of Asia in the manufacturing capacities of the world was also enormous. Indeed, during the seventeenth and eighteenth centuries, the world economy was characterized by a flow of manufactured goods from Asia to Europe that was paid for by a flow of silver from Europe to Asia (Findlay and O'Rourke, 2007). Trade in spices was just one part of the story. Cotton textiles from India and porcelains or silks from China were much sought after in Europe. And some of the most dynamic sectors in eighteenth-century Europe were seeking to imitate and compete against goods from Asia (Parthasarathi, 2011).

In a study of industrialization levels across the world since 1750, Bairoch (1982) provides estimates of manufacturing production for selected regions, country-groups and countries. Table 1.4, based on these estimates, outlines the changes in the distribution of manufacturing production in the world economy from 1750 to 1963. It makes a distinction between two groups of continents and countries: the first is made up of Europe, North America, and Japan, described by Bairoch as 'Developed Economies', while the second is made up of Asia, Africa, and Latin America, described by Bairoch as the 'Third World'. Manufacturing production covers the entire range of output without differentiating between technology levels or organizational structures. Thus, it includes both the traditional sector with production by craftsmen, and modern industry with production in factories. The figures are based on triennial or quinquennial annual averages to eliminate the impact of short-term fluctuations.

Table 1.4 Distribution of manufacturing production in the world economy: 1750–1963 (in percentages)

Year	Europe, North America, and Japan	Latin America, Africa, and Asia	(of which) China and India	World
1750	27.0	73.0	57.3	100
1800	32.3	67.7	53.0	100
1830	39.5	60.5	47.4	100
1860	63.4	36.6	28.3	100
1880	79.1	20.9	15.3	100
1900	89.0	11.0	7.9	100
1913	92.5	7.5	5.0	100
1928	92.8	7.2	5.3	100
1938	92.8	7.2	5.5	100
1953	93.5	6.5	4.0	100
1963	91.5	8.5	5.3	100

Source: Bairoch (1982).

Table 1.4 shows that Asia, Africa, and Latin America, taken together, accounted for almost three-fourths of world industrial output in 1750, much of it in Asia, since just China and India accounted for almost three-fifths of world industrial output. These shares remained high, even if lower, at 68 per cent in 1800 (with China and India contributing 53 per cent) and 61 per cent in 1830 (with China and India contributing 47 per cent), but plummeted to 21 per cent in 1880 (with China and India contributing 15 per cent) and a mere 7.5 per cent in 1913 (with China and India contributing 5 per cent). For the next forty years, these proportions remained around that level, and rose just a little over the next ten years in the early post-colonial era. The distribution of industrial output between China and India was roughly in the proportion 60:40 during 1750–1860 and 1913–1963, while it was 75:25 during 1860–1913, which suggests that deindustrialization in India was even more than in China.[15] Over the same period, the share of Europe, North America, and Japan in world industrial output rose from 27 per cent in 1750 to 40 per cent in 1830, 79 per cent in 1880 and 92.5 per cent in 1913. In fact, the proportional contribution of the two groups of continents and countries to world manufacturing production was almost reversed in just thirty years, between 1830 and 1860. Yet, in 1860, China ranked second and India third, just below Britain ranked first, but above France fourth, United States fifth and Germany sixth, in the world in terms of total manufacturing output (Bairoch, 1982, p. 284). Surprisingly, in total manufacturing output in the world, China ranked seventh in both 1913 and 1953, while India ranked eleventh in 1913 and tenth in 1953, essentially because of their size.

It is not possible to compare how productivity per worker in manufacturing changed over time in these two parts of the world because there is no evidence on the number of persons employed in the industrial sector. Thus, Bairoch studied levels of industrialization in terms of manufacturing production per capita. The results of this exercise are just as striking. The ratio of manufacturing production per capita in Asia, Africa, and Latin America to that in Europe, North America, and Japan, dropped from 7:8 in 1750 and 3:4 in 1800 to 1:4 in 1860, 1:8 in 1880, 1:17.5 in 1900, and 1:27.5 in 1913, but this ratio did not worsen thereafter at 1:27 in 1953 and 1:24 in 1963. In the same selected years, these ratios were almost the same for China and India, although India fared somewhat worse from 1860 to 1913.[16] But in terms of manufacturing output per capita, China and India were not even among the top twenty countries in the world in 1860, let alone in 1913 or 1953, given their large populations.

The revolutionary change in methods of manufacturing, which were developed in Britain in the late eighteenth century and spread to countries in Western Europe through the early nineteenth century, meant profound changes in the economic life of Europe.[17] Innovation, followed by continuous improvements in technologies, yielded sharp increases in productivity, output and incomes. The rapid diffusion of the new technologies, combined with their geographical spread, brought about rapid industrialization in Britain, Belgium, Netherlands, France, and Germany. This industrialization in Western Europe, associated with scale economies that sharply reduced prices of manufactured goods, led to the demise of traditional industries in Asia, particularly India and China, so that the outcome was deindustrialization in Asia except for Japan.[18] Consequently, the knowledge and skills that had been developed in Asia over centuries were slowly but surely eroded and diminished. Thus, the nineteenth century witnessed a divergence not just in incomes but also in labour productivity, skill levels, and technological capabilities. The consequent path dependence had long-term consequences for development.

The obvious cause of this deindustrialization in Asia was the much greater competitiveness of industry in Britain and Western Europe. But that was not all. The transport revolution of the nineteenth century dismantled the natural pro-tection, which was provided by the distance and time implicit in geographical barriers, to handicrafts or manufacturing industries in countries such as India and China (Nayyar, 2006; Findlay and O'Rourke, 2007). The advent of the steamship reduced the cost of ocean freight by two-thirds between 1870 and 1900 (Lewis, 1978). The spread of the railways, everywhere, brought the hinterland of countries into the world economy, not only to source raw materials but also to sell manufactured goods (Nayyar, 2006). It would have required high tariffs, possibly even an exclusion of imports through prohibitive protection, for India and China, or countries in Asia, to neutralize the impact of the revolutions in industry and transport on prices of manufactures imported from Britain or Western Europe. Of course, colonialism and imperialism meant that countries in Asia did not have the freedom to use tariffs for protecting domestic industries. The mix of gunboat diplomacy and colonial dominance, as noted above, imposed free trade on China, India, Indonesia, Japan, and Korea.[19] There was sustained productivity growth with industrialization in Western Europe and a steady productivity decline with deindustrialization in Asia. This widening productivity gap was the basic factor underlying the divergence in per capita incomes between Western Europe and Asia.

The world economy was divided into countries (mostly with temperate climates) that industrialized and exported manufactures, and countries (mostly with tropical climates) that did not industrialize and exported primary commodities. The 'Great Divergence' in incomes between these countries was closely related to the 'Great Specialization' in division of labour between countries. Slowly but surely, these countries became dependent on the industrializing countries in Western Europe, not simply for markets and finance but also as their engine of growth (Lewis, 1978). Much of Asia, except Japan, was colonized *de jure* or *de facto*, placing it on the wrong side of this divide, which led to its deindustrialization and underdevelopment.

4. Initial conditions in post-colonial Asia

Initial conditions prevalent in countries must relate to a specific point in time. For our purpose, it was the end of the colonial era. These conditions always matter in any process that shapes trajectories of development. After all, where a country starts out from is bound to exercise some influence on the journey and the destination. Initial conditions are shaped by history embedded in the past. Initial conditions could be influenced by their context in the present. And initial conditions do, in turn, shape outcomes in the future. Of course, this cannot be reduced to a deterministic view that initial conditions are immutable, or given once and for all, for these might have to be, and often are, reshaped, reconstructed, or recreated to kick-start development.

It is no surprise then that *Asian Drama* placed a strong emphasis on initial conditions. In an interactive mode, these could be a powerful constraint which might even perpetuate underdevelopment through cumulative causation by creating vicious circles such that poor countries and poor people remain poor.[20] Myrdal's focus, however, was on differences in initial conditions between South Asia, as a proxy for Asia, and Western Europe, before the Industrial Revolution, at comparable stages of development. The choice of a comparable period posed a dilemma for Myrdal (1968, p. 675):

> One thing is certain: at the beginning of what we recognize as the industrial revolution—or, more precisely, their industrial revolutions—the Western countries had behind them many years—in some cases centuries—of social, political

and also incipient economic development; in a number of ways they were already much more favourably situated than South Asia is today. In many respects, therefore the period of comparison should be fixed centuries before the industrial revolutions in the West.

Thus, the period of comparison in the history of Western countries was left vague but, in effect, it was *circa* 1750.

Some initial conditions, such as natural resource endowments and climate, Myrdal thought, were near-constants over time. Even so, he was concerned that most countries in Asia except for a few, were natural-resource-scarce, and that much of Asia had tropical climates while industrialization and development had always been concentrated in temperate climates. He was also concerned that population growth rates in Asia were so much higher than in the West two centuries earlier, which could only constrain possibilities of development. International trade and capital movements were seen as an important difference. While rapid trade expansion and significant private capital movements had facilitated development in the West, for Asia 'the epoch of rapidly growing export markets has ended' (p. 683) and he saw little prospect of international private capital movements at the time. The comparison led him to argue that economic levels (income, savings, and investment), institutions (political, social, and economic) and attitudes (to work and life) constituted initial conditions that were a formidable obstacle to development in Asia. Two centuries later, the availability of modern technology was an opportunity but it was also a challenge because of skill shortages and learning capacities in Asia, or the inappropriate nature of such technologies, particularly in agriculture. The problem, he believed, was accentuated by the rapid pace of technical progress.[21]

Myrdal was absolutely right in stressing the importance of initial conditions. But his perspective, which chose to compare Asia, *circa* 1950 with Western Europe, *circa* 1750, had serious limitations. First, he failed to recognize that Asia became what it was, *circa* 1950, precisely because of what Europe did in Asia for two centuries. Second, it considered two different eras, separated in time, and two different continents, separated in space, without sufficient recognition that trajectories of development in Asia over the next fifty years might be different from, rather than similar to, patterns of development in Western Europe over the past 200 years. Third, he did not show any awareness that latecomers to industrialization, such as Russia and Japan, narrowed the gap in much shorter periods,[22] which was a surprising blind spot in his vision of development. As it turned out, there was an economic transformation in Asia despite its relatively poor natural endowment of resources and climates. Population growth slowed down. There was a rapid growth in exports and an increase in private capital movements. Economic levels—incomes, savings and investments—rose much faster than might have been expected from history of the West. Institutions evolved even if this process was characterized by considerable diversity rather than broad uniformity. Attitudes to work and life also witnessed change uneven though it was. The opportunities provided by modern technologies were exploited, as these were absorbed, adapted, or even developed, not only to foster industrialization but also to transform agriculture.

It is more appropriate to focus on initial conditions in Asia *circa* 1965, around the time that Gunnar Myrdal wrote *Asian Drama*, which could be considered in themselves, or in comparison with other parts of the world at the time. This is also more logical as most Asian countries were independent by 1965, which was not so in 1950. Table 1.5 presents a compilation of available evidence on initial conditions in Asia in terms of demographic, social, and economic indicators. This evidence is also disaggregated by its four constituent sub-regions: East, Southeast, South and West Asia.

The evidence on demographic and social indicators relates to 1965. It shows that Asia was the most populous continent, home to more than half the people in the world. It was also the most land-scarce continent, with a population density of 117 persons per square kilometre. Its birth rate, at 40 per 1000, and fertility rate, at 6 births per woman, were very high. The social indicators show that life expectancy in Asia was just fifty years, while infant mortality rates were 159 per 1000 live births, reflecting the poor health status of people. Literacy rates at 43 per cent were low, and significantly lower in South Asia. There was also a strong gender bias, obvious from a comparison of male–female literacy rates. The picture in the sub-regions was broadly similar, except for Southeast Asia, which fared better. Sub-Saharan Africa apart, demographic and social indicators in Asia were the worst in the world.

The evidence on economic indicators relates to 1970 because it is the earliest year for which data are available. It shows that, in current prices at market exchange rates, Asia contributed just 8 per cent of world GDP (although it had 54 per cent of world population), of which East Asia and South Asia accounted for 3 per cent each, while Southeast Asia and West Asia accounted for 1 per cent each. GDP per capita in Asia was only 5 per cent of GDP per capita in industrialized countries. This proportion would have been even lower were it not for West Asia where GDP per capita in the oil producing countries was much higher. In the same year, 1970, GDP per capita in Latin America was more than four times that in Asia while GDP per capita in Africa was 60 per cent higher than that in Asia (Nayyar, 2013).

For Asia, in 1970, the primary sector—agriculture, forestry, animal husbandry—accounted for just over one-fourth of GDP.[23] But four-fifths of the population lived in the rural sector. The share of manufacturing value added in GDP was one-tenth. However, the share of the industrial sector was larger because of mining, construction, and utilities. For Asia, merchandise exports plus merchandise imports, were the equivalent of about two-fifths of GDP. These proportions were lower at about one-fifth of GDP in East Asia and one-sixth of GDP in South Asia, but were significantly higher at close to one-half in Southeast Asia. Investment, gross capital formation, was just over one-fifth of GDP in Asia, with

Table 1.5 Selected indicators of initial conditions in Asia: 1965 and 1970

	Asia	East Asia	Southeast Asia	South Asia	West Asia
DEMOGRAPHIC	1965	1965	1965	1965	1965
Population (millions)	1749	782	245	637	86
Density (per sq. km)	125	103	89	178	30
Birth rate (per 1000)	40	38	42	42	45
Fertility rate(births per woman)	6	6	6	6	7
SOCIAL	1965	1965	1965	1965	1965
Life expectancy (years)	49	50	55	45	49
Literacy rate (per cent)	43	52	52	28	30
Literacy rate Male: Female (per cent)	51:33	58:47	63:42	40:15	42:19
Infant mortality rate (per 1000 live births)	160	196[a]	83	154	92
ECONOMIC	1970	1970	1970	1970	1970
Income					
GDP (in current US$ billion)	276	114	24	85	54
as a percentage of world	8.1	3.3	0.7	2.5	1.6
GDP per capita (Current US$)	139	127	85	119	546
as a percentage of industrialized countries	4.7	4.3	2.9	4	18.4
Structure and Openness					
Primary sector share in GDP	27	46	30	49	9
Manufacturing Value Added–GDP ratio (in percentages)	10	5	15	14	14
Merchandise Trade (Exports plus Imports)—GDP ratio	43	21	46	17	65
Investment					
Gross capital formation as a percentage of GDP	21.6	30.7	24.2	20.2	16.9
Infrastructure					
Electricity consumption per capita(in kwh)[b]	647	1355	757	81	–
Road kms per 100 sq km of land area	25	67	8	30	20
Urban: Rural population	21:79	20:80	21:79	19:81	42:58

Notes:

[a] This figure in the column for 1965 relates to 1960.

[b] The figures in the columns for 1970 relate to 1980. Statistics for West Asia are not available.

Source: Author's calculations based on several sources, see Appendix.

some variation between regions. Although available evidence is incomplete, in 1960, in most Asian countries, gross domestic savings were in the range of 8–12 per cent of GDP while gross domestic investment was in the range 12–15 per cent of GDP. Infrastructure, reflected in electricity consumption per capita and roads relative to land area, was poor though it was distinctly better in East Asia as compared with other sub-regions.

Clearly, *circa* 1965–1970, around fifty years ago, Asia was the poorest continent in the developing world. If the evidence presented in Table 1.5 was available for earlier years, say 1950, which it is not, it would show that underdevelopment in Asia was even more pronounced.

5. Shaping and reshaping of initial conditions

The initial conditions observed in Asian countries in the early post-colonial era, around 1950, were shaped mostly by the history embedded in their pasts. Of course, given the diversity of Asia, geography also mattered, since the size and location of a country exercised an influence on its past and its evolution. But the history, with its layers in time, is far more complex. There are centuries of history in Asia much before colonialism. But there is also a colonial history of at least 150 years. Both influences shaped the reality observed in the mid-twentieth century, even if the imprint of colonialism was more recent and more visible. There were two closely intertwined dimensions of the past before the European intrusion into Asia. Cultures, societies, and identities were one dimension, while economies were the other dimension. The influence of the colonial era differed across countries, as the legacies of different colonialisms—British, French, Dutch, American, and Japanese—were different.

Asian countries were characterized by a diversity attributable to their cultures, societies, and identities. There was a social stratification everywhere. There were religious, ethnic, and language divides. In South Asia, especially India, there were caste divides. In East Asia, particularly China, there was more cultural homogeneity, although there were minority identities and social divides. In Southeast Asia, there were religious divides (Buddhism and Islam) as well as ethnic diversity (with significant Chinese and Indian populations). Some divides were old, while some were new. Yet, given their long history, Asian countries were able to forge, or reclaim, national identities in their struggles for independence against colonial rulers, and strengthen these in the early post-colonial era. Most Asian countries did have a long history of well-structured states, and cultures, which were not entirely destroyed by colonialism. In this respect, Asia was very different from Latin America, or Africa, where colonialism had eroded indigenous cultures and identities.

There was also an economic dimension to initial conditions that was embedded in history, which was some sort of manufacturing experience from their past so that the origins of such experience differed across Asia (Amsden, 2001). For the two Asian giants, China and India, this experience was pre-capitalist, coming from artisans and craftsmen, and from an era when these countries were the main exporters of manufactures in the world. In some economies, such as Indonesia, Malaya, Taiwan, and Thailand, this experience originated in migrants, mostly from China but partly from India, while in Turkey it came from European migrants (Nayyar, 2013). But colonialism was also a source of manufacturing experience, from the British in India and Malaya, from the Dutch in Indonesia, and from the Japanese in Manchuria (China), Korea, and Taiwan. This process was inevitably strengthened during the two World Wars when manufactured goods were not readily available from the usual sources.

Even so, it must be recognized that deindustrialization and underdevelopment in Asia were in large part a consequence of colonialism. Much of Asia was colonized. The solitary exception was Thailand. China was not colonized in a formal sense. It had a semblance of indigenous political rule with large foreign enclaves and spheres of influence (mostly British) to control the economy, which was in effect not very different from colonization. India, Ceylon, Burma, and Malaya (Malaysia and Singapore) were colonized by the British, Indonesia by the Dutch, Indochina (Vietnam, Cambodia, and Laos) by the French, Manchuria (Manchukuo in China), Korea, and Taiwan by the Japanese, and Philippines by the Spanish followed by the United States. There were essential similarities insofar as all the colonizers were exploitative in economics and authoritarian in politics, subordinating the colonies to serve their own economic and political interests. The models were also similar. The Europeans—British, Dutch, and French—followed their political conquests of countries in Asia with an acquisition of control over economies that existed, which were then integrated in subordinate roles with own their respective economies. But their legacies were somewhat different.

The limited concern here is how different legacies shaped initial conditions.[24] The British opted for direct rule with relatively few expatriates to govern by creating new local elites and an intermediate class in their own image (replacing old feudal elites), for whom they created schools, colleges, or training facilities. Institutions—legal, administrative or economic—were established to help govern, using the axiom of divide and rule. Infrastructure was developed—hinterland to ports—to integrate economies of colonies with the economies of their colonial rulers. The spread of education or the development of infrastructure for ordinary people was simply not on the agenda. But the transfer of power, except in Malaya where it was delayed, was voluntary. In contrast, the Dutch and the French resisted parting with their colonies and were ultimately ousted through wars. The Dutch opted for indirect rule in Indonesia, through hereditary local leaders, to disturb traditional society as little as possible. But they did nothing to curb the power and greed of Dutch people or firms who dominated the colonial economy, or to eliminate discrimination against the local population in government and business. Yet, the Dutch believed that they would rule forever. The French in Indochina also did not think that their colonies would ever be separated from France, while their subjects could even dream of becoming French citizens. French colonialism was ostensibly on a civilizing mission to spread their culture, ideas, and language among indigenous peoples in Asia. Yet, local people were treated as second-class citizens in their own countries, excluded from the modern sector of the economy and from government (except at subordinate levels), which were for the French alone. In addition, French settlers from the lower ranks of their army and of peasant origins, acquired large amounts of land, while internal trade and commerce was run by local Chinese. During 1898–1946, Philippines was a colony of the United States, which sought to create a democracy in its own image, but without disturbing the essentially Spanish colonial legacy of local landed elites that had evolved over three centuries. For that reason, perhaps, Philippines in Asia resembles the erstwhile Spanish colonies in Latin America.

The Japanese were latecomers to industrialization and imperialism. Taiwan and Korea became colonies in 1895 and 1910 respectively, while Manchuria was formally colonized starting 1928. But Japanese colonialism was different from European colonialism in Asia, even though its authoritarian and repressive nature is etched in memories. Its military and police presence was much greater. So was the presence of Japanese civilians.[25] But there were substantial investments in manufacturing and infrastructure. In Manchuria, manufacturing more than quadrupled between 1929 and 1941 and, by 1945, it was producing half of the total manufacturing output in China (Maddison, 2007, p. 153). And there was an emphasis on education. By 1940, 50 per cent of schoolchildren in Korea and Taiwan received elementary education, compared with 2 per cent in Vietnam at the time (Duara, 2019).[26] These attributes were an important part of initial conditions, which had significant implications for development in the post-colonial era in Korea, Taiwan, and China.

The conjuncture in time also influenced initial conditions in post-colonial Asia. Land reforms were carried out in Korea after the Second World War, under the supervision of the United States occupation forces, and in Taiwan, soon after 1950, once again under the supervision of the United States, after the Nationalist Kuomintang government fled there from China. Following the revolution, in 1950, the Chinese Communist Party led by Mao Zedong carried out land reforms in China. Similarly, the Communist Party in Vietnam led by Ho Chi Minh started land reforms in 1945, which were completed after the French were forced to leave in 1954. During the early 1950s, the geopolitics of the Cold War also reshaped initial conditions in the so-called front-line states, especially Korea and Taiwan, which received massive economic assistance, plus a preferential access to its market, from the United States. Some time later, during the Vietnam War, such support was extended to some Southeast Asian countries, particularly Thailand and, to some extent, Philippines. On the other side of this Cold War divide, the USSR provided economic and military support, but governments in China and Vietnam were also conscious of their geopolitical vulnerabilities, which motivated them to address problems embedded in their legacy of initial conditions. It is clear that the conjuncture, in the national or international context, also reshaped initial conditions in some Asian countries, which in turn shaped trajectories of development for these countries in subsequent decades.

Conclusion

This chapter provides a historical perspective on Asia in the world economy with a focus on the colonial era, and sketches a profile of the prevalent initial conditions when Asian countries became independent, to set the stage for the book. In 1820, two centuries ago, Asia accounted for two-thirds of world population and almost three-fifths of world income, where just two countries, China and India, accounted for one-half of world population and world income. The colonial era witnessed a precipitous decline in this economic significance. By 1962, the share of Asia in world population diminished to 50 per cent, while its share of world income plummeted to 15 per cent. For China and India, taken together, these shares plunged to 35 per cent and 8 per cent respectively. The outcome was the 'Great Divergence'. Income per capita in Asia, as a proportion of that in the West, dropped from one-half in 1820 to less than one-tenth in 1962. This was associated with the 'Great Specialization', which meant that Western Europe produced manufactured goods while Asia produced primary commodities. Consequently, the share of China and India in world manufacturing production collapsed from 47 per cent in 1830 to 5 per cent in 1963. The decline and fall of Asia was attributable to its integration with the world economy, through trade and investment, shaped by colonialism and driven by imperialism. The industrialization of Western Europe and the deindustrialization of Asia were, in fact, two sides of the same coin, which had a devastating impact on China and India.

It is no surprise that, *circa* 1965–1970, around fifty years ago, in terms of income levels, Asia was the poorest continent in the world. Its demographic and social indicators of development, among the worst anywhere, epitomized its underdevelopment. Such initial conditions, inherited from the past, were the starting point in its journey to development. Even so, most Asian countries did have a long history of well-structured states, and cultures, which were not entirely destroyed by colonialism. Given the diversity of Asia, there were differences between countries embedded in their own histories and shaped by different colonial legacies. These diverse national contexts were juxtaposed with an international context in which the Cold War was larger than life and reshaped initial conditions in some countries. As it turned out, this past also influenced future outcomes in development.

2

The rise of Asia

The preceding chapter situated the subject of this book in its wider historical context to highlight the overwhelming significance of Asia in the world economy until the mid-eighteenth century, followed by its rapid decline through the nineteenth century, culminating in a fall that was almost complete by the mid-twentieth century, to reach a nadir in the early 1960s. It also set out the initial conditions which epitomized the underdevelopment of Asia at the time, making it the poorest continent in the world. The object of this chapter is to outline the broad contours of the story of development in Asia since then, situated in the wider context of the world economy. In doing so, it sketches a picture of the phenomenal transformation of Asia in terms of economic progress, even if it has been uneven across countries and unequal among people, over such a short time span in history. Indeed, five decades ago, such change would have been thought of as imagination running wild.

The structure of the chapter is as follows. Section 1 outlines the broad contours of the social and economic transformation of Asia, reflected in demographic, social, and economic indicators, by comparing the initial conditions *circa* 1965 with the situation half a century later in 2016. Section 2 considers the changes in the relative importance of Asia in terms of its shares of world population and world GDP, and compares changes in its per capita income levels with developing countries, industrialized countries, and the world. Section 3 disaggregates Asia into its four constituent sub-regions, to examine the differences in their relative importance within the continent and their economic performance over time in a global context, in terms of output shares and income levels. Section 4 presents the evidence on growth rates of GDP and GDP per capita underlying the changing shares of Asia and its sub-regions in world GDP, to explain the end of divergence and beginnings of convergence in per capita incomes. Section 5 sets out the trends in industrial production in Asia as a continent, divided into sub-regions, compared with other parts of the world, reflected in its rapidly rising share of world manufacturing value-added and world exports of manufactured goods, which suggests catch up in industrialization although its distribution was unequal among sub-regions. Section 6 traces the rapid increase in the engagement of Asia, as well as its constituent sub-regions, with the world economy, through international trade, international investment and international migration. Section 7 builds a bridge to the discussion in the chapters that follow by explaining why disaggregated analysis must move beyond sub-regions to selected countries.

Resurgent Asia: Diversity in Development. Deepak Nayyar, Oxford University Press (2019). © United Nations University World Institute for Development Economics Research. DOI: 10.1093/oso/9780198849513.001.0001

In comparing Asia with the world, the analysis in this chapter, as well as the book, makes a distinction between two country-groups. 'Industrialized Countries', described as developed-market-economies or developed countries in United Nations statistics, are made up of North America, Western Europe, Japan, Australia, and New Zealand. 'Developing Countries', described in the past as 'under-developed countries' or 'less developed countries', are made up of Africa, Asia, and Latin America including the Caribbean. There is a third country-group in the world, described as 'transition economies', made up of Eastern Europe and the former USSR, a residual group that is not part of the analysis, whose significance in the world economy has diminished rapidly since late 1991 when the erstwhile USSR was dissolved to create fifteen independent countries.

At the outset, it is just as essential to specify the geographical coverage of the study. It is an ambitious exercise because Asia is such a large continent, which has forty-seven countries. This chapter makes a beginning by disaggregating Asia into four sub-regions: East, Southeast, South, and West Asia. The constituent economies in each of these four sub-regions are: (a) East Asia: China, Democratic People's Republic of Korea, Hong Kong, Macao, Mongolia, Republic of Korea, and Taiwan; (b) Southeast Asia: Brunei Darussalam, Cambodia, Indonesia, Laos, Malaysia, Myanmar, Philippines, Singapore, Thailand, Timor-Leste, and Vietnam; (c) South Asia: Afghanistan, Bangladesh, Bhutan, India, Maldives, Nepal, Pakistan, and Sri Lanka; and (d) West Asia: Bahrain, Iran, Iraq, Jordan, Kuwait, Lebanon, Oman, Palestine, Qatar, Saudi Arabia, Syria, Turkey, United Arab Emirates, and Yemen. The focus is on developing countries in Asia. Therefore, Japan and Israel, which are both high-income industrialized countries in Asia, and were even fifty years ago, are not part of the study. Even so, this coverage includes thirty-seven countries.[1] This sub-regional classification is essentially geographical. Yet, it serves an analytical purpose, and there are similarities between countries within sub-regions. But there are also significant differences between countries within sub-regions, which are analysed later in the book.

It is worth noting that the above classification covers the entire continent of Asia but is not exhaustive because it does not include two sets of countries. It excludes thirteen Pacific islands that are part of the Asia-Pacific region.[2] These are mostly small island economies with very small populations that are not quite in Asia. It also excludes eight transition economies that were part of the former USSR but are now part of Asia. Of these, in the UN classification, Armenia, Azerbaijan, and Georgia are in West Asia, whereas Kazakhstan, Kyrgyzstan, Tajikistan, Turkmenistan, and Uzbekistan are in Central Asia. These countries are not part of the study, since they were part of the former USSR for about half of the fifty-year period and statistical information on these countries is available only from the mid-1990s. Moreover, the scope of the present study, already vast, needs to be kept within manageable proportions.

The title of the Gunnar Myrdal magnum opus, *Asian Drama*, was deceptive in terms of its country-coverage. The focus of that study was on the erstwhile British India, made up of India, Pakistan, and Ceylon. Burma and Indonesia were paid some attention. But Malaysia, Philippines, and Thailand were grouped together as the rest of Southeast Asia, while Cambodia, Laos, and South Vietnam were touched upon when some information of interest was available. Myrdal described all these countries broadly as South Asia.[3] However, Japan, Korea, China, Formosa (Taiwan), Hong Kong, and Singapore were excluded. So was West Asia. And, it is no surprise that the central Asian economies, then part of the USSR, were also excluded. It is clear that *Asian Drama* was both selective and restricted in terms of the countries studied. This book attempts a much larger country coverage in terms of range, although it cannot match the depth of that study published half a century ago.

1. Economic transformation of Asia

For Myrdal (1968), the fundamental point of departure from conventional think-ing about development was that 'economic problems cannot be studied in isola-tion but only in their own demographic, social and political setting' (p. ix). In this worldview, development was a multidimensional process of circular causation and cumulative change in which economy, polity, and society interacted not only with technology, history, and culture but also with each other. Cumulative causation could create vicious circles through negative feedbacks, keeping countries in a state of underdevelopment, or virtuous circles through positive feedbacks, placing countries on the path to development. This approach and conceptualization was both perceptive and correct. But his analysis of the prevalent situation in under-developed Asia sought to focus on output and incomes, conditions of production, levels of living, attitudes towards life and work, institutions, and policies. Taken together, these constituted a social system that represented a powerful constraint on development, which meant that poor countries and poor people would remain poor.[4] The interaction of these conditions, Myrdal believed, would lead to 'either an unchanged level of underdevelopment, which is to say stagnation, or else development to a higher level or a regression to a lower level' (p. 1864).

The challenge of development, then, was intervention in the form of policies and planning to transform the process of cumulative causation so that it could create virtuous circles through positive feedbacks and spread effects. However, his assessment of the possibilities in the countries studied led him to a deep pessim-ism about development prospects in Asia.[5] In sum, economic problems were intractable, political problems were formidable, while solutions that could trans-form the possible into the probable, or the desirable into the feasible, were exceedingly difficult if not elusive. Myrdal's conception of drama, speeding towards a climax in which economic, social, and political tensions are mounting, captured the essence of this narrative (1968, p. 34). Yet, he recognized that the outcome at the end was not predetermined by the playwright as it would be in a theatre. 'History, then, is not taken to be predetermined, but within the power of man to shape. And the drama thus conceived is not necessarily tragedy' (Myrdal, 1968, p. 35). The wisdom of this sentence is perhaps the unintended escape clause, as the reality of development that unfolded in Asia over the next fifty years was so strikingly different. It was, of course, contrary to what Myrdal expected. But, to be fair, it would have been just as difficult for anyone at the time to expect or even imagine.

The broad contours of the remarkable transformation of Asia emerge clearly from Table 2.1, which compares selected demographic, social, and economic indicators in 2016 with the initial conditions five decades ago in terms of the same indicators. The demographic and social transformation was remarkable. In terms of demographics, the population of Asia and its sub-regions in 2016 was two to three times its size in 1965, so that population density in a land-scarce continent also rose by the same multiple. Yet, birth rates in 2016 came down sharply to much less than one-half of their levels in 1965, while fertility rates came down even more to one-third of their 1965 levels. Between 1965 and 2016, social development in Asia was also impressive, as life expectancy at birth rose from forty-nine years to seventy-two years, and infant mortality rates dropped from 160 to twenty-three per 1000 live births, while literacy rates rose from 43 per cent to 82 per cent. There was a gender bias reflected in the female–male ratio for literacy rates, which diminished but persisted. Inevitably, there were variations in performance across the four sub-regions, but the similarities were much greater than the differences and there was much progress everywhere. Of course, it must be recognized that such indicators are arithmetic averages that cannot measure the well-being of the poor.

The economic indicators also reveal some transformative changes. The comparison is between 1970, the earliest year for which national accounts statistics compiled by the United Nations are available, and 2016. If evidence on these selected economic indicators were available for an earlier year such as 1960, or even 1965, it would show even more pronounced changes in Asia. The following comparison considers Asia as a whole to focus on the big picture. Much like the social indicators, there were broad similarities across sub-regions in terms of change and progress. Yet, there were also some significant differences between the four sub-regions, which are noted here and considered later in this chapter or in subsequent chapters.

Between 1970 and 2016, the share of Asia in world GDP, measured in constant 2010 dollars, rose from less than one-twelfth to more than one-fourth, by almost 20 percentage points, but GDP per capita in Asia as a proportion of that in

Table 2.1 Social and economic transformation in Asia: 1965–2016

	Asia		East Asia		Southeast Asia		South Asia		West Asia	
	1965	2016	1965	2016	1965	2016	1965	2016	1965	2016
DEMOGRAPHIC										
Population (millions)	1749	4239	782	1514	245	642	637	1766	86	318
Density (per sq. km)	125	320	103	202	89	257	178	486	30	92
Birth rate (per 1000)	40	17	38	12	42	18	42	20	45	20
Fertility rate (births per woman)	6	2	6	2	6	2	6	2.5	7	2.5
SOCIAL	1965	2016	1965	2016	1965	2016	1965	2016	1965	2016
Life expectancy (years)	49	72	50	76	55	71	45	69	49	74
Literacy rate (per cent)[a]	43	82	52	95	52	91	28	66	30	84
Literacy rate Male:Female (per cent)[a]	51:33	89:76	58:47	97:92	63:42	94:88	40:15	78:53	42:19	89:78
Infant mortality rate (per 1000 live births)	160	23	196[b]	8	83	21	154	37	92	16
ECONOMIC	1970	2016	1970	2016	1970	2016	1970	2016	1970	2016
Income										
GDP (in constant 2010 US$ billion)	1416	20,763	303	11,652	212	2644	272	2975	629	3493
as a percentage of world	*7.5*	*26.8*	*1.6*	*15.0*	*1.1*	*3.4*	*1.4*	*3.8*	*3.3*	*4.5*
GDP per capita (in constant 2010 US$)	714	4898	340	7695	755	4119	382	1684	6362	11,009
as a percentage of industrialized countries	*3.8*	*11.1*	*1.8*	*17.5*	*4.0*	*9.4*	*2.0*	*3.8*	*34.1*	*25.0*
Structure and Openness										
Primary sector share in GDP	27.4	8	45.8	6.8	29.7	10.4	48.5	14.5	8.6	4.7
Merchandise trade (Exports plus Imports) to GDP ratio	43	70	21	66	46	118	17	40	65	70
Investment										
Gross capital formation as a percentage of GDP	21.6	37.6	30.7	43.6	24.2	28.9	20.2	32.1	16.9	28.7
Infrastructure										
Electricity consumption per capita (in Kwh)[c]	647	3394	1355	6216	757	3366	81	1663	–	–
Road kms per 100 sq. km of land area[d]	25	100	67	113	8	103	30	84	20	100
Urban:Rural population	21:79	47:53	20:80	58:42	21:79	48:52	19:81	33:67	42:58	72:28

Notes:
[a] The figures in the columns for 2016 relate to 2010.
[b] The figure in the column for 1965 relates to 1960.
[c] The figures in the columns for 1970 relate to 1980 and in the column for 2016 to 2015. Statistics for West Asia are not available.
[d] The figures in the columns for 2016 relate to 2015.

Source: Author's calculations based on various sources, see Appendix.

industrialized countries, in constant 2010 dollars, increased far less. This catch-up in aggregate output and average income levels was uneven between the sub-regions, which is analysed in Section 3. There was structural change in Asia as the share of the primary sector in GDP fell from 27 per cent to 8 per cent. This decline varied across sub-regions. In West Asia, there was little agriculture to start with. In fact, for East Asia, Southeast Asia, and South Asia, taken together, the share of the primary sector in GDP fell from 42 per cent to 9 per cent.[6] The share of manufacturing value added in GDP more than doubled, rising rapidly in East Asia, moderately in Southeast Asia and marginally in South Asia, while falling in West Asia.

The degree of openness in Asia defined as the ratio of merchandise trade (exports plus imports) to GDP increased significantly over this period from 43 per cent to 70 per cent, increasing far more in East Asia and Southeast Asia than it did in South Asia and West Asia (where it was already high). Investment rates in Asia shot up. Gross capital formation, as a proportion of GDP, rose from around one-fifth to almost two-fifths, broadly similar across sub-regions, except East Asia and West Asia where these were higher and lower respectively to start with, in 1970. The indicators on infrastructure also reveal transformative change. For Asia, the road density multiplied by four while electricity consumption per capita multiplied by five, with some variations in levels between sub-regions in which East Asia was ahead and South Asia was behind. The ratio of urban to total population in Asia rose from about one-fifth to one-half over this period, although this urbanization was somewhat less in South Asia, somewhat more in East Asia and the most in West Asia.

The remarkable transformation of Asia in fifty years is reflected in its demographic transition (a sharp drop in birth rates and fertility rates), its social progress (the spread of education as literacy rates reached much higher levels and improved health status as life expectancy rose and infant mortality rates fell) and its economic development (output growth, income levels, structural change, investment rates, infrastructure, and urbanization). In this process of transformation, East Asia was the leader and South Asia was the laggard, with Southeast Asia in the middle, while progress in West Asia did not quite match its high incomes per capita.

2. Output shares and income levels in Asia

The preceding discussion paints a broad brush picture of social and economic change in Asia through a simple point-to-point comparison between then and now, fifty years apart, largely within the continent. But the economic transformation of Asia needs to be situated in its wider context of the world economy, to reveal how its importance and performance have changed over these five decades.

Table 2.2 presents evidence on population, GDP and GDP per capita in Asia, in current prices at market exchange rates, compared with developing countries, industrialized countries and the world economy, at ten-year intervals from 1970 to 2010, plus 2016, to keep the statistics within manageable proportions. It starts in 1970, rather than 1965, because national accounts statistics compiled by the United Nations are available only from 1970.

It is worth beginning with a perspective on population changes. The total population of Asia more than doubled between 1970 and 2016, as its share of world population returned to its 1870 level. This was attributable to demographic factors. As death rates dropped because of improvements in public health systems that eliminated epidemic diseases, birth rates did not at the same pace because poverty and illiteracy persisted. However, with rising levels of income and

Table 2.2 Asia in the world economy: 1970–2016

	1970	1980	1990	2000	2010	2016
Population (in billions)						
Asia	2.0	2.5	3.0	3.6	4.1	4.3
Developing Countries	2.6	3.3	4.1	4.9	5.6	6.1
Industrialized Countries	0.8	0.9	0.9	1.0	1.0	1.1
World	3.7	4.5	5.3	6.1	7.0	7.5
Percentage Share of Asia in						
Developing Countries	*75.4*	*74.6*	*73.8*	*73.9*	*72.1*	*70.5*
World	*53.8*	*55.4*	*56.8*	*58.6*	*58.4*	*57.3*
GDP						
(US$ billion in current prices at market exchange rates)						
Asia	296	1405	2343	4550	15,112	22,582
Developing Countries	580	2727	4003	7279	21,810	29,273
Industrialized Countries	2372	8554	18,107	25,943	42,094	44,578
World	3402	12,293	22,985	33,601	66,010	75,649
Percentage Share of Asia in						
Developing Countries	*51.0*	*51.5*	*58.5*	*62.5*	*69.3*	*77.1*
World	*8.7*	*11.4*	*10.2*	*13.5*	*22.9*	*29.9*
GDP per capita						
GDP per capita (US$ in current prices at market exchange rates)						
Asia	149	569	773	1263	3718	5211
Developing Countries	220	824	975	1495	3874	4792
Industrialized Countries	2974	9956	19,920	26,622	40,933	42,390
World	919	2757	4312	5468	9487	10,131
GDP per capita in Asia						
as a percentage of that in						
Developing Countries	*67.7*	*69.1*	*79.3*	*84.5*	*96.0*	*108.7*
Industrialized Countries	*5.0*	*5.7*	*3.9*	*4.7*	*9.1*	*12.3*
World	*16.2*	*20.6*	*17.9*	*23.1*	*39.2*	*51.4*

Note: The percentages have been calculated.

Source: United Nations, National Accounts Statistics and Population Statistics.

education, birth rates in Asia did come down significantly so that its population growth between 2010 and 2016 was modest. In fact, between 1970 and 2016, Asia's share in the population of developing countries dropped by 5 percentage points, essentially because Africa's population grew more rapidly as it lagged behind in the demographic transition.

From 1970 to 2016, the share of Asia in world GDP jumped by 21 percentage points from less than one-tenth to three-tenths, while its share in the GDP of developing countries rose by 26 percentage points from one-half to more than three-fourths. Over this period, the share of industrialized countries in world GDP fell from 70 per cent to 59 per cent, while that of developing countries rose from 17 per cent to 38 per cent. It would seem that Asia accounted for almost the entire increase in the share of developing countries in world GDP, while the increase in Asia's share of world GDP was at the expense of industrialized countries (11 per cent) and transition economies (10 per cent).

Figure 2.1a outlines trends in Asia's share of world population and world GDP based on time-series data from 1970 to 2016. It shows a large asymmetry in 1970 when Asia's population share exceeded its income share by 45 percentage points. This asymmetry persisted until 1990 to diminish slowly until 2000 after which it narrowed significantly. Yet, in 2016, Asia's population share was 27 percentage points higher than its income share.

The story is different for per capita income. Table 2.2 shows that, GDP per capita in Asia as a proportion of GDP per capita in the world economy rose from less than one-sixth to more than one-half. The comparison with developing countries appears even more impressive. GDP per capita in Asia relative to that in the developing world rose from two-thirds in 1970 to exceed it in 2016. However, the reality check lies in a comparison with industrialized countries. The ratio of GDP per capita in Asia to GDP per capita in industrialized countries was just 1:20 in 1970 and 1:21 in 2000 but, as a consequence of rapid growth thereafter, it was higher at 1:8 in 2016. Yet, convergence was modest.

Figure 2.1b, based on time series data, clearly outlines these trends in GDP per capita for Asia, as a percentage of GDP per capita in industrialized countries, developing countries, and the world economy during the period from 1970 to 2016. It shows that GDP per capita in Asia, as a proportion of GDP per capita in industrialized countries, witnessed a modest convergence from 2000, while, as a proportion of GDP per capita in developing countries, it increased steadily throughout the period, gathering pace after 2000, to catch up and surpass it in 2013. It is also clear that GDP per capita in Asia converged towards the world average income level from the late 1990s.

In sum, the precipitous decline in its share of world GDP and the massive divergence in its GDP per capita experienced by Asia during the preceding 150 years came to an end by 1970. A reversal started thereafter. In fact, beginning around 2000, Asia witnessed a rapid increase in its share of world GDP and a

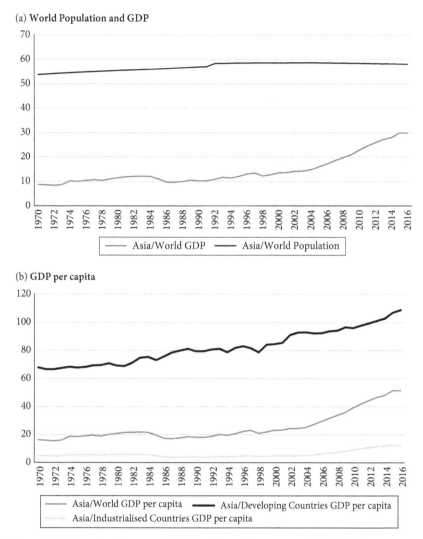

(a) World Population and GDP

Asia/World GDP ——— Asia/World Population

(b) GDP per capita

——— Asia/World GDP per capita   ——— Asia/Developing Countries GDP per capita
········ Asia/Industrialised Countries GDP per capita

Figure 2.1 Rising significance of Asia in the world economy: 1970–2016 (in percentages)

Note: The percentages have been calculated.

Source: United Nations, National Accounts Statistics and Population Statistics.

significant convergence in per capita incomes in comparison with the world economy although this convergence was at best modest in comparison with industrialized countries. It is obvious that the decline and fall of Asia during 1820–1950 occurred under some form of colonialism, or dependence, which was accentuated from 1870 in the age of imperialism. This changed, in the period from the late 1940s to the early 1960s, as Asian countries regained their political independence, which restored their economic autonomy, enabling them to pursue their national development objectives.

It would be instructive to compare the substantial increase in Asia's share of world GDP, and the relatively modest increase in its per capita income levels, during the period 1970–2016, with the past. The Maddison PPP statistics show that the share of Asia in world GDP reached its lowest level of 14.9 per cent in 1962 (Table 1.1), while its GDP per capita as a proportion of that in Western Europe and North America also reached its lowest level of 9.2 per cent in 1962 (Table 1.2). It is obviously not possible to compare these proportions with income shares and levels in current prices at market exchange rates. Fortunately, the Maddison statistical database has recently been extended up to 2016, from which it has been estimated that Asia's share of world GDP, in 1990 international (Geary–Khamis) dollars, was 43.1 per cent in 2016.[7] This proportion was 36.1 per cent in 1870 and 56.5 per cent in 1820 (Table 1.1). It has also been estimated that GDP per capita in Asia as a proportion of that in Western Europe, North America, and Oceania was 26.4 in 2016.[8] This proportion was 26.6 per cent in 1870 (Table 1.2). Therefore, it is reasonable to infer that the share of Asia in world GDP returned to its level *circa* 1850, whereas its per capita income as a proportion of that in industrialized countries returned to its level in 1870.

3. Uneven development among sub-regions

Asia is a large and diverse continent. It is, therefore, essential to provide an analysis of output shares and income levels by disaggregating Asia into its four constituent sub-regions. Table 2.3 makes a distinction between East Asia, Southeast Asia, South Asia, and West Asia to present evidence on the share of each of these sub-regions in world population and world GDP, while comparing their GDP per capita with that in the world economy and in industrialized countries.

More than three-fourths of the people in Asia live in the East and the South. Between 1970 and 2016, as a proportion of world population, the share of East Asia decreased from one-fourth to one-fifth while the share of South Asia increased from one-fifth to one-fourth. The shares of Southeast Asia and West Asia in world population were much smaller and witnessed little change. Over this period, the share of Asia in world GDP rose by about 21 percentage points, of which more than two-thirds was attributable to East Asia, while less than one-third was attributable to Southeast, South and West Asia taken together. This unequal distribution of the rise in Asia's share of world GDP is confirmed by Figure 2.2a, which uses time-series data to outline the trends in the shares of Asia and its constituent sub-regions in world GDP.

A comparison of the asymmetries in shares of world population and world GDP for each of the four sub-regions is also revealing. In 1970, the population

Table 2.3 Asia disaggregated by sub-regions: population, GDP and GDP per capita in comparison with the world: 1970–2016

	1970	1980	1990	2000	2010	2016
Population						
East Asia	24.1	24.1	23.7	22.5	21.1	20.3
Southeast Asia	7.6	8.0	8.3	8.5	8.6	8.6
South Asia	19.3	20.2	21.3	22.6	23.1	23.7
West Asia	2.7	3.0	3.4	3.7	4.1	4.2
Asia	*53.7*	*55.4*	*56.8*	*58.6*	*58.4*	*58.0*
GDP						
East Asia	3.3	3.7	4.1	6.8	11.9	17.9
Southeast Asia	1.1	1.7	1.6	1.9	3.0	3.4
South Asia	2.5	1.9	1.8	1.8	3.1	3.8
West Asia	1.6	3.9	2.4	2.5	4.1	3.9
Asia	*8.7*	*11.4*	*10.2*	*13.5*	*22.9*	*29.9*
GDP per capita						
as a percentage of GDP per capita in the world						
East Asia	13.9	15.3	17.3	30.4	56.6	88.4
Southeast Asia	14.6	21.0	19.4	21.7	35.0	39.4
South Asia	12.9	9.6	8.5	8.0	13.3	16.2
West Asia	59.4	131.2	70.3	67.3	100.1	91.6
Asia	*16.2*	*20.6*	*17.9*	*23.1*	*39.2*	*51.4*
as a percentage of GDP per capita in the industrialized world						
East Asia	4.3	4.2	3.7	6.2	13.1	21.1
Southeast Asia	4.5	5.8	4.2	4.5	8.1	9.4
South Asia	4.0	2.7	1.8	1.6	3.1	3.9
West Asia	18.4	36.3	15.2	13.8	23.2	21.9
Asia	*5.0*	*5.7*	*3.9*	*4.7*	*9.1*	*12.3*

Note: The percentages have been calculated. The data used for GDP and GDP per capita are in US dollars at current prices and market exchange rates.

Source: United Nations, National Accounts Statistics and Population Statistics.

share exceeded the income share by 20.8 percentage points in East Asia, 6.5 percentage points in Southeast Asia, 16.8 percentage points in South Asia, and 1.1 percentage points in West Asia. In 2016, the population share exceeded the income share by a far narrower 2.4 percentage points in East Asia, a marginally lower 5.2 percentage points in Southeast Asia, a clearly wider 19.9 percentage points in South Asia, and a mere 0.3 percentage points in West Asia. It would seem that, over this period, population and income shares became almost symmetrical for East Asia and even more asymmetrical for South Asia. For West Asia, with its concentration of oil-exporting countries, these shares were always close and its income share exceeded its population share when world oil prices rose in 1973 and 1979. For Southeast Asia, this asymmetry diminished a little but remained significant.

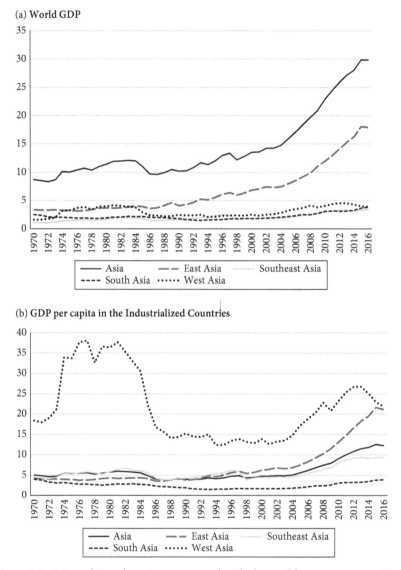

Figure 2.2 Asia and its sub-regions compared with the world economy: 1970–2016 (in percentages)

Note: The percentages have been calculated. The data used for GDP and GDP per capita are in US dollars at current prices and market exchange rates.

Source: United Nations, National Accounts Statistics and Population Statistics.

Trends in GDP per capita set out in Table 2.3 mirror this uneven development in Asia. A comparison of GDP per capita for each of the sub-regions with GDP per capita in the world economy, or in industrialized countries, in 1970 and 2016, shows that East Asia fared the best and South Asia fared the worst, with Southeast

Asia in between, while West Asia, fluctuations apart, stayed roughly where it was. However, point-to-point comparisons conceal the trends, which emerge clearly from Figure 2.2b, which plots these proportions using time series data. It shows that, starting around 1990, the enormous gap in per capita income vis-à-vis industrialized countries diminished significantly in East Asia and moderately in Southeast Asia. In West Asia, where the gap was always narrower, this proportion was never stable and fluctuated sharply with world oil prices, rising from 1973 to 1981, falling thereafter until 2001, to rise again until 2013 and fall again until 2016. South Asia was the real outlier in this story, as the enormous gap widened even more for twenty-five years, so much so that the ratio of GDP per capita to that in industrialized countries dropped from 1:25 in 1970 to 1:66 in 1995 to recover partly and reach 1:33 in 2010 but, forty-six years later, this ratio was still a fraction less than 1:25 in 2016.

To recapitulate, it is clear that, from 1970 to 2016, the increase in Asia's share of world GDP was attributable in large part to East Asia but in part also to other sub-regions, among which the contribution of South Asia was the least. The asymmetry in world income and population shares, which was always small for West Asia, diminished greatly for East Asia and just a little for Southeast Asia, but increased moderately for South Asia. The convergence towards the per capita income level in the world economy was striking in East Asia, modest in Southeast Asia, and the least in South Asia, while per capita incomes in West Asia fluctuated around the world average. In comparison with per capita incomes in industrialized countries, there was a significant convergence for East Asia and a modest convergence for Southeast Asia, particularly after 2000, but the income gap remained large, South Asia witnessed a divergence for three decades followed by a recovery after 2000 but no convergence over the entire period, while West Asia experienced fluctuations driven by oil prices to stay roughly where it was.[9]

4. Growth, convergence, and divergence

The changes in the global significance of Asia over time depend upon its economic performance as compared with the rest of the world. It is obvious that differences in GDP growth rates, in real terms, underlie the changing share of any country-group, or continent, in world GDP. It is simple arithmetic that differences in growth rates of GDP and population determine differences in growth rates of GDP per capita, which in turn shape convergence or divergence in per capita incomes. Therefore, Table 2.4 sets out growth rates in GDP and GDP per capita for Asia, and its constituent sub-regions, compared with Africa, Latin America, developing countries, industrialized countries, and the world economy from 1970 to 2016, also subdivided in time for the periods 1971–1980, 1981–1990, 1991–2000, 2001–2008 and 2009–2016. It is logical to choose decades for this purpose. However,

Table 2.4 Growth rates in the world economy by country-groups and regions compared with growth rates in Asia and its sub-regions: 1970–2016 (per cent per annum)

	1971–1980	1981–1990	1991–2000	2001–2008	2009–2016	1971–2016
GDP						
World	3.70	3.45	2.96	3.56	2.81	2.96
Industrialized Countries	3.22	3.41	2.76	2.25	1.65	2.47
Developing Countries	5.36	3.59	4.66	6.48	4.96	4.53
Latin America	5.74	2.03	2.98	4.21	2.12	2.83
Africa	4.05	2.45	2.81	5.72	3.32	3.28
Asia	5.38	5.14	5.99	7.57	6.04	5.80
East Asia	7.24	9.39	8.21	8.95	6.77	8.21
Southeast Asia	6.89	5.10	4.41	5.70	5.07	5.33
South Asia	3.54	5.34	5.56	7.38	6.48	5.43
West Asia	4.66	1.30	3.78	5.93	4.44	3.20
GDP per capita						
World	1.93	1.44	1.12	1.75	1.28	1.10
Industrialized Countries	2.48	2.85	2.15	1.70	1.26	1.86
Developing Countries	3.13	1.42	2.99	5.03	3.59	2.72
Latin America	3.03	–0.76	0.47	1.72	–0.46	0.21
Africa	1.72	0.44	1.17	4.43	2.18	1.57
Asia	3.25	3.07	4.40	6.35	4.96	4.10
East Asia	5.46	7.71	7.37	8.38	6.24	7.12
Southeast Asia	4.51	2.92	2.77	4.40	3.86	3.56
South Asia	1.17	2.97	3.58	5.75	5.14	3.41
West Asia	1.64	–1.59	1.39	3.44	2.22	0.57

Note: GDP and GDP per capita are measured in constant 2010 US$. The average annual growth rates for each of the periods have been calculated by fitting a semi-log linear regression equation LnY = a + bt and estimating the value of b.

Source: United Nations, National Accounts Statistics.

the dividing line for the last two sub-periods is different, as the global economic crisis that surfaced in late 2008 led to a sharp slowdown in growth across the world. This evidence reveals clear differences in the growth performance of Asia compared with other parts of the world and of its sub-regions compared with each other.

It shows that GDP growth rates in Asia were consistently higher than in Africa, Latin America, developing countries, industrialized countries, and the world economy. This was so throughout in every sub-period. The differences vis-à-vis Africa and Latin America were most pronounced during 1981–1990 and 1991–2000, their lost decades, and during 2009–2016 after the slump in 2008. The differences vis-à-vis the industrialized countries increased during 1991–2000 and 2001–2008 but were most pronounced during 2009–2016 because of the Great Recession. Over a period that spanned almost five decades, 1970–2016, the GDP growth rate in Asia was 5.8 per cent per annum compared with 3 per cent per annum in the world economy, 2.5 per cent per annum in industrialized countries, 4.5 per cent per annum in developing countries (attributable essentially to Asia) and around 3 per cent per annum in Africa and Latin America. It is no surprise that, in world GDP, Asia increased its share at the expense of industri-alized countries and accounted for almost the entire increase in the share of developing countries.

Similarly, GDP per capita growth rates in Asia were consistently higher than in other country-groups and the world economy throughout in every sub-period. The differences vis-à-vis Africa and Latin America were small in the 1970s but became substantial during 1981–1990 and 1991–2000, their lost decades, and mounted even further thereafter. The differences vis-à-vis industrialized countries were modest during 1971–1980 and 1981–1990, but as population growth slowed down in Asia and economic growth slowed down in the West, these differences grew wider, so much so that during 2009–2016, GDP per capita growth in Asia, at 5 per cent per annum, was almost four times that in industrialized countries at 1.3 per cent per annum. Over the entire period, 1970–2016, the GDP per capita growth rate in Asia was 4.1 per cent per annum, compared with 1.1 per cent per annum in the world economy, 1.9 per cent per annum in industrialized coun-tries, 2.7 per cent per annum in developing countries (driven largely by Asia), 0.2 per cent per annum in Latin America, and 1.6 per cent per annum in Africa. Consequently, starting around 1990, GDP per capita in Asia witnessed a signifi-cant convergence towards GDP per capita in the world economy and caught up with and surpassed GDP per capita in developing countries, but the convergence towards GDP per capita in industrialized countries was far more limited. Insofar as Asia was a constituent of developing countries, the faster growth in its GDP per capita inevitably created divergences elsewhere in that country-group. Over this period, Africa experienced a significant divergence in per capita incomes, to replace Asia as the poorest continent in the world, while Latin America, at much higher per capita income levels, witnessed neither convergence nor divergence to stay roughly where it was (Nayyar, 2013).

The disparities in GDP growth rates within Asia, between its constituent sub-regions, are just as striking, which are reflected in changes in their respective shares of GDP in developing countries and in the world. GDP growth rates in East Asia were much higher than in Asia, which in turn were significantly higher than elsewhere in the world, in every sub-period. GDP growth rates in Southeast Asia and South Asia were lower than in East Asia and Asia but were mostly higher than elsewhere in the world and that difference became larger after 2000. GDP growth rates in West Asia fluctuated. During 1970–2016, the GDP growth rate was 8.2 per cent per annum in East Asia, 5.3 per cent per annum in Southeast Asia, and 5.4 per cent per annum in South Asia, all distinctly higher than elsewhere in the world, while West Asia at 3.2 per cent per annum was closer to the rest of the world. Thus, while every sub-region of Asia increased its share in world GDP, of the total increase in Asia's share, East Asia contributed two-thirds.

The disparities in GDP per capita growth rates within Asia were even more pronounced, which are reflected in the timing, degree, and pace of convergence in per capita incomes for each of its constituent sub-regions relative to industrialized countries and the world. GDP per capita growth rates in East Asia were far higher than elsewhere in Asia, and the world outside, in every sub-period without exception. In Southeast Asia, GDP per capita growth rates were moderate by Asian standards and were lower than the Asian average during 1981–1990 and 1991–2000. In South Asia, GDP per capita growth rates were the lowest in Asia and in the world during 1971–1980, lower than the average for Asia and developing countries during 1981–1990, closer to the Asian average and higher than developing countries during 1991–2000, but were the highest in the world, excepting East Asia, during 2001–2008 and 2009–2016. West Asia was the exception insofar as GDP per capita growth rates were lower than almost every other part of Asia and the world. Over the entire period, 1970–2016, the GDP per capita growth rate was spectacular at 7.1 per cent per annum in East Asia (on average doubling its per capita income every ten years), respectable at 3.6 per cent per annum in Southeast Asia and 3.4 per cent per annum in South Asia (on average doubling per capita incomes every twenty years), but poor at 0.6 per cent per annum in West Asia (the lowest in the world except for Latin America where it was a mere 0.2 per cent per annum).

Thus, as the gap in GDP per capita growth rates widened, East Asia converged towards world per capita income, starting 1990, and almost caught up with it in 2016, just as it witnessed some convergence relative to industrialized countries starting 1990, which gathered pace after 2000 as industrialized countries slowed down but its extent was circumscribed by the initial income gap that was wide. Starting around 2000, Southeast Asia witnessed a significant convergence towards the world average and a rather limited convergence relative to industrialized countries, despite its modest growth in GDP per capita, as their growth experienced a sharp slowdown. South Asia experienced a divergence in per capita incomes relative to both industrialized countries and the world economy during 1970–2000, despite its high GDP growth rates during 1981–2000 because of population growth, as its share in world population rose by 3.3 percentage points over three decades, so that the rapid growth in GDP per capita during 2000–2016 only reversed the earlier divergence, returning South Asia's per capita income, relative to industrialized countries, in 2016 to where it was in 1970. West Asia was the other outlier, even if its per capita income levels were far higher than in the other sub-regions, as its GDP per capita fluctuated mostly in consonance with world oil prices, with no discernible convergence or divergence over the entire period.

5. Manufacturing and industrialization

The most visible outcome of industrialization is in output. But it is difficult to find time series evidence on industrial production for country-groups in the world economy. And there are problems that arise from the comparability of data over time. It is, therefore, simplest to consider manufacturing value-added in Asia for a comparison with other parts of the world. It is also useful to make such a comparison for manufactured exports, insofar as it reflects the ability of the industrial sector in Asia to compete in world markets.

Table 2.5 sets out the evidence on manufacturing value added in the world economy, industrialized countries and developing countries compared with Asia and its sub-regions, for selected benchmark years. Between 1970 and 2016, in current prices at market exchange rates, the share of industrialized countries fell from 70 per cent to 50 per cent while the share of developing countries rose from 10 per cent to 48 per cent. The share of developing countries rose by 38 per cent, of which 20 per cent was at the expense of industrialized countries while 18 per cent was at the expense of Eastern Europe and the former USSR. Asia's share rose from 4 per cent to 41 per cent, which accounted for almost the entire increase in the developing-countries share, so that the share of Latin America and Africa taken together increased by only 1 percentage point. These trends emerge with much greater clarity from Figure 2.3a. It uses time series data to reveal two distinct phases: a steady increase during 1970–2003, followed by a step jump and a rapid rise thereafter so much so that, in 2015, the share of developing countries matched that of industrialized countries.

The distribution of the rapidly rising manufacturing value-added within Asia was just as unequal between its sub-regions. Between 1970 and 2016, Asia's share in the world rose by just over 37 percentage points, of which East Asia contributed more than three-fourths, while Southeast, South and West Asia together contributed one-fifth. Once again, these trends show up even more clearly in

Table 2.5 Manufacturing value added in the world economy by country-groups compared with manufacturing value added in Asia and its sub-regions: 1970–2016

	1970	1980	1990	2000	2010	2016
(in US$ billion)						
World	*846*	*2679*	*4575*	*5557*	*10,501*	*12,088*
Industrialized Countries	*594*	*1913*	*3623*	*4438*	*5866*	*6030*
Developing Countries	*83*	*385*	*705*	*1048*	*4359*	*5819*
Asia	*30*	*154*	*381*	*607*	*3444*	*4937*
(as a percentage of World)						
Industrialized Countries	70.2	71.4	79.2	79.9	55.9	49.9
Developing Countries	9.8	14.4	15.4	18.9	41.5	48.1
Asia	3.6	5.8	8.3	10.9	32.8	40.8
East Asia	0.6	1.4	3.0	4.4	22.5	29.9
Southeast Asia	0.7	1.4	1.9	2.9	4.3	4.4
South Asia	1.4	1.4	1.5	1.7	3.1	3.5
West Asia	0.9	1.5	1.9	2.0	2.9	2.9

Note: The data on manufacturing value added are in current prices at market exchange rates. The percentages have been calculated.

Source: United Nations, UNCTAD Stat, based on UN National Accounts Statistics.

Figure 2.3b. It reveals three discernible phases. During 1970–1985, the shares of the four sub-regions were very similar and moved together. East Asia began to move ahead starting 1985 and Southeast Asia began to move ahead starting 1990. Even so, until 2003, the shares of the sub-regions were close to each other, so that South Asia and West Asia were not much behind. There was a dramatic change beginning 2004 when East Asia raced ahead leaving the others far behind, so that, in 2016, just over a decade later, the share of East Asia in world manufacturing value-added exceeded the share of the other three sub-regions put together by 19 percentage points.

The story is similar for exports of manufactured goods, which were an outcome of industrialization in Asia. Table 2.6 presents available evidence on manufactured exports from Asia and its sub-regions compared with the world economy, industrialized countries and developing countries for selected benchmark years from 1995 to 2016. Over this period, the share of industrialized countries in world manufactured exports fell from 74 per cent to 55 per cent while that of developing countries rose from 25 per cent to 44 per cent. The entire increase in the share of developing countries was at the expense of industrialized countries. Asia's share rose from 21 per cent to 39 per cent, so that the share of Latin America and Africa taken together increased from just 4 per cent to 5 per cent. Figure 2.4, which uses time-series data, shows that, over the two decades, there was a steady decrease in the share of industrialized countries and a steady, almost matching increase, in the share of developing countries, with much of the latter attributable to Asia.

(a) Country-Groups

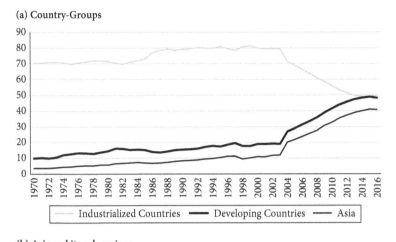

(b) Asia and its sub-regions

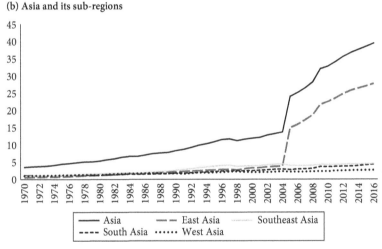

Figure 2.3 Distribution of world manufacturing value added: 1970–2016 (in percentages)

Source: Same as Table 2.6.

This rapid growth in exports of manufactured goods from Asia was distributed in a most unequal manner among its sub-regions. Between 1995 and 2016, Asia's share in the world rose by over 18 percentage points, of which East Asia contributed more than three-fourths, while Southeast Asia, South Asia and West Asia together contributed less than one-fourth. Figure 2.4b depicts the trends over time with clarity. The share of East Asia rose at a rapid pace starting in 2000. The share of Southeast Asia was stable, while the shares of South Asia and West Asia, at far lower levels, increased slowly.

The quarter century since 1990 witnessed a dramatic increase in the share of Asia in world manufacturing value added, at the expense of industrialized

Table 2.6 Manufactured exports in the world economy by country-groups compared with manufactured exports in Asia and its sub-regions: 1995–2016

	1995	2000	2005	2010	2016
(in US$ billion)					
World	*3.7*	*4.7*	*7.4*	*10.0*	*11.3*
Industrialized Countries	*2.7*	*3.3*	*4.8*	*5.8*	*6.2*
Developing Countries	*0.9*	*1.4*	*2.5*	*4.0*	*5.0*
Asia	*0.8*	*1.1*	*2.1*	*3.5*	*4.4*
(as a percentage of World)					
Industrialized Countries	73.8	69.7	65.6	58.5	54.9
Developing Countries	25.3	29.3	33.2	40.3	44.0
Asia	21.5	24.2	28.5	35.5	39.2
East Asia	13.5	15.2	19.1	25.0	27.5
Southeast Asia	6.1	7.0	6.4	6.7	7.2
South Asia	0.8	0.9	1.2	1.6	1.9
West Asia	1.0	1.1	1.9	2.3	2.5

Note: The data on manufactured exports are in current prices at market exchange rates. In this table, manufactured exports are defined as *the sum of* SITC 5 (chemicals), SITC 6 (manufactured goods), SITC 7 (machinery and transport equipment), SITC 8 (miscellaneous manufactured articles) *less* SITC 68 (non-ferrous metals) and SITC 667 (pearls, precious and semi-precious stones). The percentages have been calculated.

Source: United Nations, UNCTADStat.

countries and transition economies, and in world manufactured exports largely at the expense of industrialized countries. This catch-up in industrialization was led and dominated by East Asia. Southeast Asia was a distant second, while South Asia and West Asia made progress that was, at best, modest. A comparison with the past is instructive. There are no separate estimates for the share of Asia, but the share of China and India taken together in world manufacturing production is estimated at 47.4 per cent in 1830 and 28.3 per cent in 1860 (Table 1.4), so that the share of Asia was probably a little higher. By comparison, in 2016, the share of Asia in world manufacturing valued added was 41 per cent. Therefore, it is plausible to suggest that, in 2016, the share of Asia in world industrial production was close to its level around 1850.[10] Clearly, the end of colonialism, which meant political independence for Asian countries, made an enormous difference in their pursuit of industrialization. Of course, this would not have been possible without a sustained increase in agricultural productivity, which is discussed later in the book.

6. Engagement with the world economy

The economic significance of Asia in the global context is also shaped by the nature and degree of interaction with the outside world. The broad contours of the

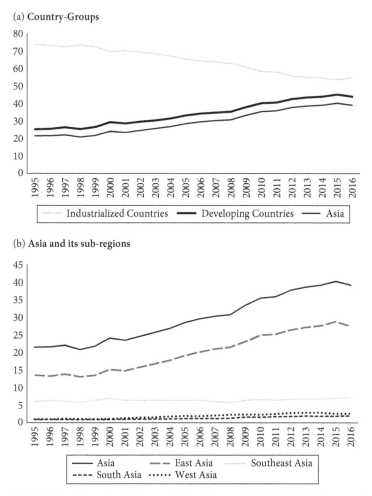

Figure 2.4 Distribution of world manufactured exports: 1995–2016 (in percentages)

Source: Same as Table 2.7.

main channels of engagement—international trade, international investment, and international migration—are explored briefly in this section.

On international trade, Table 2.7 sets out data on the value of merchandise exports and imports in the world economy, industrialized countries and developing countries compared with Asia and its sub-regions, for selected benchmark years.[11]

Between 1970 and 2016, the share of Asia in world exports rose from 8 per cent to 36 per cent, the share of developing countries rose from 19 per cent to 44 per cent, while the share of industrialized countries fell from 76 per cent to 53 per cent. Thus, the increase in Asia's share of world exports was largely at the expense

Table 2.7 Merchandise trade in the world economy compared with merchandise trade in Asia and its sub-regions: 1970–2016

	1970	1980	1990	2000	2010	2016
				Exports		
(in US$ billion)						
World	*318*	*2050*	*3496*	*6452*	*15,302*	*15,986*
Industrialized Countries	*243*	*1356*	*2534*	*4243*	*8255*	*8550*
Developing Countries	*61*	*608*	*843*	*2060*	*6438*	*6988*
Asia	*27*	*373*	*590*	*1538*	*5016*	*5743*
(as a percentage of World)						
Asia	8.4	18.0	17.0	24.0	33.0	36.0
East Asia	2.2	3.8	8.0	12.1	17.8	21.3
Southeast Asia	2.0	3.5	4.1	6.7	6.9	7.2
South Asia	1.1	0.7	0.8	1.0	1.8	2.1
West Asia	3.1	10.2	3.9	4.1	6.3	5.4
	1970	1980	1990	2000	2010	2016
				Imports		
(in US$ billion)						
World	*330*	*2091*	*3609*	*6655*	*15,421*	*16,150*
Industrialized Countries	*255*	*1505*	*2669*	*4645*	*8947*	*9183*
Developing Countries	*61*	*502*	*800*	*1918*	*6020*	*6591*
Asia	*28*	*279*	*575*	*1393*	*4631*	*5154*
(as a percentage of World)						
Asia	8.4	13.3	15.9	20.9	30.0	31.9
East Asia	2.7	4.2	7.4	11.2	16.4	17.3
Southeast Asia	2.5	3.1	4.5	5.7	6.2	6.7
South Asia	1.3	1.2	1.1	1.2	2.9	3.0
West Asia	2.0	5.0	2.9	2.8	4.6	4.9

Note: The data on absolute values of merchandise exports and imports are in current prices at market exchange rates. The percentages have been calculated.

Source: United Nations, UNCTADStat, based on UN International Trade Statistics.

of industrialized countries (23 per cent), but it was also at the expense of other developing countries (Latin America and Africa, 3 per cent) and of the residual country-group made up of Eastern Europe and the former USSR (2 per cent). The distribution of the massive increase in exports within Asia was just as unequal between its sub-regions. Between 1970 and 2016, of the 28 percentage points increase in Asia's share of world exports, East Asia contributed two-thirds, while Southeast Asia, South Asia and West Asia together contributed one-third. Over time, the share of Asia and East Asia rose rapidly, and the share of Southeast Asia increased steadily, while the share of South Asia stagnated until 2000 to increase modestly thereafter, and the share of West Asia fluctuated with oil prices.

The picture is similar on the other side of the trade coin. Between 1970 and 2016, the share of Asia in world imports rose from 8 per cent to 32 per cent, the share of developing countries rose from 18 per cent to 41 per cent, while the share of industrialized countries fell from 77 per cent to 57 per cent. The increase in Asia's share of world imports was largely at the expense of industrialized countries (20 per cent) and the residual country-group made up of Eastern Europe and former USSR (3 per cent), but in very small part also at the expense of other developing countries (Latin America and Africa, less than 1 per cent). The distribution of the increased import share of Asia among its sub-regions was less unequal. Between 1970 and 2016, of the 23.5 percentage points increase in Asia's share of world imports, East Asia contributed three-fifths, while Southeast Asia, South Asia and West Asia together contributed two-fifths. East Asia was dominant but not as much as in exports. Over time, the share of Asia as a whole rose faster than that of East Asia, the share of Southeast Asia increased until the late 1990s to stabilize thereafter, while the share of South Asia remained unchanged for decades to increase from 2000, and the share of West Asia fluctuated presumably as changes in oil prices affected incomes.

On international investment, Table 2.8 presents evidence on trends in foreign direct investment, inward and outward, in terms of average annual inflows and outflows, during the periods 1981–1990, 1991–2000, 2001–2010 and 2010–2015, in the world economy, industrialized countries and developing countries, compared with Asia and its sub-regions. It shows that Asia was not as dominant as it was in the sphere of trade although East Asia was just as dominant among its sub-regions.

Between 1981–1990 and 2010–2015, the share of industrialized countries in average annual inflows fell from 78 per cent to 51 per cent, while the share of developing countries rose from 21 per cent to 45 per cent and the share of Asia rose from 13 per cent to 29 per cent. The share of industrialized countries dropped by 27 percentage points, which accrued mostly to developing countries (24 per cent) and in small part to the residual country-group of Eastern Europe and former USSR (3 per cent). Of the increase in the share of developing countries, Asia accounted for two-thirds (16 per cent) while Latin America and Africa accounted for one-third (8 per cent). The share of Asia as a destination for foreign direct investment inflows in the world rose by 16 percentage points, of which East Asia contributed two-thirds.

Between 1981–1990 and 2010–2015, the share of industrialized countries in average annual outflows decreased from 94 per cent to 68 per cent, while the share of developing countries increased from 6 per cent to 29 per cent, of which the share of Asia rose from 5 per cent to 25 per cent while the share of Latin America and Africa increased from 1 per cent to 4 per cent. Yet, for outward flows of foreign direct investment, industrialized countries remained the primary source in the world, and Asia remained the main source from the developing world

Table 2.8 Flows of foreign direct investment in Asia and the world economy (1981–2015: in US$ billion: annual averages)

	1981–1990	1991–2000	2001–2010	2011–2015
	Inward Flows			
(in US$ billion)				
World	108.0	513.1	1097.6	1545.0
Industrialized Countries	84.7	373.9	663.1	783.0
Developing Countries	23.2	134.6	385.9	698.0
Asia	14.0	82.1	251.5	446.0
(as a percentage of World)				
Asia	13.0	16.0	22.9	28.9
East Asia	5.2	10.3	11.9	16.1
Southeast Asia	4.7	4.6	4.6	7.6
South Asia	0.3	0.5	2.0	2.4
West Asia	2.9	0.6	4.4	2.8
	1981–1990	1991–2000	2001–2010	2011–2015
	Outward Flows			
(in US$ billion)				
World	127.2	554.6	1210.9	1418.0
Industrialized Countries	119.8	500.4	965.4	958.0
Developing Countries	7.4	52.4	212.4	412.0
Asia	6.2	45.3	169.1	356.0
(as a percentage of World)				
Asia	4.8	8.2	14.0	25.1
East Asia	3.8	6.1	8.7	17.9
Southeast Asia	0.6	1.9	2.8	4.5
South Asia	0.0	0.1	0.9	0.5
West Asia	0.3	0.1	1.5	2.3

Note: The percentages have been calculated from absolute values in US$.

Source: United Nations, UNCTAD, Foreign Direct Investment Online Database.

accounting for four-fifths. The distribution among sub-regions of Asia was unequal. The share of Asia as a source of foreign direct investment outflows in the world rose by 20 percentage points, of which East Asia contributed more than two-thirds.

On international migration, statistical information is scarce. There is some evidence on the numbers of international migrants across country-groups and regions in the world and on their proportion in the total population of host countries (Nayyar, 2013). But there is no evidence on flows of international migrants by destination or source. To some extent, however, the relative importance of countries of origin is reflected in remittances from international migrants.

Table 2.9 Remittances in world economy by country-groups compared with remittances to Asia and its sub-regions: 1980–2016

	1980	1990	2000	2010	2016
(in US$ billion)					
World	*35*	*63*	*125*	*464*	*581*
Industrialized Countries	*17*	*32*	*47*	*117*	*141*
Developing Countries	*18*	*31*	*74*	*312*	*405*
of which					
Africa	5.7	8.7	9.4	53.9	61.9
Latin America	1.8	5.8	21.0	58.5	77.4
Asia	10.5	16.5	43.6	199.9	265.9
(as a percentage of World)					
Asia	29.9	26.3	34.8	43.1	45.8
East Asia	1.6	3.9	4.2	12.8	11.8
Southeast Asia	2.9	4.5	9.3	8.8	11.0
South Asia	15.0	8.9	13.7	17.7	19.0
West Asia	10.4	9.0	7.5	3.9	4.0

Note: The figures on remittances are in current prices and at market exchange rates.

Source: United Nations, UNCTADStat, based on IMF Balance of Payments Statistics, World Bank Migration and Remittances, Economist Intelligence Unit Country Data, and national sources.

Table 2.9 presents available evidence on remittances in the world economy, by country-groups, compared with Asia and its sub-regions, during the period from 1980 to 2016. Over this period, the share of industrialized countries fell from 49 per cent to 24 per cent, while the share of developing countries rose from 51 per cent to 70 per cent. The share of Asia rose from 30 per cent to 46 per cent, once again at the expense of industrialized countries. Yet the story was different from that of trade and investment. For one, the share of other developing countries—Latin America and Africa—was significant and rose from 21 per cent to 24 per cent. For another, the share of the residual country-group—Eastern Europe and former USSR—rose from zero in 1980 to 6 per cent in 2016. Figure 2.5a using time-series data shows clearly that Asia, while significant, was not dominant, as the absolute value of remittances to developing countries rose faster than remittances to Asia throughout the period. The distribution of remittances within Asia, among its constituent sub-regions, was also rather different from that in trade and investment. Figure 2.5b, based on time-series data, shows that in total remittances to Asia, South Asia had the largest share throughout, while Southeast Asia was next until 2005 when East Asia picked up, and the share of West Asia declined after 2000. It would seem that the story of remittances is different from that of trade and investment, insofar as Asia was not dominant in the developing world and East Asia was not dominant in Asia. This might be partly attributable to the fact that international migration, driven by 'push' or 'pull' factors, could be concentrated in low-income countries that send out more

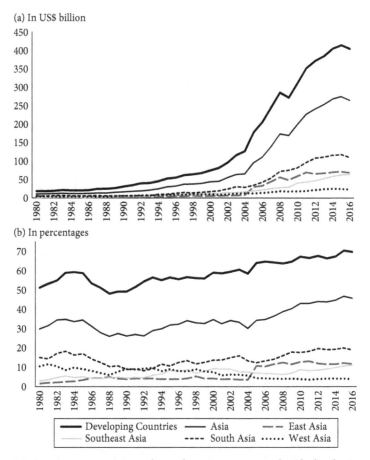

(a) In US$ billion

(b) In percentages

Developing Countries — Asia — — East Asia
Southeast Asia — — — South Asia •••••• West Asia

Figure 2.5 Remittances to Asia and its sub-regions compared with developing countries and the world economy: 1980–2016

Source: Same as Table 2.10.

migrants. But it cannot be a complete explanation, because the factors underlying international migration during the post-colonial era are more complex and have changed over time.

During the period 1950–1975, international migration from Asian countries, was made up of unskilled or semi-skilled workers destined for Western Europe to meet the demand for labour-shortages. Colonial ties and a common language were the factors that shaped these flows. For example, Britain imported workers from the Indian sub-continent, while the Netherlands imported workers from Indonesia. During 1975–2000, there have been two streams of international migration from Asian countries. First, there was a permanent emigration of people with professional qualifications or technical skills to the United States, made possible by a change in immigration laws, which extended to Canada and Australia. Second, there was a temporary migration of unskilled or semi-skilled workers in manual or clerical occupations from South Asian and Southeast Asian countries to the high-income, labour-scarce, oil-exporting countries in West Asia, followed by more recent imports of temporary workers by labour-scarce countries in East Asia. This international migration from Asia was an important factor underlying productivity increase and economic dynamism in industrialized countries, while remittance inflows from migrants eased macroeconomic constraints on growth in their home countries.

The spread of globalization, which gathered momentum from 1990, has also made it easier to move people across borders, whether guest workers or illegal immigrants, many of whom come from Asia and some of them stay on in industrialized countries often in an incarnation of small entrepreneurs. On a smaller scale, there is a movement of professionals from developing countries who can migrate permanently, live abroad temporarily, or stay at home and travel frequently for business. These people are almost as mobile as capital. This phenomenon is associated with their rise as managers to the top echelons of the corporate world in the age of shareholder capitalism. The most striking example is the substantial presence of professionals from India in the United States and Europe. For example, the CEOs of Google, and Microsoft at present are persons of Indian origin. This has also been so for Pepsi and Deutsche Bank in the recent past. Of course, there are similar professionals from other Asian countries, such as South Korea, Vietnam, Philippines, and now China too, particularly in the United States.[12]

It is interesting to juxtapose the past and the present in international migration. There is a connection that is attributable to the diaspora from the past and to globalization in the present. The diaspora from India and China, beyond its traditional meaning of Jews in exile, has its historical origins in indentured labour. There is a significant presence of this diaspora from the two Asian giants across the world not only in industrialized countries but also in developing countries. This is associated with entrepreneurial capitalism, Indian and Chinese, across the world. Migrants from other Asian countries are entrepreneurs too but, for historical reasons, the number of people whose origins lie in India or China is so much larger.

In sum, it would seem that there has been a remarkable increase in Asia's engagement with the world economy over the past fifty years, which is reflected in its growing relative importance in every dimension. The dominance of Asia, led by East Asia, is particularly striking in international trade flows, where both have expanded at the expense of all other country-groups and regions of the world. However, even though Asia and East Asia are significant in other spheres, such a dominance is not visible in international investment and international migration.

7. From regions to countries

It is important to recognize that aggregates for Asia could be deceptive because it is such a large and diverse continent. Therefore, the analysis in this chapter also disaggregated Asia into its four constituent sub-regions. It revealed that changes in aggregate output and income levels over time were uneven between East, Southeast, South and West Asia. The rising share of Asia in world industrial production and manufactured exports, too, was distributed in a most unequal manner among these sub-regions. Their growing engagement with the world economy, despite many similarities, was inevitably characterized by significant differences. It should come as no surprise if development was just as uneven between countries within, or across, the sub-regions. Clearly, a further disaggregation beyond regions, by countries, is as necessary. This is indeed essential because a meaningful analysis of development, which is difficult for sub-regions defined by geography, is both more feasible and more appropriate at the level of countries.

The choice of countries is based on three simple criteria: economic significance in development, demographic size in terms population, and representative of diversity. If the number is to be kept within manageable proportions, this choice is almost automatic, although there could be minor differences in judgement about inclusion and exclusion. Based on these criteria, the study will focus on fourteen selected economies in Asia: China, South Korea, and Taiwan in East Asia; Indonesia, Malaysia, Philippines, Singapore, Thailand, and Vietnam in Southeast Asia; Bangladesh, India, Pakistan, and Sri Lanka in South Asia; and Turkey in West Asia, which are described as the Asian-14.

Table 2.10 presents evidence on the share of the selected fourteen countries in the population and GDP of Asia for 1970, 1990, and 2016. Over this period, taken together, these countries accounted for around 90 per cent of population and more than 80 per cent of GDP in Asia. Between 1970 and 1990, seven economies (Korea, Taiwan, Indonesia, Malaysia, Singapore, Thailand, and Turkey) increased their share in Asia's GDP, while seven economies (China, Philippines, Vietnam, Bangladesh, India, Pakistan, and Sri Lanka) experienced a decrease in their share of Asia's GDP. This reflects differences in rates of economic growth for the two sets of countries. Between 1990 and 2016, only China increased its share in Asia's GDP, whereas all other countries witnessed a decrease in their share. This reflects the rapid growth in, and the economic size of, China as its share in Asia's GDP rose from 17 per cent to almost 50 per cent, so that diminished shares for others were inevitable, although Asia's share in world GDP also rose rapidly during 1990–2016.

The oil-exporting countries of West Asia are not included because, as natural-resource-based economies, they are very different from the rest of Asia. Bahrain,

Table 2.10 Economic significance of the selected 14 countries in Asia (as a percentage of the total for Asia)

	1970		1990		2016	
	Population	GDP	Population	GDP	Population	GDP
China	41.5	30.3	38.7	17.0	32.4	49.7
Korea	1.6	3.0	1.4	11.9	1.2	6.2
Taiwan	0.7	2.0	0.7	7.1	0.5	2.3
Indonesia	5.8	3.5	6.0	5.7	6.0	4.1
Malaysia	0.5	1.3	0.6	1.9	0.7	1.3
Philippines	1.8	2.5	1.3	2.1	2.4	1.4
Singapore	0.1	0.6	0.1	1.7	0.1	1.3
Thailand	1.9	2.5	1.9	3.8	1.6	1.8
Vietnam	2.2	0.9	2.3	0.3	2.2	0.9
Bangladesh	3.3	2.1	3.5	1.2	3.8	1.0
India	27.9	20.2	28.7	13.5	30.6	10.0
Pakistan	2.9	4.4	3.6	2.2	4.5	1.3
Sri Lanka	0.6	1.0	0.6	0.4	0.5	0.4
Turkey	1.8	8.5	1.8	8.9	1.8	3.8
Total above	92.6	82.8	91.0	77.6	88.2	85.5
Asia	100.0	100.0	100.0	100.0	100.0	100.0

Note: The percentages have been calculated.

Source: United Nations, National Accounts Statistics and Population Statistics.

Iran, Iraq, Kuwait, Oman, Qatar, Saudi Arabia, and United Arab Emirates accounted for just over half the population of West Asia, while their share in its GDP, significantly influenced by world oil prices, was higher at roughly three-fourths in 1990 compared with about two-thirds in 2016. These eight countries accounted for around 3.5 per cent of Asia's population, contributing 14 per cent of its GDP in 1990 and 9 per cent of its GDP in 2016, determined essentially by oil prices.

There is a high degree of concentration among the Asian-14, not only in terms of their size, reflected in population and GDP, but also in terms of industrialization, reflected in manufacturing value added, and engagement with the world economy, reflected in international trade, investment, and migration. Such concentration among a few is matched by a diversity within the few in terms of the very same attributes. Moreover, this group of countries is diverse in the three dimensions of history, geography, and economics, so that it represents the diversity of Asia. It needs to be said that a focus on the Asian-14 serves an analytical purpose to foster an understanding of the economic transformation in Asia over the past fifty years, but the study will refer to the sub-regions, as also other countries, whenever necessary and appropriate.

Conclusion

The transformation of Asia over the past fifty years, reflected in its demographic transition, social progress, and economic development, has been phenomenal. In 1970, it was the poorest continent in the world, marginal except for its large population. By 2016, there was a striking change in its relative importance. Its share of world GDP rose from less than one-tenth to three-tenths, while its income per capita surpassed that of developing countries and converged towards the world average income level, although this convergence was at best modest compared with industrialized countries because the initial income gap was so enormous. Growth in GDP and GDP per capita in Asia was much higher than in the world economy, industrialized countries and the developing world, both Africa and Latin America. Over this period, the share of Asia in world industrial production jumped from a miniscule 4 per cent to more than 40 per cent. Its share of world merchandise trade rose from one-twelfth to one-third. Its engagement with the world economy through international investment, as a destination and a source, witnessed similar change.

This transformation provides a sharp contrast with the decline and fall of Asia in the world economy during 1820–1960 in the colonial era. For Asian countries, political independence, which restored their economic autonomy and enabled them to pursue their national development objectives, made this possible. However, economic and social development was most unequal between the constituent sub-regions of Asia. East Asia was the leader and South Asia was the laggard, with Southeast Asia in the middle, while progress in West Asia did not match its high income levels. Economic growth was faster than elsewhere in the world, not only in East Asia but also in South Asia and Southeast Asia through much of the period. Yet, East Asia contributed about two-thirds of the increase in Asia's share of world GDP, while Southeast Asia, South Asia, and West Asia together contributed the remaining one-third. The proportions were similar in merchandise trade. Industrialization was even more concentrated in East Asia which accounted for more than three-fourths of the increase in Asia's share of world manufacturing value added. And it was East Asia that witnessed a significant convergence in incomes per capita.

3

Macroeconomics of growth

The pessimism of Gunnar Myrdal in *Asian Drama* turned out to be wrong, as the continent has witnessed remarkable rates of economic growth during the past five decades, which provide a sharp contrast with the preceding century in Asia and with the growth experience of industrialized countries at comparable stages of their development. The object of this chapter is to provide a macroeconomic analysis of the growth process in Asia. In analysing growth, orthodox economics seeks to focus on the supply-side. However, the demand-side, which is often neglected, also matters. What is more, the interaction between the supply-side and the demand-side in the process of growth is just as important. In fact, the macroeconomic objectives pursued, and the macroeconomic policies adopted, by governments also influence the pace of growth. In most Asian countries, which have surplus labour, the transformation of growth in economies at the macro-level into development for people at the micro-level depends upon the creation of employment and livelihoods. The discussion that follows seeks to address this range of issues.

It is obviously not possible to do so at the level of the continent as a whole, or even its sub-regions, partly because of the enormous diversity and partly because growth processes are inevitably country-specific. Moreover, the differences between countries within sub-regions are just as significant as differences between countries across sub-regions. Therefore, a meaningful analysis is possible only at the level of countries. For this purpose, I have selected fourteen economies spanning the four constituent sub-regions: China, South Korea, and Taiwan in East Asia; Indonesia, Malaysia, Philippines, Singapore, Thailand, and Vietnam in Southeast Asia; Bangladesh, India, Pakistan, and Sri Lanka in South Asia; and Turkey in West Asia. This set of economies is described as 'The Asian-14'. The logic underlying the choice of countries is explained towards the end of the preceding chapter. Taken together, these countries accounted for nine-tenths of Asia's population and contributed more than four-fifths of its income.

Section 1 provides an analytical narrative of economic growth, to highlight the differences between countries and the changes in their performance over time. Section 2 considers investment, savings, and education, important drivers of growth on the supply-side, recognizing that investment also stimulates growth on the demand-side, and pointing briefly to the underlying factors. Section 3 decomposes aggregate demand into private consumption expenditure, government final consumption expenditure, investment, and net exports, to analyse the

Resurgent Asia: Diversity in Development. Deepak Nayyar, Oxford University Press (2019). © United Nations University World Institute for Development Economics Research. DOI: 10.1093/oso/9780198849513.001.0001

implications of long-term changes in each of these components as a stimulus to growth on the demand-side. Section 4 explores the nexus between investment and exports at the macro-level, through an interaction between the supply-side and the demand-side, in the process of growth, which provides an analytical explanation of differences in performance across countries. Section 5 discusses macroeconomic objectives, which extended beyond balanced budgets and price stability to economic growth and employment creation, and macroeconomic policies, which were much broader in their use of instruments, thereby departing from orthodoxy in both thinking and practice. Section 6 compares output growth with employment growth across countries and over time, to examine the nature of the relationship between economic growth and job creation.

1. Economic growth in the Asian-14

The growth performance of Asia and its sub-regions since 1970 has been stunning. However, an analytical narrative of this process would not be complete unless it examines country-level experiences.

Tables 3.1 and 3.2 present the evidence on growth rates in GDP and GDP per capita, respectively, for the Asian-14 from 1970 to 2016, subdivided in time for the periods 1971–1980, 1981–1990, 1991–2000, 2001–2008 and 2009–2016. The dividing line for the last two sub-periods is not decadal, because the financial crisis and the Great Recession led to an economic slowdown in the world starting in 2009. It also provides a longer-term perspective, by presenting average annual growth rates for each of these countries in the periods 1971–1990, 1991–2016 and 1971–2016. The evidence on growth rates in the sub-regions, discussed earlier, is set out only as a point of reference for comparison.

Table 3.1 shows that China, South Korea, Taiwan, and Singapore witnessed the most rapid GDP growth, in the range of 7–9 per cent per annum over a period spanning almost five decades. China was the star performer with GDP growth rates of 8–10 per cent per annum during 1981–2016. In South Korea and Taiwan, average annual GDP growth rates were almost 9 per cent during 1971–1990 but less than 5 per cent during 1991–2016, whereas in Singapore these growth rates were 7.5 per cent and 5.6 per cent respectively. In the Southeast Asian countries, except for Philippines, GDP growth rates were in the range of 5–6 per cent per annum during 1971–2016. In Indonesia, Malaysia, and Thailand, these growth rates were significantly lower in 1991–2016 as compared with 1971–1990 (a consequence of the reforms introduced after the Asian financial crisis), while the opposite was true for Vietnam and Philippines. In South Asia, over the entire period 1971–2016, the GDP growth rate was almost 6 per cent per annum in India, but lower in the range of 4.5–5 per cent per annum in Bangladesh, Pakistan,

Table 3.1 GDP growth rates in the Asian-14: 1970–2016 (per cent per annum)

	1971–1980	1981–1990	1991–2000	2001–2008	2009–2016	1971–1990	1991–2016	1971–2016
East Asia	7.24	9.39	8.21	8.95	6.77	8.21	7.94	8.19
China	5.79	9.95	9.89	10.67	7.72	8.07	9.41	9.14
South Korea	9.53	9.91	3.20	4.49	3.20	8.86	4.67	6.85
Taiwan	9.54	8.48	6.17	5.10	3.08	8.63	4.45	6.42
Southeast Asia	6.89	5.10	4.41	5.70	5.07	5.81	4.64	5.33
Indonesia	7.47	5.74	3.49	5.29	5.39	6.58	4.30	5.37
Malaysia	7.52	5.02	6.40	5.64	5.24	6.29	5.00	5.98
Philippines	5.87	1.00	3.49	5.20	6.05	3.14	4.44	3.43
Singapore	7.76	6.64	6.75	6.88	4.72	7.49	5.61	6.69
Thailand	7.11	7.60	3.50	5.14	3.41	6.77	3.74	5.62
Vietnam	4.80	5.13	7.62	6.91	6.91	5.03	6.61	6.16
South Asia	3.54	5.34	5.56	7.38	6.48	4.46	6.29	5.43
Bangladesh	2.64	3.83	4.74	5.89	6.12	3.31	5.49	4.53
India	3.49	5.65	6.09	7.80	6.83	4.51	6.73	5.73
Pakistan	4.93	6.04	3.51	5.50	3.89	5.85	3.93	4.72
Sri Lanka	4.59	3.80	5.15	5.99	5.89	4.67	5.25	4.83
West Asia	4.66	1.30	3.78	5.93	4.44	1.58	4.18	3.20
Turkey	4.39	5.21	3.85	6.58	6.88	4.08	4.38	4.18
Asia	5.38	5.14	5.99	7.57	6.04	4.50	6.30	5.80

Note: GDP is measured in constant 2010 US dollars. The average annual growth rates for each of the periods have been calculated by fitting a semi-log linear regression equation LnY = a + bt and estimating the value of b.

Source: Author's calculations from United Nations, National Accounts Statistics.

and Sri Lanka. Unlike most other Asian countries, in India, Bangladesh, and Sri Lanka, these growth rates were significantly higher in 1991–2016 as compared with 1971–1990, although Pakistan conformed to the opposite. In Turkey, GDP growth rates were in the range of 4 per cent per annum during 1971–1990, 1991–2016 and 1971–2016, but much higher in the range of 6.5 per cent per annum during 2001–2016.

Table 3.2 shows that the story of GDP per capita growth is similar but not quite the same, since the timing and pace of the slowdown in population growth differed across these countries. Over the entire period, 1971–2016, growth in GDP per capita was 8 per cent per annum in China, while it was close to 6 per cent per annum in South Korea and Taiwan. It was in the range 4–4.5 per cent per annum in Vietnam, Singapore, and Thailand, in the range 3.5–3.75 per cent per annum in India, Sri Lanka, Indonesia, and Malaysia, and in the range of 2–2.5 per cent per annum in Turkey, Bangladesh, and Pakistan, with Philippines at just 1 per cent per annum. However, during 1991–2016 as compared with 1971–1990, average annual growth rates of GDP per capita were more than 3 percentage points lower in South Korea and Taiwan, 2.5 percentage points lower in Singapore, 1.5–2 percentage points lower in Indonesia, Malaysia, and Thailand, and 1 percentage point lower in Pakistan. In sharp contrast, during 1991–2016 as compared with 1971–1990, average annual growth rates of GDP per capita were 3.75 percentage points higher in Vietnam, 3 percentage points higher in India and Bangladesh, 2 percentage points higher in Philippines, 1.5 percentage points higher in Sri Lanka, and 1 percentage point higher in Turkey. China's spectacular performance was about the same in both periods. It would seem that, between 1971–1990 and 1991–2016, growth in income per capita slowed down in the East Asian Tigers (South Korea, Taiwan, and Singapore) and their second-tier followers in Southeast Asia (Malaysia, Thailand, and Indonesia), which was attributable to the long-term effects of the Asian financial crisis, whereas it gathered pace in India, Vietnam, Bangladesh, and Sri Lanka. Philippines and Turkey picked up whereas Pakistan slowed down, but their per capita income growth was the slowest in Asia.

This analytical narrative of economic growth in the Asian-14 could have more clarity and precision, if it is supported by a country classification that makes a distinction between high, medium and low growth in GDP, and GDP per capita, during 1971–1990, 1991–2016 and 1971–2016. In such an exercise, it is necessary to select thresholds that define categories. For GDP growth, more than 6.5 per cent per annum is defined as high growth, 5 to 6.5 per cent per annum is defined as medium growth, and less than 5 per cent per annum is defined as low growth. For growth in GDP per capita, in view of declining population growth rates, the thresholds are lowered by 1.5 percentage points, so that more than 5 per cent per annum is high growth, 3.5 to 5 per cent per annum is medium growth, and less

Table 3.2 GDP per capita growth rates in the Asian-14: 1970–2016 (per cent per annum)

	1971–1980	1981–1990	1991–2000	2001–2008	2009–2016	1971–1990	1991–2016	1971–2016
East Asia	5.46	7.71	7.37	8.38	6.24	6.56	7.31	7.12
China	4.01	8.24	9.06	10.09	7.18	6.43	8.78	8.04
South Korea	7.92	8.75	5.16	4.05	2.79	7.45	4.08	5.91
Taiwan	7.73	7.14	5.55	4.49	2.75	7.03	3.89	5.46
Southeast Asia	4.51	2.92	2.77	4.40	3.86	3.56	3.27	3.53
Indonesia	4.98	3.70	1.98	3.91	4.15	4.30	2.92	3.65
Malaysia	5.05	2.28	3.90	3.72	3.48	3.75	2.93	3.60
Philippines	3.08	−1.70	1.20	3.34	4.42	0.40	2.50	1.11
Singapore	6.34	4.41	4.17	4.17	2.96	5.64	3.16	4.36
Thailand	4.65	5.83	2.44	4.49	2.99	4.69	2.99	4.35
Vietnam	2.58	2.86	6.05	5.97	4.66	2.78	5.48	4.47
South Asia	1.17	2.97	3.58	5.75	5.14	2.07	4.62	3.41
Bangladesh	0.37	1.17	2.62	2.34	4.97	0.74	3.88	2.41
India	1.18	3.44	4.19	6.22	5.59	2.23	5.13	3.81
Pakistan	1.95	2.82	1.06	3.44	1.81	2.68	1.74	2.08
Sri Lanka	2.75	2.39	4.41	5.23	5.39	3.06	4.58	3.78
West Asia	1.64	−1.59	1.39	3.44	2.22	−1.40	1.78	0.57
Turkey	2.08	3.20	2.26	5.60	5.01	1.89	2.93	2.45
Asia	3.25	3.07	4.40	6.35	4.96	2.50	5.00	4.10

Note: GDP per capita is measured in constant 2010 US dollars. The average annual growth rates for each of the periods have been calculated by fitting a semi-log linear regression equation $LnY = a + bt$ and estimating the value of b.

Source: Author's calculations from United Nations, National Accounts Statistics.

than 3.5 per cent per annum is low growth. These thresholds might seem high when compared with average annual growth rates for the industrialized countries and the world economy during 1971–2016, which were 2.5 per cent and 3 per cent per annum respectively for GDP and 1.9 per cent and 1.1 per cent per annum respectively for GDP per capita (Table 2.4), with similar or lower average annual growth rates in Latin America and Africa. Growth rates in Asia were far higher. Thus, if thresholds for Asia were selected based on averages in the rest of the world, each of the Asian-14 would be a high-growth country in terms of both GDP and GDP per capita. Quite apart from yielding a classification that is normal rather than skewed, the selected thresholds also have their own underlying logic. A growth rate of 6.5 per cent per annum would double GDP in just over one decade. A growth rate of 5 per cent per annum would double GDP, or GDP per capita, in fourteen years. A growth rate of 3.5 per cent per annum would double GDP per capita in twenty years. These examples based on the arithmetic of compound growth rates fit the experience of many countries in the Asian-14.

The results of this exercise are set out in Table 3.3, which presents a classification of countries into three groups—high, medium and low growth in GDP and GDP per capita—for the periods 1971–1990, 1991–2016 and 1971–2016. It is important to point out that, in each category for each period, the names of the countries are in descending order of growth rates in GDP, and GDP per capita, respectively.

The table is self-explanatory. It clearly shows the movement of countries from one category to another. In terms of GDP growth, between 1971–1990 and 1991–2016, South Korea and Taiwan moved from high to low, as did Indonesia and Thailand, Singapore moved from high to medium, while Pakistan moved from medium to low. In terms of GDP per capita growth, South Korea and Taiwan moved from high to medium, Singapore moved from high to low, while Thailand, Malaysia, and Indonesia moved from medium to low. Movements were in the opposite direction too. In terms of GDP growth, between 1971–1990 and 1991–2016, India moved from low to high, Vietnam from medium to high, while Bangladesh and Sri Lanka from low to medium. In terms of GDP per capita growth, India moved from low to high, while Sri Lanka and Bangladesh from low to medium. During both these periods, for GDP as well as GDP per capita, China was in the high growth category, while Philippines and Turkey were in the low growth category. The entire period from 1971 to 2016 reflects the outcome of both sets of movements. During 1971–2016, China, South Korea, and Singapore were in the high GDP growth category, while China, South Korea, and Taiwan were in the high GDP per capita growth category, but Turkey, Bangladesh, Pakistan, and Philippines were in the low growth category for both GDP and GDP per capita. During 1971–2016, around half the countries among the Asian-14 were in the medium growth space for GDP as well as GDP per capita.

Table 3.3 Country classification of the Asian-14 by growth rates (per cent per annum)

	1971–1990	1991–2016	1971–2016
GDP			
High (more than 6.5)	South Korea Taiwan China Singapore Thailand Indonesia	China India Vietnam	China South Korea Singapore Taiwan
Medium (5 to 6.5)	Malaysia Pakistan Vietnam	Singapore Bangladesh Sri Lanka Malaysia	Vietnam Malaysia India Thailand Indonesia
Low (less than 5)	Sri Lanka India Turkey Bangladesh Philippines	South Korea Taiwan Philippines Turkey Indonesia Pakistan Thailand	Sri Lanka Pakistan Bangladesh Turkey Philippines
GDP per capita			
High (more than 5)	South Korea Taiwan China Singapore	China Vietnam India	China South Korea Taiwan Vietnam
Medium (3.5 to 5)	Thailand Indonesia Malaysia	Sri Lanka South Korea Taiwan Bangladesh	Singapore Thailand India Sri Lanka Indonesia Malaysia
Low (less than 3.5)	Sri Lanka Vietnam Pakistan India Turkey Bangladesh Philippines	Singapore Thailand Turkey Malaysia Indonesia Philippines Pakistan	Turkey Bangladesh Pakistan Philippines

Source: Tables 3.1 and 3.2.

2. Investment and savings as drivers of growth

It is widely accepted, across the spectrum of different ideological perspectives, that high rates of investment and saving were among the most important drivers of economic growth in Asia.[1] This section examines the trends in investment and saving among the Asian-14 during the period from 1970 to 2016, to analyse the factors underlying the high investment rates and savings rates. In addition, it emphasizes the importance of education as a driver of growth in Asia.

In a closed economy, investment is possible only if there are savings, so that, by definition the two must be equal. This must be so *ex post*. However, *ex ante*, investors and savers are not the same. It is firms that invest and households that save. Thus, firms must have access to credit from commercial banks or the financial system, an institutional setting that Hicks (1937) describes as an 'over-draft economy', which allows investment to be financed in advance of, and independent of, the level of savings in the economy. In an open economy, investment can exceed savings if the country borrows abroad, and savings can exceed investment if the country exports capital. Therefore, the difference between investment and saving in an open economy must, *ex post*, be equal to the difference between imports and exports (of goods and services).[2] Thus, an economy can invest more than it saves by borrowing from abroad. Ultimately, however, investment rates will come down if domestic savings are not enough, because external debt will accumulate, which in turn must be repaid from domestic savings. Thus, both investment and savings matter for growth.

Table 3.4 outlines the trends in investment rates (gross capital formation as a proportion of gross domestic product) as a percentage of GDP in the Asian-14 during the period 1970–2016. In order to keep the statistics within manageable proportions, the figures are averages for three-year periods centred on the selected

Table 3.4 Investment in the Asian-14: 1970–2016 (as a percentage of GDP)

	1971	1980	1990	2000	2010	2015
China	34.4	35.4	35.9	35.2	47.4	45.2
South Korea	24.4	35.0	39.4	31.8	31.1	29.1
Taiwan	26.7	32.7	25.7	25.0	22.8	21.2
Indonesia	15.0	22.1	29.3	18.4	32.5	34.4
Malaysia	19.9	31.4	33.3	24.5	21.5	25.4
Philippines	23.9	33.9	25.0	19.8	19.2	22.0
Singapore	39.7	44.0	34.6	31.8	27.7	26.9
Thailand	26.4	29.8	39.7	21.9	24.3	22.7
Vietnam	14.5	14.5	14.7	29.5	34.2	27.0
Bangladesh	4.0	20.4	17.4	22.8	26.6	29.0
India	21.0	27.0	28.8	27.0	39.4	32.7
Pakistan	14.2	16.8	17.8	14.8	15.8	15.1
Sri Lanka	19.8	32.6	24.0	27.4	30.3	30.7
Turkey	18.0	18.4	23.2	21.1	27.1	28.5

Note: The figures in this table are a three-year average centred around the benchmark year specified in the table.

Source: Author's calculations from UN National Accounts Statistics based on gross capital formation and GDP in current market prices.

benchmark years. This also smoothens out short-term year-to-year fluctuations. Moreover, figures in the table are based on eighteen observations, rather than just six for the selected benchmark years, over a period that spans forty-seven years. It shows that investment rates were stable at a high level of around 35 per cent in China during 1970–2000 to rise significantly thereafter, while investment rates in South Korea, Taiwan, and Singapore rose until the late 1990s but fell after the Asian financial crisis. The Southeast Asian countries—Indonesia, Malaysia, and Thailand—also witnessed a significant increase in investment rates during 1970–1990, which dropped sharply in 2000 following the Asian financial crisis to recover only in part thereafter. Interestingly enough, 1980 was the peak in investment rates for Philippines and Sri Lanka, which did not recover after the financial crisis in the former but returned to earlier levels from 2010 in the latter. Between 1970 and 2010, investment rates in India and Vietnam doubled, to drop in 2016, while investment rates in Bangladesh rose steadily throughout. Investment rates stagnated at a level of about 15 per cent in Pakistan over the entire period, but rose significantly after 1980 in Turkey. These trends in investment rates, for the Asian-14, are mirrored in differences in their growth performance across countries over time.

In economics, the relationship between investment and growth in an economy is measured by the incremental capital-output ratio (ICOR), which is the ratio of the investment rate to the GDP growth rate. Thus, the higher the ICOR, the lower the productivity of investment. If the ICOR rises over time, any given investment rate will mean a lower growth rate, while the investment rate would have to be higher just to maintain the growth rate. ICORs, estimated for the Asian-14 during 1970–2016, are set out in Table A.3.1 in the Appendix. It shows that, during 1991–2016, rising investment rates in China, India, Vietnam, Bangladesh, and Sri Lanka, with stable ICORs, meant higher growth rates, whereas falling investment rates in South Korea, Taiwan, Malaysia, Thailand, and Indonesia, with rising ICORs, meant significantly lower growth rates. Investment rates in Philippines dropped but the ICOR also did, yielding a higher growth rate.

Given the diversity of Asia, it is obviously difficult to provide generalized hypotheses about investment behaviour. Even so, it is possible to highlight some underlying factors that were common to the Asian-14, although their relative importance may have differed across countries and changed over time. Public investment, particularly in infrastructure but also elsewhere, played a leading role in the earlier stages of development as a driver of growth.[3] In many of the Asian-14, governments also established large public sector firms, for example, in petroleum, steel, telecommunications, transport, or energy, going even further into commercial banks and development banks. To begin with, this might have been driven by the absence of private investment in these sectors because of the lumpiness, risk, or gestation lags associated with such investments. But such public investment reduced the cost of inputs used by the private sector or increased the demand for goods produced by the private sector. In the process, public investment crowded-in private investment pushing up investment rates.[4] At the same time, development banks provided long-term financing on concessional terms, for private investment in infrastructure, manufacturing and services, which might not have been forthcoming without such support.[5] Over time, the expansion of private sectors led to profits that were reinvested, creating a profits–investment nexus forming a virtuous circle, also described as profit-led growth.[6] This was reinforced by strategic support in the form of industrial policy, for example through access to credit at low interest rates, or trade policy, for example through protection for domestic manufacturing in earlier stages followed by promotion or incentives for manufactured exports in later stages.[7]

UN national accounts statistics do not provide data on domestic savings. The only source for cross-country data, then, is the World Bank, which estimates gross domestic savings as GDP minus final consumption expenditure using the residual method. This is, at best, a rough approximation, which is not comparable with the investment rates discussed above.[8] Table 3.5 sets out these estimates of gross domestic savings as a percentage of GDP. In order to keep the statistics within manageable proportions, it uses time-series data to present five-year averages for nine sub-periods during 1971–2015. A comparison between 1971–1975 and 2011–2015 is instructive. Gross domestic savings as a proportion of GDP rose from one-fifth, or less from around one-eighth, to one-third in South Korea, Taiwan, Indonesia, Malaysia, Thailand, and India. The high-saving economies were Singapore, where this proportion rose from one-fourth to more than one-half, and China, where this proportion rose from one-third to almost one-half. In Vietnam and Sri Lanka, these proportions rose to one-fourth, and in Bangladesh to one-fifth. However, savings rates dropped in Philippines from one-fourth to one-sixth and in Turkey from three-tenths to one-fourth. In Pakistan, the savings rate in 1971–1975 and 2011–2015 was exactly the same at 8 per cent although it averaged around 15 per cent during 1991–2005. A comparison between 1991–1995 and 2001–2005 is also instructive. It shows that, following the Asian financial crisis, savings rates dropped sharply in South Korea, Taiwan, Indonesia, Malaysia, Philippines, and Thailand. Evidence for some of the Asian-14, which is available for 1960 even if is not quite comparable, suggests a phenomenal increase in savings rates for some but not all countries. In 1960, gross domestic savings as a proportion of GDP were 1 per cent in South Korea, 13 per cent in Taiwan, 8 per cent in Indonesia, 27 per cent in Malaysia, 16 per cent in Philippines, 14 per cent in Thailand, 8 per cent in Bangladesh, 14 per cent in India, 5 per cent in Pakistan, 11 per cent in Sri Lanka, and 13 per cent in Turkey.[9]

What can we learn from macroeconomic theory about savings behaviour in Asian countries? The Keynes (1936) hypothesis suggests that the marginal propensity to consume falls as income levels rise so that the average savings rates in an

Table 3.5 Estimated gross domestic savings in the Asian-14: 1970–2015 (as a percentage of GDP)

	1971–1975	1976–1980	1981–1985	1986–1990	1991–1995	1996–2000	2001–2005	2006–2010	2011–2015
China	36.5	36.5	33.8	36.5	40.6	38.8	42.1	50.1	49.3
South Korea	19.1	28.1	30.0	39.3	38.5	36.6	33.9	33.7	34.5
Taiwan	–	–	32.2	34.4	28.5	27.7	28.3	29.8	31.1
Indonesia	18.7	24.7	25.1	27.8	29.9	27.9	26.3	30.9	34.0
Malaysia	21.6	31.1	30.0	34.9	37.8	45.8	42.8	41.8	35.4
Philippines	25.8	27.3	24.4	20.0	14.9	14.9	15.7	16.9	16.0
Singapore	26.9	34.5	43.9	43.0	48.4	50.0	45.3	53.0	53.6
Thailand	21.2	22.4	22.9	31.3	36.5	34.5	30.9	32.1	31.0
Vietnam	–	–	–	17.9	15.2	22.1	28.5	26.5	27.9
Bangladesh	–	–	12.6	14.9	13.4	18.2	20.8	20.5	21.6
India	11.0	14.1	14.8	18.3	23.7	24.4	28.0	33.1	32.0
Pakistan	8.0	7.9	7.2	10.3	16.4	14.9	16.5	10.6	8.4
Sri Lanka	14.3	17.1	18.4	17.2	17.8	18.3	16.9	17.9	24.0
Turkey	30.9	30.6	30.6	27.4	18.0	21.5	22.4	23.5	24.3

Note: The figures in this table are quinquennial averages for the period specified in the table.

Source: World Bank, World Development Indicators, except for Taiwan where the data are from the Asian Development Bank SDBS database starting from 2000 and national sources prior to 2000. Vietnam's figure for 1986–1990 is also from national sources.

economy would rise as its income rises. This idea, developed for short-run macroeconomic analysis, clearly does not explain long-term savings behaviour, for savings rates do not continue to rise as countries become richer. The Friedman (1957) hypothesis argues that permanent income, defined as expected long-term income based on the assets and education of individuals, determines the stable consumption levels that people wish to maintain over a lifetime, saving only if and when they expect that their permanent income will be less than their current income. This idea, about how people spread consumption over their lifetimes also cannot explain long-term savings behaviour in Asian countries, beginning in the 1960s when expected long-term incomes must have been very low. The Modigliani (1970 and 1976) hypothesis suggests that people plan their consumption and savings behaviour over a lifetime, evening out consumption levels, saving when they work and dis-saving when they retire, so that aggregate savings in an economy depend on its rate of growth rather than income levels. This idea provides the most plausible explanation of savings rates in the Asian-14, where populations were young and growth rates were high. As a corollary, it follows that savings rates will come down as populations age and growth slows. Of course, institutional settings would have influenced savings behaviour as well. In countries where social protection was absent or negligible, which was the case in most of the Asian-14 for much of the period, the precautionary motive would have reinforced saving habits above critical minimum levels of income. Similarly, the spread of commercial banking and the evolution of financial markets, which enabled people to save in the form of financial assets, would also have strengthened Asian saving habits.

In the context of industrialized countries, orthodox neoclassical economics explains long-run economic growth in terms of capital accumulation (investment in physical capital), labour or population growth augmented by education (human capital formation), and increases in productivity attributable to technological progress.[10] Technical progress matters far less in developing countries where growth is about catching up. And investment has been the focus of the preceding discussion. Given surplus labour, population growth is also not a driver of economic growth until these countries attain full employment. However, education, which leads to human capital formation, can drive growth through increased productivity. This proposition is also a basic tenet in the Solow model. In the new growth theories, technical progress, in which education contributes to R&D as well as learning, is endogenous.[11] In agriculture, too, education raises productivity by enabling farmers to adopt modern technologies.[12] It is no surprise that education was among the important drivers of growth on the supply-side in Asia. In fact, the step up in growth rates in post-colonial Asia was in part attributable to the spread of education in society, particularly in East and South-east Asian countries that were success stories.[13]

3. Long-run changes in the composition of aggregate demand

The simplest macroeconomic analysis of possible drivers of economic growth from the demand-side is a decomposition exercise which examines the relative importance of its principal components. For this purpose, it is useful to begin with the national income accounting identity which postulates that, for an economy, income (Y) is equal to expenditure (E). The latter has four principal components: private consumption expenditure (PCE or C_p), government final consumption expenditure (GFCE or C_g), investment, described as gross capital formation (GCF or I), and net exports (X − M, or NE, exports minus imports of goods and services). For an economy, then, the identity is: $Y = (C_{p + } C_g) + I + (X − M)$. It could also be written as Y = PCE + GFCE + GCF + NE. Thus, *ex post*, the growth in GDP, on the demand-side, can be decomposed into these four components of aggregate expenditure.

Such a decomposition was first used for Keynesian short-term analysis, in advanced economies below full employment where output was constrained only by aggregate demand. Thus, it is not strictly appropriate for developing countries, which are below full employment and output is constrained on the supply-side, when considering the long term. Yet, each of these components matters for growth. Consumption is the main source of well-being of people. Government expenditure provides for law and order, public goods, economic institutions, and infrastructure without which growth would be impossible. Investment drives growth not only on the supply-side but also from the demand-side. Exports are vital for importing capital goods and consumption goods. Thus, long-term changes in the composition of aggregate demand are a useful analytical construct, which can help understand what drives growth from the demand-side over longer periods of time. A decomposition of aggregate demand into its four components, reveals whether economic growth was private-consumption led, government-final-expenditure led, investment led, or net exports led from the demand-side.

This section analyses long-term changes in the composition of demand in the Asian-14 during the period from 1970 to 2016, subdivided into five periods 1971–1980, 1981–1990, 1991–2000, 2001–2008 and 2009–2016, for each of the countries, so that results can be presented within a manageable space. The data for this exercise are obtained from UN National Accounts Statistics. The contribution of each of the four components of aggregate demand to GDP growth is calculated from their respective share of the increase in GDP for every year during a period and then averaged for the period. The percentage share of the four components must add up to 100. Thus, if the contribution of any one component is negative, which could be so for net exports, the other three components add up to more than 100, to offset the negative.[14] The results are presented in Figure 3.1, as bar charts, with three countries in each panel. The brief discussion that follows

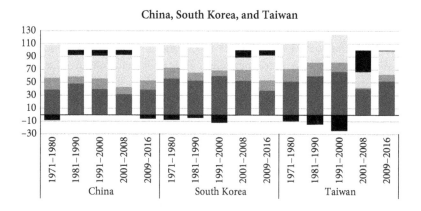

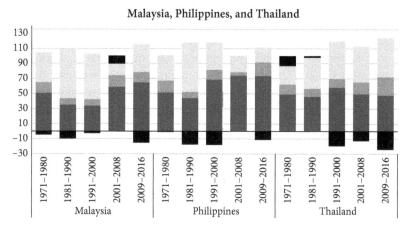

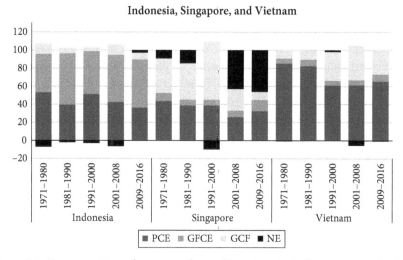

Figure 3.1 Decomposition of aggregate demand into its principal components for the Asian-14 (percentages)

Source: Author's calculations from United Nations National Accounts Statistics, see Appendix.

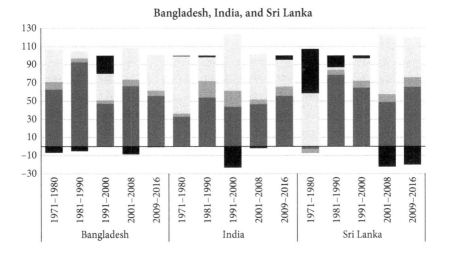

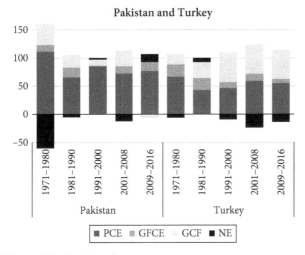

Figure 3.1 Continued

highlights the relative importance of each component as a stimulus to growth across countries in the Asian-14, pointing to changes over time.

Private consumption expenditure was an important, if not dominant, stimulus for economic growth on the demand-side in most of the Asian-14. Over the entire period, on an average, its contribution to GDP growth in the decomposition was as high as three-fourths in Pakistan, one-half to three-fourths in Philippines, two-thirds in Bangladesh, Sri Lanka, and Vietnam, more than half in South Korea, Taiwan, and Turkey, around one-half in India, Indonesia, Malaysia, and Thailand, and almost two-fifths in China. It was the lowest at just over one-third in Singapore.

Government final consumer expenditure was not a significant stimulus for growth on the demand-side in most of the Asian-14. In the decomposition, its contribution to GDP growth was in the range of one-tenth to one-fifth and, on an average, around 15 per cent. Indonesia was the striking exception where its average contribution was more than 50 per cent. At the other end, in a few countries, such as Sri Lanka and Vietnam, it contributed just about 5 per cent so that it was almost insignificant as a source of growth. However, in most countries, except South Korea, Malaysia, Bangladesh, and Turkey, its share rose during 2009–2016 perhaps as part of the fiscal stimulus in response to the recession.

Gross capital formation, or investment, was the most important stimulus for economic growth on the demand-side, as it was on the supply-side, in the Asian-14 particularly in countries with a strong growth performance, and where public investment in infrastructure might have been critical. The decomposition exercise shows that its contribution to GDP growth over the entire period was, on average, 45 per cent in both China and India, but this average was lowered by dips during 1981–2000 in China and during 1981–1990 and 2009–2016 in India. This propor- tion was on average around 40 per cent in Thailand and Turkey too, picking up in Thailand from 1981 and in Turkey from 1991. It was just as important in South Korea, Taiwan, and Singapore, but diminished greatly in significance as invest- ment dropped after the Asian financial crisis of 1997–1999 and recovered only partly in 2009–2016. Malaysia and Philippines were afflicted by the same problem after the late 1990s. Sri Lanka, Vietnam, and Bangladesh provide a contrast during 1991–2016, when the contribution of investment to their GDP growth rose to about one-third on average. The striking exception was Indonesia, where the contribution of investment to GDP growth on the demand-side averaged a mere 8 per cent over the entire period. Pakistan witnessed a steady decline in the contribution of investment to GDP growth starting in the 1980s.

The contribution of net exports to aggregate demand was either small or negative in most of the Asian-14. It was negative almost throughout in Indonesia, Malaysia, Philippines, Thailand, Vietnam, Bangladesh, Pakistan, and Turkey. Sri Lanka was different as the contribution of net exports as a stimulus to GDP growth from the demand-side was almost one-half during 1971–1980 and one-eighth during 1981– 1990 (possibly attributable to its plantation exports, especially tea, and the boom in prices of primary commodities), but turned negative during 2001–2016 given low commodity prices and the import intensity of its clothing exports. Singapore was the exception as the contribution of net exports was essentially positive over the entire period and reached a level of more than 40 per cent during 2001–2016, which was probably attributable to its size and openness to begin with and its success at industrialization thereafter. In South Korea and Taiwan it was negative until 2000 but turned positive thereafter as these economies succeeded at industrialization. In China, the contribution of net exports was positive at around 8 per cent during 1981–2008, driven by the surge in its manufactured exports, but turned negative during 2009–2016 with the Great Recession in industrialized countries that were the major markets for China's exports. In India, the contribution of net exports, mildly positive or negligible until 1990 and after 2008, turned negative during 1991–2000 (as much as −23 per cent) with a surge in imports attributable to liberalization.

It is clear that private-consumption-expenditure-led growth was an important, and for some countries a leading, stimulus on the demand-side. In contrast, government-final-consumption-expenditure-led growth was not significant in the Asian-14, with the exception of Indonesia. Gross capital formation was a crucial stimulus to growth on the demand-side, so that there was investment-led growth in most of the Asian-14, particularly in countries where economic growth was rapid. However, the contribution of net exports to growth from the demand-side was either small or negative, with the exception of Singapore and a few countries in specific sub-periods.

The observed relationship between net exports as a component of aggregate demand and as a source of growth must be interpreted with caution. It does not reflect either the degree of openness of economies or the contribution of openness to the process of development including economic growth. It is simply that exports add to aggregate demand while imports subtract from aggregate demand in the economy. The component net exports measures this difference. In terms of short-run macroeconomic analysis, exports increase the size of the base on which the foreign trade multiplier operates while imports reduce the size of the foreign trade multiplier, so that both are determinants of the income level. However, if the focus shifts to the medium term, exports are a source of demand and a means of transforming domestic resources into foreign resources which are necessary to finance development. Imports, so financed by exports, are essential to sustain desired levels of consumption, investment, and production in the economy, which in turn generate multiplier effects, so that both influence growth outcomes.[15] The section that follows illustrates other aspects of the positive relationship between trade and growth which surface over time.

4. Investment–exports–growth nexus

So far, this chapter has sought to consider possible drivers of growth either on the supply-side or on the demand-side. The discussion in this section seeks to focus on the interaction between the supply-side and the demand-side in the process of growth.

There is an important nexus between investment and exports at the macro-level that could drive economic growth. Investment creates a domestic market on the demand-side and transforms the industrial structure on the supply-side, whereas exports provide an external market on the demand-side and enforce a cost discipline on the supply-side. Hence, there is a possible cumulative causation that arises from the interaction between an expansion of demand in the domestic as well as external markets, and the restructuring of supply through capacity-creation combined with cost-efficiency. On the demand-side, investment growth and export growth together induce market expansion and could be conducive to output growth. On the supply-side, rapid investment growth may provide flexibility through a more rapid supply-side adjustment, while rapid export growth may provide discipline by enforcing cost-efficiency. The cumulative causation outlined here may lead to a virtuous circle, if investment growth coincides with export growth. Of course, this assumes that investment growth is not neutralized by an increase in the capital-output ratio reflecting a declining productivity of investment at the margin.

Table 3.6 sets out average annual growth rates, for gross domestic product, gross capital formation, and exports of goods and services, in the Asian-14, all estimated from time-series data in constant 2010 US dollars, during the periods 1971–1990 and 1991–2016. The rationale for the division into two sub-periods is that the entire period of almost five decades is too long for such an analysis, given the considerable structural change in most of these economies. What is more, the analytical narrative of growth in the Asian-14 showed that this division was appropriate in discerning phases of growth while highlighting differences in growth performance across countries over time. The evidence presented in the table suggests that when rapid investment growth and rapid export growth coincided, it was associated with rapid GDP growth.

This relationship emerges with much greater clarity from the bubble diagrams in Figure 3.2, for 1971–1990 and 1991–2016, which measure investment growth on the horizontal axis and export growth on the vertical axis. For every country, there is a distinct point on the diagram which shows its rates of growth of investment and of exports. At this point, the GDP growth rate of the country is plotted in the form of a bubble, where the size of the bubble represents the GDP growth rate, thus introducing a third dimension into the diagram.

Consider Figure 3.2a for the period 1971–1990. Apart from the bubbles, it also plots a regression line based on the observations, which has a positive slope. It would seem that higher investment growth rates were associated with higher export growth rates. But for a few outliers, the size of the bubble—GDP growth—also increases as export and investment growth rates increase. South Korea, Taiwan, and China, with the highest export-investment-GDP growth rates are in the northeast corner, clearly above the regression line. Singapore, Malaysia, and Thailand, with similar growth rates in the three dimensions, are bunched close together on the regression line. India, Pakistan, and Vietnam are the next cluster also close to the trend line. Sri Lanka and Philippines are in the southwest corner, reflecting their respective growth rates. The three outliers are Bangladesh, Indonesia, and Turkey. Investment and export growth rates in Bangladesh were high possibly because of the low base in 1971 which coincided with the liberation

Table 3.6 Growth rates in the Asian-14: gross domestic product, gross capital formation and exports (per cent per annum)

	Gross Domestic Product		Gross Capital Formation		Exports	
	1971–1990	1991–2016	1971–1990	1991–2016	1971–1990	1991–2016
East Asia						
China	8.07	9.41	8.34	10.69	13.41	12.40
South Korea	8.86	4.67	11.91	3.33	13.97	10.35
Taiwan	8.63	4.45	8.36	1.97	11.77	6.93
Southeast Asia						
Indonesia	6.58	4.30	9.22	2.48	2.62	5.25
Malaysia	6.29	5.00	7.56	3.27	8.71	5.54
Philippines	3.14	4.44	2.38	4.16	3.14	4.44
Singapore	7.49	5.61	6.77	4.83	7.49	5.61
Thailand	6.77	3.74	7.10	0.86	6.77	3.74
Vietnam	5.03	6.61	5.16	9.93	5.00	12.06
South Asia						
Bangladesh	3.31	5.49	10.65	8.46	8.59	10.03
India	4.51	6.73	4.95	8.90	5.71	12.02
Pakistan	5.85	3.93	5.50	2.17	5.75	3.88
Sri Lanka	4.67	5.25	3.78	6.81	4.09	4.33
West Asia						
Turkey	4.08	4.38	4.22	6.65	9.83	7.21

Note: The data on gross domestic product, gross domestic capital formation and exports are all in constant 2010 US dollars. Exports include goods and services. The average annual growth rates for each of the periods have been calculated by fitting a semi-log linear regression equation LnY = a + bt and estimating the value of b.

Source: Author's estimates from United Nations National Accounts Statistics.

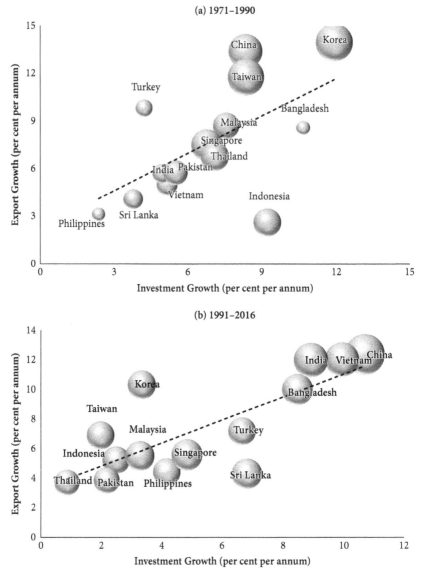

Figure 3.2 Investment growth, export growth and GDP growth: per cent per annum

Note: The size of the bubble represents the GDP growth rate. Export growth is of goods and services.

Source: Table 3.6.

war, while its GDP growth was slow. Indonesia did have a high GDP growth rate, close to that of Malaysia and Thailand, with an investment growth rate that was even higher, but its export growth rate was abysmally low. In Turkey, the export growth rate was high but both investment and GDP growth rates were low.

The story that emerges from Figure 3.2b for the period 1991–2016, which also plots the bubbles and the regression line, is somewhat different. It is China, Vietnam, India, and Bangladesh that are in the northeast corner bunched together, close to the trend line, because their high investment and export growth rates coincided in time and were associated with high GDP growth rates. In Turkey, the higher investment growth rate matched the export growth rate raising its GDP growth. Singapore was close to the trend line but its investment and export growth rates were significantly lower than in the earlier period as was the GDP growth rate. South Korea and Taiwan still had rather high export growth rates but their investment growth rates dropped very sharply from the 1971–1990 levels, as did the GDP growth rate, which was attributable to the long-term effects of the Asian financial crisis. It is possible that Singapore, South Korea, and Taiwan also experienced an increase in capital-output ratios reflecting a decline in the productivity of investment. Sri Lanka and Philippines fared better than in 1971–1990, as all three growth rates were higher, with investment and export growth rates closer together. Malaysia, Indonesia, Pakistan and Thailand were close to the trend line but in the southwest corner at the tail-end, essentially because their investment growth rates slumped even if their export growth rates did not drop as much.

The discussion on Figure 3.2, together with the evidence presented in Table 3.6, for the periods 1971–1990 and 1991–2016, does provide support for the hypothesis that there is nexus between investment and exports at the macro-level that could have driven economic growth. The experience of the Asian-14 seems to confirm that there was a virtuous circle of cumulative causation in countries where rapid investment growth coincided in time with rapid export growth, leading to rapid GDP growth. But this virtuous circle of cumulative causation did not materialize in countries where, or during periods when, there was rapid growth in either investment or exports but not in both together. It also shows that where investment growth and export growth were both slow, so was GDP growth. The contrast between Figures 3.2a and 3.2b also shows why, among the Asian-14, the growth performance of some countries—South Korea, Taiwan, Singapore, Malaysia, and Thailand—was so much better during 1971–1990, while the growth performance of other countries—India, Vietnam, Bangladesh, and Turkey—was distinctly better during 1991–2016. It also explains the consistently good growth performance of China and the relatively poor growth performance of Philippines over the entire period.

5. Macroeconomic stability and macroeconomic policies

In conventional thinking, the economic success of Asian countries, reflected in their growth and development, is attributed in part to maintaining macroeconomic stability through orthodox macroeconomic management. This view might have originated in the academic literature on the subject, but it became far more influential once it was adopted and propagated by the World Bank.[16] The countries identified as the success stories in Asia, apart from Japan, were Hong Kong, Singapore, South Korea, and Taiwan (the East Asian Tigers) and Indonesia, Malaysia, and Thailand (Newly Industrializing Countries or NICs), also described as the first-tier and second-tier NICs respectively (World Bank, 1993). The same seven plus China, in addition to Japan, were included in a worldwide selection of thirteen success stories in growth and development (World Bank, 2008).[17] Of these, China, South Korea, Singapore, Taiwan, Indonesia, Malaysia, and Thailand, are also seven among the Asian-14.

In such analysis, the orthodox characterization of macroeconomic stability is balanced budgets and price stability to ensure that volatility or unpredictability does not disrupt private investment that drives growth. Similarly, orthodoxy in macroeconomic management prescribes that fiscal deficits be kept within prudent limits, often specified as a percentage of GDP, not only to restrain inflation but also to manage internal and external debt. These are narrow perspectives in thinking about macroeconomics and inaccurate, if not misleading, characterizations of the success stories in Asia. There is, in fact, an extensive literature in heterodox macroeconomics which questions this worldview.[18] In many countries among the Asian-14, the idea of macroeconomic stability was different because it was not independent of their macroeconomic objectives. It was just as much, if not more, about economic growth and employment creation as sustainable processes. Similarly, macroeconomic policies were thought of as much broader in scope, so that fiscal policy was not simply an instrument for balancing budgets, and monetary policy was not simply an instrument for attaining price stability through inflation targeting. In fact, for much of the time, most of the Asian-14 did not conform to orthodox prescriptions in choosing their macroeconomic objectives, just as their policies and practices were non-conformist rather than conformist.

The experience of the Asian-14 over the past five decades suggests that their macroeconomic objectives extended much beyond price stability and balanced budgets, reflecting the fact that economic growth and employment creation were considered crucial in their quest for development. Thus, the use of macroeconomic policies was not confined to the management of inflation and the elimination of macroeconomic imbalances, but sought to support economic growth and foster employment creation. This heterodox, sometimes unorthodox, approach also extended to policy instruments. Fiscal policy was not reduced to a means of reducing government deficits or restoring macroeconomic balances. It was used, whenever necessary, as a potent instrument in the pursuit of economic growth and job creation, without being obsessive about fiscal deficits. Monetary policy was not reduced to a means of controlling inflation through interest rates. It was used, wherever appropriate, as a versatile instrument in which both the price (interest rate) and the volume of credit (access or allocation) were manipulated in the pursuit of directing investment or promoting industrialization, without being obsessive about inflation rates. In sum, countries that succeeded in Asia adopted a developmental approach to macroeconomic policies, which was based on an integration of short-term countercyclical fiscal and monetary policies with long-term development objectives.

Table 3.7 presents evidence on macroeconomic balances, gross fiscal balance and current account balance, in the Asian-14. The earliest year for which data on gross fiscal balances in these countries are available is 1985. Thus, the table sets out the trends in gross fiscal deficits (or surpluses) of central governments and current account deficits (or surpluses) in the balance of payments, as a percentage of GDP, over the period 1985–2016. In order to keep the statistics within manageable proportions, the figures are averages for three-year periods centred on the selected benchmark years.[19] The average annual rates of inflation, measured in terms of the consumer price index, are for the sub-periods used in the earlier narrative of growth. The following discussion considers these macroeconomic imbalances.

The gross fiscal balance for any government is the difference between its total income (from tax and non-tax revenue) and its total expenditure (on consumption and investment), which must be financed by borrowing. Orthodoxy believes that reducing gross fiscal deficits is both necessary and desirable for maintaining macroeconomic stability and managing public debt. This is a myth. The size of the fiscal deficit, or the amount of government borrowing, is the symptom and not the disease. And there is nothing in macroeconomics which stipulates an optimum level to which the fiscal deficit must be reduced as a proportion of GDP. Indeed, it is perfectly possible that a fiscal deficit at 5 per cent of GDP is sustainable in one situation while a fiscal deficit at 3 per cent of GDP is not sustainable in another. The real issue is the allocation and use of government expenditure in relation to the cost of borrowing by the government. Thus, government borrowing is always sustainable if it is used to finance investment and if the rate of return on such investment is greater than the rate of interest payable. However, government borrowing is sometimes used, at least in part, to support consumption expenditure. In that case, the rate of return on investment financed by the remainder of the borrowing must be high enough to meet the burden of servicing the entire debt, which is always difficult; it may be impossible if a large proportion of government borrowing is used to support consumption, since that yields no future income flow to the exchequer. It would seem that this simple macroeconomics was recognized in the Asian-14, despite influential orthodox thinking that stressed limits on the size of fiscal deficits as a percentage of GDP.

Table 3.7 shows that gross fiscal deficits ranged from 3 per cent to 8 per cent of GDP across countries over time, although they were lower or higher for a few countries in some periods. There were exceptions at both ends. At one end, Singapore had a fiscal surplus throughout, while South Korea was close to a fiscal

Table 3.7 Macroeconomic balances in the Asian-14: 1985–2016

	Gross Fiscal Balance (+/−) (as a percentage of GDP)					Current Account Balance (+/−) (as a percentage of GDP)					Inflation (in per cent per annum)			
	1985	1990	2000	2010	2015	1985	1990	2000	2010	2015	1981–1990	1991–2000	2001–2008	2009–2016
China	−5.6	−2.6	−2.7	−1.7	−3.0	−1.8	+1.8	+1.6	+3.5	+2.2	11.8	7.5	2.4	2.3
South Korea	−0.6	−0.7	−0.1	+0.4	+0.5	−2.4	+2.0	+4.7	+1.9	+6.5	6.4	5.1	3.3	2.0
Taiwan	−0.5	+0.3	−5.3	−2.5	−0.3	+10.0	+6.5	+2.2	+7.7	+11.9	3.1	2.6	1.2	0.8
Indonesia	−3.4	−1.0	−1.8	−1.1	−2.4	−2.6	−2.0	+4.0	+0.9	−2.3	8.6	14.1	9.6	5.2
Malaysia	−8.1	−2.7	−4.6	−5.5	−3.2	−2.4	−3.2	+10.9	+12.2	+3.3	3.2	3.6	2.5	2.1
Philippines	−3.5	−2.6	−3.7	−3.1	−1.3	−0.3	−3.5	−2.8	+3.7	+2.2	15.0	8.4	4.8	3.0
Singapore	+1.8	+9.5	+7.2	+6.1	+5.5	−0.1	+9.4	+13.9	+20.8	+19.0	2.3	1.8	1.6	1.8
Thailand	−4.0	+4.6	−5.0	−2.8	−1.3	−2.7	−6.4	+7.2	+4.6	+7.8	4.4	4.5	3.0	1.6
Vietnam	−6.2	−5.9	−3.7	−2.2	−4.3	−22.8	−5.0	+3.2	−3.2	+3.2	–	3.7	7.7	7.4
Bangladesh	+0.6	−3.3	−3.9	−3.2	−3.8	−2.7	−1.8	−0.9	+1.7	+0.8	7.4	5.3	6.3	7.2
India	−5.1	−6.2	−5.5	−5.7	−3.8	−1.6	−2.0	−0.5	−2.9	−1.0	9.0	9.1	5.1	8.6
Pakistan	−7.9	−7.6	−4.9	−5.8	−4.8	−2.4	−2.7	+0.4	−1.4	−1.6	7.0	9.2	7.7	8.8
Sri Lanka	−10.2	−8.8	−8.7	−7.7	−6.2	−3.9	−4.6	−3.2	−3.1	−2.4	12.4	9.7	12.2	5.2
Turkey	–	–	−10.1	−3.3	−1.7	−1.4	−0.2	−0.7	−5.9	−4.8	45.7	76.7	20.8	7.7

Note: (a) Gross Fiscal Balance relates to central governments and is estimated as a three-year average centred on the specified benchmark year (except in 1985 where the average is of 1985 and 1986). (b) Inflation rates for decades in the table are calculated from annual data on the consumer price index.

Source: For gross fiscal balance, Asian Development Bank, SDBS database, starting from 2000, and national statistical sources for earlier years. For Turkey the gross fiscal balance figures are from the IMF database. For current account balance, UNCTAD Stat. For inflation, UN National Accounts Statistics.

balance through much of the period. At the other end, some countries such as Malaysia, Thailand, Vietnam, India, Pakistan, and Sri Lanka had fiscal deficits at around 5 per cent of GDP in many periods. These fiscal deficits might have been even higher for most of the Asian-14 during 1965–1985 for which data are not available. This was probably so in China, Malaysia, Philippines, Thailand, India, Pakistan, and Sri Lanka. The fiscal deficit in Malaysia peaked at 18 per cent of GDP in 1982; during the 1980s, it was 7.5 per cent of GDP in India and 6 per cent of GDP in Thailand.[20] In general, however, fiscal deficits remained within prudent limits and corrective action was taken when there was a danger of moving out of control.

It was only India, Pakistan, Bangladesh, and Sri Lanka in the 1980s, and Turkey in the 1990s, that experienced macroeconomic management problems attributable to fiscal imbalances, as government borrowing was used to support consumption, even if it was balance of payments crises in the current account that were the triggers.[21] A decade later, in the late 1990s, Indonesia, Malaysia, Philippines, and Thailand in Southeast Asia, along with South Korea and Taiwan, were hit by the Asian financial crisis, attributable to a premature integration into international financial markets, excessive short-term borrowing abroad with a maturity mismatch, and weak domestic financial sectors. This was triggered by a balance of payments crisis in the capital account, as boom was followed by bust, leading to capital flight and a run on national currencies.[22] The underlying profligacy was in private sectors and not in fiscal deficits of governments.

In general, fiscal deficits were not the culprits implicit in the dominant orthodoxy of macroeconomics that borders on a deficit fetishism. In fact, the experience of the Asian-14 suggests that fiscal deficits were used, whenever necessary, as a part of countercyclical macroeconomic policies to provide a stimulus in economic downturns. Following the Asian financial crisis, in 2000 as compared with 1990, the fiscal deficit rose in Taiwan, Indonesia, Malaysia, Philippines, and Thailand. Similarly, following the global financial crisis that surfaced in late 2008, fiscal deficits increased almost everywhere in the Asian-14. However, three-year averages do not reveal the magnitudes. A time-series plot of fiscal deficits, not presented here given the space constraint, shows a sharp increase in their size as a percentage of GDP almost everywhere in East and Southeast Asia during 1998–2001, rising to peak levels of 3 per cent in China, 3.6 per cent in South Korea, 6.2 per cent in Taiwan, 5.5 per cent in Malaysia, 5 per cent in Philippines, and 9.5 per cent in Thailand, while the fiscal surplus in Singapore dropped from 11 per cent in 1997 to 3 per cent in 1998. The same time-series plot of fiscal deficits shows that, in 2009, as a percentage of GDP, the fiscal deficit was 2 per cent in China and South Korea, 3.5 per cent in Taiwan, 6.7 per cent in Malaysia, 4 per cent in Philippines, Thailand, and Vietnam, 6.5 per cent in India, and 10 per cent in Sri Lanka, while the fiscal surplus in Singapore dropped from 11 per cent in 2007 to 2 per cent in 2009. Such an approach has meant that the internal public debt of central governments was significant in most of the Asian-14, but it was sustainable as their GDP growth rates were higher than the interest rates.[23]

Table 3.7 shows that inflation in the Asian-14 was moderate, as compared with Latin America, during the period 1981–2016.[24] In fact, Taiwan, Singapore, and Malaysia had low inflation rates comparable with industrialized countries. At the other end, Turkey was the only exception with its high inflation rates through much of this period. China, Indonesia, Philippines, Bangladesh, India, Pakistan, and Sri Lanka had higher inflation rates particularly during 1981–2000. In decadal averages, however, double-digit inflation was not common after 1980 in the Asian-14. South Korea and Thailand had moderate inflation rates. Yet, average consumer price inflation was far higher in South Korea at 17 per cent per annum in the 1960s and 20 per cent per annum in the 1970s (Chang, 2003). Similarly, consumer price inflation in China during 1981–1990 was 12 per cent per annum, and it reached 25 per cent per annum in the mid-1990s. Inflation rates in the South Asian countries were lower but averaged around 8 per cent per annum during 1991–2016. It would seem that periods of high growth in most of the Asian-14 coincided with inflation rates that were high by Asian standards but remained within limits of political tolerance, in which double-digit inflation was an unstated threshold for economies where most people did not have index-linked incomes. Clearly, these countries did not allow obsessive concerns about inflation to stifle economic growth, so that their essential macroeconomic object-ive was not lost sight of in the orthodox fetishism about price stability. And, it would seem that large fiscal deficits did not fuel inflation in Asia as they did in Latin America.

It is now fashionable for central banks everywhere to engage in inflation targeting so that money supply and interest rates are captive policy instruments. Even so, in the past many countries among the Asian-14 used monetary policy to support their industrialization and development objectives. It is worth citing two examples. Following Japan, the East Asian Tigers used differential interest rates and preferential credit allocation to guide the allocation of scarce investible resources in market economies as instruments of strategic industrial policy.[25] So did India for lending through development banks (Nayyar, 2017). Somewhat later, China used low interest rates for individuals or households as depositors in banks, to provide industrial finance for state-owned enterprises and firms or entrepre-neurs in the private sector for investment in manufacturing at low interest rates.

Given the export performance of the Asian-14, and the large remittance inflows in many among them, current account deficits were not a significant problem. The only exceptions revealed by Table 3.7 are the deficits in Malaysia, Philippines, Thailand, and Vietnam around 1990, and in Turkey starting in 2010. From 1980 to 1990, most of the Asian-14 did run persistent current account deficits in the balance of payments, which remained within manageable proportions and were not allowed to constrain their pursuit of economic growth,[26] but this was associated with an increase in external debt.[27] Capital account liberalization during the 1990s led to the Asian financial crisis in 1997–1999. The situation has changed since then. Lessons have been learnt from the balance of payments crises in South Asia and the financial crisis in East and Southeast Asia. First, there has been a systematic attempt across the Asian-14 to reduce long-term external debt of the public sector which has succeeded.[28] Second, some of the Asian-14 used heterodox interventions in foreign exchange management by introducing controls to regulate external capital flows and established the Chiang Mai Initiative of a multi-currency swap arrangement as an insurance for the future.[29] Third, China, South Korea, Taiwan, and Singapore have run large and growing current account surpluses for twenty-five years, making them capital-exporting countries which save more than they invest. But lessons of the Asian financial crisis also induced most Southeast Asian countries—particularly Malaysia and Thailand but also Indonesia, Philippines, and Vietnam—to accumulate foreign exchange reserves as a form of self-insurance by running current account surpluses. South Asian countries still run current account deficits but have attempted to reduce these. India has also accumulated large foreign exchange reserves.[30] The progressive reduction of external debt, the management of current account deficits and the accumulation of foreign exchange reserves in the Asian-14 were all conscious decisions, motivated by strategic objectives to minimize risks associated with mounting external debt and capital account liberalization, even if it sacrificed some growth.

In sum, it is clear that most of the Asian-14 did not follow orthodoxy in its prescriptions for macroeconomic stability and macroeconomic management. Their primary macroeconomic objectives were economic growth and employment creation. Their macroeconomic policies were also much broader and more versatile in the use of policy instruments. In pursuit of development objectives, they used orthodox policies for heterodox or unorthodox objectives, such as interest rates to influence the allocation of scarce resources in market economies, or heterodox policies for orthodox objectives, such as expansionary fiscal policies in an economic downturn, without hesitating to depart from orthodox prescriptions which advocated balanced budgets and price stability whenever such departures were necessary to foster economic growth. Similarly, they use unorthodox policies for unorthodox objectives in imposing controls on capital flows to manage the consequences of capital account liberalization. Yet, their approach was almost always characterized by a mix of pragmatism and prudence that did not hesitate to introduce correctives whenever needed. It is worth noting that their success in maintaining high growth rates increased their degrees of freedom in the use of macroeconomic policies, which enabled them to finance government deficits and raise sustainable levels of domestic borrowing, while making higher inflation rates politically more acceptable, none of which would have been possible if economic growth was slow.

6. Economic growth and employment creation

The creation of employment opportunities matters because it transforms economic growth into meaningful development by providing livelihoods which improve the well-being of people. Thus, growth is pro-poor if it generates employment. There are no either–or trade-offs between output growth and employment growth, implicit in orthodoxy that emphasizes efficiency and productivity. In fact, there are strong complementarities. Macroeconomics in developing countries is, in part, about mobilizing and creating resources—not only financial resources, but also real resources—for development. Employment creation can both mobilize and create resources. It constitutes resource-mobilization insofar as it mobilizes the most abundant yet underutilized resource, people, for development. The absorption of surplus labour, then, is an important source of economic growth (Lewis, 1954). It also constitutes resource-creation insofar as it increases the productivity of labour, for any given level of technological development, introducing another source of economic growth. The same people who constitute resources on the supply-side provide markets on the demand-side. Thus, growth can create jobs through the absorption of surplus labour in employment. Jobs creation can drive growth since wages are incomes that expand the size of the market. Indeed, the two can reinforce each other, through such interaction between the supply-side and the demand-side, to create a virtuous circle of cumulative causation.[31]

The past five decades have witnessed unprecedented economic growth in most of the Asian-14. What has such rapid growth in output meant for growth in employment in these countries? This section attempts to address the question. It is easier said than done for two reasons. First, there are conceptual problems in the definition of employment. Unlike industrialized countries, in developing countries the distinction between employment and unemployment is unclear. People are too poor to be unemployed. Everyone works in some way or the other. However, a significant proportion of people are underemployed, not by the time criterion but by the income or productivity criterion of employment. Most of them might work very hard, or for long hours, but do not earn enough for a living. It is no surprise that open unemployment rates in developing countries are low. Second, there are empirical problems that arise partly because employment statistics in developing countries are not readily available and partly because the quality of existing statistics is not reliable enough.

National employment statistics for so many countries are difficult to access. These are reported in the ILO database, which provides information starting only in 1991, but statistics are available for all countries in the Asian-14. For earlier years, the Groningen Growth and Development Centre has compiled national employment statistics, but this information is available for just nine countries among the Asian-14. Therefore, the discussion that follows considers two time periods: 1971–1990 for nine countries in the Asian-14 and 1991–2016 for all countries in the Asian-14.

Table 3.8 presents evidence on the average annual growth in employment in the agriculture (primary), industry (secondary) and services (tertiary) sectors, and in total employment, for each of the countries, juxtaposed with their respective GDP growth rates in the two periods. It shows that total employment growth rates were much lower than GDP growth rates for almost all countries in both periods. This is only to be expected as productivity increases. During 1971–1990, agricultural employment growth was negative in South Korea, Malaysia, Singapore, and Thailand, while in China, India, Indonesia, Philippines, and Thailand, it was clearly slower than the total employment growth. During 1991–2016, agricultural employment growth was negative or negligible in twelve of the Asian-14, while it was significantly positive only in Pakistan and Singapore (which did not quite have an agricultural sector). It is obvious that the contribution of the agricultural sector to employment growth was minimal, if not negligible, throughout 1971–2016, so that employment was created essentially in the industry and services sectors. Therefore, the following analysis seeks to focus on employment growth in industry and services taken together. Figure 3.3 plots GDP growth and employment growth for each of the countries in scatter diagrams. It also charts the median growth rates for GDP and employment.

Figure 3.3a considers the relationship between GDP growth and employment growth during 1971–1990 in nine countries among the Asian-14. Employment growth was higher than the median in China, South Korea, Thailand, and Indonesia, on the median in Malaysia, and lower than the median in Taiwan, Singapore, India, and Philippines. GDP growth was higher than the median in South Korea, Taiwan, China, and Singapore, on the median in Thailand, and lower than the median in Malaysia, India, and Philippines. There were only two countries in the northeast quadrant—China and South Korea—where both employment growth and GDP growth were higher than the median values, while there were two countries in the southwest quadrant—India and Philippines—where both employment growth and GDP growth were lower than the median values. If a regression line was fitted in this scatter diagram, it would have a mildly positive slope, suggesting that rapid GDP growth is associated with some employment growth but the latter is much less than proportionate.

Figure 3.3b considers the relationship between GDP growth and employment growth during 1991–2016 in the Asian-14. Employment growth was higher than the median in Vietnam, Bangladesh, India, Malaysia, Philippines, and Pakistan, on the median in China and Turkey, and lower than the median in Sri Lanka, South Korea, Taiwan, Indonesia, and Thailand. GDP growth was higher than the median in China, India, Vietnam, Bangladesh, Singapore, Malaysia, and Sri Lanka, and lower than the median in South Korea, Taiwan, Turkey, Indonesia, Philippines, and Pakistan. There were four countries in the northeast quadrant—India, Vietnam, Bangladesh, and Malaysia—where both employment growth and GDP growth were higher than the median values, while there were four economies

Table 3.8 Growth in GDP and in employment by sectors (per cent per annum) 1971–1990

	GDP Growth	Agriculture Employment	Industry Employment	Services Employment	Industry and Services Employment	Total Employment
China	8.1	1.0	6.8	7.4	7.1	2.7
South Korea	8.9	−2.9	6.0	5.3	5.7	2.9
Taiwan	8.6	−2.7	4.6	4.2	4.5	3.1
Indonesia	6.6	2.6	6.2	5.5	5.8	3.8
Malaysia	5.9	−0.5	5.7	5.1	5.2	3.4
Philippines	3.1	2.2	3.0	4.5	4.2	3.3
Singapore	7.5	−6.4	4.5	3.7	3.9	3.4
Thailand	6.8	2.6	5.7	5.3	5.7	3.3
India	4.5	2.4	3.6	4.1	3.9	2.8
Median	**6.8**	**1.0**	**5.7**	**5.1**	**5.2**	**3.3**

Note: The figures for Malaysia are for the period 1975–1990.

Source: For GDP growth, UN National Accounts Statistics. For employment growth, Groningen Growth and Development Centre (GGDC) database. See Appendix.

1991–2016

	GDP Growth	Agriculture Employment	Industry Employment	Services Employment	Industry and Services Employment	Total Employment
China	9.4	−3.7	0.8	9.9	3.2	0.7
South Korea	4.7	−3.0	−0.4	2.6	1.6	1.2
Taiwan	4.5	−3.2	0.6	3.9	1.4	1.1
Indonesia	4.3	0.3	3.1	3.1	3.1	1.9
Malaysia	5.0	0.2	2.2	4.1	3.4	2.9
Philippines	4.4	0.7	2.4	4.0	3.6	2.5
Singapore	5.6	7.1	0.3	4.0	3.1	3.1
Thailand	3.7	−0.9	2.0	3.7	3.0	1.2
Vietnam	6.6	−0.2	6.2	5.0	5.5	2.1
Bangladesh	5.5	0.1	5.2	5.3	5.2	2.3
India	6.7	0.1	3.9	3.1	3.5	1.7
Pakistan	3.9	2.6	4.3	3.4	3.8	3.3
Sri Lanka	5.3	−0.5	1.9	2.4	2.2	1.2
Turkey	4.4	−2.3	2.5	3.7	3.2	1.4
Median	**4.8**	**0.1**	**2.3**	**3.8**	**3.2**	**1.8**

Source: For GDP growth, UN National Accounts Statistics. For employment growth, ILO Stat based on national employment statistics. See Appendix.

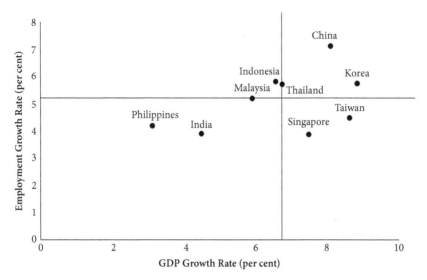

Figure 3.3a GDP growth and employment growth in industry and services for nine Asian countries: 1971–1990: per cent per annum

Source: Table 3.8.

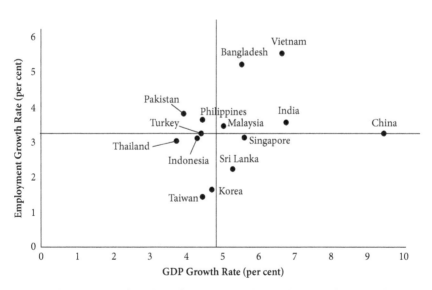

Figure 3.3b GDP growth and employment growth in industry and services for the Asian-14: 1991–2016: per cent per annum

Source: See Table 3.8.

in the southwest quadrant—South Korea, Taiwan, Indonesia, and Thailand—where both employment growth and GDP growth were lower than the median values. It is not possible to fit a regression line in this scatter diagram, essentially because there are many outliers, particularly China with much the highest GDP growth rate and the median employment growth rate. The relationship between GDP growth and employment growth during this period was obviously weak and inconsistent, except for the four countries in the northeast quadrant, and China, where it was mildly positive. In India, Malaysia, and China, employment growth was much slower than GDP growth, whereas in Vietnam and Bangladesh employment growth was much closer to GDP growth.

The differences between the two sub-periods are worth noting. First, both GDP growth and employment growth were significantly slower during 1991–2016 as compared with 1971–1990, which is clear even from the respective median values. Second, the relationship between GDP growth and employment growth was discernibly weaker during 1991–2016 as compared with 1971–1990. Third, the countries where employment growth was higher than the median changed between the two periods: during 1971–1990, it was China, South Korea, Thailand, and Indonesia, whereas during 1991–2016, it was India, Vietnam, Bangladesh, and Malaysia, although China was on the median in 1991–2016 while Malaysia was on the median in 1971–1990. This difference was partly but not wholly mirrored in GDP growth. And there was an asymmetry. Slower GDP growth was almost always associated with even slower employment growth but rapid economic growth was not always associated with commensurate employment creation.

Conclusion

Economic growth over fifty years in most of the Asian-14 has been stunning. China was the star performer throughout. Growth rates of both GDP and GDP per capita were high in South Korea, Taiwan, Singapore, Indonesia, Malaysia, and Thailand during 1971–1990 but slowed down significantly during 1991–2016, whereas these growth rates were lower in India, Vietnam, and Bangladesh during 1971–1990 but were much higher during 1991–2016. In comparison, the growth performance of Sri Lanka was respectable, while that of Turkey was average, but that of Philippines and Pakistan was poor. The slowdown in growth, during 1991–2016, experienced by South Korea, Taiwan, Singapore, Indonesia, Malaysia, and Thailand was attributable to the long-term effects of the Asian financial crisis. In countries where growth was impressive, investment and savings which rose rapidly, were the main drivers of growth on the supply-side. Thus, trends in investment rates, and savings rates, mirrored differences in growth performance across countries over time. Education, which contributed to human capital formation, was a sustained driver of growth in countries that were success stories. An analysis of long-term changes in the composition of aggregate demand shows that, from the demand-side, growth was primarily private-consumption-expenditure led and investment led in most of the Asian-14. It was government-consumption-expenditure led only in Indonesia. The contribution of net exports as a demand stimulus to growth was in general small or negative, except in Singapore and, to some extent, in China, South Korea, and Taiwan but only for limited time periods.

The interaction between the supply-side and the demand-side in the Asian-14 suggests that there was a virtuous circle of cumulative causation, where rapid investment growth coincided in time with rapid export growth, leading to rapid GDP growth. This was so in China throughout, in South Korea, Taiwan, Singapore, Indonesia, Malaysia, and Thailand during 1971–1990, and in India, Vietnam, and Bangladesh during 1991–2016. But this did not happen in countries where rapid investment growth and rapid export growth did not coincide, or where growth in both was slow.

It is clear that many of the Asian-14 did not follow orthodox prescriptions of balanced budgets and price stability for macroeconomic management. In fact, they were heterodox in their objectives and policies. Their primary macroeconomic objectives were economic growth and employment creation. Their macroeconomic policies were also much broader and more versatile in their use of policy instruments. Their success in maintaining high growth rates increased their degrees of freedom, which enabled them to finance government deficits and raise sustainable levels of government borrowing, while making higher inflation rates politically more acceptable, none of which would have been possible if economic growth was slow.

During 1991–2016, as compared with 1971–1990, both GDP growth and employment growth were significantly slower, while the relationship between them was clearly weaker. Slower GDP growth was always associated with even slower employment growth, but rapid economic growth was not always associated with rapid employment creation.

4

Structural change and economic transformation

The process of industrialization and development is associated with a structural transformation of economies, which is a multidimensional phenomenon. In a long-term perspective, its most important dimension is structural change in the composition of output and employment over time. This is reflected in changing shares of the primary sector, secondary sector, and tertiary sector in national income and total employment for an economy. The primary sector is made up of agriculture, livestock, forestry, and fishing, although it is often described simply as agriculture. The secondary sector is made up of manufacturing, mining, construction, and utilities (electricity, gas, water), although it is often described simply as industry. The tertiary sector is made up of a diverse range of services, as distinct from goods, and is often described simply as services. In the literature on the subject, the words 'structural change' and 'structural transformation' are frequently used interchangeably. Strictly speaking, however, the former is a process while the latter is an outcome.

The object of this chapter is to analyse the process of structural change in Asian countries and analyse their paths to structural transformation. Section 1 develops an analytical framework to examine the relationship between economic growth and structural change, in theory and history, to discuss the direction of causation. Section 2 considers development experience, with a focus on structural change in Asia, Africa, and Latin America, in comparison with the industrialized countries, to discern what we can learn from the wider international context. Section 3 outlines the broad contours of structural change in the composition of output and employment in the Asian-14, distinguishing between agriculture, industry, and services as sectors, since meaningful analysis is possible only at the country level, while highlighting peak shares of the industrial sector in output and employment. Section 4 explores the relationship between structural change and economic growth in the Asian-14, by analysing the contribution of labour transfer between sectors and productivity increase within sectors to GDP growth in agriculture, industry, and services, across countries. Section 5 discusses the different paths of structural transformation within sectors and between sectors, characterized by striking diversities across the Asian-14, to reflect briefly on future pathways as the ongoing transformations in most countries are uneven and incomplete.

Resurgent Asia: Diversity in Development. Deepak Nayyar, Oxford University Press (2019). © United Nations University World Institute for Development Economics Research. DOI: 10.1093/oso/9780198849513.001.0001

1. Analytical constructs and stylized facts

In the literature on structural transformation, analytical constructs are derived mostly from stylized facts rather than from economic theorizing or analytical abstractions. Thus, patterns of structural change observed in the process of development provide the analytical foundations.

In the earlier stages of development, when income levels are low, the share of the agricultural sector in both output and employment is overwhelmingly large. At the next stage, as industrialization proceeds, the share of the manufacturing sector in output and employment rises, while that of the agricultural sector falls. At an advanced stage of development, after industrialization, the share of the manufacturing sector in both output and employment diminishes, while that of the services sector rises. This is the classical pattern, observed by Fisher (1935), Clark (1940) and Kuznets (1966), from the experience of countries that industrialized during the second half of the nineteenth century and the first half of the twentieth century.

The focus of such conventional thinking is on economic growth in which structural change is an associated outcome. It is postulated that the income elasticity of demand for industrial goods is higher than that for agricultural goods, while the income elasticity of demand for services is even higher than that for industrial goods (Fisher, 1935). The expansion of markets creates new demands, so that new production activities follow. And growing economies almost always follow the sequence of moving, in terms of relative importance, from the primary sector to the secondary sector and then to the tertiary sector. After a stage, when labour is no longer available from agriculture or from domestic personal services, the share of the services sector increases at the expense of the manufacturing sector, more in employment than in output. In the already industrialized countries, such outcomes have been described as deindustrialization (Rowthorn and Wells, 1987). In this characterization, productivity growth in the services sector is slower than in the manufacturing sector, because the scope for attaining it through capital accumulation, scale economies, or technical progress is much less (Baumol, 1967). This provides an explanation for why the share of the services sector in total employment increases further (Rowthorn and Wells, 1987). At the same time, the increase in its share of total output is attributable mostly to an increase in the relative price of services (Baumol, 1967). In sum, irrespective of different hypotheses about the increasing significance of the services sector, economic growth drives structural change from the demand-side.

For developing countries, then, it is possible to make an analytical distinction between three stages in the structural transformation of economies (Nayyar, 1994). In the first stage, there is absorption of surplus labour from the agricultural sector into manufacturing at existing levels of real wages and productivity.[1]

This is associated with a decline in the share of agriculture and a rise in the share of manufacturing, in output and in employment. The process can be described as labour absorption at the extensive margin. In the second stage, there is a transfer of labour from low productivity to higher productivity occupations in manufacturing, while, at the same time, there is an increase in the average productivity of labour in both sectors, so that real wages rise in both. There is a further increase in the share of manufacturing and a further decrease in the share of agriculture, more pronounced in output than in employment. The process can be described as labour use at the intensive margin. In the third stage, the share of the agricultural sector continues to decline, even as the share of the manufacturing sector is maintained while that of the services sector rises but, after a point, when labour is no longer readily available from the agricultural sector, the share of the services sector increases at the expense of the manufacturing sector, particularly in employment but also in output.

It is essential to recognize that patterns of structural change are not simply an associated outcome of economic growth. Indeed, the causation might also run in the opposite direction. In fact, the unconventional, heterodox, perspective stresses that structural change drives economic growth.[2] It does so by moving labour from low productivity sectors to higher productivity sectors, thus pushing up GDP growth from the supply-side.

This proposition was also implicit in the Lewis (1954) model. It starts from the premise that, in countries at low levels of income and at early stages of development which are capital scarce, there is surplus labour that is underemployed, irrespective of their endowments of land or natural resources. In these situations, the marginal productivity of labour in the agricultural sector, as also the social opportunity cost of labour, is zero or close to zero, so that its withdrawal does not lead to any reduction in output, while it mobilizes their most abundant yet underutilized resource—people—for development. The transfer of such surplus labour from the agricultural sector to the manufacturing sector, at a subsistence-plus wage,[3] increases the profits of capitalists, reinvestment of which is the key source of capital accumulation and economic growth. In effect, the transfer of surplus labour with near-zero marginal productivity in traditional agricultural sectors to modern industrial sectors is a source of economic growth.

The Kaldor (1966) model went much further in developing this causation to suggest that the manufacturing sector is the engine of growth in economies. This was set out in terms of three laws. First, there is a positive relationship between the growth of manufacturing output and the growth of GDP, which is explained by the absorption of surplus labour from the agricultural sector into the manufacturing sector. Second, growth of manufacturing output leads to growth of productivity in manufacturing, which is attributable to static and dynamic scale economies, where the former depend on plant size or output levels at any point in time, while the latter derive from learning-by-doing that is a function of cumulative past output (Arrow, 1962) or cumulative production experience (Kaldor, 1962) over time. Third, growth of manufacturing output is associated with an overall increase in productivity in the economy driven by spillover effects elsewhere.

It is important to recognize that the world has changed, particularly in the services sector, from the time that stylized facts about structural change were formulated by the aforesaid pioneers.[4] Given the massive increase in the size of firms, it is more profitable to procure services, such as those in the spheres of law, accounts, transport, or finance, from specialist providers rather than produce them within the firm.[5] Indeed, telecommunications, financial, software, or business services are now organized in a manner that strongly resembles the manufacturing sector, for scale economies or technical progress are easily incorporated to increase efficiency in providing these services.[6] The revolution in transport, communication, and information technologies has meant that hitherto non-traded services now enter into cross-border transactions in international trade (Nayyar, 1988, and Gaurav Nayyar, 2012). In this changed world, the services sector could also drive economic growth in terms of Kaldor's first two laws, by raising growth in GDP and in manufacturing productivity, with some possibility of spillover effects in the economy as a whole implicit in the third law.[7]

It is clear that, in the relationship between economic growth and structural change, the causation runs in both directions. Economic growth drives structural change on the demand-side, while structural change drives economic growth on the supply-side. Such an interaction between the demand-side and the supply-side could create a virtuous circle of cumulative causation. It is also plausible to suggest that structural change implicit in the transfer of labour between sectors drives growth in the earlier stages of development, while rising labour productivity within sectors drives growth in the later stages of development.

2. Development experience and structural change

The experience of latecomers to industrialization, beginning during the second half of the twentieth century, suggests that the pattern and sequence of structural change has been different from that in the earlier industrializers. It has followed different paths. And it has not been uniform across economies. It would seem that during the second half of the twentieth century and the first decade of the twenty-first century, most developing countries moved from the first stage, in which agriculture dominates, to the third stage, in which services dominate, without necessarily going through the second stage in which manufacturing dominates. There were some exceptions to this pattern but not many. To begin with, of course, the share of the industrial sector in both output and employment did increase almost everywhere, perhaps less than in the classical Clark–Kuznets worldview, but then stabilized or even declined. In contrast, the share of the services sector began to rise along with the fall in the share of the agricultural sector but, after a point, its share in both employment and output rose at the expense of the industrial sector. The former is not surprising as the services sector is a source of labour absorption and employment creation in developing countries, but the latter is unexpected because it is widely believed that manufacturing is the engine of productivity growth. In conformity with this observed sequence of change, it has been argued that there may be two waves of growth in the services sector: the first wave made up of traditional services in countries with low per capita incomes, and a second wave made up of modern services in countries with higher per capita incomes (Eichengreen and Gupta, 2013).

The contrast between industrialized countries and developing countries is no surprise. In industrialized countries, from 1970 to 2010, the share of agriculture in GDP dropped from 5 per cent to 1.5 per cent, the share of industry declined from 38 per cent to 24 per cent (of which manufacturing declined from 27 per cent to 15 per cent), and the share of services rose from 57 per cent to 74 per cent. For developing countries taken together, between 1970 and 2010, the share of agriculture in GDP declined from 25 per cent to 10 per cent, the share of industry increased from 33 per cent to 39 per cent (of which manufacturing remained unchanged at 21 per cent), and the share of services increased from 42 per cent to 51 per cent (Nayyar, 2013).

There were also significant differences between continents in the developing world.[8] In Asia, between 1970 and 2010, the share of agriculture in GDP dropped by 23 percentage points, the share of industry increased by 10 percentage points (of which manufacturing was just 2 percentage points while mining, utilities, and construction contributed 8 percentage points but that was supportive of industrial production) and the share of services rose by 13 percentage points. This structural change was conducive to economic growth and reflected progress in industrialization. For Latin America and the Caribbean, between 1970 and 2010, the share of agriculture in GDP declined by 6 percentage points but so did the share of industry by 3 percentage points (in which the share of manufacturing dropped by more than 7 percentage points so that mining, utilities, and construction compensated for some of the decline), while the share of services increased by 9 percentage points. It is no surprise that the region witnessed a slowdown in growth and experienced some deindustrialization. Between 1970 and 2010, in Africa, the share of agriculture in GDP decreased by 9 percentage points, the share of industry rose by 8 percentage points (although the share of manufacturing fell by 3 percentage points and mining possibly contributed to much of the increase), and the share of services increased by just 1 percentage point. For a span of four decades, this structural change was, at best, modest. It did not drive economic growth and it did not reflect industrialization, despite the increased share of industry in total output. Thus, during 1970–2010, structural change in Asia fostered economic growth, because it moved labour from low-productivity sectors to high-productivity sectors, but structural change in Latin America and Africa was not conducive to economic growth, because it did not.[9]

In examining structural transformation, it is worth considering available evidence on the nature of causation. In a study based on data for a cross section of fifty-seven developing countries and transition economies, grouped into twelve regions, during the period 1970–2006, Ocampo et al. (2009), analyse the relationship between structural change and economic growth. The annual growth rate of GDP per capita is juxtaposed with changes in the shares of agriculture and industry in total GDP. The scatter plots for the period show a negatively sloped regression line for decreases in the agricultural output share and a positively sloped regression line for increases in the industrial output share for the entire sample of twelve country-groups. However, the relationship between falling agricultural shares or rising industrial shares and economic growth is clear only for four country-groups in Asia (East Asia, Southeast Asia, China, and South Asia) that registered sustained growth. In contrast, the other eight country-groups that experienced slow growth (semi-industrialized countries mostly from Latin America but including South Africa and Turkey, Central America and the Caribbean, Middle East and North Africa, and Eastern Europe) or stagnant growth (smaller Andean countries, Sub-Saharan Africa, other Africa, and former USSR), reveal a random scatter. Similarly, the fast growth regions also had rapidly rising service sector shares. However, there was no apparent relationship between industrial-sector shares or service-sector shares and economic growth for the lagging regions. It would seem that structural change and economic growth are necessary but not sufficient to drive each other. The direction of causation does run in both directions but is strong and positive only in countries where there are virtuous circles of cumulative causation that reflect success in development, while it is weak or absent elsewhere.[10]

In another cross-country study which examines evidence until 2010, Diao, McMillan and Rodrik (2017) analyze growth boom experiences in developing economies in Africa and Latin America compared with Asia,[11] for selected periods in different countries, to draw three conclusions. First, in Africa, growth accelerations were based on growth-promoting structural change which moved labour from low-productivity activities to high-productivity sectors. This structural change originated on the demand-side through external resource transfers or increases in agricultural incomes but was often associated with declining labour-productivity growth in modern sectors of economies. Second, in Latin America, growth accelerations were based on rapid labour-productivity growth within sectors, but growth-promoting structural change was weak or negative. Third, there was a strong negative correlation between the two components (labour transfer between sectors and labour-productivity increase within sectors) as sources of growth across countries, so that the former was present and the latter was absent in Africa, while the latter was present and the former was absent in Latin America. This provides a sharp contrast with the East Asian experience (South Korea, Taiwan, and China) in which both components were drivers of growth. In some other Asian countries too (particularly India but also Bangladesh, Vietnam, Cambodia, and Laos), both components—growth-promoting structural change and labour-productivity increases within sectors—were factors underlying the growth acceleration. The relative importance of the latter component increased over time everywhere although, in terms of industrialization, the South Asian and Southeast Asian countries were no match for the East Asian countries.

Generalizations from cross-country studies serve an important purpose but cannot suffice, because unfolding reality at the country-level is neither as uniform nor as simple as the stylized facts. There are some latecomers to development in Asia such as South Korea and Taiwan, followed by Malaysia, China, and possibly Indonesia later, that conform to the more classical pattern of structural change where the decline of agriculture is juxtaposed with the rise of manufacturing followed by an increase in the relative importance of services. However, other latecomers to development in Asia, such as India, have followed the non-traditional pattern of structural change, where the decline of agriculture has been juxtaposed with some increase in manufacturing but a much greater increase in services. Most countries in Asia conform to this pattern.

3. Contours of structural change in the Asian-14

The wider context set out above is necessary but cannot suffice, because meaningful analysis of structural change is possible only at the country level. Hence, this section outlines the contours of such change in the Asian-14, with a focus on changes in the composition of output and employment over time.

Table 4.1 presents evidence on changes in the composition of output, distributed between agriculture, industry (of which, manufacturing) and services, for each of the Asian-14, during the period 1970 to 2016. It selects three benchmark years at intervals of two decades, plus the latest year for which data are available, to limit the statistics to manageable proportions, which is both adequate and appropriate since structural changes are slow and easier to discern over longer periods.

The share of agriculture in GDP declined rapidly almost everywhere. Between 1970 and 2016, it fell from around 40 per cent to less than 20 per cent in China, Indonesia, Vietnam, Bangladesh, and India (dropping to 9 per cent in China), while it fell from around 30 per cent to less than 10 per cent in South Korea, Malaysia, Philippines, Thailand, Sri Lanka, and Turkey, but fell the least in Pakistan from 40 per cent to 25 per cent. The exceptions were Taiwan, where it fell from an already low 17 per cent to 2 per cent, and Singapore where the share was always negligible.[12]

Table 4.1 Structural change in the composition of output in the Asian-14: 1970–2016 (as a percentage of GDP)

	Agriculture				Industry				Manufacturing				Services			
	1970	1990	2010	2016	1970	1990	2010	2016	1970	1990	2010	2016	1970	1990	2010	2016
China	35.1	26.8	9.8	8.9	40.4	41.2	46.6	40.0	–	–	31.6	27.5	24.5	32.0	43.6	51.2
South Korea	28.9	8.4	2.5	2.2	26.9	39.6	38.3	38.6	18.8	27.3	30.7	29.3	44.3	51.9	59.3	59.2
Taiwan	17.1	4.2	1.6	1.9	37.3	41.1	34.8	36.1	29.8	32.6	29.9	31.1	45.6	54.7	63.6	62.0
Indonesia	42.7	16.2	14.3	14.0	17.2	35.9	43.9	40.8	9.6	20.8	22.6	21.3	40.1	47.9	41.8	45.3
Malaysia	29.8	15.0	10.2	8.9	28.2	41.5	40.9	40.2	15.2	23.8	23.7	23.1	41.9	43.5	48.9	50.9
Philippines	26.0	19.0	12.3	9.7	34.9	37.5	32.6	30.9	27.0	26.6	21.4	19.6	39.1	43.5	55.1	59.5
Singapore	2.7	0.3	0.0	0.0	28.5	32.3	27.6	26.1	18.5	25.6	21.4	19.6	68.8	67.3	72.3	73.8
Thailand	25.9	10.0	10.5	8.3	25.3	37.2	40.0	35.8	15.9	27.4	31.1	27.4	48.8	52.8	49.5	55.8
Vietnam	38.8	35.1	21.0	18.1	21.3	20.6	36.7	36.4	14.5	11.0	14.8	15.9	39.9	44.3	42.2	45.5
Bangladesh	41.8	31.5	17.8	14.8	12.6	21.4	26.1	28.8	8.4	13.4	16.9	17.9	45.6	47.2	56.0	56.5
India	44.0	30.7	18.9	17.4	23.2	32.2	32.5	28.8	15.6	19.7	17.5	16.5	32.8	37.1	48.7	53.8
Pakistan	39.7	28.1	24.3	25.2	16.9	19.5	20.6	19.2	10.9	11.9	13.6	12.7	43.3	52.3	55.1	55.6
Sri Lanka	31.8	20.8	9.5	8.2	25.5	33.2	29.7	29.6	18.6	22.9	20.1	16.9	42.7	46.0	60.9	62.2
Turkey	31.1	14.0	10.3	7.0	29.3	38.7	28.0	32.0	20.6	28.4	17.2	18.8	39.6	47.2	61.8	61.0

Note: Agriculture includes livestock, forestry, and fishing. Industry includes manufacturing, mining, construction, and utilities.

Source: Author's calculations from UN National Accounts Statistics.

The share of industry in GDP in China and Taiwan was already about 40 per cent by 1970 and stayed in that range until 2016. This share, which was in the range of 25–30 per cent in South Korea, Malaysia, Philippines, Singapore, Thailand, India, Sri Lanka, and Turkey in 1970, rose to 30–40 per cent by 1990 and stabilized in that range thereafter, except for Philippines where it declined. Starting from lower levels, it increased steadily in Indonesia, Vietnam, and Bangladesh throughout. Pakistan was the exception, where this share remained less than 20 per cent. Between 1970 and 1990, the share of manufacturing in GDP increased significantly in South Korea, Taiwan, Indonesia, Malaysia, Philippines, Singapore, Thailand, Bangladesh, India, Sri Lanka, and Turkey, while it was roughly the same in Pakistan and decreased in Vietnam.[13] Between 1990 and 2016, the share of manufacturing in GDP stabilized or diminished in most of these countries, including China, except Indonesia, Bangladesh, and Vietnam where, starting from lower levels, it witnessed an increase. In general, the GDP share of manufacturing was the highest in East Asia and the lowest in South Asia, with Southeast Asia (and Turkey) in the middle.

The share of services in GDP increased rapidly almost everywhere except in Indonesia and Vietnam. In 1970, this share was already in the range of 40 per cent (or more) everywhere, except in China at 25 per cent and in India at 33 per cent. By 2016, this share was in the range of 50–60 per cent in most of the Asian-14, except Indonesia and Vietnam at 45 per cent. The other striking exception was Singapore, where the GDP share of services, at 74 per cent, was comparable to that in industrialized countries.

Table 4.2 sets out evidence on the distribution of employment between agriculture, industry and services for each of the Asian-14 during the period from 1991 to 2016. It selects three benchmark years at decadal intervals, plus the latest year for which data are available, to limit the statistics to manageable proportions, which is also appropriate if the object is to discern changes in the composition of employment. Unfortunately, such data are not available for earlier years, while data on employment in manufacturing are sparse and limited.[14] Even so, the table provides figures on employment by sectors for nine countries in 1971 from another source which is not strictly comparable but is useful for comparisons over a longer time period.

The share of agriculture in total employment declined rapidly everywhere. Between 1971 and 2016, in terms of percentage points, it dropped by about 50 in China, 45 in Thailand, 40 in South Korea, 35 in Indonesia and Malaysia, 30 in Taiwan and India, and 20 in Philippines. Between 1991 and 2016, in terms of percentage points again, it dropped by about 30 in Vietnam and Turkey, 25 in Bangladesh, and 15 in Sri Lanka, all of which would have been greater if there were data on 1971 for these countries. The solitary exception was Pakistan where this share was almost unchanged. Yet, in 2016, in most of these countries 25–40 per cent

Table 4.2 Composition of employment by sectors in the Asian-14: 1971–2016 (in percentages)

	Agriculture					Industry					Services				
	1971	1991	2000	2010	2016	1971	1991	2000	2010	2016	1971	1991	2000	2010	2016
China	80.9	59.7	50.0	36.7	27.7	10.0	21.4	22.5	28.7	28.8	9.1	18.9	27.5	34.6	43.5
South Korea	48.0	16.4	10.6	6.6	4.8	17.5	36.0	28.1	25.0	25.0	34.5	47.7	61.3	68.4	70.2
Taiwan	35.1	13.4	7.7	5.2	4.9	27.5	41.1	36.5	35.9	35.9	37.4	45.5	55.8	58.8	59.2
Indonesia	66.1	54.0	45.3	39.1	31.8	9.9	14.6	17.4	18.7	21.7	24.1	31.4	37.3	42.2	46.5
Malaysia	47.6	26.6	18.4	14.2	11.4	14.8	27.7	32.2	27.7	27.5	37.6	45.8	49.5	58.1	61.1
Philippines	49.4	45.3	37.1	28.8	27.0	16.0	16.0	16.2	13.6	17.4	34.6	38.7	46.7	57.6	55.5
Singapore	3.8	0.3	0.2	0.1	0.1	31.5	35.2	33.8	30.4	16.3	64.7	64.6	66.0	69.5	83.6
Thailand	77.2	60.3	48.8	38.2	31.2	7.1	15.4	19.0	20.6	23.7	15.8	24.2	32.2	41.1	45.2
Vietnam		75.1	65.3	48.7	41.9		9.2	12.4	21.7	24.8		30.6	22.3	29.6	33.4
Bangladesh		69.5	64.8	47.3	42.7		13.6	10.7	17.6	20.5		16.9	24.5	35.1	36.9
India	72.6	63.6	59.6	51.5	43.4	11.0	14.8	16.3	21.7	23.7	16.4	21.6	24.0	26.8	32.8
Pakistan		47.5	48.4	43.4	42.3		19.8	18.0	21.4	23.6		32.7	33.5	35.2	34.1
Sri Lanka		42.8	41.3	33.6	27.1		26.6	23.4	24.9	26.4		30.6	35.4	41.5	46.5
Turkey		47.8	36.0	24.0	19.0		20.2	24.0	26.0	27.0		32.0	40.0	50.0	54.0

Note: ILO STAT does not provide data on the manufacturing sector which is included in Industry.
The figures for 1971, from the Groningen Growth and Development Centre, are available only for nine countries and are not strictly comparable with figures for subsequent years.

Source: Author's calculations from ILO STAT.

of total employment was still in agriculture; the exceptions were the economies of South Korea and Taiwan at 5 per cent and Malaysia at just above 10 per cent.

The share of industry in total employment did rise almost everywhere, but this was much less than the fall in the share of agriculture. Between 1971 and 1991, it rose by large proportions in South Korea and Taiwan, and modestly in Singapore, to decline somewhat thereafter during 1991–2016. Malaysia witnessed a significant increase during 1971–2000, followed by a decline. This employment share of industry increased steadily throughout the period 1971–2016 in China, Indonesia, Thailand, and India, while it remained almost unchanged in Philippines. In countries where the data start in 1991, the employment share of industry increased steadily in Vietnam, Bangladesh, and Turkey, while it changed little in Pakistan and Sri Lanka. It is worth noting that industry includes manufacturing, mining, utilities and construction. Thus, it does not reveal the differences between countries in the employment share of manufacturing, for which statistics are not available. In most of the Asian-14, construction might have made a significant contribution to employment, just as mining might have contributed significantly to employment in a few.

The share of services in total employment increased rapidly everywhere, which is no surprise, given that the sharp contraction in the employment share of agriculture was not compensated for by an expansion in the employment share of industry in any of the Asian-14. In the nine countries for which 1971 figures are available, between 1971 and 2016, the employment share of services increased by 20–35 percentage points. The proportionate increase was much greater in countries where this share was low to start with. In the remaining five countries, between 1991 and 2016, the employment share of services increased by 15–20 percentage points in Bangladesh, Sri Lanka, and Turkey, but remained almost unchanged in Vietnam and Pakistan.

It is important to recognize that there were asymmetries between changes in output shares and employment shares for each of the three sectors. There was a sharp drop in the share of the agricultural sector, but this decline was far greater in its share of output when compared to its share of employment. Of course, its employment share was always higher than its output share, and, although the gap between the two shares diminished, it persisted among the Asian-14. There was a significant increase in the share of the industrial sector, but this increase was more pronounced in its share of employment as compared with its share of output in most of the Asian-14, which was attributable not only to manufacturing but also to construction. The exceptions were Philippines and Sri Lanka, where there was no increase in its employment share, and Singapore, where its employment share dropped sharply. There was a substantial rise in the share of the services sector, but this rise was much greater in its employment share as compared with its output share in most of the Asian-14. The exceptions were Philippines and Turkey, where the increase in employment and output shares was almost equal, and India and Sri Lanka, where the output share increased more than the employment share. Yet, in 2016, the services sector's output share was higher than its employment share in most of the Asian-14; this difference was the largest at 20 percentage points in India and Bangladesh, with Sri Lanka not far behind. The exceptions were South Korea, Malaysia, and Singapore where the employment share of services was higher than the output share, and Taiwan where it was close, much like industrialized countries.

Economic development was associated with an increase in the relative importance of the industrial sector across countries. Table 4.3 presents available evidence on peak shares of the industrial sector in output (since 1970) and employment (since 1991) for the Asian-14, to highlight turning points in the process of structural change. It shows that, in the Asian-14, the peak share of the industrial sector in total output was in the range of 40–50 per cent for eight countries, 35–39 per cent in five countries and less than 25 per cent in just one country. In sharp contrast, the peak share of the industrial sector in total employment was more than 40 per cent in only one country, 35–40 per cent in four countries, 20–30 per cent in eight countries and less than 20 per cent in one country. In effect, these are peak shares of the industrial sector in employment for all the Asian-14, since 1970, because peak shares in the nine economies for which data are available from another source—China, South Korea, Taiwan, Indonesia, Malaysia, Philippines, Singapore, Thailand, and

Table 4.3 Peak shares of the industrial sector in output and employment for the Asian-14 (in percentages)

	Output		Employment	
	Peak share	Peak Year	Peak Share	Peak Year
China	48.2	1980	30.2	2010
South Korea	40.2	1991	36.0	1991
Taiwan	48.1	1986	41.1	1991
Indonesia	44.8	2008	22.0	2015
Malaysia	47.4	2004	33.7	1997
Philippines	42.4	1981	17.5	2016
Singapore	36.5	1984	35.2	1991
Thailand	40.0	2010	23.7	2015
Vietnam	38.6	2006	24.8	2016
Bangladesh	28.8	2016	20.8	2016
India	34.5	2007	24.4	2012
Pakistan	22.3	2008	24.0	2015
Sri Lanka	38.5	1978	27.3	2005
Turkey	41.4	1989	27.9	2014

Note: For peak shares in output, data used start in 1970. For peak shares in employment, data used start in 1991.

Source: Author's calculations from UN National Accounts Statistics for output, and ILO STAT for employment.

India—were lower during the period 1970–1990 when compared with 1991–2016,[15] while peak shares in the other five economies—Vietnam, Bangladesh, Pakistan, Sri Lanka, and Turkey—were attained well after 2000. Given higher productivity in the industrial sector, as compared with the agricultural sector, this asymmetry in its peak shares of output and employment across countries is not surprising.

It was only in South Korea, Taiwan, and Singapore that peak shares of the industrial sector in output and employment were attained without significant time lags and were close to each other. The time lag between attaining the peak output share and peak employment share was twenty-five years or more in China, Philippines, Sri Lanka, and Turkey, ten years in Vietnam, seven years in Indonesia, Malaysia, and Pakistan, five years in Thailand and India, while the two coincided in Bangladesh. This time lag simply confirms that structural change in employment was much slower than in output. For most countries, the peak output share was distinctly higher than the peak employment share, by as much as 15–20 percentage points in China, Indonesia, Malaysia, Thailand, and Vietnam, and by about 10 percentage points in India, Sri Lanka, and Bangladesh. The outliers were Pakistan, where the peak shares were similar at low levels, and Philippines, where the peak output share was 25 percentage points higher than the peak employment share. The difference between the two peak shares was the real issue. Given the negligible or declining employment opportunities in agriculture, and the long time lags between attaining peak output and peak employment shares in industry, it is no surprise that the services sector progressively became the largest employer in the Asian-14.

In this context, the literature on premature deindustrialization deserves mention, although it would mean too much of a digression to enter into a discussion here.[16] The share of manufacturing in employment has begun its decline at much lower levels of per capita income in many among the Asian-14, as compared with advanced economies during their industrialization, while there is the related phenomenon of jobless growth in the formal manufacturing sector in both the fast-growth and the slow-growth economies in the Asian-14. At the same time, the services sector has witnessed rapid increases, not only in employment but also in output, to boost, if not lead, economic growth in many of the Asian-14.

4. Structural change and economic growth in the Asian-14

In the context of structural change, there is an important question that arises. Economic growth in the Asian-14 was attributable in part to a transfer of labour from low-productivity sectors to higher-productivity sectors and in part to productivity increases within sectors. Did the relative importance of these two sources differ across countries? In an attempt to address this question, Table 4.4 presents

Table 4.4 Growth rates of GDP, employment and output per worker in the Asian-14: 1991–2016 (per cent per annum)

	Agriculture			Industry			Services		
	GDP growth	Employment growth	Growth in output per worker	GDP growth	Employment growth	Growth in output per worker	GDP growth	Employment growth	Growth in output per worker
China	4.0	−3.7	7.7	10.5	0.8	9.7	9.9	5.3	4.6
South Korea	1.3	−3.0	4.3	5.2	−0.4	5.6	4.3	2.6	1.7
Taiwan	−0.04	−3.2	3.2	5.3	0.6	4.7	3.9	2.0	1.9
Indonesia	3.0	0.3	2.7	3.8	3.1	0.7	5.0	3.1	1.9
Malaysia	2.3	0.2	2.1	4.1	2.2	1.9	6.3	4.1	2.2
Philippines	2.6	0.7	1.9	4.1	2.4	1.7	5.2	4.0	1.2
Singapore	−2.1	7.1	−9.2	5.4	0.3	5.1	5.8	4.0	1.8
Thailand	2.5	−0.9	3.4	3.8	2.0	1.8	3.8	3.7	0.1
Vietnam	3.6	−0.2	3.8	7.6	6.2	1.4	6.1	5.0	1.1
Bangladesh	3.7	0.1	3.6	7.4	5.2	2.2	5.3	5.2	0.1
India	2.9	0.1	2.7	6.8	3.9	2.9	8.2	3.1	5.1
Pakistan	3.1	2.6	0.5	4.6	4.3	0.3	4.4	3.4	1.0
Sri Lanka	2.8	−0.5	3.3	5.8	1.9	3.9	5.3	2.4	2.9
Turkey	2.0	−2.3	4.3	4.9	2.5	2.4	4.0	3.7	0.3

Source: Author's calculations from UN National Accounts Statistics and ILO STAT. See Appendix.

evidence on average annual growth in GDP, employment, and output per worker, disaggregated by sectors—agriculture, industry, and services—during the period from 1991 to 2016, for which employment statistics are also available.

It shows that, in the agricultural sector, employment growth was negligible or negative in twelve of the Asian-14. The only exceptions were Singapore, where there was virtually no agriculture, and Pakistan where employment growth nearly matched GDP growth. In all the other countries, GDP growth in agriculture was attributable entirely, or almost entirely, to productivity growth, rather than an increase in employment, reflected in rising output per worker. This is no surprise given the exit of workers from agriculture throughout.

In the industrial sector, employment growth was negligible in South Korea, Taiwan, Singapore, and China, so that GDP growth was essentially attributable to increases in output per worker, reflecting within-sector productivity growth, where labour transfer from low-productivity to higher-productivity sectors contributed little. In sharp contrast, the employment growth rate in Indonesia, Vietnam, Bangladesh, and Pakistan was as much as 75–90 per cent of the GDP growth rate, so that economic growth was attributable largely to the transfer of labour from low-productivity agriculture to higher-productivity industry, while the contribution of increases in output per worker was small. The other six countries – Malaysia, Philippines, Thailand, India, Sri Lanka, and Turkey—were in the middle, where the employment growth rate was more than half the GDP growth rate (except Sri Lanka where it was one-third), so that the contribution of labour transfer from a low-productivity to a higher-productivity sector and within-sector productivity increase was roughly equal. The differences between these groups of countries in the Asian-14 broadly validate the proposition that labour transfer from low to higher productivity sectors drives growth in the earlier stages of development whereas within-sector productivity increase drives growth in later stages of development.[17]

The story in the services sector is somewhat more complex, with two features that are different and worth noting. For one, the employment growth rate in services was higher than in industry for most of the Asian-14. For another, employment growth in services contributed more to GDP growth than did increases in output per worker in most of the Asian-14. In Thailand, Bangladesh, and Turkey, the employment growth rate was almost the same as the GDP growth rate, while it was 75–80 per cent of the GDP growth rate in Philippines, Vietnam, and Pakistan. In these six countries, it would seem that GDP growth in the services sector was driven mostly by a labour transfer from a low-productivity to a higher-productivity sector, and not by a within-sector productivity increase reflected in output per worker. Indonesia was similar, with an employment growth rate around two-thirds of its GDP growth rate, so that within-sector productivity increase contributed somewhat more but labour transfer between sectors was still far more important. In China and Sri Lanka, the employment growth rate was about half the GDP growth rate so that the contribution of labour transfer between sectors and within-sector productivity increase was roughly equal. In four economies, the employment growth rate was high as a proportion of the GDP growth in the services sector—South Korea (60 per cent), Taiwan (50 per cent), Singapore (70 per cent) and Malaysia (65 per cent) – but this probably represented a labour transfer from a high-productivity industry to higher-productivity services as employment contracted in industry (particularly manufacturing), so that this group in the Asian-14 was similar to industrialized countries.

India was the outlier, with an employment growth rate that was less than 40 per cent of the GDP growth rate in its services sector. Unskilled rural labour drawn from low-productivity occupations in agriculture to higher-productivity occupations in the urban informal services sector (segments in wholesale and retail trade, hotels and restaurants, transport and storage, or personal services which were labour-intensive, could use almost unskilled labour, and had no barriers to entry for job-seekers) contributed to economic growth through labour transfer between sectors. At the same time, skill-intensive, human-capital-intensive and capital-intensive services (such as communication, financial, business, education, and health services), contributed to economic growth through within-sector productivity increases reflected in an impressive growth in output per worker. This dichotomization of the services sector in India was unusual, making it a special case.[18]

It is time to return to the questions posed at the outset. Did economic growth drive structural change, or did structural change drive economic growth in the Asian-14? The answers are clear enough. In countries that were success stories, at least in terms of their growth performance, where there was rapid economic growth and significant structural change, the causation ran strongly in both directions, creating a virtuous circle of cumulative causation. In contrast, there were two countries among the Asian-14, Pakistan and, to some extent, Philippines, in which both economic growth as well as structural changes in the composition of output and employment were relatively slow, so that the causation was weak in both directions.

The virtuous circle is apparent from the development experience of South Korea, Taiwan, Singapore, China and, to some extent, Malaysia, that followed the classical pattern of structural change, as well as from the development experience of most others among the Asian-14, particularly India, Thailand, Vietnam, Bangladesh, and Turkey, that followed the non-traditional pattern of change. Of course, there was an exit of labour from agriculture everywhere, which moved from low-productivity employment in rural areas, to higher-productivity employment either in manufacturing, or into other industrial sub-sectors such as construction, or into the informal services sector. Such structural change, associated with labour transfer between sectors, drove economic growth from the supply-side in the Asian-14, perhaps more in countries where surplus labour moved into manufacturing. However, the growth-push was also significant in countries such as India where surplus labour moved into services.

At the same time, economic growth also drove structural change from the demand-side, as the composition of output and employment moved from agriculture towards manufacturing, or into other industrial sub-sectors and, then, in sequence or in parallel to different services sub-sectors. Economic growth raised income levels. The higher income elasticity of demand for manufactured goods, as compared with agricultural goods, and the higher income elasticity of demand for services as compared with manufactured goods, drove structural change, as rising incomes created new demands and new production activities followed. Obviously, this push for structural change was much less in countries where and when economic growth was slow.

The relative importance of the direction of causation in this relationship between economic growth and structural change was a function of the stage of development. In the earlier stages, the transfer of labour between sectors from low-productivity to higher-productivity occupations drove economic growth from the supply-side. In the later stages, increases in productivity within sectors drove economic growth from the supply-side with a stimulus from the demand-side. The mix differed across countries, which is apparent from the preceding discussion on the relative contribution of employment growth and output per worker growth to GDP growth in the agricultural, industrial, and services sectors of the Asian-14 during 1991–2016.

5. Different paths to structural transformation

The reality that has unfolded in Asia does not quite conform to stylized facts or analytical constructs based on the experience of industrialized economies. South Korea and Taiwan were the exceptions. To some extent, Malaysia, China, and even Indonesia, followed similar paths later. Singapore was different. It had no agriculture. The remaining eight countries just did not follow the classical pattern of structural change. And there were significant differences in the nature of, and paths to, structural transformation in the Asian-14. The crucial common factor was the rapid decline in the share of agriculture, more pronounced in output than in employment, although the timing and pace of change differed across countries. In most countries, to begin with, surplus labour was absorbed in the industrial sector, not only in manufacturing but also in mining and construction. However, in many countries, it was not long before surplus labour moved directly to the services sector. Soon thereafter, in the countries where manufacturing reached its peak shares in output and employment, much like in industrialized countries, labour moved from manufacturing to services. It is no surprise that the share of the services sector in total employment rose faster than in total output. Even so, in the Asian-14, except for South Korea, Taiwan, Singapore, and Malaysia, the share of services in output was higher than in employment. The transition from a situation, *circa* 1970, when the agricultural sector was dominant to a situation, in 2016, when the services sector was dominant, in terms of shares in output and employment, was far from uniform in the Asian-14. There was an exit of labour from agriculture everywhere (which was a remarkably similar pattern) in some countries to manufacturing, in other countries to industry outside manufacturing (particularly construction), in yet other countries to services, and these three sorts of labour transfers often overlapped in time and space. The story is complicated further by the differences in the timing and the speed of these changes or shifts.

The process of structural transformation is associated with a migration of rural workers to urban settings, a falling share of agriculture in output and employment, and a rising share of economic activities—industry and services—in modern urban sectors. Agriculture is critical in this process, because it provides the surplus of labour, food, and savings in the early stages but, as the productivity-gap between the agricultural and non-agricultural sector widens, it also requires investments that raise productivity in agriculture so as to eradicate poverty in the rural sector and provide food for the urban sector. With rising income levels in societies, agriculture also experiences a dietary transformation since the share of food in household budgets declines, while sources of calories and proteins in diets diversify beyond cereals and root crops.[19]

The past fifty years have witnessed rapid agricultural transformations in most Asian countries, which have helped kick-start development in ways outlined in the preceding paragraph. But the nature and speed of this change has differed sharply across countries. In East Asia—South Korea, Taiwan and China—agricultural productivity growth, driven in part by Green Revolution technologies which led to a spurt in yields, facilitated the transfer of labour, savings and food, thus supporting industrialization and urbanization. Institutional change, particularly land reforms, in agriculture, creation of a rural infrastructure, public expenditure on the farm sector, and supportive policies (such as R&D, extension networks, and price incentives) reinforced the process. Government intervention and market forces complemented each other. This, in turn, induced deeper agrarian changes as well as dietary transformations in food systems. Southeast Asia, particularly Malaysia, traversed a similar path, but the transformation was not comparable with that in East Asia. Indonesia, Philippines, Thailand, and Vietnam were in the middle-tier, where the gap between the share of agriculture in employment and in GDP persisted. In India, and much of South Asia, which constitute the bottom-tier, such transformative changes were lagged, but these countries now seem to have turned the corner, with the beginnings of change in agriculture and an acceleration in economic growth, although the challenges implicit in widespread poverty, food insecurity, rapid urbanization, and changing dietary patterns remain.[20]

Economic history suggests that no country has attained high-income status without a period of sustained industrialization, except for resource-rich high-income economies. The peak shares of the industrial sector in GDP and total employment are impressive in most of the Asian-14. But this is deceptive. Apart from manufacturing, industry includes mining, utilities, and construction, which have also grown rapidly in developing Asia. In fact, performance is far more unequal in terms of manufacturing for industrialization, in which East Asian countries have led the process, Southeast Asian countries are somewhere in the middle, and South Asian countries bring up the rear. The trajectory of Asia shows that success at industrialization does require a rapid growth of output and employment in manufacturing, combined with high levels of investment (reflected in investment–GDP ratios) that are maintained over time. This is necessary but not sufficient. There are two other conditions that must be met. First, the rapid expansion in manufacturing output needs to be sustained for long, well beyond the peak share of manufacturing in employment. Second, industrial production needs upgrading, which depends on technological learning and capabilities, and vertical diversification, which requires a capacity to develop backward and forward linkages in production processes.[21]

South Korea, Taiwan, and Singapore have industrialized in terms of these criteria and China is on that path. But the industrial dynamism of Malaysia, Thailand, and Indonesia has waned, as their manufacturing output growth has not even kept pace with their GDP growth. In India, where the share of manufacturing in output peaked decades ago, at lower levels, is a similar story, although it continues to sustain high GDP growth rates. Vietnam and Bangladesh do show a rapid growth of output and employment in manufacturing but are in the early stages. Turkey, which has experienced a sharp contraction in the share of manufacturing in GDP, seems to have prematurely deindustrialized. Philippines, Pakistan, and Sri Lanka are not quite on the path to industrialization. In sum, manufacturing and industrialization were significant in the process of growth and development in Asia, far more so than in Latin America or Africa, but their contribution to structural change did not conform to the established sequential patterns.[22] It differed across countries and changed over time.

In most of the Asian-14, the falling share of the agricultural sector in output and employment was matched by the rising share of the services sector in output and employment. The increase in its share of total employment began much before the industrial sector attained its peak shares in output and employment. In general, this pattern was not sequential as it had been in the industrialized countries. What is more, in most countries, the output share of the services sector was consistently higher than its employment share. South Korea, Taiwan, and Singapore (which had no agriculture) were the only exceptions to these two generalizations. Given this reality, it has been argued that there may be two waves of growth in the services sector: the first wave, made up of traditional services, is when a country moves from low-income to middle-income status, while the second wave, made up of modern communication and financial services, is when a country moves from a middle-income to high-income status (Eichengreen and Gupta, 2013). But this idea is not borne out by the Asian experience, where these waves surfaced almost in parallel rather than in sequence. It would seem that there is a dualism in the services sector.

In much of Asia, during 1970–2016, GDP growth in the services sector was faster than GDP growth in the economy. The consequent rise in the share of the services sector in total output was associated with higher rates of GDP growth across the Asian-14. Of course, this was partly attributable to the fact that the services were an increasingly important component of GDP in most countries. The rapid GDP growth in the services sector, in turn, was attributable almost entirely, or in large part, to the labour transfer from low-productivity agriculture to higher-productivity services in seven of the Asian-14. In the remaining seven countries, this growth was attributable in part to labour transfer from elsewhere and in part to productivity increase within the sector.

For an understanding of this process, it is necessary to disaggregate the sub-sectors in services into two categories.[23] The first includes wholesale and retail trade, hotels and restaurants, transport and storage, and social, community, or personal services, while the second includes communication services, financial services, business services, real estate services, public administration, education, and health. The former are essentially labour-intensive services characterized by low barriers to entry for job-seekers and low technological levels for service provision. The latter are essentially skill-intensive, human-capital-intensive or capital-intensive, characterized by high barriers to entry for job-seekers and high technological levels for service provision. Of course, such a generalization is not without its limitations, because there is a dualism in each of these sub-sectors. Yet, this distinction helps as such dualism is far greater in the former. The absorption of unskilled surplus labour from low-productivity occupations in rural areas to higher-productivity occupations in the urban informal services sector, mostly in the first category sub-sectors, led to GDP growth through labour transfer between sectors, which conforms to the Lewis (1954) model with a slight twist. In the second category sub-sectors, GDP growth was attributable to prod-uctivity increases within sectors, even where there was labour transfer from the manufacturing sector.

On the demand-side, growth in the services sector was driven by private final consumption expenditure on education, health, entertainment, communication, transport, and personal services, which absorbed a larger share of household budgets. In other words, the income elasticity of demand for these consumer services was high, as both income levels and income inequalities rose in these economies. On the supply-side, technological change, deregulation, and privat-ization in sectors such as communications, business, financial, education, and health services provided a stimulus to growth not only in producer services but also consumer services.[24]

The preceding discussion suggests that, despite the rapid pace of structural change, the process of structural transformation in Asia is uneven and incomplete, except in South Korea, Taiwan, Singapore, and, to some extent, Malaysia. The transformation of the agricultural sector has progressed the most in East Asia. Yet, in China the agriculture employment share exceeds its output share by 19 percentage points. There is an ongoing transformation in Southeast Asia, uneven across countries, as well as in South Asia, where progress has been slower. But both these regions have some distance to traverse, as the gap between the share of agriculture in employment and output remains large, and productivity in the agricultural sector is much lower than in the non-agricultural sector. In most countries, there is a significant transformation reflected in the rising share of the industrial sector, more in output than in employment but, except for East Asia, there is much less progress in manufacturing for industrialization, particularly in South Asia, while industrial dynamism has waned in Southeast Asia, and there are countries in both regions—Pakistan and Philippines—that are laggards. The striking aspect of structural change in Asia is the increasing relative importance of the services sector, which has driven economic growth in many countries, but there could be limits to this process. In most of the Asian-14, the services sector has led economic growth in large part through labour absorption at the extensive margin but might not be able to sustain it through labour absorption at the intensive margin, since the possibilities of moving unskilled labour from the informal labour-intensive services sector to the formal skill-intensive or capital-intensive formal services sector are very limited.

The structural transformation of economies in Asia cannot be completed by more of the same. It needs correctives and interventions. The transformation of the agricultural sector requires support through institutional reform, rural infrastructure, and supportive policies, such that markets and governments complement each other. In many countries, it is necessary to renew the focus and emphasis on manufacturing, since it is the path to employment creation in better jobs and a potential source of economic growth through absorption of surplus rural labour, with a potential for moving workers from lower- to higher-productivity employment within manufacturing. Economic development is not only about economic growth. It is also about the capabilities of an economy to organize and transform its productive activities. This is simply not possible without industrialization (Nayyar, 2013). The economic history of the now developed high-income countries provides confirmation (Chang, 2002). Indeed, the experience of success stories in development since 1950 also shows that no country has achieved middle-income status without industrialization.[25] Manufacturing also shows faster growth in lower-income countries, so that it narrows the productivity gap between industrialized and developing countries more rapidly, suggesting an unconditional convergence to the frontier (Rodrik, 2013). Moreover, evidence available suggests that productivity gains for unskilled labour are unlikely to occur in the same services sub-sector,[26] while, as argued above, the possibilities of moving to a higher-productivity sub-sector are very limited. The importance of manufacturing, then, cannot be stressed enough.

In fact, the services and manufacturing sectors are no longer strictly separable from each other. There is an increasing integration of, and a growing interdependence between, services and manufacturing.[27] In this changing world, manufacturing and services should be thought of as complements rather than substitutes, with potential synergies that can be exploited. Rapid output growth in manufacturing and services would provide an impetus to employment creation in both sectors on the demand-side, just as it would enhance productivity increases in both sectors through exploiting static and dynamic scale economies on the supply-side. The moral of the story is that, while economic growth might be led by a sector, the process of structural transformation cannot be completed if there is a sector, or sectors, whether agriculture or manufacturing, that are laggards.

Conclusion

Over the past fifty years, development in Asia has been associated with a structural transformation of economies. In this process, economic growth drove structural change from the demand-side as incomes rose and production activities followed, while structural change drove economic growth from the supply-side as labour moved from low-productivity to higher-productivity activities.

There were significant differences among the Asian-14 in their paths to structural transformation. South Korea, Taiwan, and Singapore, followed by Malaysia, China, and possibly Indonesia later, conformed to the classical pattern of structural change from agriculture through manufacturing, or industry, to services. India, Turkey, Thailand, Philippines, Pakistan, and Sri Lanka, followed by Bangladesh and Vietnam later, did not conform to this traditional sequence. The transition from a situation, *circa* 1970, when the agricultural sector was dominant to a situation, in 2016, when the services sector was dominant, was far from uniform in the Asian-14. Yet, there was an exit of labour from agriculture everywhere, in some countries to manufacturing, in other countries to industry outside manufacturing (particularly construction), in yet other countries to services, and these three sorts of labour transfers overlapped in time and space. In earlier stages of development, such labour transfer between sectors was growth-promoting. In later stages of

Continued

Conclusion: Continued

development, productivity increase within sectors was growth-promoting. The relative importance of these two drivers differed across countries, as well as sectors, and changed over time. Given the negligible or declining employment opportunities in agriculture, and the long time lags between attaining peak output and peak employment shares in industry, it is no surprise that the services sector progressively became the largest employer, with the highest output share, across the Asian-14.

It is clear that, apart from South Korea, Taiwan, Singapore, and perhaps Malaysia, the process of structural transformation in the Asian-14 is uneven and incomplete. The transformation of the agricultural sector remains incomplete in China, and even more so in Southeast Asia, while South Asia has a considerable distance to traverse. There is much less progress in manufacturing for industrialization, particularly in South Asia, while industrial dynamism has waned in Southeast Asia. The services sector has led economic growth so far in several countries, largely through absorption of unskilled labour, but this might not be sustainable. In many of the Asian-14, it is necessary to address the neglect of agriculture and renew the emphasis on manufacturing, just as it is essential to exploit the synergies and complementarities between manufacturing and services. Economic growth cannot be sustained and structural transformation cannot be completed even if one of three sectors is a weak link in the chain.

5

Openness and industrialization

Over the past fifty years, the evolution of thinking about openness and industrialization, in the wider context of development, has seen some twists and turns. These changes have been shaped by history, ideology, and experience. The ideological spectrum spans the entire range, from a strong belief in the magic of markets and openness at one end, to a strong conviction about the necessity of strategic intervention and calibrated openness at the other, in the pursuit of industrialization. It is striking that both such polar opposite ideological perspectives invoke the story of industrialization in Asia to support their worldviews. However, the development experience of Asia is much too diverse and far too complex for simple prescriptive generalizations. There are significant differences between countries. And there are significant changes within countries over time. Even so, the degree of openness of economies and the nature of strategic intervention in markets have remained the critical issues in the debate on industrialization.

The object of this chapter is to analyse openness and industrialization, which have been centre-stage in the process of economic development in Asia over the past fifty years. Section 1 outlines the contours of economic openness in the Asian-14, situated in the wider context of Asia and the world economy, with a focus on international trade and capital flows, to consider how these changed over time and differed across countries. Section 2 traces the trajectories of industrialization in the Asian-14, using Asia and the world economy as points of reference, to examine transformations in industrial production and the related changes in trade patterns across countries over time. Section 3 discusses the enormous diversity in the nature of openness and process of industrialization among the Asian-14, touching upon their intersections, to highlight the similarities and differences between countries. Section 4 analyses the very different paths to industrialization in the Asian-14, exploring how or why the relationship between economic openness, industrial policy, and effective government was a determinant of success. Section 5 concludes with a brief discussion on the critical importance of technology in the process of industrialization.

1. Contours of openness

During the period from the mid-nineteenth century to the mid-twentieth century, international trade with Europe locked Asian countries into an international

Resurgent Asia: Diversity in Development. Deepak Nayyar, Oxford University Press (2019). © United Nations University World Institute for Development Economics Research. DOI: 10.1093/oso/9780198849513.001.0001

division of labour that inhibited industrialization and stifled growth. Indeed, there was a causal connection between the Great Specialization and the Great Divergence. For that reason, perhaps, in the early post-colonial era, starting around 1950, most Asian countries adopted strategies of development that provided a sharp contrast with the preceding hundred years. There was a conscious attempt to limit the degree of openness and of integration with the world economy because open economies of the colonial past were associated with deindustrialization and underdevelopment. Industrialization was seen as an imperative in catching up, which had to begin with import substitution in the manufacturing sector, but was, in effect, state-led industrialization. This approach also represented the consensus in thinking about development at the time. In such a milieu, the possibilities that economic openness could also create development opportunities were simply not recognized. Gunnar Myrdal's thinking in *Asian Drama* was similar, where the entire discussion on foreign trade was based on the premise of export pessimism, while the elaborate discussion on capital flows argued that international capital movements could not be a source of investment in Asia as they had been in Europe.[1] It would seem that export pessimism and capital immobility were accepted as characteristics of the world economy that would remain forever. However, it was not long before the actual industrialization experience in Asia—in which the impressive economic performance of South Korea, Taiwan, Singapore, and Hong Kong, at the time attributed to markets and openness by mainstream economists, was juxtaposed with the disappointing economic performance of other Asian countries, attributed to excessive state intervention and restricted openness, even though such attributions were questioned by critics—led to changes in both thinking and policies beginning *circa* 1980. The spread of markets and the gathering momentum of globalization reinforced changes in thinking. It led to a marked increase in the degree of economic openness in Asian countries. This began with international trade, to be followed by capital flows in the form of investment and finance.

1.1 International trade

International trade is the most visible form of openness in terms of engagement with the world economy. During the early post-colonial era, the share of Asia in world trade dropped from 14 per cent in 1950 to 8.4 per cent in 1970, reaching its lowest level in the early 1970s (Nayyar, 2013). Over the next four decades, increasing openness in Asia led to a transformation in the significance of international trade.

Tables 5.1 and 5.2 set out evidence on merchandise exports from, and imports into, each of the Asian-14, as a percentage of GDP, which reflects their economic openness in the national context, and as a percentage of world trade, which shows

Table 5.1 Merchandise exports from the Asian-14: 1970–2016

	(as a percentage of GDP)						(as a percentage of world exports)					
	1970	1980	1990	2000	2008	2016	1970	1980	1990	2000	2008	2016
China	2.6	5.9	15.6	20.5	31.1	18.7	0.73	0.88	1.78	3.86	8.86	13.12
South Korea	9.3	26.9	23.3	30.7	42.1	35.1	0.26	0.85	1.86	2.67	2.61	3.10
Taiwan	24.7	46.9	40.3	45.7	61.3	52.9	0.45	0.97	1.92	2.35	1.58	1.75
Indonesia	10.6	25.8	19.2	37.1	25.7	15.5	0.35	1.07	0.73	1.01	0.86	0.91
Malaysia	43.6	52.9	66.9	104.7	86.4	63.9	0.53	0.63	0.84	1.52	1.23	1.18
Philippines	14.0	16.0	16.5	47.0	28.2	18.8	0.33	0.28	0.23	0.59	0.30	0.36
Singapore	80.9	160.4	135.6	143.8	175.9	113.9	0.49	0.95	1.51	2.14	2.09	2.11
Thailand	9.6	19.4	26.1	54.7	61.0	52.9	0.22	0.32	0.66	1.07	1.10	1.35
Vietnam	–	14.1	37.1	46.5	63.2	86.1	–	0.02	0.07	0.22	0.39	1.11
Bangladesh	–	4.5	5.9	14.1	16.8	15.8	–	0.04	0.05	0.10	0.10	0.22
India	3.4	4.8	5.7	9.3	15.5	11.7	0.64	0.42	0.51	0.66	1.21	1.65
Pakistan	3.4	8.4	10.8	11.7	13.5	7.2	0.14	0.13	0.16	0.14	0.13	0.13
Sri Lanka	12.1	21.7	20.4	28.4	18.1	12.7	0.11	0.05	0.05	0.08	0.05	0.06
Turkey	2.4	3.1	6.2	10.2	17.3	16.5	0.2	0.1	0.4	0.4	0.8	0.9
Asian-14	*5.7*	*14.8*	*20.7*	*30.4*	*34.9*	*23.1*	*4.4*	*6.7*	*10.8*	*16.8*	*21.3*	*27.9*
Asia	*9.3*	*27.0*	*25.8*	*35.2*	*40.0*	*26.2*	*8.4*	*18.2*	*16.9*	*23.8*	*29.9*	*35.9*
Developing Countries	*10.5*	*22.3*	*21.1*	*28.3*	*34.3*	*23.9*	*19.1*	*29.7*	*24.1*	*31.9*	*39.0*	*43.7*
Industrialized Countries	*10.2*	*15.9*	*14.0*	*16.4*	*21.2*	*19.2*	*76.3*	*66.2*	*72.5*	*65.8*	*56.5*	*53.5*
World	*9.4*	*16.7*	*15.2*	*19.2*	*25.4*	*21.1*	*100.0*	*100.0*	*100.0*	*100.0*	*100.0*	*100.0*

Note: The percentages have been calculated from data on merchandise exports and GDP in current prices and market exchange rates. The share of developing countries and industrialized countries in world exports does not add up to 100. The residual is attributable to the transition economies of Eastern Europe and the former USSR.

Source: Author's calculations from United Nations, UNCTAD Stat based on UN International Trade Statistics, and UN National Accounts Statistics.

Table 5.2 Merchandise imports into the Asian-14: 1970–2016

	(as a percentage of GDP)						(as a percentage of world imports)					
	1970	1980	1990	2000	2008	2016	1970	1980	1990	2000	2008	2016
China	2.5	6.5	13.4	18.5	24.6	14.2	0.7	1.0	1.5	3.4	6.9	9.8
South Korea	22.0	34.3	25.0	28.6	43.4	28.8	0.6	1.1	1.9	2.4	2.6	2.5
Taiwan	26.4	46.7	32.8	42.4	57.7	43.5	0.5	0.9	1.5	2.1	1.5	1.4
Indonesia	9.6	12.8	16.3	24.7	23.5	14.6	0.3	0.5	0.6	0.7	0.8	0.8
Malaysia	36.2	44.0	66.5	87.4	67.7	56.8	0.4	0.5	0.8	1.2	0.9	1.0
Philippines	16.7	23.1	26.5	45.7	34.7	28.2	0.7	0.4	0.4	0.6	0.4	0.5
Singapore	128.2	198.8	156.6	140.4	166.4	98.3	0.7	1.1	1.7	2.0	1.9	1.8
Thailand	17.6	27.5	37.4	49.1	61.5	47.7	0.4	0.4	0.9	0.9	1.1	1.2
Vietnam	–	54.9	42.5	50.2	81.4	84.9	0.0	0.1	0.1	0.2	0.5	1.1
Bangladesh	–	15.5	12.9	19.5	26.0	20.3	0.0	0.1	0.1	0.1	0.1	0.3
India	3.6	8.3	7.4	11.4	25.6	15.9	0.6	0.7	0.7	0.8	1.9	2.2
Pakistan	5.9	17.3	14.3	14.1	28.0	16.7	0.2	0.3	0.2	0.2	0.3	0.3
Sri Lanka	13.7	41.7	28.6	32.8	29.9	23.9	0.1	0.1	0.1	0.1	0.1	0.1
Turkey	3.8	8.4	10.8	20.0	26.4	23.0	0.3	0.4	0.6	0.8	1.2	1.2
Asian-14	*7.1*	*17.1*	*21.9*	*28.9*	*33.8*	*20.4*	*5.3*	*7.6*	*11.0*	*15.5*	*20.3*	*24.4*
Asia	*9.5*	*20.2*	*25.2*	*31.9*	*35.9*	*23.5*	*8.4*	*13.3*	*15.9*	*20.9*	*26.3*	*31.9*
Developing Countries	*10.6*	*18.4*	*20.0*	*26.3*	*31.3*	*22.5*	*18.5*	*24.0*	*22.2*	*28.8*	*34.9*	*40.8*
Industrialized Countries	*10.7*	*17.6*	*14.7*	*17.9*	*23.6*	*20.6*	*77.0*	*72.0*	*74.0*	*69.8*	*61.7*	*56.9*
World	*9.7*	*17.0*	*15.7*	*19.8*	*25.9*	*21.3*	*100.0*	*100.0*	*100.0*	*100.0*	*100.0*	*100.0*

Note: The percentages have been calculated from data on merchandise imports and GDP in current prices and market exchange rates. The share of developing countries and industrialized countries in world imports does not add up to 100. The residual is attributable to the transition economies of Eastern Europe and the former USSR.

Source: Author's calculations from United Nations, UNCTAD Stat based on UN International Trade Statistics, and UN National Accounts Statistics.

their relative importance in the global context, during the period from 1970 to 2016. In order to keep the statistics within manageable proportions, the figures are presented for selected benchmark years, at decadal intervals. The exceptions are 2008, as the global economic crisis led to a sharp contraction in trade flows thereafter, and 2016, the latest year for which data are available. For the purpose of reference and comparison, the tables also present the corresponding figures in percentages for the Asian-14, Asia, developing countries, industrialized countries, and the world.

The tables show that, for Asia as a whole, the share of exports and imports in GDP rose rapidly from less than one-tenth in 1970 to about two-fifths in 2008 but, in the aftermath of the financial crisis and the Great Recession, contracted to roughly one-fourth in 2016. This reflected a substantial increase in the degree of openness in trade until 2008 that was dampened by the global economic crisis. During 2009–2016, these trade–GDP ratios witnessed a contraction that was modest in industrialized countries and significant in developing countries but substantial in Asia. The export–GDP ratios for Asia were consistently higher than the import–GDP ratios, which suggests asymmetrical openness, but that was partly attributable to West Asia's oil-exporting countries.[2] Among the Asian-14, Indonesia was the only country that was a major oil-exporter.[3]

The export–GDP and import–GDP ratios in the Asian-14 also rose between 1970 and 2008 but fell in 2016, in most economies except for Vietnam where these ratios continued to rise. The degree of openness increased rapidly in China, South Korea, Taiwan, Singapore, and Vietnam, slowly in India, Bangladesh, Pakistan, Sri Lanka, with Indonesia, Malaysia, Philippines, Thailand, and Turkey somewhere in the middle. In general, except for Indonesia, these trade–GDP ratios were the highest in the Southeast Asian countries. This is no surprise, because the ratio of exports or imports to GDP is bound to be the highest in small economies (Taiwan, Malaysia, and Singapore, although it was not so for Sri Lanka) and the lowest in large economies (China, India, and Indonesia). For medium-size countries, trade–GDP ratios were high (South Korea, Thailand, and Vietnam) or not high (Philippines, Bangladesh, Pakistan, and Turkey) depending upon their degree of openness. There were asymmetries between export–GDP and import–GDP ratios for the Asian-14. Starting 1990, the export–GDP ratio in Taiwan, South Korea, and China was significantly higher than the import–GDP ratio, as these economies ran trade surpluses. So did Malaysia and Indonesia (an oil-exporter). In Philippines, Singapore, and Thailand, the import–GDP ratio exceeded the export–GDP ratio, except after the financial crisis when they sought to accumulate foreign exchange reserves through trade surpluses. In India, Pakistan, Bangladesh, and Sri Lanka, as well as Vietnam and Turkey, the import–GDP ratio was mostly higher than the export–GDP ratio, as these countries ran trade deficits.

Given that the share of countries in world exports or world imports essentially depends on their size, it is no surprise that the distribution trade flows within Asia was unequal. The share of the Asian-14 in Asia's merchandise trade was three-fourths in 2016 as compared with one-half in 1970. There was also a concentration among a few countries in the Asian-14. In 2016, in total world trade, the share of China was 11 per cent, the shares of South Korea, Taiwan, Singapore, and India were in the range of 2–3 per cent, while the shares of Malaysia, Thailand, and Vietnam were around 1 per cent.[4] The share of China was about the same as that of the other seven countries taken together. In 1970, such concentration in a few was somewhat less, and China was just one among eight countries.

The focus so far has been on merchandise trade, as exports and imports of goods were always the primary form of international trade.[5] Of course, services such as shipping and insurance, which are intimately linked with merchandise trade, were always traded, and there was tourism. But the past three decades have witnessed real change in the possibilities of trade in services. The technological revolution in transport and communication has made hitherto non-traded services tradable, either by a dramatic reduction in the cost of transport, which increases the mobility of producers and consumers of services, or by developing a means of communication, which eliminates the need for physical proximity between producers and consumers of services. There is now a flourishing trade in software. In addition, financial services, business services, education services, and health services, which are skill-intensive or technology-intensive, have become so much more tradable.[6]

Table 5.3 outlines the increasing significance of trade in services by presenting evidence on exports and imports of services, as a percentage of GDP and as a percentage of world trade, for the Asian-14, in three benchmark years—1980, 2000, and 2013—while providing corresponding figures for the Asian-14, Asia, developing countries, industrialized countries, and the world for purpose of comparison. It shows that for Asia as a whole, and for the Asian-14, trade in services as a proportion of GDP was much smaller than merchandise trade, as it was for developing countries, industrialized countries, and the world. There was a modest increase in this share between 1980 and 2000 followed by a slight drop in 2013. The distribution of trade in services across countries was unequal. In 1980, the Asian-14 accounted for about one-half of Asia's trade in services. In 2013, this proportion had increased to almost three-fourths. And there was, by then, a further concentration within the Asian-14. The countries with the largest shares (in descending order), China, India, Singapore, and South Korea, taken together, accounted for more than one-half of Asia's trade in services. The shares of Thailand and Taiwan were distinctly lower, while the shares of the others were negligible. In fact, exports of services from China, India, Singapore, and South Korea constituted one-eighth of world exports in 2013, and were largely skill-intensive or technology-intensive.

Table 5.3 International trade in services for the Asian-14: 1980–2013

| | (as a percentage of GDP) | | | | | | (as a percentage of world trade) | | | | | |
| | Exports | | | Imports | | | World Exports | | | World Imports | | |
	1980	2000	2013	1980	2000	2013	1980	2000	2013	1980	2000	2013
China	–	2.5	2.1	–	3.0	3.4	–	2.0	4.4	–	2.4	7.4
South Korea	7.6	5.6	8.7	5.8	6.0	8.2	1.2	2.1	2.4	0.8	2.2	2.4
Taiwan	4.6	6.0	10.1	6.0	8.0	8.3	0.5	1.3	1.1	0.6	1.8	0.9
Indonesia	–	3.0	2.4	–	8.9	3.8	–	0.3	0.5	0.6	1.8	0.9
Malaysia	4.6	14.9	12.4	12.1	17.9	14.0	0.3	0.9	0.8	0.7	1.1	1.0
Philippines	4.0	4.2	8.0	4.0	6.5	5.4	0.4	0.2	0.5	0.3	0.4	0.3
Singapore	40.2	29.8	40.5	24.1	31.4	42.5	1.2	1.9	2.6	0.7	2.0	2.9
Thailand	4.5	11.0	14.0	4.9	12.3	13.1	0.4	0.9	1.2	0.4	1.0	1.2
Vietnam	–	8.7	6.1	–	10.4	7.7	–	0.2	0.2	–	0.2	0.3
Bangladesh	1.3	1.8	2.5	2.9	3.6	4.3	0.1	0.1	0.1	0.1	0.1	0.2
India	1.7	3.7	7.9	1.7	4.2	6.6	0.8	1.1	3.2	0.7	1.3	2.8
Pakistan	2.1	1.8	2.2	2.8	2.9	3.5	0.2	0.1	0.1	0.2	0.2	0.2
Sri Lanka	4.7	4.9	6.3	7.2	8.5	4.7	0.1	0.1	0.1	0.08	0.1	0.1
Turkey	0.8	7.5	5.0	0.6	3.3	2.5	0.2	1.3	1.0	0.1	0.6	0.5
Asian-14	*2.2*	*5.3*	*5.0*	*2.2*	*6.0*	*5.0*	*5.2*	*12.5*	*18.2*	*5.3*	*14.2*	*20.9*
Asia	*2.9*	*5.9*	*5.7*	*5.8*	*6.9*	*6.4*	*10.3*	*16.8*	*24.5*	*17.8*	*19.7*	*28.6*
Developing Countries	*2.7*	*4.8*	*4.9*	*5.1*	*5.7*	*5.9*	*18.5*	*23.1*	*30.1*	*31.2*	*27.4*	*37.7*
Industrialized Countries	*3.7*	*4.4*	*7.0*	*3.5*	*4.1*	*5.8*	*79.0*	*75.5*	*67.2*	*66.1*	*70.8*	*58.1*
World	*3.2*	*4.5*	*6.1*	*3.6*	*4.5*	*5.8*	*100.0*	*100.0*	*100.0*	*100.0*	*100.0*	*100.0*

Note: Comparable data are not available after 2013. The share of developing countries and industrialized countries in world exports and world imports does not add up to 100. The residual is attributable to the transition economies of Eastern Europe and the former USSR.

Source: United Nations, UNCTAD Stat, based on IMF Balance of Payments Statistics.

1.2 Capital flows

There have been significant changes not only in the nature of capital flows but also in the degree of openness to foreign capital in Asia over the past fifty years. The changes were sequential with some overlaps. In the first phase, beginning around 1960, concessional development assistance was the most important form of capital flows to Asia, which diminished in relative importance after 1990. In the second phase, starting around 1980, foreign direct investment surfaced and progressively became the most important form of capital flows to Asia. In the third phase, that began around the turn of the century, portfolio investment in the newly industrializing countries of Asia emerged as a new form of capital flows, enabled by capital account liberalization and driven by internationalization of finance.

In earlier stages of the post-colonial era in Asia, international capital movements were almost negligible. During this period, large trade deficits were common in most Asian countries, so that external resources were necessary to finance development. It was foreign aid that bridged this gap. Table 5.4 presents evidence on concessional development assistance to the Asian-14, from donor countries and multilateral institutions, as a percentage of gross capital formation in each of these countries, during the period 1961–2016, which is divided into decades so that the statistics remain within manageable proportions. It shows the macroeconomic significance of foreign aid, which could have been an important source of financing investment in many countries, not just in the earlier decades 1961–1980, when it was the only

Table 5.4 Concessional development assistance to the Asian-14 as a percentage of gross capital formation (annual averages)

	1961–1970	1971–1980	1981–1990	1991–2000	2001–2010	2011–2016
China	–	0.6	2.0	2.3	0.5	0.1
South Korea	37.3	14.5	3.3	1.2	–	–
Taiwan	–	7.7	2.0	0.6	–	–
Indonesia	51.8	19.7	9.1	14.9	5.1	1.6
Malaysia	5.7	7.4	6.2	4.1	3.4	1.6
Philippines	9.2	9.8	12.7	15.6	6.7	3.1
Singapore	3.4	5.9	3.6	3.9		
Thailand	8.0	6.1	6.1	8.1	2.9	1.6
Vietnam	–	72.5	26.5	15.9	9.3	11.7
Bangladesh	–	56.8	22.8	13.7	6.2	3.8
India	11.8	4.5	2.8	2.8	1.2	0.9
Pakistan	39.5	22.9	11.0	11.2	7.6	6.5
Sri Lanka	12.4	18.9	26.7	13.0	7.6	2.9
Turkey	14.5	6.2	5.9	3.9	2.7	1.7

Source: Author's calculations from: (i) OECD DAC database for Concessional Development Assistance, and (ii) UN National Accounts Statistics for Gross Capital Formation. See Appendix.

significant source of capital flows, but also in the later period 1981–2000. The critical importance of foreign aid in the Cold War era is obvious. During 1961–1970 and 1971–1980, aid as a proportion of investment was 37 per cent and 15 per cent respectively in South Korea, 52 per cent and 20 per cent in Indonesia, 40 per cent and 23 per cent in Pakistan, 15 per cent and 6 per cent in Turkey, while it was in the range of 5–10 per cent in Malaysia, Philippines, Singapore, and Thailand. For Taiwan and Vietnam, during 1971–1980, these proportions were 8 per cent and 73 per cent respectively.[7] Even at a later stage, during 1981–2000, foreign aid was large as a proportion of investment in Indonesia, Pakistan, Philippines, and Vietnam. Similarly, foreign aid was important for Bangladesh and Sri Lanka throughout these decades. India and China also received foreign aid but, given the large size of their economies, it was modest as a proportion of investment, except in India during 1961–1970. The significance of foreign aid as a source of capital inflows diminished rapidly during 2001–2010 in most of the Asian-14, except in Indonesia, Philippines, Vietnam, Bangladesh, Pakistan, and Sri Lanka. By 2010–2016, it was significant only in Vietnam and Pakistan.

International investment by large firms from industrialized countries surfaced in the 1970s as regimes for capital exports were liberalized. Asian countries had always been a destination for their investments to obtain natural resources and primary commodities. It began in the nineteenth century with the large trading firms from Europe, and continued in the post-colonial era with their modern corporate counterparts. The increasing openness of Asian countries to private foreign capital, beginning around 1980, turned them into destinations for transnational corporations to manufacture for domestic markets or export markets or both. It was not long before such investments also came to the services sector.

Table 5.5 sets out available evidence on the flows of foreign direct investment, inward and outward, as a percentage of gross capital formation, in each of the Asian-14, with annual averages for the periods 1981–1990, 1991–2000, 2001–2008, and 2009–2016, while providing corresponding figures for the Asian-14, Asia, developing countries, industrialized countries, and the world for the purpose of comparison. Once again, 2008 is used in the periodization, since the global economic crisis led to a downturn in foreign direct investment thereafter. Table 5.6, in the same format, provides statistics on stocks of foreign direct investment, inward and outward, as a percentage GDP, for each of the Asian-14, in 1980, 1990, 2000, 2008, and 2016. Taken together, the two tables sketch a complete picture.

The inward flows of foreign direct investment, as a percentage of gross capital formation, increased in Asia, developing countries, and industrialized countries, between 1981–1990 and 2001–2008, but these inflows contracted everywhere during 2009–2016, most sharply in Asia. However, even at their peak, this proportion was less than 10 per cent in Asia. The trends over time were similar

Table 5.5 Flows of foreign direct investment into and from the Asian-14: 1981–1990 to 2009–2016 (annual averages as a percentage of gross capital formation)

	Inward Flows				Outward Flows			
	1981–1990	1991–2000	2001–2008	2009–2016	1981–1990	1991–2000	2001–2008	2009–2016
China	1.6	11.0	6.8	3.0	0.4	0.8	1.6	2.6
South Korea	1.3	2.4	3.5	2.5	1.1	1.9	3.8	7.2
Taiwan	2.6	2.5	4.5	2.7	7.6	5.0	8.6	11.9
Indonesia	1.4	3.3	4.2	5.1	0.03	1.4	3.0	1.1
Malaysia	11.3	17.5	13.8	13.4	2.3	6.0	15.4	17.6
Philippines	3.7	7.5	6.8	7.0	0.3	0.9	2.7	5.5
Singapore	26.9	36.8	71.1	73.8	4.7	20.6	48.1	43.7
Thailand	4.5	6.8	13.0	7.8	0.2	0.8	1.4	8.3
Vietnam	3.5	26.1	16.5	20.1	0.0	0.0	0.4	2.5
Bangladesh	0.0	3.2	3.9	3.4	0.0	0.03	0.06	0.08
India	0.2	1.9	5.3	5.1	0.01	0.1	2.7	1.5
Pakistan	1.5	3.9	13.2	4.7	0.2	0.04	0.3	0.2
Sri Lanka	2.1	4.0	4.3	3.5	0.04	0.2	0.4	0.3
Turkey	0.9	1.4	8.3	5.3	0.0	0.4	0.9	1.4
Asian-14	*2.1*	*7.2*	*7.4*	*4.6*	*0.9*	*2.0*	*3.3*	*3.5*
Asia	2.9	7.7	9.3	6.2	1.3	4.3	5.7	4.3
Developing Countries	*3.0*	*8.6*	*10.6*	*7.6*	*0.9*	*3.4*	*5.3*	*4.1*
Industrialized Countries	2.8	6.9	8.6	8.7	4.0	9.2	12.3	9.5
World	2.6	7.0	9.4	8.3	3.1	7.8	10.2	6.9

Note: The annual averages in percentages have been calculated.

Source: UNCTAD Foreign Direct Investment Online Database and UN National Accounts Statistics.

Table 5.6 Stocks of foreign direct investment for the Asian-14: 1980–2016 (as a percentage of GDP)

	Inward Stock					Outward Stock				
	1980	1990	2000	2008	2016	1980	1990	2000	2008	2016
China	0.4	5.2	15.9	8.2	12.1	–	1.1	2.3	4.0	11.4
South Korea	1.8	1.9	7.8	9.5	13.1	0.2	0.8	3.8	9.8	21.7
Taiwan	5.7	5.8	5.9	10.9	14.2	30.8	18.2	20.1	39.2	60.6
Indonesia	5.4	6.5	14.2	13.3	25.2	0.0	0.1	3.9	0.5	6.3
Malaysia	21.1	23.4	56.2	31.9	41.0	1.2	1.7	16.9	29.0	42.8
Philippines	3.6	6.7	17.0	12.5	21.1	0.2	0.8	1.3	3.3	14.9
Singapore	44.3	78.3	115.4	238.7	369.2	6.4	20.1	59.2	165.5	229.8
Thailand	2.9	9.3	24.5	32.4	46.3	0.0	0.5	2.6	3.6	21.0
Vietnam	0.4	3.8	47.3	41.8	56.2	–	–	–	0.6	4.9
Bangladesh	2.8	1.7	4.8	5.3	6.6	–	0.2	0.1	0.1	0.1
India	0.3	0.5	3.6	10.0	14.1	0.0	0.0	0.4	5.0	6.4
Pakistan	2.2	3.7	9.0	10.9	13.8	0.1	0.5	0.6	1.3	0.7
Sri Lanka	4.7	7.2	13.1	11.4	12.0	–	0.1	0.3	0.6	1.4
Turkey	9.3	5.4	6.9	10.6	15.4	–	0.6	1.3	2.3	4.4
Asian-14	*3.5*	*6.2*	*15.4*	*15.3*	*20.5*	*1.5*	*2.6*	*5.7*	*9.5*	*16.1*
Asia	*15.4*	*14.9*	*24.1*	*21.9*	*28.5*	*1.2*	*2.9*	*13.7*	*15.1*	*22.6*
Developing Countries	*10.8*	*12.7*	*22.9*	*22.1*	*31.0*	*2.6*	*3.5*	*10.2*	*12.1*	*19.8*
Industrialized Countries	*4.8*	*9.3*	*22.2*	*25.4*	*37.9*	*5.7*	*11.7*	*25.8*	*31.6*	*44.8*
World	*5.7*	*9.6*	*22.3*	*24.2*	*35.3*	*4.5*	*9.8*	*22.2*	*25.2*	*34.6*

Note: For the Asian-14 outward stock, in 1980, figures for Bangladesh, China, Sri Lanka, Turkey, and Vietnam are not available.

Source: Author's calculations from UNCTAD Foreign Direct Investment Online Database and UN National Accounts Statistics.

for most of the Asian-14. Malaysia, Singapore, and Vietnam were the exceptions, with much higher proportions which did not drop in 2009–2016. In fact, for most of the Asian-14, during 1981–2000, as a proportion of gross capital formation, foreign aid inflows were greater than foreign direct investment inflows; Malaysia and Singapore were exceptions throughout, while China and Vietnam were exceptions during 1991–2000. In Bangladesh, Pakistan, and Sri Lanka, foreign aid was larger than foreign direct investment even after 2000. The inward stocks of foreign direct investment, as a proportion of GDP, increased rapidly in Asia, developing countries, and industrialized countries throughout the period from 1980 to 2016. There was a similar uninterrupted increase in the Asian-14. However, this proportion differed significantly across countries. In 2016, it was in the range of 12–15 per cent in China, South Korea, Taiwan, India, Pakistan, Sri, and Turkey, 20–25 per cent in Indonesia and Philippines, and 40–50 per cent in Malaysia, Thailand, and Vietnam, while Singapore at 370 per cent and Bangladesh at 6 per cent were the outliers. Clearly, there was a steady increase in economic openness to foreign direct investment in Asia, which gathered momentum after 2000.

The outward flows of foreign direct investment, as a percentage of gross capital formation, also increased in Asia, and the Asian-14, in consonance with developing countries and less than industrialized countries, from 1981–1990 to 2001–2008, but contracted during 2009–2016. However, in most of the Asian-14, except Indonesia, India, and Singapore, this increase was uninterrupted. Of course, the proportions were low or negligible during 1981–2000, except for Taiwan, Malaysia, and Singapore. These proportions did rise in most of the Asian-14 during 2001–2016 but were still at low levels. The proportions were higher in South Korea, Taiwan, Malaysia, and Singapore, where outflows were also greater than inflows. The outward stocks of foreign direct investment, as a proportion of GDP, increased rapidly in Asia, from 1 per cent in 1980 to 23 per cent 2016. There was a similar uninterrupted increase in the Asian-14. In 2016, this proportion was high in Taiwan, Malaysia, and Singapore (small economies), medium in South Korea, Thailand, and Philippines (mid-size economies), and low in China, India, and Indonesia (large economies), while it was even lower in the remaining Asian-14. The emergence of Asian countries as origins of foreign direct investment lends another dimension to their increasing openness.[8]

There is yet another form of international investment which has emerged with capital account liberalization, that is, portfolio investment. Unfortunately, it is exceedingly difficult to find evidence on distribution by countries of origin and destination or inflows and outflows. But there can be little doubt that it has grown in significance as mutual funds and pension funds from industrialized countries have searched worldwide for financial assets that would yield higher capital appreciation or higher returns on their investible resources. Much of this placement is still in industrialized countries but many economies among the Asian-14 are also destinations for these footloose and volatile capital flows.[9]

2. Trajectories of industrialization

The nineteenth century witnessed rapid deindustrialization in Asia, Africa, and Latin America, as their total share in world manufacturing production fell from 60.5 per cent in 1830 to 7.5 per cent in 1913 and was just 8.3 per cent in 1963, of which the share of China and India was 47.4 per cent in 1830, 5 per cent in 1913, and 5.3 per cent in 1963 (Table 1.4). This process was driven by the economics of colonialism and the politics of imperialism. It led to the demise of traditional industries in Asia, particularly China and India, reducing their skill levels and technological capabilities over time. Thus, in the early post-colonial era, it is no surprise that industrialization was seen as an imperative in Asia. The essential ideas were developed then and the rationale was set out, at some length, in *Asian Drama*.[10] The spread effects of industrialization were associated with higher invest-ment levels on the demand-side and scale economies on the supply-side, together with backward and forward linkages within and between sectors, which recognized the importance of capturing externalities that would arise in the process.

Since 1950, there have been three discernible phases in terms of dominant thinking about how to pursue industrialization as an objective, which were shaped and reshaped by outcomes in development. During the first phase, 1950–1975, the widely accepted Development Consensus emphasized industrialization as a neces-sity in the quest for catching-up with the rich countries, starting with import substitution in the manufacturing sector, fostered by a supportive, if not leading, role for the state. In the second phase, 1975–2000, as the Washington Consensus gathered momentum, influence and acceptance, the emphasis shifted to markets and openness as the only path to an efficient industrialization, relegating state intervention and industrial policy to the dustbin. In the third phase, beginning around 2000, there is rethinking yet again, induced by actual development experi-ence and the global economic crisis, that seeks to highlight the importance of industrial policies and strategic interventions in the pursuit of industrialization. Interestingly enough, the industrialization experience of Asia is the arena for contending, often conflicting, views on the subject.

2.1 Industrial production

The most visible outcome of industrialization is in output.[11] Table 5.7 sets out evidence on manufacturing value added in each of the Asian-14, as a percentage of GDP, which reflects their industrialization in the national context, and as a percentage of world manufacturing value added, which shows their relative importance in the global context, during the period 1970–2016, for selected benchmark years at decadal intervals, providing corresponding figures in percent-ages for the Asian-14, Asia, developing countries, industrialized countries and the

Table 5.7 Manufacturing value added in the Asian-14: 1970–2016

	(as a percentage of GDP)						(as a percentage of World MVA)					
	1970	1980	1990	2000	2010	2016	1970	1980	1990	2000	2010	2016
China	(7.9)	(5.5)	(14.7)	(27.3)	31.7	27.5	(0.8)	(0.6)	(1.3)	(6.0)	18.3	25.5
South Korea	17.2	21.6	24.6	26.0	27.8	26.6	0.2	0.5	1.5	2.6	2.9	3.1
Taiwan	28.1	34.3	31.2	25.7	29.0	30.0	0.2	0.5	1.1	1.5	1.2	1.3
Indonesia	9.0	11.6	20.5	24.7	22.0	20.5	0.1	0.4	0.6	0.8	1.6	1.6
Malaysia	14.7	21.9	24.2	30.9	23.4	22.8	0.07	0.2	0.2	0.5	0.6	0.6
Philippines	26.7	27.6	26.6	24.5	21.4	19.6	0.2	0.4	0.3	0.4	0.4	0.5
Singapore	17.5	26.5	24.4	25.9	20.2	18.4	0.04	0.1	0.2	0.5	0.5	0.5
Thailand	15.9	21.5	27.4	28.6	31.1	27.4	0.1	0.3	0.5	0.7	1.0	0.9
Vietnam	16.0	16.0	12.2	18.4	12.9	14.3	0.05	0.01	0.02	0.1	0.1	0.2
Bangladesh	7.9	16.6	12.9	14.7	16.1	17.0	0.06	0.1	0.08	0.1	0.2	0.3
India	14.9	17.2	18.0	16.8	16.2	14.9	1.1	1.2	1.3	1.4	2.6	2.8
Pakistan	10.1	9.9	10.7	9.9	13.1	12.0	0.2	0.1	0.1	0.1	0.2	0.3
Sri Lanka	13.5	17.0	16.2	17.5	18.1	15.5	0.05	0.03	0.03	0.06	0.1	0.1
Turkey	17.6	19.7	25.3	18.8	15.1	16.6	0.5	0.7	1.2	0.9	1.1	1.2
Asian-14	*9.8*	*12.9*	*18.0*	*14.9*	*26.3*	*24.3*	*2.8*	*4.5*	*7.1*	*9.6*	*30.8*	*38.8*
Asia	*10.4*	*11.2*	*16.7*	*13.9*	*23.6*	*22.5*	*3.6*	*5.8*	*8.3*	*10.9*	*32.8*	*40.8*
Developing Countries	*14.2*	*14.1*	*17.6*	*14.4*	*20.0*	*19.9*	*9.8*	*14.4*	*15.4*	*18.9*	*41.5*	*48.1*
Industrialized Countries	*25.1*	*22.4*	*20.0*	*17.1*	*13.9*	*13.5*	*70.2*	*71.4*	*79.2*	*79.9*	*55.9*	*49.9*
World	*24.9*	*21.8*	*19.9*	*16.5*	*15.9*	*16.0*	*100.0*	*100.0*	*100.0*	*100.0*	*100.0*	*100.0*

Notes:

[a] The percentages have been calculated from data on manufacturing value added and GDP in current prices at market exchange rates.

[b] The figures for China, in 1970, 1980, 1990, and 2000, are calculated from the Groningen Growth and Development Centre online database and are not strictly comparable with figures for subsequent years.

[c] The share of developing countries and industrialized countries in world manufacturing value added does not add up to 100. The residual is attributable to the transition economies of Eastern Europe and the former USSR.

Source: Author's calculations from UNCTAD Stat based on UN National Accounts Statistics.

world, as a point of comparison. It shows that, between 1970 and 2016, in Asia, the share of manufacturing value added in GDP rose from 10 per cent to 23 per cent, while its share in world manufacturing value added jumped from 4 per cent to 41 per cent, which was a remarkable transformation. Over this period, the corresponding shares for developing countries also rose, which was also attributable almost entirely to Asia.

In the Asian-14, between 1970 and 2016, the share of manufacturing value added in GDP increased from 10 per cent to 24 per cent. It rose everywhere, peaked at different times in different countries at different levels and fell thereafter. This peak level was reached for Taiwan, Philippines, and Singapore in 1980, for India and Turkey in 1990, for Indonesia, Malaysia, and Vietnam in 2000, for China, South Korea, Thailand, Pakistan, and Sri Lanka in 2010, and for Bangladesh in 2016.[12] It is worth noting that, in 1970, for most of the Asian-14, the share of manufacturing value added in GDP was higher than in Asia as a whole except in China, Indonesia, Bangladesh, and Pakistan, whereas in 2016 it was higher than in Asia as a whole only for China, South Korea, Taiwan, Malaysia, and Thailand, but it was lower for Indonesia, Philippines, Singapore, Vietnam, Bangladesh, India, Pakistan, Sri Lanka, and Turkey.

The share of the Asian-14 in world manufacturing value added increased from 3 per cent in 1970 to 39 per cent in 2016. This share rose much more in some countries than in others, so that its inter-country distribution became far more unequal. In 1970, there was only one country—India—which had a share of more than 1 per cent, while China and Turkey had shares of more than 0.5 per cent, the three together accounting for more than two-thirds of the share of Asia in world manufacturing value added. In 2016, there were six economies—China, South Korea, India, Taiwan, Indonesia, and Turkey—which had a share of more than 1 per cent, accounting for almost nine-tenths of the share of Asia in world manufacturing value added. It is important to recognize the importance of China in this story. In 2016, China alone accounted for 25.5 per cent of world manufacturing value added, distinctly higher than the share of the United States at 17.6 per cent, the European Union at 19.4 per cent and Japan at 8.5 per cent. It is surprising that this stunning dominance has surfaced in such a short span of time. In 2000, the share of China in world manufacturing value added was just 6 per cent, compared with the United States at 25.4 per cent, the European Union at 24.5 per cent, and Japan at 18.1 per cent.[13] It would seem that the entire increase in China's share was at the expense of the United States, the European Union, and Japan.[14] In fact, the share of Asia, excluding China, in world manufacturing value added also increased from 4 per cent in 2000 to 15 per cent in 2016. Clearly, this transformation was not only about China. The decline of manufacturing in industrialized countries, relative rather than absolute, was attributable partly to the Great Recession but mostly to the continuing structural change, with manufacturing giving way to services as per capita incomes rose. Even so, the stunning transformation in such a short period of time, reflected in the statistics, is difficult to explain.

The share of countries in world manufacturing value added depends upon their size. For that reason, the preceding discussion considered manufacturing value added as a percentage of GDP, which normalized for differences in income size, as a measure of industrialization. However, manufacturing value added (MVA) per capita, which normalizes for differences in population size, might be even more appropriate for cross-country comparisons.

Figure 5.1 plots trends in manufacturing value added per capita in constant 2010 dollars, for each of the Asian-14 during 1970–2016 using time series data, on a logarithm scale to highlight differences in growth across countries over time. It confirms the rapid and sustained industrialization in Singapore, South Korea, and

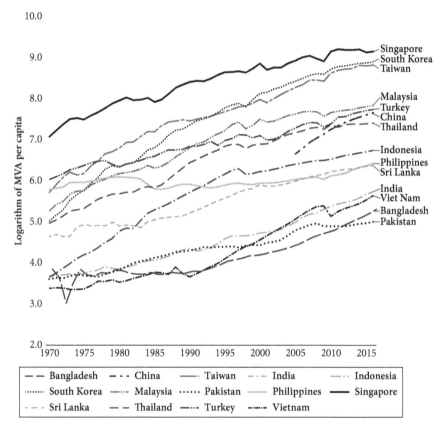

Figure 5.1 Growth in manufacturing value added per capita in the Asian-14: 1970–2016 (in constant 2010 US$)

Note: For China, the data are available only for the period 2004–2016.

Source: Author's calculations from United Nations, National Accounts Statistics, and Population Statistics.

Taiwan. China has followed the same path during 2004–2016 for which data are available. However, growth in MVA per capita witnessed a distinct slowdown in Indonesia, Malaysia, Philippines, and Thailand since the late 1990s; their loss of industrial dynamism was attributable to the financial crisis.[15] India (since 1980), Bangladesh, and Vietnam (since 1990), where MVA per capita is lower but its growth has been respectable and sustained, provide a sharp contrast. Turkey and Sri Lanka, at somewhat higher levels of MVA per capita, have also sustained this growth, albeit at a slower pace. Pakistan, with sluggish growth throughout, is the outlier.

2.2 Trade patterns

The rising share in world manufacturing output was reflected in the emergence of Asian countries as important sources of manufactured exports in the world economy, which suggests that their industrial sectors also became competitive in international markets.

Table 5.8 presents available evidence on manufactured exports from each of the Asian-14, as a percentage of their total merchandise exports and as a percentage of world manufactured exports, during the period 1970–2016, for selected benchmark years at decadal intervals. It shows that, over this period, the share of manufactured goods in total exports increased everywhere in the Asian-14. In 1970, this share exceeded 50 per cent only in South Korea, Taiwan, India, and Pakistan, whereas this share was less than 10 per cent in Indonesia, Malaysia, Philippines, Thailand, Sri Lanka, and Turkey. By 1990, it was higher than 50 per cent in all the Asian-14, including Bangladesh, except Indonesia and Philippines. In 2016, it was in the range of 70–90 per cent in all of the Asian-14. It is worth noting that peak shares were often attained earlier than 2016: South Korea as early as 1990, Taiwan, Indonesia, Malaysia, Philippines, Singapore, Thailand, India, Pakistan, Sri Lanka, and Turkey in 2000, with only China and Vietnam in 2016.[16] Between 1970 and 2016, most of the Asian-14 increased their share in world manufactured exports, but much more for a few than for others, while the shares of some countries such as Philippines, Bangladesh, Pakistan, and Sri Lanka remained miniscule. In 1970, there were only two economies—India and Taiwan—which had a share of 0.6 per cent, while South Korea had a share of 0.4 per cent. In 2016, there were five economies that had shares higher than 1.5 per cent: China, South Korea, Taiwan, Singapore, and India. Of these, China alone had a share of 17.5 per cent, which was far larger than others but not quite as dominant as it was in world manufacturing value added.

It is also important to examine how industrialization changed the composition of trade. In doing so, it is necessary to make the obvious distinction between primary commodities and manufactured goods, but it is just as important to distinguish between different categories of manufactures depending upon the

Table 5.8 Manufactured exports from the Asian-14: 1970–2016

	(as a percentage of total merchandise exports)						(as a percentage of world manufactured exports)					
	1970	1980	1990	2000	2010	2016	1970	1980	1990	2000	2010	2016
China	–	–	71.4	88.2	93.6	93.7	–	–	1.9	4.7	14.7	17.5
South Korea	76.6	89.4	93.2	89.9	88.3	89.9	0.4	1.6	2.5	3.3	4.1	4.0
Taiwan	75.8	–	92.2	93.2	89.1	91.3	0.6	–	2.6	3.0	2.4	2.3
Indonesia	1.1	2.3	35.2	53.9	37.0	46.7	0.01	0.05	0.4	0.7	0.6	0.6
Malaysia	6.5	18.7	53.9	80.4	67.1	68.0	0.06	0.2	0.7	1.7	1.3	1.1
Philippines	7.6	21.3	38.1	91.3	56.3	82.7	0.04	0.1	0.1	0.7	0.3	0.4
Singapore	27.5	46.7	71.1	85.4	72.2	76.4	0.2	0.9	1.6	2.5	2.5	2.3
Thailand	5.4	25.0	63.2	74.9	73.2	74.5	0.02	0.2	0.6	1.1	1.4	1.4
Vietnam	–	0.0	0.0	42.6	64.0	82.1	0.0	0.0	0.0	0.1	0.5	1.3
Bangladesh	–	66.0	72.2	77.8	91.9	–	–	0.05	0.1	0.1	0.2	0.0
India	51.9	51.4	69.7	77.7	63.8	73.1	0.6	0.4	0.5	0.7	1.4	1.7
Pakistan	57.2	48.8	78.6	86.4	74.5	78.7	0.2	0.1	0.2	0.2	0.2	0.1
Sri Lanka	1.6	18.5	53.2	75.2	64.2	72.4	0.0	0.02	0.0	0.1	0.1	0.1
Turkey	8.9	26.9	67.7	80.4	79.2	80.1	0.03	0.08	0.4	0.5	0.9	1.0
Asian-14	*22.5*	*32.0*	*69.3*	*83.0*	*81.9*	*85.2*	*1.6*	*3.7*	*8.9*	*16.4*	*28.1*	*31.5*
Asia	*26.7*	*17.1*	*61.4*	*72.7*	*71.0*	*76.1*	*4.0*	*6.3*	*15.1*	*23.8*	*35.5*	*39.0*
Developing Countries	*15.5*	*14.3*	*48.6*	*65.7*	*62.7*	*70.3*	*5.3*	*8.6*	*17.1*	*28.7*	*40.2*	*43.8*
Industrialized Countries	*67.8*	*66.6*	*76.0*	*77.2*	*70.4*	*71.6*	*92.3*	*89.6*	*80.5*	*69.6*	*57.9*	*54.5*
World	*56.1*	*49.1*	*68.4*	*73.0*	*65.5*	*70.2*	*100.0*	*100.0*	*100.0*	*100.0*	*100.0*	*100.0*

Note: The share of developing countries and industrialized countries in world manufactured exports does not add up to 100. The residual is attributable to the transition economies of Eastern Europe and the former USSR. Manufactured goods are defined as the sum of SITC 5 (chemicals), SITC 6 (manufactured goods), SITC 7 (machinery and transport equipment), and SITC 8 (miscellaneous manufactured articles) less 68 (non-ferrous metals).

Source: Author's calculations from United Nations COMTRADE online database.

degree of processing and the level of technology. For this purpose, it is both appropriate and valuable to use the well-known classification, based on the natural-resource content and the technological content of merchandise exports, developed by the late Sanjaya Lall (2000). It is, however, necessary to recognize a significant limitation of the Lall-classification. At the time it was developed, in 2000, high-technology manufactures included computers and electronic goods. Subsequently, these became an integral part of assembly operations that drove international trade flows. Hence, such a definition tends to overstate the high-technology component in manufactured exports from, and imports into, Asian countries, particularly China and the smaller Southeast Asian economies. Even so, this classification serves an important analytical purpose.

Figure 5.2 outlines the changes in the composition of exports from the Asian-14, making a distinction between primary products, resource-based manufactures, low-technology manufactures, medium-technology manufactures and high-technology manufactures, during the period from 1980 to 2016, for selected benchmark years at decadal intervals. The primary source used does not provide data on Taiwan and Bangladesh, while the data for China, Pakistan, and Turkey are available starting 1990 and for Vietnam starting 2000.

These statistics suggest a structural transformation that confirms the impact of industrialization on trade. During the period under review, in general, the share of primary products in total exports dropped sharply, the share of resource-based manufactures fell, the share of low-technology manufactures declined or changed little, while the share of medium-technology and high-technology manufactures, taken together, rose significantly. There were, of course, exceptions. The share of resource-based manufactures increased in India, Indonesia, Thailand, and Turkey, while the share of low-technology manufactures increased in Indonesia, Malaysia, Thailand, Pakistan, Sri Lanka, and Vietnam. There were also important differences between countries. In China, South Korea, and Singapore, industrialization is far more visible as the share of medium- and high-technology manufactures in total exports jumped from just over one-third to almost three-fourths, although there must have been an assembly component in such exports from China. In Malaysia, Philippines, and Thailand, the share of primary products and resource-based manufactures in total exports dropped from 80 per cent to a range of 20–30 per cent. The share of medium- and high-technology manufactures in total exports, in 2016, was more than 50 per cent in Malaysia and Thailand and almost 75 per cent in Philippines. These high proportions were obviously attributable to assembly operations, rather than a deepening of industrialization.[17] In Indonesia and Sri Lanka, the share of primary products in total exports fell from 80 to 30 per cent and 60 to 20 per cent respectively, while the share of resource-based and low-technology manufactures rose from 18 to 50 per cent and 35 to 70 per cent respectively. In India and Turkey, the share of resource-based and low-technology manufactures in total exports remained almost unchanged around 55 per cent, while the share of

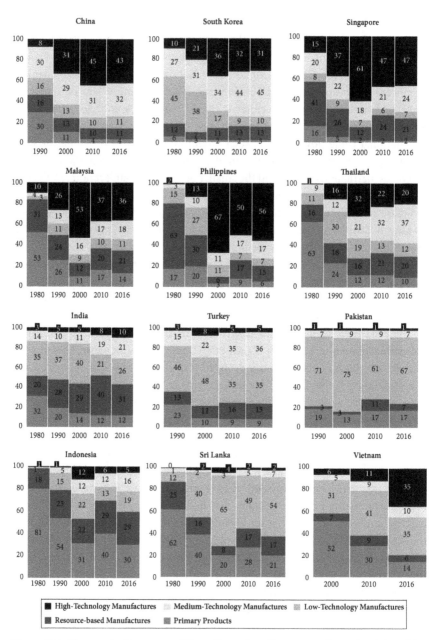

Figure 5.2 Changes in the composition of merchandise exports from the Asian-14: 1980–2016 (in percentages)

Note: The classifications are based on Lall (2000). The figures in the bars may not add up to 100 because of rounding-off to the nearest whole number.

Source: Author's calculations from United Nations COMTRADE online database.

medium- and high-technology manufactures rose from roughly 15 to 30 per cent and 20 to 40 per cent respectively. In Pakistan, during 1990–2016, the share of resource-based and low-technology manufactures in total exports remained almost the same at 75 per cent. In Vietnam, during 2000–2016, the share of primary products and resource-based manufactures dropped from 60 per cent to 20 per cent.

Industrialization should also be reflected in the structure of imports. Figure 5.3 traces the changes in the composition of imports in the twelve Asian countries, based on the same classification for the same periods and years. This shows that, in general, the share of primary products in total imports diminished, the share of resource-based manufactures and low-technology manufactures changed little, while the share of medium- and high-technology manufactures rose. Once again, there were exceptions. The share of primary products in total imports increased in China and Vietnam, the share of resource-based manufactures decreased in India and Vietnam, while the share of low-technology manufactures rose in Thailand and Vietnam. The differences between countries were consistent with changes in export patterns, reflecting similarities in the level or nature of industrialization within each of the following country-groups: China, South Korea, and Singapore; Malaysia, Philippines, and Thailand; Indonesia and Sri Lanka; and India and Turkey. Once again, the significance of high-technology manufactures in the imports of China, Malaysia, Philippines, and Thailand is overstated because of imports for assembly operations.

2.3 Manufacturing for world markets

There were three phases in the growth of manufactured exports from Asia that started in the early-1970s, the mid-1980s, and the early 2000s, respectively, which were interconnected but sequential with the progressive integration of Asia into the world economy over time (Nayyar, 2013).

In the first phase, external markets became increasingly important in the process of industrialization for Asian countries. It was a litmus test for domestic firms seeking to become competitive in international markets. In large countries, exports were the end rather than the beginning of the market expansion path for such firms. However, in some small countries, particularly in specific sectors, transnational corporations played an important role in developing manufactured exports.[18] This process gathered momentum in South Korea, Taiwan, Singapore, and Hong Kong, where firms manufactured for the world market rather than domestic markets and relied more on large international firms as manufacturers, partners, or buyers. Malaysia and Thailand followed in their footsteps, manufacturing for home-county markets of transnational corporations.

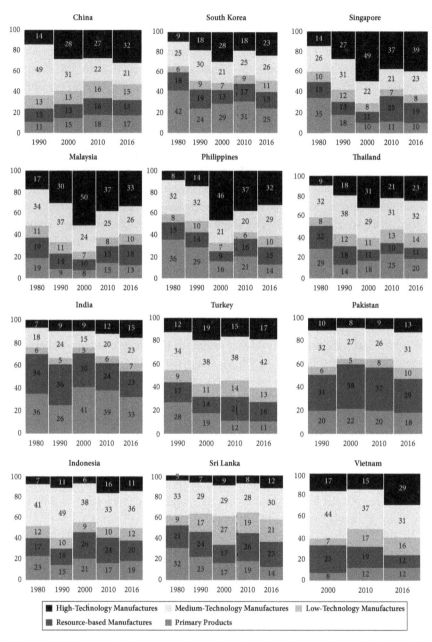

Figure 5.3 Changes in the composition of merchandise imports from the Asian-14: 1980–2016 (in percentages)

Note: The classifications are based on Lall (2000). The figures in the bars may not add up to 100 because of rounding-off to the nearest whole number.

Source: Author's calculations from United Nations COMTRADE online database.

During the second phase, there was a progressive internationalization of production. This began with transnational corporations from industrialized countries engaging in offshore assembly operations under special tariff provisions, relocating production through international sub-contracting.[19] The essential underlying factor was large differences in wages. In fact, even wage costs per unit of output in these developing countries were distinctly lower despite much lower levels of productivity. But the process was driven by the competition for markets between large international firms from industrialized countries seeking to reduce costs. Transnational manufacturing firms relocated assembly operations or component manufacture. Transnational buying groups sourced simple labour-intensive consumer goods such as clothing through sub-contracting from Asian countries.[20]

In the third phase, as globalization gathered momentum, reinforced by the revolution in transport and communication, there was a growing interdependence and deepening integration between countries in the world economy. Such global economic integration led to an increasing worldwide relocation of parts of production processes, which became more feasible, in terms of rapid technological change and declining transport costs, to Asian countries with relatively skilled labour and low wages. This, in turn, led to a massive expansion of world trade in manufactures, especially in components for assembly or intermediates for processing. The phenomenon is described as the rise of global value chains.[21] It was not as new as it is sometimes made out to be, but was the culmination of a process that began two decades earlier.

Given the nature of international trade statistics, it is not possible to find empirical evidence on such cross-border trade at a macro-level. It is, however, widely known that global value chains are particularly important in three sectors: textiles, clothing, leather, and footwear; computer, electronic, and optical equipment; and motor vehicles. The OECD and the WTO have estimated domestic value added in manufactured exports from each of these three sectors, for the period 1995–2011, in countries where such trade is significant. Table 5.9 presents this evidence, which is available for eleven countries among the Asian-14 for 1995 and 2011. For the eleven countries taken together, using statistics on their manufactured exports, the share of these three sectors in the gross value of total manufactured exports is estimated at 50.5 per cent in 1995 and 41.5 per cent in 2011.[22] Thus, the sectors in which global value chains were important accounted for a large proportion of total manufactured exports from these eleven Asian countries.

Table 5.9 suggests some generalizations. First, net foreign exchange earnings were much less than the gross value of manufactured exports for all sectors and all countries. Second, of the three sectors, domestic value added was the highest by a wide margin in textiles, clothing, leather, and footwear, and clearly the lowest in computer, electronic, and optical equipment, with motor vehicles in the middle.

Table 5.9 Domestic value added in the gross value of exports of manufactured goods in Asian countries for selected sectors: 1995 and 2011

	Total Exports of Manufactures		Textiles, Textile Products, Leather, & Footwear		Computer, Electronic, & Optical Equipment		Motor Vehicles, Trailers, & Semi-Trailers	
	1995	2011	1995	2011	1995	2011	1995	2011
China	55.6	59.9	61.6	73.5	32.9	45.0	47.7	66.9
South Korea	72.7	53.1	78.7	64.7	72.2	57.8	75.5	62.3
Taiwan	62.6	49.0	71.6	56.9	55.5	55.4	62.0	52.2
Indonesia	80.7	81.4	82.2	81.8	65.2	72.9	66.7	74.5
Malaysia	61.3	47.6	62.6	50.8	54.2	33.2	61.3	40.9
Philippines	58.8	71.0	67.3	84.4	49.1	71.5	57.3	59.7
Singapore	48.1	51.0	52.2	44.2	47.5	59.9	37.1	51.7
Thailand	68.2	49.0	81.9	56.9	51.1	55.4	57.1	52.2
Vietnam	68.2	51.7	64.5	74.1	42.1	34.8	54.2	43.6
India	87.4	63.8	90.2	80.2	84.6	68.8	87.2	67.5
Turkey	87.7	64.8	91.5	77.3	81.9	61.1	83.9	55.8

Source: OECD-WTO TIVA Database.

Third, between 1995 and 2011, the proportion of domestic value added in the gross value of manufactured exports from the three sectors rose in China, Indonesia, Philippines, and Singapore while it fell in South Korea, Taiwan, Malaysia, Thailand, Vietnam, India, and Turkey. Fourth, the proportion of domestic value added in all three sectors in Indonesia, India, and Turkey was far higher than elsewhere in 1995 and despite the subsequent decline in India and Turkey, in 2011, it was still higher than in most countries. Some plausible inferences follow. China and Singapore probably moved up the value chain,[23] while Indonesia and Philippines reduced the import content of exports in these sectors. South Korea and Taiwan possibly increased outsourcing of components in these sectors. Malaysia and Thailand perhaps enhanced their insertion into global value chains. India and Turkey were probably the least integrated with global value chains in their manufactured exports.

3. Diversity across Asia

The preceding discussion on the contours of openness and the trajectories of industrialization in Asia over the past fifty years highlights the enormous diversity across countries in this vast continent, which is juxtaposed with changes within countries over time that make cross-country analysis even more difficult. There were differences in size, endowments, and drivers, that influenced both openness and industrialization.

The geographical and economic size ranged from small (Taiwan, Malaysia, Singapore, and Sri Lanka) through medium (South Korea, Philippines, Thailand, Vietnam, Bangladesh, Pakistan, and Turkey) to large (China, India, and Indonesia). There were different endowments. Most of these countries were resource-poor and land-scarce, except for Indonesia, Malaysia, and Turkey that were resource-rich and land-abundant, while the large countries, China and India, were also endowed with natural resources. But all of these countries were labour-abundant. There were different drivers. In the early stages, many of the Asian-14 might have relied on primary commodities or natural resources as the basis for manufacturing, but it was not long before they moved to rely on cheap labour which was their most abundant resource.

Initial conditions, particularly infrastructure and education, mattered since a critical minimum in both was necessary to kick-start industrialization. To begin with, there were differences in levels between the Asian-14 attributable to different colonial legacies. In this respect, East Asia was much better endowed than South Asia. Of course, even if initial conditions were bequeathed by history, government intervention could, and did, improve that legacy, every-where, most effectively in East Asian countries, followed by Southeast Asian countries, and then South Asian countries. But there was a third dimension to initial conditions, relevant even if less critical, which was some sort of manu-facturing experience embedded in history. For some economies, this experience was pre-capitalist, coming from artisans or handicrafts, as in China, India, and Turkey. For other economies such as Indonesia, Malaysia, Singapore, Taiwan, and Thailand, this experience originated in migrants mostly from China but partly from India, while in Turkey it came from European migrants. But colonialism was also a source of manufacturing experience, from the British in India, Pakistan, Bangladesh, Sri Lanka, Malaysia, Singapore, and China, from the Dutch in Indonesia, from the Americans in Philippines, or from the Japanese in Manchuria (China), South Korea,[24] and Taiwan. Such manufactur-ing experience, which might have made some difference in the earlier stages for countries, did exist in most of the Asian-14.[25]

The relative importance of, and emphasis on, external markets and external resources as compared with domestic markets and domestic resources, which is an important aspect of openness and industrialization, differed among the Asian-14. This was, in part, a function of the size of countries, but was also shaped by strategies and policies that changed over time. Yet, it is possible to classify the Asian-14 into four broad groups. There were several countries—Indonesia, Malaysia, Philippines, Singapore, Thailand, and Vietnam—where external mar-kets and resources were much more important than domestic markets and resources. There were two economies—South Korea and Taiwan—that empha-sized external markets and domestic resources. There were some countries—Bangladesh, Pakistan, and Sri Lanka—that relied mostly on domestic markets but were significantly dependent on external resources. In the two largest countries—China and India—domestic markets and domestic resources were far more important than external markets and resources. In Turkey, too, domestic markets and domestic resources were more important, except for some reliance on external resources in the earlier stages.

Until the early 1970s, when industrialization was state-led, based on import substitution in the manufacturing sector, except in Singapore and Hong Kong, openness was restricted in most of the Asian-14. This situation was transformed by the early 1990s. Yet, there were differences in the nature and degree of openness across economies. It is possible to distinguish between four broad groups. There was unrestricted openness only in Singapore. There was moderated openness in Indonesia, Malaysia, Philippines, and Thailand, which meant largely open economies with few restrictions in some spheres. There was calibrated openness, in South Korea and Taiwan, characterized by asymmetries in openness by design manifest in strategic trade policy that was open for the export sector but restrictive for other sectors, with limits on openness to foreign capital and tight curbs on foreign brand names, which has been dispensed with since these countries have industrialized. There was controlled openness, in China, India, Pakistan, Bangladesh, Sri Lanka, Turkey, and Vietnam, which was much more extensive than in other countries, not only in trade but also with respect to foreign investment and foreign technology and that has been progressively liberalized since the early 2000s, although openness continues to be regulated in most of these countries.

There were different models of industrialization, in terms of the relative importance of the foreign sector, as the extent of reliance on foreign capital, foreign technology, and foreign markets differed across the Asian-14. The Southeast Asian countries—Malaysia, Philippines, Singapore, Thailand, and Vietnam—relied far more on foreign capital, foreign technology, and foreign markets. This is, of course, a general characterization, for there were domestic firms that were a part of the industrialization process in each of these countries. The East Asian economies—South Korea and Taiwan—relied on foreign markets but mobilized domestic resources and developed domestic technological capabilities, so that it was domestic firms that led the process of industrialization. The mega-economy model, followed by China and India, relied mostly on domestic markets, domestic resources, and domestic technologies in the earlier stages of industrialization but at later stages both countries joined the quest for external markets with a selective approach to foreign capital and foreign technology. The South Asian countries—Pakistan, Bangladesh, and Sri Lanka—relied mostly on domestic markets but were dependent on foreign capital (more foreign aid than foreign direct investment) and used foreign technology. Turkey sought to find a blend of domestic and foreign in capital, technology, and markets, which evolved over time, moving towards increasing openness in all three spheres.[26]

It is essential to recognize the diversity of Asia reflected in forms of openness and paths to industrialization, which also changed over time. Even so, it seems that there are some discernible patterns in this diversity which make the task of cross-country analysis somewhat less difficult.

4. Paths to industrialization

It is clear that, during the past fifty years, industrialization has been a key driver of economic growth and structural transformation in most of the Asian-14. This role has acquired even greater significance in the past quarter century. Economic openness has performed a critical supportive role in the process, wherever it has been in the form of strategic integration with, rather than passive insertion into, the world economy. The guiding role of governments, as catalysts or leaders, has been at the foundation of success at industrialization. This success, although uneven across countries, has been remarkable. It would have been difficult to imagine in 1950, or even in 1970. In retrospect, this industrialization experience of Asia is often cited by scholars, with polar opposite ideological views, in support of their worldviews. It must be stressed that prescriptive, often oversimplified, generalizations which follow are misleading. The most important lesson from the Asian experience is that there are no magic wands: whether markets and openness or state intervention and controls. The paths to industrialization varied and the recipes for success were country-specific.

Interestingly enough, paths to industrialization were broadly similar across countries in Asia during 1950–1975, except in the city states of Hong Kong and Singapore, when most Asian countries sought to industrialize based on import substitution in the manufacturing sector with governments in a leading role. The actual industrialization experience of this era led to a mounting critique from orthodox economics.[27] The essential argument was that industrialization policies, which protected domestic industries from foreign competition and led to excessive or inappropriate state intervention in the market, were responsible for the high cost and the low growth in most economies. Inward-looking policies driven by import substitution, particularly in the sphere of trade, were seen as the prime culprit. The prescription followed from the critique. More openness and less intervention would impart both efficiency and dynamism to the process. And outward-looking policies, particularly in the sphere of trade, were seen as the prime saviour, because trade policies were perceived as critical. This approach to trade and industrialization was narrow in its focus. It did not recognize that there is more to trade policies than the distinction between import substitution and export promotion, just as there is much more to industrialization than simply trade policies.[28] This critique was juxtaposed with the impressive economic performance of South Korea, Taiwan, and

Singapore which was attributed to markets and openness. The unqualified enthusiasm for free(r) trade in mainstream economics, unmindful of the distinction between statics and dynamics, or the formal exposition of the free-trade argument in economic theory with its careful assumptions, proofs, and exceptions, was indeed puzzling.[29] Heterodox critics argued that the characterization of these countries as free-trade and laissez-faire economies was caricature history, for their export-orientation was not the equivalent of free trade, just as the visible hand of the state was more in evidence than the invisible hand of the market.[30] Thus, industrialization was not so much about getting prices right as it was about getting state intervention right.

It was also not recognized that this period, when protection or promotion was provided to domestic industry, witnessed rapid industrialization in Asia, with rates of growth in manufacturing output that revealed a sharp contrast with their past of deindustrialization from the mid-nineteenth to the mid-twentieth century, when they practiced free trade. Indeed, during this period, which coincided with the golden age of capitalism, industrial growth in Asia kept pace with that in industrialized countries. Of course, there were problems that surfaced. Infant industries did not come of age in many countries. Government interventions in the form of 'operational controls' tended to be 'negative rather than positive', or 'discretionary rather than uniform', without any co-ordination, which was akin to 'driving a car with the accelerator pushed to the floor but the brakes on', which served vested interests and incumbent firms (Myrdal, 1968, p. 925). It happened in India but not everywhere in Asia. Yet, this was also a phase of learning to industrialize, through developing managerial capabilities in individuals and technological capabilities in firms, to become competitive in world markets. Such learning takes time so that outcomes in industrialization surface with a time lag. This accounts for the acceleration of growth in manufacturing output in Asia that became visible in the early 1970s. It was not the magic of markets that produced the sudden spurt in industrialization. It came from the foundations that had been laid in the preceding quarter century.[31] Obviously, it is not appropriate to focus on that earlier phase, 1950–1975, in isolation. In fact, an analysis of the Asian industrialization experience since then clearly shows that proactive industrial policy was instrumental in success.[32]

Industrial policy, in some form or the other, is an integral part of starting, as also sustaining, the process of industrialization in countries that are latecomers to development.[33] It is essential for creating some initial conditions. It is necessary for creating enabling institutions. It is the basic foundation for the supportive role of governments, whether as leaders or catalysts. Such intervention can and does come in different forms at different stages of development. But industrial policy always matters, because industrialization is about learning-by-doing. The counterfactual validates this proposition. For some countries, in the past, deindustrialization was about unlearning-by-not-doing. For many countries, in the present, the absence of industrial policy, which has adverse consequences for industrialization, is also industrial policy.

It is possible to think of industrial policy in Asia at the macro-level, meso-level and micro-level. This blurs the distinction between *general* and *selective* interventions but it reflects observed realities in practice. At the macro-level, for the economy as a whole, governments sought to foster industrialization through industrial protection and import substitution to manufacture for the domestic market or industrial promotion through export orientation to manufacture for the world market. The stress on the former in large countries was motivated by the object of learning to industrialize, not only in consumer goods but also in intermediate goods and capital goods, so that exports were the end of the market expansion path for firms. The emphasis on the latter in small countries was also motivated by the object of learning to industrialize, but with a focus on labour-intensive manufactured consumer goods, so that exports were the beginning of the market expansion path for firms. At the meso-level, for particular industries, government intervention sought to develop sunrise industries or retrench sunset industries. Strategic government support for industries to be developed was possible through a range of policy instruments. But the withdrawal of such support, always possible in principle, required effective governments in practice. At the micro-level, always for selected firms, government support in the domestic market, or in the world market, sought to nurture their managerial or techno-logical capabilities, or encourage their horizontal and vertical expansion, so that they were able to realize scale economies, not only in production but also in marketing to develop global brand names and create large international firms. This was about picking winners and creating champions. The complexity of government intervention necessary increased progressively in moving from the macro-level through the meso- to the micro-level.

Success or failure, in terms of outcomes, depends upon the nature and the quality of intervention. Thus, industrial policy is no panacea. There are benefits and there are costs. However, outcomes are not binary. More often than not, outcomes are a mix of success and failure. This mix changes over time. Moreover, in the process of learning to industrialize, the costs surface earlier while the benefits accrue after a time lag. It follows that industrial policy must be assessed not at a point in time but over a period of time. The real question, then, is how to make industrial policy more effective for intended outcomes. It could slip into rents and patronage. Its success depends upon the nature of the state and the effectiveness of administrative systems. This, in turn, requires institutionalized control mechanisms. At the same time, the risks associated with industrial policy must be balanced against the risks associated with no industrial policy.

The pioneering success stories of industrialization in Asia during the past fifty years—South Korea, Taiwan, and Singapore—are striking examples of the critical importance of industrial policy.[34] Governments in South Korea and Taiwan intervened at the macro-, meso- and micro-levels. Trade policy was characterized by an asymmetry, as it was open for the export sector but restrictive for other sectors, while exchange rates were undervalued over long periods, so that domestic industries could become competitive in the world market for manufactured goods. The allocation of scarce investible resources to selected sectors was influenced by the strategic use of differential interest rates in South Korea and by tax credits in Taiwan. Both countries preferred to access foreign technology through licensing rather than foreign investment. Infant industry protection was progressively scaled down as domestic firms were induced to export so as to become competitive in world markets. For selected firms, governments sought to nurture their managerial and technological capabilities, foster their horizontal and vertical expansion, or encourage technological upgrading, so that they were able to realize scale economies and technological learning in production, without which their industrialization could have stopped at labour-intensive consumer goods as wages rose. This also helped realize scale economies in marketing, to develop global brand names and create large international firms such as Samsung and LG in South Korea (which was helped by a ban on the use of foreign brand names), or Foxconn in Taiwan. Singapore was somewhat different. It followed free trade and welcomed transnational corporations. However, while relying on foreign direct investment, it was selective, even strategic, in choosing the firms and the sectors. At the same time, it relied heavily on state-owned-enterprises, which still account for roughly one-fifth of GDP, as a means of influencing the shape of industrialization. In addition, the government owned nine-tenths of the land, which was used for strategic bargaining with international firms in pursuit of industrial policy objectives. In all three countries, successful industrialization was driven by industrial policy that was implemented by effective governments.

The more recent success story of industrialization in Asia is that of China, which adopted a gradualist approach in transition to a market economy, with some economic decentralization in its highly centralized political system.[35] For one, it adopted a dual-track pricing system, which protected state-owned enterprises from market forces during the transition by allowing them to sell for profit while learning to compete in the market. For another, it attracted foreign direct investment into export-processing zones, using tax incentives, that were enclaves which provided an excellent infrastructure and disciplined workers, while encouraging domestic firms to set up in these zones to integrate with international firms and global value chains. Unlike South Korea and Taiwan, China relied far more on foreign direct investment and did not impose formal conditions in terms of export obligations or local sourcing. But it engaged in strategic bargaining with transnational corporations by using its high-quality infrastructure, disciplined skilled workers, and large domestic market as levers, to impose informal conditions on local sourcing, export commitments, or technology-transfer. Once such industrialization gathered momentum, the government turned its attention to the strategic long-term objectives of building domestic managerial and technological capabilities, R&D capacities, vertical diversification, and technological learning. At a much earlier stage of industrialization, Vietnam is attempting to follow in the footsteps of China, using industrial policy to attract foreign direct investment and connect with global value chains to promote manufacturing for world markets.[36] Both countries have effective governments that can implement industrial policy.

Apart from Singapore and Vietnam, the other Southeast Asian countries among the Asian-14 are Indonesia, Malaysia, Philippines, and Thailand.[37] Over the past fifty years, the structural transformation of these economies, reflected in the changed composition of output and employment, the diversification of trade patterns, and the growth in manufacturing value added, suggests that industrialization has been impressive. Of course, there were differences among countries. Industrialization in Malaysia and Thailand made much more progress than in Indonesia, while Philippines lagged behind. There were also differences that have surfaced over time. Until around 2000, Malaysia, Thailand, and Indonesia, described as the second-tier NICs, were seen as success stories in the footsteps of the East Asian Tigers. In this phase, industrial policy and the guiding role of governments were important underlying factors. But, after the Asian financial crisis, the four economies have all experienced a distinct slowdown in industrialization and growth. Investment levels have dropped sharply. Industrial dynamism has waned. Growth in MVA per capita has slowed down significantly. It is plausible to suggest, though impossible to prove, why industrialization was not sustained. The growth in industrial output and manufactured exports was driven by foreign direct investment, in which low-cost docile labour was the prime attraction for global value chains. However, the proportion of domestic value added in the gross value of manufactured exports which was never high dropped further in this slowdown phase, surprisingly enough more in Malaysia and Thailand than in Indonesia or Philippines. Insofar as manufacturing was led by exports based on an assembly of imported components or parts, linkages with domestic economies were weak, while learning was limited. Consequently, these economies witnessed a horizontal spread of manufacturing activities rather than vertical diversification or technological upgrading. Clearly, industrialization in these countries could have sustained longer and progressed further if industrial policy had been more purposive and effective. Once again, Malaysia and Thailand are probably better placed than Indonesia and Philippines to revive the momentum of industrialization.

In comparison with East Asian countries, which have led the process of industrialization in Asia, and Southeast Asian countries, which simply did not match that performance, South Asian countries—India, Pakistan, Bangladesh, and Sri Lanka—were laggards in industrialization.[38] During 1950–1980, industrial growth was impressive, as it was a real departure from deindustrialization in the colonial era, but its quality and sustainability were subjected to question.

It was not cost-efficient, largely because infant industries did not grow up to become competitive in world markets. The implementation of industrial policy, even if well-intentioned, left much to be desired. Myrdal's concerns about the nature and effectiveness of state intervention in South Asian countries were broadly correct. This might have been a phase of learning to industrialize that laid the foundations. However, for subsequent, more successful industrialization, economic reforms and increased openness, beginning around 1990, also did not lead to the expected turnaround in performance, simply because governments never used industrial policy to upgrade the economy. In fact, industrial policy was abandoned in the hope that markets would do the trick.

In the pursuit of industrialization, the performance of Pakistan was perhaps the worst, in terms of vertical diversification of industrial production or trade patterns, while growth in MVA per capita was the slowest. Sri Lanka's performance was much better in terms of growth in MVA per capita and manufactured exports, made possible by an increased openness, leading to some integration with global value chains, particularly in garments. However, it could have done far better since, in terms of social indicators of development, fifty years ago, it was more like Southeast Asia than the other South Asian countries. It did not, possibly because of the prolonged civil war. Bangladesh made impressive strides in industrialization from 1980, reflected in the sustained growth in MVA per capita, plus rapidly rising shares of manufacturing in GDP and of manufactures in merchandise exports. The garments sector was the driver, in whose development industrial policy played a critical role. Bangladesh, which had preferential access to quota-protected markets as a least-developed country, entered into an agreement with the South Korean firm, Daewoo, to transfer a percentage of future sales revenues to Daewoo if it could create export capabilities in its Bangladesh partner-firm Desh. The rents so promised were a credible incentive. Desh became a competitive global firm. Its supply-chain model was imitated by thousands of Bangladeshi entrepreneurs leading to an explosive growth in the garments sector.[39]

The story of industrialization in India is complex. It would mean too much of a digression to enter into a discussion here. Even so, it is important to recognize that the essential foundations were laid during 1950–1980 as India learnt to industrialize (Lall, 1987). There were limitations implicit in the implementation, rather than the design, of industrial policy during that period. Yet, peak shares of manufacturing in GDP and manufactures in merchandise exports were attained before economic liberalization. It is ironical that increased economic openness, beginning in 1991, seems to have worsened, rather than improved, India's performance in industrialization. Clearly, economic openness, while necessary, was not sufficient. The government almost dispensed with industrial policy without creating the conditions or the ecosystem that might have enabled the manufacturing to become competitive in world markets. The pace and the sequence of import liberalization, followed by the rush to join free-trade agreements, led to the beginnings of some deindustrialization. It is time to rethink and revive industrial policy, which requires a co-ordination not only of trade, investment, and technology policies, but also of interest rate and exchange rate policies, in shaping degrees of economic openness to achieve the desired objectives.[40]

In this context, it is worth pointing out that industrial policy was responsible for three success stories of industrialization in India: pharmaceuticals, automobiles, and software.[41] The industrial policy might have been intended for a different purpose in pharmaceuticals, so that the outcome might have been unintended, but it was intended, by design, in automobiles and software. This is seldom recognized. Consider each in turn.

The Patents Act of 1970 in India stipulated that, in pharmaceuticals, product patents would no longer be admissible and only process patents would be allowed. This was a real boost for the pharmaceuticals sector, which was enabled to produce medicines at affordable prices for domestic consumers, in conformity with the object of the legislation. Over the next three decades, beginning with exports, and followed by R&D, India's pharmaceutical firms developed technological capabilities that made them competitive in world markets, transforming India into a pharmacy for the developing world, well before the TRIPS agreement led to an amendment of the Patents Act to allow product patents.

In 1982, the government in India entered into an agreement with the Japanese firm, Suzuki, to enter the highly protected domestic automobile industry provided it produced a car in India with 70 per cent domestic content within five years. Maruti-Suzuki was established as a joint venture in 1982.[42] And there was no question of the capacity of the state in India to enforce this condition. Suzuki knew that if the condition was met, there would be very high profits from the lucrative domestic market that was bound to grow over time. It made the investment to develop the auto-components sector, which became globally competitive within a decade. This enabled India to transform its automobile industry and develop its own branded cars. In 2016, India produced 4.5 million motor vehicles, of which it exported 0.9 million.[43] Suzuki rapidly recovered its costs of financing through the learning period, became the majority shareholder, continued to earn lucrative profits, and built a global reputation as a manufacturer of cars.

India imposed a ban on IBM in 1977. This led to the development of computer maintenance skills. By the mid-1980s, software development began life, driven by the domestic market to begin with, followed by exports soon after in an arrangement with Texas Instruments. In 1991, the government established Software Technology Parks of India as a society to encourage and promote the export of software from India. Domestic firms could be located anywhere in India and were provided with direct satellite links. The government also exempted profits earned in software exports from income tax. This exemption continued from 1991 to 2011. In the late 1990s, there were close consultations between industry and government to chart out a road map for next steps. Software exports boomed, to reach US$111 billion in 2016, as compared with total merchandise exports at US$275 billion.[44]

Clearly, success at industrialization in Asia was driven by sensible industrial policy that was implemented by effective governments. There is, of course, a danger that the very success of the Asian-14 might lead them into dead-ends or middle-income traps, unless they can diversify manufacturing, in vertical rather than horizontal spreads, and upgrade technologies. In countries lagging behind, effective industrial policy will also require human capital and institutional quality as prerequisites. Going forward, industrial policy will need to be creative, recognizing the implications of technological changes on the horizon for labour-intensive manufactured exports, and the increasing interdependence between manufacturing and services.

5. Technology, learning, and industrialization

In the ultimate analysis, catching up is about making a transition from being a developing country to becoming an industrialized country. The simple litmus test is whether a country is able to make a transition from imports through absorption, adaptation, and diffusion of technologies, to innovation, so that it advances the technology frontier in some, even a few, industries or sectors. Thus, countries that are on the path to industrialization only through integration into global value chains cannot sustain the process. Of course, it could be an important first step in technological learning. However, unless they move up the technology ladder, they would be stuck with assembly operations or manufacturing simple components. In this sense, South Korea, Taiwan, and Singapore have completed the transition. China has moved up the technology ladder rapidly, in terms of R&D and technological capabilities, particularly in the defence sector and in robotics. It is almost there. India suggests a potential. It is competitive in information technology. It can build and launch satellites into space. Yet, it has not arrived at the technology frontier to lead innovation in any domain. The other countries have miles to go.

In an analysis of technology for industrialization in developing countries, Lall (1992) made an important distinction between firm-level technological capabilities at the micro-level and national technological capabilities at a macro-level. Firms operate not on a production function but at a point so that their technical progress, building upon their own efforts, experience, and skills, is localized around that point (Atkinson and Stiglitz, 1969). Thus, evolutionary theories, which stress investment capabilities, production capabilities, and linkage capabilities, provide a plausible explanation of firm-level technological change, which is a continuous process of absorption, learning, and innovation (Nelson and Winter, 1982). Given the nature of the learning process, such capabilities are both firm-specific and path-dependent (Rosenberg, 1994).[45] However, technological development in firms at the micro-level is also shaped by technological capabilities in the economy at the macro-level. National technological capabilities are the outcome of a complex interaction between incentives, capabilities, and institutions. Each may suffer market failure and so require corrective intervention. Such interventions, which need careful formulation and application, are necessary for industrial success (Lall, 1990, 1991 and 1992). It becomes possible for late industrializers to complete the transition once they develop technological capabilities both at the micro-level in firms and at the macro-level in the economy. The process of technological learning and the development of technological capabilities at different levels—firms, sectors and economies—are closely intertwined.[46]

R&D is a significant, observable, underlying factor that shapes technological capabilities in firms at the micro-level and economies at the macro-level. Table 5.10 sets out evidence on R&D expenditure as a percentage of GDP in the Asian-14 for selected years during 1996–2015. It reveals that South Korea, Taiwan, and Singapore were definitely comparable with, if not better than, industrialized countries in their R&D effort. In fact, in 2015, at 4.22 per cent, South Korea had almost the highest R&D–GDP ratio in the world, compared with 3.28 per cent in Japan, 2.92 per cent in Germany, 2.72 per cent in the United States, and 2.27 per cent in France.[47] It is no surprise that South Korea, Taiwan, and Singapore joined the league of industrialized nations in terms of technological capabilities.

Table 5.10 R&D expenditure as a percentage of GDP for the Asian-14

	1996	2000	2005	2010	2015
China	0.56	0.89	1.31	1.71	2.06
South Korea	2.26	2.18	2.63	3.47	4.22
Taiwan	1.80	2.06	2.30	2.80	3.05
Indonesia	–	0.07	–	–	–
Malaysia	0.22	0.47	–	1.04	1.30
Philippines	–	–	0.11	–	–
Singapore	1.32	1.82	2.16	2.01	–
Thailand	0.12	0.24	0.22	–	0.62
Vietnam	–	–	–	–	0.44
Bangladesh	–	–	–	–	–
India	0.65	0.77	0.84	0.82	0.62
Pakistan	–	0.13	0.44	–	0.25
Sri Lanka	0.18	0.14	–	0.14	0.11
Turkey	0.45	0.47	0.57	0.80	0.88

Note: R&D expenditure is made up of domestic expenditures on research and development. This includes both capital and current expenditures in the four main sectors: business enterprise, government, higher education, and private non-profit. R&D covers basic research, applied research, and experimental development.

Source: UNESCO, Institute of Statistics, online database. The statistics for Taiwan are obtained from *Taiwan Statistical Data Book*.

China increased its R&D–GDP ratio from 0.56 per cent to 2.06 per cent in just two decades. By doing so, it is catching up in technological capabilities. It is worth noting that India, the other country among the Asian-14 with a technological potential, regressed in terms of its R&D–GDP ratio, which was higher than that of China in 1996 but was less than one-third that of China in 2015, so that its falling behind in industrialization is no surprise.

In order to examine the implications for other latecomers to industrialization, it is important to consider the foundations of technological capabilities and the common policy dilemmas which surface (Nayyar, 2011). In such an exercise, some general lessons from the industrialization experience of the Asian-14 are instructive.

The level of technological development and the capacity for innovation are often country-specific, sector-specific or context-specific. Yet, there are discernible similarities in the essential foundations. First, an emphasis on higher education and science research in the early stages of industrialization created the initial conditions. This development of human resources laid the foundations of capabilities in individuals at a micro-level. Second, import substitution in manufactured goods, or manufacturing for world markets (beyond integration into global value chains), with some special effort to establish a capital goods sector, recognized the importance of learning-by-doing. Such learning was critical in the endeavour to industrialize for it created technological capabilities in firms at a meso-level. Third, industrializing late required institutional mechanisms, which were neither mutually exclusive nor exhaustive, to support catching-up. There was an attempt to foster imitation and leapfrog on the part of domestic firms, sometimes with explicit or implicit lax systems for the protection of intellectual property rights. This was often juxtaposed with a proactive technology policy in the form of strategic interventions by the government. Economic policies in the sphere of international trade and international investment were used to promote the insertion of domestic firms into global value chains. Once domestic firms became competitive in world markets, policy regimes were modified so that the acquisition of foreign firms also became a means for the acquisition of foreign technology (Nayyar, 2008). Such mechanisms were meant to create national technological capabilities at a macro-level.

The industrialization experience of the Asian-14 suggests that each of them faced some common policy dilemmas. The most important of these was striking a balance between imports of technology and indigenous technological development. There were instances where import of technologies was followed by stagnation, rather than adaptation, diffusion, and innovation at home. There were instances where indigenous technological development did not lead to widespread diffusion, let alone up-gradation. In such situations, market structures and government policies did not combine to provide an environment that would encourage the absorption of imported technology and speed up the development of indigenous technology, or create a milieu that would be conducive to diffusion and innovation. Even so, an open regime for the import of technology is not an answer, for the discipline of the market cannot restrain the recurrence of such imports by domestic firms time after time. Such firms are much like the school-boy, who can find someone else to write the examinations for him year after year and thus never learns. Domestic technological capabilities may not emerge either because there is no incentive to learn (imports are possible) or because they are stifled (imports are better). The problem may be accentuated in sectors where technical progress is rapid and obsolescence is high. There are two other common dilemmas. For one, it is difficult to foster the culture of R&D in domestic firms. This is not automatic. It needs incentives, embedded in industrial policy, for start-up and scale-up. For another, it is difficult to develop synergies between science and industry that transform scientific knowledge into marketable products. This is not automatic either. It needs institutional mechanisms to build bridges between the two worlds. Every latecomer to industrialization, at every stage in history, has confronted these dilemmas. Each has attempted to address the dilemmas in different ways. The countries that have succeeded in industrializing late, and making the transition from importation to innovation, from know-how to know-why, have done so by resolving these dilemmas.

Conclusion

The past fifty years have witnessed a marked increase in the degree of eco-nomic openness in Asia, reflected in international trade and investment flows. Between 1970 and 2008, for Asia, merchandise trade as a proportion of GDP rose from less than one-tenth to about two-fifths although, following the global economic crisis, contracted to one-fourth in 2016. Similarly, during 1970–2016, the stocks of inward and outward foreign direct investment as a propor-tion of GDP increased from one-sixth to three-tenths, and from one-hun-dredth to one-fifth, respectively. The Asian-14 mirrored these trends. There were, of course, differences between countries, depending upon their size and openness. The pace of industrialization was impressive. For Asia, and the Asian-14, the share of manufacturing in GDP rose from one-tenth in 1970 to one-fourth in 2016. This industrial transformation also led to pronounced changes in the composition of their trade as the share of primary products and resource-based manufactures fell, while the share of medium-technology and high-technology manufactures rose in both exports and imports. However, industrialization was most unequal even among the Asian-14.

Continued

Conclusion: Continued

Economic openness has performed a critical supportive role in the process, wherever it has been in the form of strategic integration with, rather than passive insertion into, the world economy. However, analysis of the industrialization experience in the Asian-14 shows that openness, while necessary, was not sufficient. It was conducive to industrialization only when combined with industrial policy. The pioneering success stories—South Korea, Taiwan, and Singapore—are classic examples of the use of industrial policy, through government intervention, to realize that scale economies foster vertical-diversification, encourage technological upgrading, and develop global brands. The more recent success story—China—has used industrial policy in a very different context in learning to industrialize and then building domestic capabilities in pursuit of long-term objectives. Vietnam is attempting to follow in its footsteps. The industrial dynamism of Indonesia, Malaysia, and Thailand waned after the Asian financial crisis, which could have sustained if industrial policy had been more purposive and effective. India, the most industrialized to start with, lagged behind the leaders, because industrial policy was poorly implemented or was simply not used, but its success in pharmaceuticals, automobiles, and software is attributable to industrial policy. Bangladesh, too, has used industrial policy to drive its garments-export-led industrialization. Clearly, success at industrialization in Asia was driven by sensible industrial policy that was implemented by effective governments. In future, however, technological learning and technological capabilities are also essential to provide the foundations for sustaining industrialization.

6

Markets, governments, and politics

It is possible to understand the evolving relationship between markets, government, and politics in Asia, over the past fifty years, only if it is situated in its wider historical context during the preceding quarter century. The end of the Second World War, in 1945, is an appropriate juncture in time, when countries in Asia, including most of the Asian-14, emerged from the crucible of their legacies of colonialism, nationalist movements, and revolutionary struggles, juxtaposed with a world war that led to the Japanese occupation of many countries in East and Southeast Asia. The incredibly complex and diverse political mosaic that straddled Asian countries at the time of their independence was shaped by these histories. This short preamble can, at best, set the stage. It would take another book to enact the play for the drama to emerge.

There were many colonialisms in Asia: the Japanese in Korea, Taiwan, and Manchuria (China), the Dutch in Indonesia, the French in Indochina, the British in India, as also China, and the United States in Philippines. Their different colonial legacies have already been discussed in an earlier chapter. There were nationalist movements in India, led by Gandhi, and in Indonesia, led by Sukarno. There were revolutionary struggles fought by communist parties in China, led by Mao Zedong, and in Vietnam led by Ho Chi Minh. There were similar communist movements in Indonesia and Malaysia that were suppressed. Political independence in Asian countries brought legendary new leaders: Jawaharlal Nehru in India, Sukarno in Indonesia, Mao Zedong with Zhou Enlai in China, and Ho Chi Minh in Vietnam. Following the departure of US occupation forces, new leaders also emerged in the erstwhile Japanese colonies: Chiang Kai-Shek in Taiwan and Park-Chung Hee in South Korea. Lee Kuan Yew became Prime Minister of Singapore on its separation from Malaysia in 1965. Deng Xiaoping succeeded Mao in China in 1978, while Mahathir Bin Mohamad became Prime Minister of Malaysia in 1981. Their leadership was, of course, representative of their political parties and ideologies. But it was almost as much about their personalities. Most of them ruled for long, on an average for twenty-five years. In doing so, they exercised an enormous influence on development strategies after independence and on the economic transformations that followed with a time lag, shaping the destiny of their nations.

The politics of Asia continued to be tempestuous until much later. Bangladesh won independence from Pakistan, in 1971, after a bloody liberation struggle, with military support from India. In this conflict, independent researchers estimate

Resurgent Asia: Diversity in Development. Deepak Nayyar, Oxford University Press (2019). © United Nations University World Institute for Development Economics Research. DOI: 10.1093/oso/9780198849513.001.0001

that 0.5 million died although Bangladesh authorities put the figure at 3 million. The Viet Cong, the National Liberation Front, ousted the powerful United States from South Vietnam, in 1975, with military support from North Vietnam, leading to the unification of Vietnam. Cambodia experienced a genocide at the hands of the Khmer Rouge led by Pol Pot, during 1975–1979, in which almost 2 million people, close to one-fourth of the total population of the country in 1975, died through mass executions, starvation, and disease. These political upheavals were followed, just two decades later, by discernible economic change. The economy of Vietnam has been a star performer since 2000. Similarly, Bangladesh and Cambodia, classified as Least Developed Countries, have witnessed rapid economic growth and a sharp reduction in absolute poverty since the turn of the century.

Apart from these dramatic political transformations in Asia during the early post-colonial era, the second half of the twentieth century also witnessed complete swings of the pendulum in economic thinking about the respective roles of states and markets in development. These turning points, which reshaped strategies, were strongly influenced by history and conjuncture, reinforced by the dominant ideology of the times. In the early 1950s, thinking about development was shaped by the experience of the colonial era, characterized by open economies and unregulated markets associated with deindustrialization and underdevelopment, and the beginnings of decolonization, when industrialization was seen as an imperative in development, motivated by nationalist aspirations of newly inde-pendent countries. The political ideology of that era also stressed the role of the state in market economies. This was the Development Consensus that dominated thinking during the quarter century from around 1950 until the mid-1970s. Outcomes in development over this period led to rethinking. The success of a few small East Asian countries was highlighted, even if the history then told was selective and partial. This was reinforced by the conjuncture in the late 1980s that witnessed the political collapse of communism. Capitalism emerged triumphant as the dominant ideology. By the early 1990s, the Washington Consensus, which stressed the virtues of markets and openness as a generalized prescription across countries, acquired a near-hegemonic status in thinking about development.[1] The swing of the pendulum was complete.

This hegemony did not last long. The belief system was somewhat shaken by the financial crises in Asia and Latin America. Development experience during the 1990s also belied expectations. Economic growth was slower and more volatile than earlier. The orthodox prescriptions were subjected to increasing questions.[2] The real dampener, however, was unfolding outcomes. Countries that were con-formists and liberalizers did not perform well, whereas countries that were non-conformists did far better.[3] Most countries in Latin America, Sub-Saharan Africa and Eastern Europe adopted the reform agenda of the Washington Consensus almost in entirety. Yet, their performance, in terms of economic growth, industrial development, and distributional outcomes, was not only much worse than other parts of the world but also distinctly worse than their own performance in the preceding quarter century. In sharp contrast, countries in Asia modified, adapted, contextualized, and paced their reform agenda, to use unorthodox or heterodox policies for orthodox objectives. They turned out to be the star performers in terms of growth and industrialization, even if not in terms of distributional outcomes.[4] More was to come. The global financial crisis that surfaced in late 2008, and the Great Recession that followed in its aftermath, eroded the triumph of capitalism and undermined the ideological faith in markets. In this context, the remarkable economic performance of Asia, which was discernible *circa* 2000 and gathered momentum thereafter, has changed perceptions and thinking about the role of the state in development yet again.

The object of this chapter is to analyse the economic and the political roles of the state in the process of development in Asia. It is divided into two parts. The first part, constituted by Sections 1 to 3, explores the relationship between states and markets in the economic sphere. Section 1 sets out an analytical approach. Section 2 examines the economic interaction between states and markets in Asia. Section 3 discusses the diversity of Asia to focus on lessons that emerge. The second part, constituted by Sections 4 to 6, considers the relationship between governments and markets to highlight its mediation through politics. Section 4 is about governments and politics in Asia, which reveals an enormous diversity across countries. Section 5 examines the checks and balances in political processes that could make governments more development-friendly. Section 6 explores how market economy and political democracy might interact with each other in the context of Asian development, as the future unfolds, and why democracy could be important for Asia.

1. Analytical approach

In retrospect, it is clear that the economic role of the state—as a leader, catalyst, or supporter—was critical in the transformation of Asia. However, fifty years ago, this was not quite anticipated in *Asian Drama*. Gunnar Myrdal believed that markets could not work in Asia, as they did in Europe, because of cultures, attitudes, and institutions, which led him to argue that governments must intervene. Thus, he emphasized the importance of planning in market economies as the way forward, which was also a part of the consensus in thinking about development at the time. Yet, this vital role of governments was diluted by his notion of 'soft states', which meant that some real-world governments did not have the willingness or ability to do what was necessary in the pursuit of development objectives because they could neither resist nor coerce powerful vested interests. And if such governments were not capable of interventions that were necessary, they could end up making matters worse. The emphasis, then, was on failures of governments. This was responsible for Myrdal's pessimism about development prospects. Surprisingly, he ignored markets, and hence their failures that needed correction.

Economic theory recognizes that governments and markets are both prone to failure. The word 'failure' is used to describe outcomes that are inefficient or undesirable with reference to some idealized state of an economy. Most textbooks in economics elaborate on such failures.[5] Even so, a brief explanation of how or why governments and markets fail might be worthwhile for the reader.

Government failure takes different forms and is attributable to several factors. Governments make mistakes because they do not have adequate information about a problem or do not understand the nature of the problem. Without adequate information and necessary understanding, governments are neither able to predict nor able to control the consequences of their actions. Hence, government intervention may not resolve the problem it intends to. Instead, it may lead to unwanted adverse effects that are unintended. There is, often, a divergence between the conception and the design of intervention by the govern-ment. The divergence between the design and the implementation of policies is, perhaps, even greater. All this may be true even with the best intentions of governments. But governments do not always act in the interests of people at large. Indeed, governments are frequently sectarian in their actions and interven-tions as they seek to promote the interests of classes, or groups, whom they represent. More narrowly, they might manipulate on behalf of groups who can exercise influence. These reasons lead orthodox economics to the conclusion that intervention in markets is inefficient because governments are incapable of inter-vening efficiently.

There are many dimensions of market failure. Consider some that are cited often. First, in the absence of adequate competition, where there is monopoly (one producer) or oligopoly (few producers), the amount of the good produced may be too little and the price charged may be too high compared with competitive situations. Economists describe such situations as *imperfect markets*, in contrast with their theoretical ideal of perfect markets. Second, an economic activity may impose costs on society that are not reflected in the costs incurred by individual producers or consumers undertaking those activities (e.g. pollution caused by chemical plants or cars). Economists characterize such effects, which impose costs (or impart benefits) to society but are not reflected adequately in market prices (formed through individual buying or selling decisions) as *externalities*. Third, there are goods and services that are considered desirable, even essential, from the viewpoint of society. But these will not or cannot be supplied by markets because they cannot be easily charged for (e.g. street-lights). Economists describe these as *public goods*. Fourth, markets tend to under-produce information, access to which cannot be restricted or priced. Economists describe this as *information failure*. It has many facets. The most important, perhaps, is *asymmetric information*, wherever there are economic transactions in which one party (the seller) has more or better information than the other (the buyer), leading to inefficient outcomes, compared with a situation where both have the same information.

In many economic situations, where the whole is different from the sum total of the parts, market decisions may widen the divergence between private and social costs or benefits. The pursuit of profit-maximizing behaviour on the part of firms, or utility-maximizing behaviour on the part of individuals, may lead to the over-production or overuse of goods (too many cars on the roads or too much pesticide in agriculture) which could impose substantial costs on society in the form of environmental problems. Similarly, the atomistic pursuit of self-interest by individuals may lead to undesirable social outcomes where co-operative solutions would lead to clearly superior outcomes (common property rights). Insofar as such market failures arise at a macro-level, are discernible only over time, or impose costs on society at large, they may go unnoticed by individuals who are not directly affected. But the failures are for real and so are the costs they impose on society.

Government failures are visible and tangible. Most people are familiar with these failures through their experiences. And governments, as entities, are prone to blame when things go wrong. Thus, governments are accountable to people as citizens. However, most people are much less conscious of market failures because these are more difficult to recognize. Even when the consequences are experienced, these are perceived to be natural events or system failures, since markets are not entities. Thus, markets are not accountable to people.

It is important to recognize that the juxtaposition of government failure and market failure, or judgements about which is worse, as if there is a choice to be made, is misleading because it diverts us into a false debate.[6] Both government failure and market failure are facts of life. For neither markets nor governments are, or can ever be, perfect. Indeed, markets are invariably imperfect and governments are, without exception, fallible. Markets, as much as governments, are human institutions which need careful monitoring. The important thing is to introduce corrective devices against both market failure and government failure. These failures are seldom absolute and a reasonable degree of correction is possible in either case.

Economic history also sheds light on the relationship between states and markets in capitalism. Historians tracing the evolutionary course of the market under early capitalism noted repeatedly that the market could become the organizing principle of capitalism only when it was embedded in the regulatory mechanism of the nation state.[7] The very extension of the scope of the free market necessitated, at each stage, the imposition of new regulations by the state to ensure further growth of the market. Thus, any characterization of the state and the market in opposition to one another is a misreading of history.

My understanding of the role of states and markets in the process of development relies upon economic theory and draws upon economic history.[8] It can be set out most simply in the form of two basic propositions. First, the state and the market are not substitutes for each other; instead, they must complement one another in many spheres. Second, the relationship between the state and the market cannot be specified once and for all in any dogmatic manner; instead the two institutions must adapt to one another in an interactive, co-operative, manner over time. These propositions explain the difference between success and failure at development. Success is observed mostly in countries where the state and the market complement each other and adapt to one another as circumstances change at different stages of development. This is borne out both by the history of capitalism among the early industrializers during the nineteenth century and by the more recent experience of late industrializers in Asia during the past fifty years.

The role of the state in market economies that are latecomers to development evolves over time. In the earlier stages, state intervention creates the conditions for the development of industrial capitalism. It creates a physical infrastructure through government investment in energy, transport, and communication, which reduces the cost of inputs used by the private sector or increases the demand for goods produced by the private sector. It develops human resources through education, which raises private profitability as it lowers the private cost of training workers. It facilitates institutional change, in some countries through agrarian reform, which increases productivity and incomes in the agricultural sector to foster industrialization through supply–demand linkages.

In the later stages of development, it is not only the degree but also the nature of state intervention that must change. For the purpose of analysis, this different role of intervention by the state in the market can be classified as *functional, institutional,* and *strategic*. Functional intervention by the state seeks to correct for market failures insofar as prices give the wrong signals. It can be specific or general. That depends on the nature of the failure of the price mechanism. The debate in such cases is about the availability of alternative market-based solutions or the ability of governments to design and implement correct solutions. Nevertheless, the logic of such intervention is sound. Institutional intervention by the state seeks to better govern the market. It does so by setting the rules of the game for players in the market. In particular, it creates frameworks for regulating markets and creates institutions to monitor the functioning of markets. The essential idea is that market economies need rules of the game to pre-empt a free-for-all and to ensure a level playing field. Fair competition requires anti-trust laws. Import liberalization requires anti-dumping rules. Financial liberalization requires matching regulatory laws. Consumer protection requires laws that curb restrictive trade practices, ensure quality control, and check misinformation in advertising. Strategic intervention by the state seeks to guide the market. It is interlinked across activities or sectors in an attempt to attain broader long-term development objectives. The most important is industrial policy, which co-ordinates economic policies across the board to foster industrialization. In the financial sector, there may be preferential access to credit for selected sectors, or the structure of interest rates may be a strategic instrument for guiding the allocation of scarce investible resources in a market economy, in accordance with a long-term perspective of comparative advantage or national priorities. Exchange rates could be put to strategic use if undervalued domestic currencies provide an entry into the world market for differentiated manufactured goods.

2. States and markets in Asia

The role of the state in the economic transformation in Asia—ranging from leader to catalyst or supporter—was proactive, often crucial, in the process of development,[9] although its degree or nature differed between countries and changed over time within countries. To begin with, there were strong similarities across countries, as states almost everywhere sought to create initial conditions and establish enabling institutions. Later, there were significant differences between countries in the role of states, which was shaped not only by outcomes but also by politics.

Even if initial conditions were bequeathed by history, intervention could and did improve upon that reality without enormous time lags. There were two aspects to this effort. For one, governments invested in developing a physical infrastructure for energy, transport, and communication. For another, governments sought to spread education in society, where primary education provided the base and higher education provided the edge. In both, a critical minimum was necessary to kick-start the process of development. Some countries did better than others in building infrastructure. Most countries concentrated on primary and secondary school education to follow up on higher education somewhat later, which was the correct approach, while a few such as India concentrated on higher education while neglecting school education, which yielded some benefits but was not appropriate as it also imposed costs.[10] The effectiveness and quality of such interventions shaped outcomes.

At the outset, governments also sought to facilitate institutional change that would be conducive to development. Institutional change in the rural sector, characterized by significant difference between Asian countries, was critical in this sphere. In much of Asia, landed elites had both voice and influence in post-colonial governments, which enabled them to resist agrarian reforms. Consequently, legislation on redistributive land reforms was diluted or circumvented almost everywhere.[11] This was so in India, Indonesia, Malaysia, Pakistan, Philippines, Sri Lanka, Thailand, and Turkey. In fact, meaningful redistributive land reforms were carried out in only four economies: South Korea, Taiwan, China, and Vietnam. There were land reforms in South Korea during 1945–1950 under the supervision of the United States occupation forces, when land owned by the erstwhile Japanese colonial government and Japanese companies or individuals was confiscated, while Koreans with large landholdings were divested of their lands, all of which was redistributed to families who were owner-cultivators. Similarly, soon after 1950, there were land reforms in Taiwan, once again under the supervision of the United States, carried out by the Nationalist Kuomintang government that had moved to Taiwan after fleeing from China. Following the revolution, in 1950, the Chinese Communist Party led by Mao Zedong carried out land reforms in China, which were redistributive to start with but then moved to collective farms. This was followed by a second round of agrarian reforms in 1978 initiated by Deng Xiaoping with the introduction of the production responsibility system with incentives for farmers. Similarly, the Communist Party in Vietnam led by Ho Chi Minh started land reforms in 1945, which were completed after the French were forced to leave in 1954, and extended to the former South Vietnam in 1976, abolishing individual ownership to introduce collective production. The next round of agrarian reform in Vietnam was in 1986. It was part of the *Doi Moi* reforms introduced in 1986, moving towards incentives and markets for peasants. These agrarian reforms in the four economies laid the foundations of their success at development in the following decades.

In the early post-colonial era, governments also attempted institutional change elsewhere. In the quest for catch-up, development planning was the focus and industrialization was the common aspiration. Such changes were introduced by proactive governments, not only in China and India but also in Indonesia, South Korea, Malaysia, Philippines, Pakistan, Sri Lanka, Taiwan, Thailand, and Turkey. It was all about industrial promotion and industrial investment, whether through the use of industrial, trade, and technology policy or through the establishment of planning offices, industrial boards, and financial institutions. In this spectrum, development banks that provided long-term financing for investment in the industrial sector were particularly important.[12] The object was to create production, investment, and innovation capabilities in domestic firms with countries opting for different emphases on the public sector and the private sector. These institutional initiatives, in which the role of the state was critical, were an integral part of the path to industrialization, even if future transition paths and success rates turned out to be different.[13] Enabling institutions were not simply about protecting property rights, keeping transaction costs low, and maintaining law and order, as orthodoxy would have us believe.[14]

In addition, governments also fostered industrialization at a micro-level, through the nurturing of entrepreneurs in different types of business enterprises, or through the creation of managerial capabilities in individuals and technological capabilities in firms in the private sector.[15] But that was not all. Governments established large public sector firms, for example in petroleum, steel, telecommunications, energy, or civil aviation, going even further into commercial banks and development banks. In the earlier stages, this was driven by the absence of private investment in these sectors because of the risks, lumpiness, or gestation lags associated with such investments. Such firms were also a strategic form of support for industrialization in the private sector.

In the later stages of development, some forms of functional intervention to address market failures were introduced almost everywhere. This was essentially general rather than specific, for example, to ensure safety or standards. However, setting rules did not always lead to invoking rules. Effectiveness varied across countries depending on whether governments had the capacity to discipline firms that circumvented or ignored these rules. Similarly, institutional intervention to regulate or monitor the functioning of markets in some form or another was put in place in most countries, say, to ensure fair competition and consumer protection, or to regulate financial sectors following liberalization and public utilities that were natural monopolies following privatization. In this domain, there were significant differences between countries in terms of both timing of inception and quality of regulation. This worked well in a few economies, such as South Korea, Taiwan, and Singapore where there were effective governments with public systems that were transparent and accountable, or in China and Vietnam where there were strong states. In most other economies, outcomes varied depending upon the authority of governments with respect to local elites who had the power to resist. Of course, in every country, corruption and collusion provided a way out.

Strategic intervention by the state, which meant co-ordinating policies across sectors over time in pursuit of national development objectives, was the exception rather than the norm in Asia. The exceptions were South Korea, Taiwan, and Singapore. These economies followed Japan as a role model.[16] South Korea, much like Japan, used an undervalued exchange rate to enter the world market for differentiated manufactured goods, where quality is perceived in terms of established brands but lower prices of unknown brands allow initial access to markets. Similarly, it used restrictions on foreign brand names as a strategic means of buying time to develop brand names that became acceptable in world markets after a time lag, but could never have surfaced in competition with established foreign brands. Japanese cars and cameras in an earlier period, or Korean cars and consumer electronics in a later period, illustrate this strategy. Like Japan, South Korea used interest rates as a strategic device to guide the allocation of scarce resources to priority sectors, particularly manufactured exports, whereas Taiwan used tax credits. Singapore also co-ordinated policies in a strategic manner in its quest for industrialization, although it relied far more on foreign capital and foreign technology.

Based on an analysis of the impressive economic development in Japan, during 1925–1975, Johnson (1982) introduced the concept of a *developmental state* committed to the idea of national development. It had some essential attributes: a competent and coherent bureaucracy to ensure rule of law and efficient implementation of policies; a government that could create a collective belief in the quest for national development among all stakeholders; maintaining close ties with key actors in society, particularly in the private sector, as partners; avoiding political capture by business elites by orienting them towards accumulation rather than consumption; and the capacity to use both carrot and stick wherever necessary.[17]

China emulated these developmental states, in an altogether different context, starting around 1990, learning not only from South Korea and Taiwan but also from Singapore. The strategic use of interest rates and an undervalued currency was part of this learning. And Vietnam has followed China, two decades later, on a similar transition path. It is at a much earlier stage but success is discernible. China and Vietnam, with developmental states, in a somewhat different incarnation, had the will and the capacity to implement their agenda.

In other countries among the Asian-14, states did not have the same willingness and ability to intervene effectively in the pursuit of national development objectives. The essential problem was that while these states could dangle carrots by creating rents for business, they could not use sticks to enforce compliance or penalize non-compliance of the conditions on which the benefits were contingent. However, reality was not just an all-or-nothing binary option. Even if these states were less efficient and less effective in intervention, they did manage to support development in different ways although the degree of success varied across countries and over time. In several Asian countries, states and elites reached specific understandings, in sectors or on issues that served their mutual interest, which also happened to be supportive of national development objectives. Business elites who could influence economic policy through their social networks or political connections with governments provided the frameworks for co-ordination. Governments created profit opportunities for business through policy regimes, while business provided political support for governments. The *quid pro quo* was simple enough, but where the rents so created were channelled into productive uses through market forces, it was also conducive to industrialization.

There is evidence to suggest that such arrangements, whereby the state provided credible incentives to domestic or foreign firms, in the form of potential *ex post* rents (but no *ex ante* rents), the realization of which was assured, did in fact lead to the expected or desired outcomes, if the capacity of the state to enforce the conditions imposed was not in doubt. This was not the norm as it was in East Asian countries. But it did happen, at times, with specific arrangements even in South Asian countries. The emergence of such arrangements as a process of institutional evolution has been described by Khan (2019) as 'political settlements', with examples from India and Bangladesh.[18] Pritchett et al. (2018) set out a related analytical construct, which suggests that, in developing countries, where rules are selectively enforced, closed 'deals' are possible but only for those with political connections where the investor can also be confident that state officials will deliver. Based on studies of Bangladesh, Cambodia, India, Malaysia, and Thailand, it is argued that such deals can also be conducive to development even if the deal-driven growth is episodic rather than sustained. Montes (2019) describes similar arrangements between states and corporates in Cambodia, Laos, Malaysia, Philippines, and Thailand, particularly in the external sectors of these economies, often with foreign firms as partners, as 'relational contracting', which did support industrialization in these countries.

3. Diversity and lessons

The relationship between the state and the market in Asian economic development has been characterized by significant diversity, rather than broad uniformity, across countries over time. There were many country-specific circumstances, also influenced by the geographical location and the international context, which shaped alternatives in terms of respective roles. Even so, a judicious blend of states and markets was at the foundation of success in terms of development outcomes in Asia. Conversely, an inappropriate mix of states and markets led to indifferent or poor outcomes.

There were adaptive changes in the relationship between states and markets over time across countries. In the initial stages, during the quarter century from 1950 to 1975, states were more important than markets almost everywhere in Asia. This was partly a reaction to the colonial past where unregulated markets and subordinated economies were associated with underdevelopment. More importantly, state intervention for kick-starting industrialization and development was perceived as both necessary and desirable. This was also an integral part of the Development Consensus at the time. By the mid-1970s, however, there was a disappointment with development outcomes and a disillusionment with excessive or inappropriate state intervention. Following such experiences, most countries in Asia sought to reduce the economic role of the state and rely more on markets. The timing and pace of the change differed across countries.[19]

Interestingly enough, China was the first to introduce economic reforms in 1978, which started its transition from a centrally planned economy towards a market economy.[20] Indonesia, Malaysia, Philippines, Thailand, and Turkey shifted the balance to rely less on states and more on markets at different times around the mid-1980s. India also started the process with some preliminary steps in deregulation about the same time, followed by rapid economic liberalization during the early 1990s. Around then, Bangladesh, Pakistan, and Sri Lanka also moved by shifting their emphasis from states to markets. Soon after, the centrally planned economies in Southeast Asia—led by Vietnam and followed later by Cambodia and Laos—commenced their transition to market economies. In the wake of the Asian financial crisis, around the turn of the century, South Korea, Taiwan, and Singapore, where states had always guided markets in a proactive manner, also progressively reduced the economic role of the state as they joined the league of industrialized nations.

It is difficult to categorize or group countries in terms of the relative importance of the state and the market not only because of changes over time but also on account of the diversity across countries. Yet, such an exercise might be worthwhile if the idea is to consider the economic transformation of Asia over the past fifty years as a whole, recognizing that states were more important in the earlier stages while markets were more important in the later stages almost everywhere, even if both performed crucial roles at every stage. Such a categorization is, of course, a broad assessment.

The relative importance of the state, in qualitative if not quantitative terms, contrary to the characterization in orthodoxy, was clearly greater than that of the market in South Korea, Taiwan, and Singapore, where the visible hand of the state was more in evidence than the invisible hand of the market although markets performed a critical role.[21] This was also true for India, Pakistan, Bangladesh, Sri Lanka, and Myanmar, where states were far more important than markets, so much so that states were dominant while the role of markets was subsidiary if not secondary for at least half of the past fifty years. It is no surprise that the role of the state was overwhelmingly important in centrally planned economies—China, Vietnam, Cambodia, and Laos—notwithstanding economic reforms and the transition to market economies. On the whole, Indonesia, Malaysia, Philippines, Thailand, and Turkey relied more on markets than on states, although states did have a significant role in the earlier stages. Among the East Asian Tigers, as well as in Asia, Hong Kong was the solitary exception with its laissez-faire economy run entirely by markets, even if the government exercised tight political control throughout, both under British rule and on return to China.

The respective roles of the state and the market, or the public sector and the private sector, evolve in a continuum. There can be no general rules, for boundaries change over time as comparative advantage or circumstances change. Most economic activities are best left to private initiative. It is what markets can and should do. There are some activities in which the private sector and public sector can co-exist where such competition benefits the economy and people. But there are some things that only governments can and should do. If governments perform these tasks badly, it is not possible to dispense with them and replace them with markets. In such situations, governments must be made to perform better. This is possible as governments are accountable to people, whereas markets are not.

Actual outcomes in development were a complex mix of success stories in some, muddling-through in others, and poor-performance in yet others. It is not as if all countries could be classified into one of these categories at all times. The degree of success at development in Asia, which also changed within countries during the past fifty years, was about managing this evolving relationship between states and markets in terms of the mix, emphasis, and change over time. Finding the right balance in the respective roles of the state and the market did improve development outcomes.[22]

There are some lessons that emerge from the Asian development experience over the past fifty years. For countries that relied more on governments, it was about minimizing government failures and getting state intervention right. For countries that relied more on markets, it was about minimizing market failures and getting prices right. For countries—irrespective of the group they were in— that were unable to minimize such failures, development outcomes were poorer.[23] In general, for countries that succeeded in terms of outcomes in development, or fared better than others, there can be no doubt that the role of governments—as supporters, catalysts, or leaders—was critical. In countries where governments were unable to perform such a role, the social and economic transformation was much slower. It is necessary to note that such governments, which were unable to perform their roles in terms of intervention, were also unable to perform their roles in a changed context of liberalization. This is not surprising because governments that could not run enterprises well could not regulate, let alone govern or guide, markets well. At the same time, it is necessary to recognize that markets are no magic wand, that the invisible hand of the market is not visible because it is not there, and that markets are good servants but bad masters. Clearly, fallible governments and imperfect markets, taken together, could only hinder economic development. The Asian experience suggests that efficient markets and effective governments, in tandem, provided the way forward to development.

It would seem that states and markets are inseparables, as complements, in the process of development. The relationship between the two institutions is crucial in shaping outcomes. Both are institutions evolved by humankind to organize economy, polity, and society, which cannot do without each other. This is because states and markets provide mutual checks and balances, in situations when one or the other goes wrong, to function as self-correcting mechanisms. It follows that co-operation rather than conflict should define their relationship. Thus, any characterization of the state and the market in opposition to one another is a misreading of history, which can never be conducive to development. Instead, it is more useful to think of the relationship as being governed by an adaptive principle in which neither the state nor the market becomes destructively dominant to cripple the other institution. If that happens, economic systems are left without any self-correcting mechanisms. Of course, while it is important to learn from experience, it is just as important to avoid overreacting to mistakes. Indeed, the best corrective mechanism is one which manages to avoid such swings of over-reaction or under-reaction. This deserves emphasis because there must always be some room for iteration and experimentation in policies. For it is just as important to unlearn from experience. That could be about reversing an experiment in policies which did not work. That could also be about questioning long-held beliefs and thinking anew.[24] The moral of the story is clear. It is essential, and wise, to be circumspect about any generalized prescriptions or standardized solutions on the subject of states and markets in development.

It is obviously necessary to recognize the diversity of Asia in its mix of states and markets, which differed across countries and changed over time. Even so, there are discernible patterns in this diversity that emerge clearly, making a difficult task more manageable. The real question is no longer about the size of the state (how big?) or the degree of state intervention (how much?). The question now is about the nature of state intervention (what sort?) and the quality of the performance of the state (how good?).

4. Governments and politics in Asia

During the past fifty years, contrary to the expectations of Gunnar Myrdal, states performed a critical role in the economic transformation of Asia. It is also plausible to argue that countries where states were unwilling or unable to perform this role lagged behind in development. Obviously, the willingness and the ability of governments to lead, guide, or support the process was largely dependent on the nature of the state, which in turn was shaped by politics.

The diversity in the political systems of countries in Asia is just as striking as the diversity in the economies of Asia. These political systems were shaped by a wide range of factors such as colonial legacies, nationalist movements, revolutionary struggles, cultures, and religions, embedded in the past of Asian countries. But these political systems were also influenced by developments such as the geopolitics of the Cold War era, the rivalries of superpowers, the collapse of communism in the former USSR, and the spread of globalization, in the outside world.[25]

For analytical purposes, it is worth attempting a rough classification of political systems in Asia. In doing so, the scope is not limited to the Asian-14 but extends to a much larger number of countries in the continent, if only to sketch a complete picture for the reader, since their respective political systems influenced their trajectories of development. This cannot be definitive because of variations between countries within categories and changes within countries over time. It is possible to distinguish between six groups. There are a few political democracies. India is the prime example, which has functioned as a vibrant democracy for more than seven decades. So are Sri Lanka and the Philippines, which have been flawed in some respects and interrupted at times. There are four democracies that have evolved from authoritarian regimes, South Korea from 1987, Taiwan from 1992, Indonesia from 1998 and Mongolia from 1990. There are some *de jure* democracies that are *de facto* oligarchies, one-party or even one-family rule, such as Malaysia, Singapore, and Bangladesh. There are four communist countries— China, Vietnam, Cambodia, and Laos—that are in different stages of transition to market economies, with one-party political rule in common. North Korea is another communist country with a one-party, one-family rule that is a totalitarian regime. There are two countries—Pakistan and Myanmar—which have been ruled largely by the army. There are several countries that are, in effect, monarchies: Bahrain, Bhutan, Brunei Darussalam, Jordan, Kuwait, Oman, Qatar, Saudi Arabia, and United Arab Emirates. And there are a few outliers that are difficult to classify. Thailand is a constitutional monarchy, which has elections from time to time, with a history of *coups*, that has been ruled largely by the army and the King. Turkey is a *de jure* constitutional democracy that elected governments, although the army was always enormously influential, until the election of Erdogan as Prime Minister in 2003 and his subsequent election as President in 2014 transforming it into an authoritarian regime. Iran was essentially a monarchy until 1979, when the Shah was overthrown and replaced by an Islamic Republic ruled, in effect, by a religious oligarchy represented by a Council of Guardians, although it elects a President and a parliament. In Iraq, the short-lived republic formed in 1958 was ousted in a *coup* by Saddam Hussein who ruled from 1979 to 2003, and was deposed by the United States, which has been followed by political instability and deep divides. Such a broad classification is neither definitive nor exhaustive but does reveal the diversity of politics in Asia. This politics shaped the nature of the state, hence the characteristics of governments, which in turn shaped development outcomes.

In the context of development, orthodox institutional economics is influential in thinking on this subject. It emphasizes the importance of strong states, which can provide robust frameworks not only for law and order, enforcement of contracts, and security of property rights, but also for institutions that underpin markets, without becoming confiscatory.[26] Strong states are, then, defined in terms of two attributes: political centralization and a capacity to make commitments that are met. This capacity of the state has fiscal, legal and military aspects, apart from its ability to provide public goods and services. The corollary follows. States that do not possess these attributes or capacities are weak states. In this worldview, strong states can drive development whereas weak states are not conducive to development.

Such a binary distinction between strong and weak states is an oversimplification that is not appropriate. Myrdal's distinction between hard and soft states was analogous. For one, states might be characterized by asymmetric behaviour, which could be strong or hard vis-à-vis the poor but weak or soft vis-à-vis the rich. For another, the desired attributes might be there in part and might differ across countries without being present or absent in entirety. What is more, states are not born in a vacuum with uniform attributes. These attributes are shaped by historical, social, and political forces. The real world, in which the nature of the state and the underlying politics differ significantly between countries, could then turn out to be rather different from simple binary characterizations. It could lead to mixed outcomes in development across the wide range between success and failure. This proposition is borne out by the diversity of political regimes and development experiences in Asia.

In any case, strong states as defined in orthodox institutional economics are simply an analytical construct derived from a contestable understanding of history, based on hindsight, which does not quite recognize that its chosen attributes of strong states evolved over time and did not exist at the outset. Asian economic development over the past fifty years does confirm that states performed a crucial role. However, binary distinctions cannot suffice to differentiate between states across countries. The actual variations are more discernible in a continuous spectrum. Developmental states, which had a strong commitment to national development and the capacity to resist, or manage, the vested interests not only of the elites but also of the rulers themselves, were at one end of the spectrum. There were other states that could not match them in attributes but were effective states in some spheres. There were yet other states that were far less effective, but managed to support development in some ways. What states could or could not do was shaped by the nature of their political systems.

The developmental states in South Korea and Taiwan, which followed in the footsteps of the developmental state in Japan, provide the basis of many analytical constructs about the role of the state in the process of development. But it is seldom recognized that the nature of these states was an outcome of circumstances in history, context, and conjuncture that were very specific to them. In history, the Japanese colonial legacy, repressive though it was, did create initial conditions in the form of a spread of education in society that was greater than in most colonized Asian countries, the basic elements of a state-bureaucratic apparatus, some manufacturing experience, a minimal physical infrastructure, and a strong sense of nationalism.[27] The context, at the end of the Second World War, was also conducive as land reform carried out under the supervision of US occupation forces eliminated the landed elite, while the industrial elite, essentially Japanese, were evicted by defeat at war. The conjuncture, the beginning of the Cold War era, meant that the United States provided protection to these frontline states, against communism, in the form of complete security cover and substantial foreign aid, which fostered their quest for industrialization. Singapore, also a developmental state, was not at par as a frontline state but did receive security cover and modest development aid. There were other similarities too, although the underlying reasons were different. Singapore was a city state with no rural hinterland so that it did not have a landed elite. It had no local industrial capitalists either, who stayed on in Malaysia. In fact, the state in Singapore started on a clean slate with no political baggage, and the nature of its state was shaped by Lee Kuan Yew.

South Korea and Taiwan had authoritarian political regimes for at least four decades until they were almost in the league of industrialized economies. Given the unusual initial situation in which there were no landed elites or industrial capitalists, juxtaposed with a strong nationalism, motivated by anti-colonial and anti-communist sentiments in both countries, their states had far more space and freedom than states elsewhere in Asia. The task was made simpler by the egalitarian land reforms that had reduced inequalities in rural sectors. But these states also consolidated their strength among people with public provisions for education and healthcare, while economic growth created employment opportunities. Their idea of national development as a collective project found ownership among most stakeholders. In fact, these states maintained close ties with the emerging industrial elites, without being captured, while being able to discipline business elites. The rents created were channelled into productive uses in pursuit of national development objectives. This attribute, which has been described as 'embedded autonomy', was supported by a 'Weberian bureaucracy' recruited on merit with a performance-based career-progress reward system.[28] In a very different context, the story was similar in Singapore. There were either foreign firms, largely wholly owned subsidiaries, or state-owned enterprises. A bureaucratic apparatus was created in which civil servants were paid salaries that were comparable with the private sector but were subject to a strong discipline against corruption. Public provisions for education, healthcare, housing, and social protection for the vulnerable created ownership among citizens even without political rights. Clearly, South Korea, Taiwan, and Singapore were exceptions, in the nature of their states, that cannot be replicated elsewhere. Interestingly enough, in a very different political context, the states in China and Vietnam provide striking parallels. But this model of developmental states, too, cannot be replicated elsewhere, except perhaps in countries with one-party communist governments. Of course, there are lessons to be learnt from all of these experiences.

5. Checks and balances

In terms of politics, most countries in Asia have either strong authoritarian (even repressive) regimes or imperfect (sometimes flawed) democracies. Hoping for developmental states in most of these countries would be wishful thinking. But that is no reason to abandon hope. Countries can, and do, progress without developmental states, although at a much slower pace. In this imperfect real world, it is necessary to explore other possibilities, given the nature of the state shaped by politics, where governments can be supportive of, or conducive to, development. The Asian experience reflected in development outcomes suggests some reason for hope, if not optimism, rather than despair. There are two questions that arise. Are there lessons to be learnt from the experience of the past few decades? Is there something in political processes that might make governments more development-friendly in the future?

There is a negative lesson, about the protection of infant industries, through tariffs or other restrictions on imports, that is worth noting. The state protects entrepreneurs in the private sector from international competition in the domestic market. In this, the state and the market complement each other. If the objective is to be realized, the state must, after a time, progressively withdraw its protection so that infant industries grow up as healthy adults, ultimately capable of competing in the world market. Thus, the respective roles of the state and the market must undergo an adaptive change. In some Asian countries, however, the objective was not realized. There were infant industries that grew up as problem adolescents, or went from a first childhood to a second childhood without ever passing through the stage of adulthood. Such infant industries needed protection for ever, because governments could not resist political pressures and discipline the errant industrialists seeking to preserve their sheltered profits.[29] The absence of any adaptive response of states and markets to each other as time moved on, or circumstances changed, meant failure. This problem, attributable to politics and governments, which does not refute the validity of the infant industry argument, has diminished now because of the increased openness of economies during the past three decades. Before that, however, many infant industries did come of age in Asia, even in countries without strong states.

There is another lesson about economic reforms and the political process, neither negative nor positive, that deserves mention. The process of economic reform is either strategy-based or crisis-driven.[30] South Korea, Taiwan, China, and Vietnam exemplify strategy-based reform. India, Pakistan, Bangladesh, and Sri Lanka exemplify crisis-driven reform. Reforms in Southeast Asian economies were a mix that was based on learning from experience in the first phase and following the 1997–1998 financial crisis in the second phase. Economic reform that represented a natural transition in the strategy of development emerged from experience and learning within countries. It was rooted in social formations and was shaped by political processes that provided constituencies. Such reform processes could be sustained and could succeed, in part because these created a capacity to manage problems of transition. The change was acceptable to polity and society. The speed and sequence of adjustment could be accommodated or absorbed by the economy. Economic reform that was crisis-driven (often guided by the IMF and World Bank), irrespective of whether the crisis was an external shock (external debt or financial crises) or internal convulsion (economic or political), was more difficult to sustain and less likely to succeed. During such transitions, for the majority of people, the costs surfaced soon while the benefits remained a distant promise. In the absence of supportive constituencies, if reform was not absorbed by the economy or was not acceptable in the polity, disillusionment set in so that even the necessary and desirable components of reform were discredited. The social and political coalitions that supported or opposed reforms determined whether the process was sustainable. It created political strains, if the support came from the rich and the influential who were vocal and captured most of the benefits, while the opposition came from the poor and the unorganized who were silent and bore most of the costs. These problems appeared more acute in democratic regimes but were not altogether absent in authoritarian regimes.

The heterodox literature on institutions and development suggests a positive lesson that emerges, about the possibilities of understandings or arrangements between business and governments, based on mutual interest, which also contribute to industrialization and national development. This explains why similar institutions deliver different results in different settings. At the same time it addresses a question posed by Myrdal fifty years ago: why do the same policies work differently in different countries with different outcomes? The notion of 'political settlements' (Khan, 2019), or 'deals in development' (Pritchett et al., 2018) between governments and elites, mentioned earlier in this chapter, suggests that cultural norms and informal institutions do matter in situations where established norms or formal institutions do not already exist. Such processes have been part of the evolution of institutions in developing Asia.

In countries that do not have developmental states, it is only institutionalized checks and balances that could make governments more development-friendly. This is clearly more feasible in political democracies than in authoritarian regimes. Such potential corrective mechanisms might exist within political processes or in institutions that could mediate between governments and markets.

There are possibilities that political processes, in themselves, could provide checks and balances, depending on the nature of political systems. In democracies, multiparty systems characterized by political competition provide checks and balances implicit in concerns about the next electoral outcome. In one-party systems, there are checks and balances if there is intra-party democracy, which allows for consultations between factions or directly with party members; if there are no barriers to entry, potential competition is a deterrent. This would also be true in situations where one political party is dominant.[31] Federal structures with specified domains for national and provincial governments, such as in India, Indonesia, and Philippines, also provide checks and balances. This goes beyond fiscal federalism. It could facilitate democratic transitions in countries as it did in Indonesia, or facilitate coalition politics as it did in India. Decentralization that devolves power from national to provincial, or provincial to local, tiers of government, provides similar checks and balances.[32] Of course, every tier wants devolution from above but is reluctant about devolution going below. Such decentralization could be either political or economic or both. There is a sharp dichotomy in China where strong political centralization is combined with considerable economic decentralization, in which the latter allows competition among provinces and experimentation in policies. Most important, perhaps, governments everywhere are ultimately accountable to people, more so in democracies and, to some extent, even in authoritarian regimes.

Institutions in the space between governments and markets can and do also function as correctives. Of these, social institutions such as media and civil society are among the most important. In Asia, an independent media is the exception and not the norm since it exists only in the few robust democracies. Of course, the social media and digital platforms on the Internet do provide space for people with dissenting or critical voices. In contrast, civil society organizations are active in most Asian countries except those run by communist parties. They do function as checks and balances on governments. In countries such as Bangladesh, they have performed roles that neither governments nor markets were willing or able to do. Micro-credit is the striking example where they have made an important contribution to social development.[33]

In addition, apart from the executive, which runs government, political institutions of the state, the legislature and the judiciary, are designed as checks and balances. These do function in most Asian countries that are democracies, even if imperfectly, but not in countries which have strongly authoritarian or one-party governments. Similarly, economic institutions created to regulate markets, or monitor their function, whether statutory regulators in different sectors or adjudicating entities on existing laws, are supposed to be independent mediators between governments and firms or citizens. Their independence and effectiveness varies across countries and over time depending on the leadership of institutions and the nature of the political regime.

The arguments developed above run contrary to the new orthodoxy in institutional economics. In their influential book, Acemoglu and Robinson (2012) argue that economic institutions determine whether a country is rich or poor while political institutions shape its economic institutions. Countries that succeed have inclusive economic institutions that allow participation by people in economic activities to make the best use of their talents, which are created by political institutions that distribute power across a broad coalition of groups. Countries that fail have extractive political institutions that force people to work largely for the benefit of ruling elites or dictators, which are the outcome of absolutist political institutions that concentrate power in narrow groups. This hypothesis is not convincing because Acemoglu and Robinson seek its validation by just-so stories from the history of countries, to conclude that the story explains why nations succeeded or failed. The benefit of hindsight makes this storytelling easier. The fundamental question is why some countries have inclusive institutions while other countries have extractive institutions. It is no surprise that rich countries have good institutions and poor countries have poor institutions. Of course, good institutions are always conducive to development. Yet, it could well be that good or inclusive institutions are a consequence rather than a cause of progress. These institutions did not already exist in countries that have succeeded. They evolved over time. This is borne out by the development experience of Asia over the past fifty years.

6. Democracy, economics, and politics

The interaction between states and markets in economic systems and governments and politics in political systems has shaped trajectories of development across countries in Asia. Over the past three decades, most Asian countries, including the erstwhile centrally planned economies, have chosen the market economy path to development, although governments continue to play a critical economic role. In terms of political systems, however, significant differences between Asian countries persist. Yet, the past three decades have also witnessed a discernible spread of the desire for political democracy in Asia, which is no surprise given its economic progress. The discussion that follows explores how market economy and political democracy might interact with each other in the context of Asian development as the future unfolds.

The virtues of political democracy can be traced to British and European thinking about liberalism. Its basic tenets are freedom for individuals, pluralism of values, importance of rights, and equality among people. These tenets are sacrosanct and the limits, if any, are enshrined in a social contract where individuals can be coerced by collective decisions only if they have consented to being subjected by the system.[34] The virtues of market economy, articulated more than two centuries ago by Adam Smith, are spelt out at length in orthodox economic theory.[35] It is efficient as it optimizes production (in terms of resource allocation) and consumption (in terms of utility maximization). It is democratic and libertarian insofar as it provides equal opportunity and the right to choose. For the contemporary enthusiasts, as much as Adam Smith, private initiative is the means and economic prosperity is the end.

Yet, both have limitations. Democracies function on the principle of majority rule or some variant thereof. This is clearly preferable to monarchies or oligarchies. But democracy can lead to the *tyranny of majorities*.[36] Moreover, in countries characterized by social and economic inequalities, universal adult franchise alone cannot create political equality. The proposition that markets create equal opportunities for all depends on the critical assumption that the initial distribution of property rights is equal. Thus, any defence of the market on the premise that it is good in terms of actual outcomes must rest on a most unrealistic assumption. Markets might, in fact, be about the *tyranny of minorities.*

The interaction between market economy and political democracy shapes outcomes for people. The essence of the tension between the economics of markets and the politics of democracy must be recognized. A market economy works on the basis of one-dollar-one-vote, while a political democracy works on the basis of one-person-one-vote. The distribution of votes, unlike the distribution of incomes or assets, is equal. One adult has one vote in politics, even though a rich person has more votes than a poor person, in terms of purchasing power, in the market. This tension may be compounded by a related asymmetry between economy and polity. The people who are excluded by the economics of markets are included by the politics of democracy. The rich dominate a market economy in terms of purchasing power. But the poor have a strong voice in a political democracy in terms of votes. And there is a mismatch. There is another asymmetry. Markets exclude people without incomes or purchasing power. It is in the logic of markets. Yet, markets would like to include as many people as possible. For, in the words of Adam Smith, 'the division of labour is limited by the size of the market'. Democracy includes people by a constitutional right to vote. It is the foundation of democracy. Yet, political processes seek to exclude or marginalize those without a voice. That is what the pursuit and exercise of political power is about. There is an irony in this paradoxical situation.[37]

In reconciling market economy and political democracy, a sensible compromise must be reached between the economic directions that the market sets on the basis of purchasing power and the priority that a political system sets on the basis of one-person-one-vote. It is no surprise that successive generations of economic thinkers and political philosophers have stressed the role of the state in this process of mediation. This is obvious in a democracy where governments are elected by the people. But, even in authoritarian regimes, governments need legitimation from the people, particularly if most of them are not rich or are poor.

There is an extensive literature on democracy and development. It would mean too much of a digression to enter into a discussion here. Even so, it is important to emphasize the strengths and recognize the weaknesses of democracy. This would help understand why, given the possible alternatives, democracy is the better way forward if we think about the future of development in Asia over the next twenty-five years.

In the context of market economies, democracy has three distinct virtues.[38] For its intrinsic value, democracy is an end in itself. For its instrumental contributions, democracy matters as it introduces checks and balances in economy, polity, and society. In the creations of norms and values, democracy plays a constructive role. The strengths are obvious. Democracy is constitutive of development insofar as it provides autonomy and freedom for individuals as citizens. It is instrumental in development insofar as it persuades governments to act in the interests of people. And it makes it possible for people to be centre-stage in development, not only as its beneficiaries but also as the main actors, by empowering people to participate in decisions that shape their lives. Electoral mandates from people lend stability and legitimacy to policy decisions, for which governments are ultimately accountable. Democratic political systems, with their supporting institutions, provide checks and balances when things go wrong under bad capitalisms. It is, then, plausible to suggest that democracy makes it possible to rule out the worst leaders and poorest outcomes.

The weaknesses are also clear. Electoral democracies that function without transparency and accountability are imperfect if not flawed. The competitive politics of populism, or cynical politics of opportunism, could lead to a race to the bottom. Money in politics makes matters worse. Long-term development objectives could be lost sight of in a short-termism that is concerned with the next year or, at best, with the next election. Above all, democracies work and evolve slowly. The experience of Europe and the United States confirms that the evolution of political democracies from birth through childhood and adulthood to maturity is a slow process that spans 100–150 years. In this evolution, ruling oligarchies, rampant corruption, manipulated institutions, electoral malpractices, crony capitalism, or poor governance are common occurrences. Democracies in Asia in the early twenty-first century are not very different from democracy in the United States in the late nineteenth century, 100 years after independence from colonial rule and the establishment of political democracy.[39] There are differences but these are largely a function of the era in time and geography in space. It is, therefore, premature to come to judgement about the future of democracies in Asia.

Even so, it is important to recognize democracies can be, and sometimes are, manipulated or misused. Indeed, democracies can become choice-less for voters, where or when there is almost no difference between the main contending political parties. In such situations, people sometimes elect demagogues, disguised as populist leaders, who then subvert democracy. Thus, there is a growing disillusionment with democracy, which has been reinforced by electoral outcomes in several countries across the world, in Asia, Europe, Latin America, and even in the United States. But that cannot be a reason for rejecting democracy or preferring authoritarianism. It need hardly be stressed that democracy is better than the alternatives, different forms or shades of authoritarianism, not only for the rights and the freedoms it provides for citizens, but also for the checks and balances and the self-correcting mechanisms it provides for political systems when things go wrong.

Studies on economic development in Asia often make a comparison between China and India, which shows that the economic performance of China is far better than that of India in almost every dimension. This leads ideologues of different persuasions to infer that authoritarianism is good for development or that democracy is bad for development. Both generalizations, or conclusions, are completely misleading and totally false. The reasons underlying the differences in the economic performance of the Asian giants—China and India—analysed in this book are manifold and complex. It is far-fetched, if not absurd, to reduce these to differences between authoritarian and democratic regimes.

The conventional view that democratization leads to weak states is often invoked in the Asian context. This is questionable. It might be more appropriate to suggest that, at the present stage of their evolution, political democracies in Asia are associated with states that appear far less effective in comparison with the developmental states. It is also clear that political democracy is neither necessary nor sufficient for economic development. It is just as clear that authoritarian regimes are neither necessary nor sufficient for economic development. In fact, there is another hypothesis, formulated in the Asian context, which argues that strong states lead to democratization, citing the examples of South Korea and Taiwan.[40] This is even more questionable, since it fails to explain why the strong state in Singapore, or the strong states in China and Vietnam, have not taken any step in the direction of democratization, despite their remarkable economic development.

In this debate, it is essential to recognize that the developmental states in South Korea, Taiwan, and Singapore, which are capitalist economies, or China and Vietnam, which are communist countries, are exceptions that will be exceedingly difficult to reproduce elsewhere in Asia.[41] The rest of Asia has either strong authoritarian regimes or imperfect political democracies. In my view, it is plausible to argue that, as compared with authoritarian governments, political democracies, even if far from perfect, will be more conducive to development.

On balance, democratic political systems are ultimately less fragile and more robust than authoritarian political systems, particularly in a long time horizon. In Asia, at this juncture, it might seem that democracies have limitations. Yet, for all their flaws and warts, they are democracies. The process of evolution might be slow. Even so, in a world of progressively empowered public opinion, the future of Asia, both economic and political, could be better if it chooses the path of democracy.

Conclusion

This chapter shows that governments performed a critical role, ranging from leader to catalyst or supporter, in the economic transformation of Asia spanning half a century, while their willingness and ability to do so depended on the nature of the state, which in turn was shaped by politics. It argues that the state and the market are complements rather than substitutes and that the two institutions must adapt to each other in an interactive co-operative manner over time. Success at development in Asia was about managing this evolving relationship between states and markets, by finding the right balance in their respective roles, which also changed over time. Countries, where governments did not, or could not, perform this role, and were unable to evolve their role vis-à-vis markets, lagged behind in development. The Asian experience suggests that efficient markets and effective governments, in tandem, provided the way forward to development.

The developmental states in South Korea, Taiwan, and Singapore, for whom Japan was the role model, which could co-ordinate policies across sectors over time in pursuit of national development objectives using the carrot and stick to implement their agenda, led the economic transformation of these countries, enabling them to become industrialized nations in just fifty years. However, the nature of these states was an outcome of circumstances in history and conjuncture that were very specific to them. China emulated these developmental states, in an altogether different political context with much success, and Vietnam has followed, two decades later, on the same transition path, as both countries had strong one-party communist governments, with clear objectives, that could co-ordinate and implement policies. It is not possible to replicate these states elsewhere in Asia. Even so, in the other countries in the Asian-14, where states were less effective in implementing their agenda, governments did manage to introduce economic policies and evolve institutional arrangements that were conducive to industrialization and development.

In countries that do not have developmental states, it is only institutionalized checks and balances that can make governments more development-oriented and people-friendly. There are possibilities within political processes, particularly multiparty systems, or through federalism, decentralization, and devolution. There are also non-state institutions such as the media and civil society, or even state institutions outside the government, that can perform this role. This is obviously more feasible in political democracies than in authoritarian regimes. Of course, democracies in Asia do have their flaws and warts. These might seem larger than life. But democracies evolve slowly. Over time, they are less fragile and more robust than authoritarian regimes. For Asia's continuing journey in development, during the twenty-first century, democracy is better than the alternatives, not only for the rights and the freedoms it provides for citizens, but also for the checks and balances and the self-correcting mechanisms it provides for political systems when things go wrong.

7

Unequal outcomes for countries
and people

During the past fifty years, economic growth in Asia has been impressive compared with developing economies elsewhere and the industrialized countries. It was also much faster than growth in Western Europe and North America during their Industrial Revolutions. And it was clearly far better than its own performance in the preceding century. This led to a significant increase in its share of world GDP even if convergence in levels of income per capita was modest and uneven. However, these aggregates are deceptive. The distribution was unequal among its constituent sub-regions and between countries. It was just as unequal between people and among regions within countries.

The object of this chapter is to analyse unequal outcomes in development and emerging divergences in incomes during this era of rapid economic growth in Asia. In doing so, it seeks to focus on uneven development across countries and on unequal distribution among people within countries. Section 1 examines whether per capita income in Asia converged towards, or diverged from, per capita income in industrialized countries, to situate these outcomes in the context of hypotheses in economics about convergence. Section 2 outlines the contours of inequality between countries in Asia, disaggregated by country-groups and countries, mirrored in divergences in per capita income over time, to underline its significance. Section 3 discusses the rising economic inequality within countries in Asia, reflected not only in a worsening of income distribution between people but also in growing regional disparities. Section 4 considers the extent to which rapid economic growth has helped the poor by bringing about a reduction of absolute poverty in Asia, while highlighting how much, and where, poverty persists. Section 5 analyses the impact of economic transformations in countries at a macro-level on the well-being of people at the micro-level, not only because it is the essential purpose of development but also because opportunities for people shape outcomes in development.

1. Convergence and divergence

The rapid economic growth in Asia, without precedent in history, led to an increase in its share of world GDP, in current prices at market exchange rates,

Resurgent Asia: Diversity in Development. Deepak Nayyar, Oxford University Press (2019). © United Nations University World Institute for Development Economics Research. DOI: 10.1093/oso/9780198849513.001.0001

from less than one-tenth in 1970 to almost three-tenths in 2016. Consequently, GDP per capita in in Asia, as a proportion of GDP per capita in the world economy rose from less than one-sixth to more than one-half. However, as a proportion of GDP per capita in the industrialized countries it rose only from one-twentieth to one-twelfth (Table 2.3). It would seem that convergence was significant relative to the world average but modest in comparison with industrialized countries.[1]

Such comparisons are obviously more meaningful at the level of countries rather than the continent. Figures 7.1 and 7.2 compare levels of GDP per capita in the Asian-14, divided into two groups, with levels of GDP per capita in the industrialized countries, in current prices at market exchange rates (in the top panel) and in 1990 international PPP dollars (in the bottom panel), both based on time-series data for 1970–2016. There are two sets of figures, which divide the fourteen countries into two groups, essentially because so many plotted lines in one figure would have been too cluttered for readers to discern the trends.

Figure 7.1 outlines the trends for the three East Asian and four South Asian countries in the Asian-14. At market exchange rates, there was a rapid convergence for South Korea and Taiwan. There was a significant convergence for China and a modest convergence for Sri Lanka beginning around 2000. India, Pakistan, and Bangladesh experienced a slight divergence until 2000 followed by a slight convergence thereafter, so that in 2016 they remained where they were in 1970, with India doing a shade better. In PPP terms, the trends are smoother and clearer. There was a complete convergence for South Korea and Taiwan. There was a significant convergence for China, somewhat less for Sri Lanka, from 2000. India also witnessed a modest convergence starting round 2000, while Pakistan and Bangladesh did not and were at lower levels. The trends over time were similar, though PPP figures smoothen out the fluctuations. The real difference between the two sets of statistics is in the levels. As a proportion of GDP per capita in industrialized countries, the levels of GDP per capita in each of these countries were much higher in PPP terms than at market exchange rates. For example, in 2016, at market exchange rates, GDP per capita in South Korea as a proportion of that in industrialized countries was 66 per cent, whereas in PPP terms, it was close to 100 per cent; the same proportions were 19 per cent and 37 per cent respectively in China, 9 per cent and 29 per cent respectively in Sri Lanka, or 4 per cent and 17 per cent respectively in India.

Figure 7.2 outlines the trends for the six Southeast Asian countries and Turkey in the Asian-14. At market exchange rates, there was a rapid convergence for Singapore, interrupted for some years by the Asian financial crisis, where income per capita exceeded that in industrialized countries from 2010. The convergence was significant for Malaysia and modest for Thailand. There was a slight convergence for Indonesia and Vietnam from around 2005, but almost none for the Philippines. Turkey, at higher income per capita levels, experienced a significant

(a) In current prices at market exchange rates

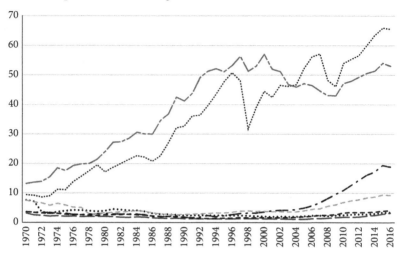

(b) In 1990 International Geary-Khamis PPP dollars

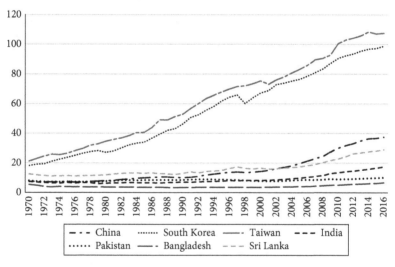

Figure 7.1 GDP per capita for the Asian-14 in East Asia and South Asia: convergence and divergence: 1970–2016 (as a percentage of GDP per capita in industrialized countries)

Source: Author's calculations from UN National Accounts Statistics and GGDC Online Maddison Project Database. See Appendix.

(a) In current prices at market exchange rates

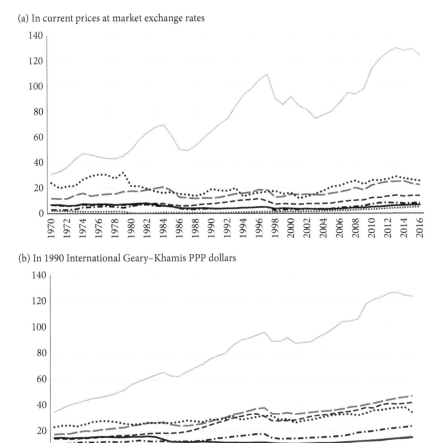

(b) In 1990 International Geary–Khamis PPP dollars

Indonesia — Malaysia — Philippines — Singapore
Thailand — Vietnam — Turkey

Figure 7.2 GDP per capita for the Asian-14 in Southeast Asia and Turkey: beginnings of convergence: 1970–2016 (as a percentage of GDP per capita in industrialized countries)

Source: Author's calculations from UN National Accounts Statistics and GGDC Online, Maddison Project Database. See Appendix.

divergence in the 1980s, from which it recovered after 2000, but did not return to its peak levels of the late 1970s, even in 2016. The trends are clearer in PPP terms. There was more than complete convergence for Singapore. There was significant convergence for Malaysia, Thailand, and Turkey, a modest convergence for Indonesia and Vietnam, but very little for Philippines. Once again, as a proportion of GDP per capita in industrialized countries, the levels of GDP per capita in each of these countries were much higher in PPP terms than at market exchange rates, except in Singapore where the two were almost the same. In 2016, at market exchange rates, GDP per capita in Malaysia as a proportion of that in industrialized countries was 22 per cent, whereas in PPP terms, it was 47 per cent; the same proportions were 14 per cent and 42 per cent respectively in Thailand, 8 per cent and 23 per cent respectively in Indonesia, or 5 per cent and 15 per cent respectively in Vietnam, while these proportions were 26 per cent and 34 per cent respectively in Turkey.

This evidence at country-level for the Asian-14 shows that, in comparison with industrialized countries, during 1970–2016, there was a rapid convergence in South Korea, Taiwan, and Singapore, with a significant convergence in China and Malaysia, also there in Thailand and Sri Lanka but somewhat less. Since 2000, there are beginnings of a modest convergence in Indonesia, and a very slight convergence in India with similar trends in Vietnam and Bangladesh starting from lower income levels. Philippines and Pakistan witnessed a divergence starting 1980 followed by a convergence after 2004, but their situation in 2016 was not quite back to 1980 levels. Turkey, at much higher levels of income than most of the Asian-14, except Singapore, South Korea, and Taiwan, has witnessed some divergence followed by convergence to stay roughly where it was.

It is worth situating these outcomes in the context of hypotheses about convergence in economics. The idea that latecomers to industrialization would, over time, catch up with countries that are leaders in the process of development does exist in the literature on the subject, but in two somewhat different strands. There is one school of thought in unconventional economic history and there is another school of thought in orthodox economic theory.

In economic history, this idea of countries that are followers catching up with leaders can be traced back to Veblen (1915) in his writing about Germany following in the footsteps of England. For the latter, it was characterized as the 'penalty of taking the lead'. This notion was conceptualized further by Gerschenkron (1962), as the 'advantages of relative economic backwardness', to consider the experience of Russia as a latecomer that was subsequently extended to include France, Italy, and Austria.

The essential hypothesis can be summed up as follows. Economic backwardness, relative to others, creates a tension between the actual stagnation and the potential prosperity. The gap provides the economic incentive to catch up, while the political process drives institutional innovation. Wider gaps create stronger incentives to leap forward. State intervention, then, creates the missing initial conditions for growth, to compensate for the scarcities of capital, skilled labour, entrepreneurship and technological capabilities. Greater backwardness needs greater intervention. The mobilization of savings for investment is critical. In Russia, this was done by the State, whereas in Germany the same role was performed by the creation of a banking system that financed industrialization. The greater degree of backwardness in Russia required an emphasis on producer goods rather than consumer goods, larger firms rather than small firms, and capital-intensive rather than labour-intensive technologies. There are benefits to be derived by learning from the mistakes of predecessors, so that economic growth for latecomers is characterized by spurts with periods of high, sometimes exceptional, growth rates. Obviously, the model has limitations, but its generalizations from history, particularly the industrialization experience in Russia, provide analytical insights into how a mix of ideology and institutions, or economics and politics, might foster success in countries that are latecomers to industrialization.

It is no surprise that the Gerschenkron mode of thinking influenced studies in the economic history of other countries, such as Japan.[2] It also led to a quantitative assessment of historical analysis across countries. Abramovitz (1986) tested the hypothesis that productivity growth rates are inversely related to productivity levels so that there is a tendency for convergence over time, to find that there was such a catch up in Western Europe with productivity levels in the United States during the quarter century that followed the Second World War. However, it is recognized that catching up is a function not only of technological opportunities but also of social capabilities, which have institutional dimensions that are slow to develop in economies, firms, and individuals. Hence, every country may not be able to realize its potential for catching up since that depends on its social history and initial conditions. In the long term, convergence is, at best, a tendency that emerges from the average experience of a group of countries, which cannot be oversimplified into generalized outcomes.[3]

In economic theory, modern theorizing about growth in the neoclassical tradition has spawned a large literature on the idea of convergence. This draws inspiration largely from the original contribution of Solow (1956), where the prediction of convergence is at the core of the model. It makes a distinction between unconditional convergence and conditional convergence. In the former, income differences between countries must wither away in the long run, if there is no tendency for countries to have differences in technical progress, savings rates, population growth, and even capital depreciation. In this world, initial conditions do not matter. Indeed, nor does history. Countries converge to their steady states. And these steady states are the same everywhere. Available evidence provides no support for this notion of unconditional, or absolute, convergence.[4] The weaker version of the hypothesis, conditional convergence, argues that countries converge to their own steady states but that these steady states can differ between countries, so that it is possible to control for differences in cross-country parameters such as differences in savings rates or population growth. The essential proposition remains the same. Convergence means a negative relationship between growth rates and initial levels of income per capita. The evidence on this latter formulation is less contrary but not sufficient to sustain any generalization. What is more, it provides no explanation about why the controlled parameters for which the statistical exercises make adjustments in fact differ across countries. It would seem that this orthodox literature reduces the complexity of the growth process to the simplicity of abstract models. It is no surprise that the notion is contradicted by stylized facts about development.

What does experience during the second half of the twentieth century suggest?[5] There are studies that focus on the industrialized countries, the original twenty-one members of OECD, which show that countries with lower levels of GDP per capita in 1950 have typically recorded higher growth rates in GDP per capita until 2000. However, if this sample is enlarged beyond the OECD to seventy countries, including countries from Asia and Africa, evidence for the period from 1960 to 2000 shows that there is no clear relationship between the level of GDP per capita in 1960 and the growth rate in GDP per capita until 2000.[6]

There are also attempts to support the convergence hypothesis by going back to the nineteenth century (Baumol, 1986) and going forward to the twenty-first century (Lucas, 2000), both of which are characterized by the limitations stressed above. The Baumol study of sixteen countries, the richest in the world at the time, from 1870 to 1979, shows a negative relationship between the initial level of GDP per capita and the growth in GDP per capita over the period. But another study for the same period from 1870 to 1979, that added just seven countries to this set of countries, all of which had higher levels of GDP per capita than Japan and Finland, which were at the bottom in the original sample of sixteen countries in 1870, reveals that the negative relationship between the initial level and growth of GDP per capita vanishes (De Long, 1988). It needs to be said that a selective focus on the rich countries that succeeded is an exercise that validates itself through its choice of countries because there were several other countries with higher levels of GDP per capita than Japan in 1870, which were not included possibly because that would have refuted the convergence hypothesis. These exercises could be described as almost tautological.[7] Clearly, studies in retrospect, when the facts about the present are known, should not be used to support generalizations that predict outcomes.

It is clear that hypothesizing about observed outcomes is one thing, but predicting future outcomes is quite another. In reality, there is nothing automatic about convergence, just as there is nothing automatic about growth. Convergence and divergence are often simultaneous. What is more, convergence is often uneven across space and over time. This may be reflected in differences between countries in rates of growth of GDP and GDP per capita but it is also important to analyse the underlying factors.

Therefore, it would be reasonable to ask whether we can learn something about this issue of convergence from the experience of the Asian-14 over the past fifty years. It does not quite validate the convergence hypothesis. In 1970, GDP per capita was among the lowest in China, India, Indonesia, Pakistan, Bangladesh, and

Vietnam. During 1970–2016, the rate of growth of GDP per capita was the highest in China, but it was among the lowest in Pakistan and Bangladesh, while it was in the medium range in India, Indonesia, and Vietnam. In 1970, the level of GDP per capita in South Korea, Taiwan, Malaysia, Philippines, Thailand, and Sri Lanka was in the middle range among the Asian-14. Yet, during 1970–2016, the rate of growth of GDP per capita was high in South Korea and Taiwan, medium in Malaysia, Thailand, and Sri Lanka, and low in Philippines. In 1970, Singapore and Turkey had the highest levels of GDP per capita among the Asian-14. However, the rate of growth of GDP per capita was close to the highest in Singapore and low in Turkey.[8] Clearly, there was no consistent relationship between the initial level of GDP per capita and the subsequent rate of growth of GDP per capita.

2. Inequality between countries

The pace of economic growth in Asia over the past fifty years was uneven across its sub-regions, country-groups and countries. It is no surprise that, over time, this led to an increasing inequality in output shares and a growing divergence in income levels within Asia.

The distribution of GDP between its constituent sub-regions became distinctly more unequal. In the total GDP of Asia, between 1970 and 2016, the share of East Asia rose from less than two-fifths to three-fifths, the share of South Asia fell from almost three-tenths to one-eighth, and the share of West Asia diminished from around one-fifth to one-eighth, while the share of Southeast Asia remained unchanged at about one-eighth (Table 2.3). Consequently, this period witnessed a growing divergence in per capita income levels between East Asia, on the one hand, and Southeast Asia, South Asia, and Asia as a whole, on the other. Of course, per capita income levels remained the highest in West Asia essentially attributable to oil-exporting countries but fluctuated with world oil prices (Figure 2.2).[9]

The discussion in the preceding chapters has sought to focus on the Asian-14, which is a group made up of economies from different constituent sub-regions of Asia. These countries accounted for more than four-fifths of Asia's GDP in both 1970 and 2016 (Table 2.10). Given the overwhelming significance of the Asian-14 in the continent, it is possible to examine divergences in per capita incomes at two levels: in comparison with other country-groups in Asia, and between countries in the Asian-14.

For this purpose, Asia is divided into four country-groups: the Asian-14, the West Asian oil-exporting countries (the high-income countries), the Asian least developed countries (LDCs, the poorest countries) and the residual of other Asian developing countries.[10] Figure 7.3 plots the trends in GDP per capita for each of these country-groups, as a percentage of GDP per capita in the world economy (perhaps the most appropriate denominator to normalize absolute values,

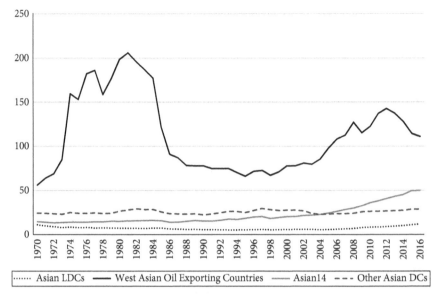

Figure 7.3 GDP per capita of selected country-groups in Asia as a percentage of GDP per capita in the world economy: 1970–2016

Note: The percentages have been calculated from data on GDP per capita in current prices at market exchange rates.

Source: Author's calculations from UN National Accounts Statistics.

spanning a wide range, for a meaningful comparison), based on time-series data for the period 1970–2016. It shows that the West Asian oil-exporting countries had the highest per capita income levels throughout, which fluctuated widely, presumably with world oil prices, but there was no systematic upward or downward trend. There was a clear upward trend with a significant convergence for the Asian-14. However, the LDCs experienced a clear divergence as the income gap between them and the rest widened progressively over time.[11] In contrast, per capita income in the Asian-14, which was distinctly lower than in other Asian developing countries in 1970, converged to their level by 2003 and increased the gap progressively thereafter. It is worth noting that, in 1970, per capita income levels for the Asian-14 and the LDCs were not far apart.

It is just as instructive to compare trends in GDP per capita among the Asian-14. Figure 7.4 plots GDP per capita, in constant 2010 dollars, for each of these fourteen countries, using time-series data, during the period 1970–2016. The emerging divergences are striking. Singapore, South Korea, and Taiwan simply pulled away far ahead of the rest. Turkey and Malaysia, at lower levels, followed to widen the gap vis-à-vis the rest. Thailand, from the mid-1980s, and China, from the mid-2000s, were some distance behind these leaders. Indonesia and Sri Lanka were just slightly better than India and Philippines barely visible at the bottom,

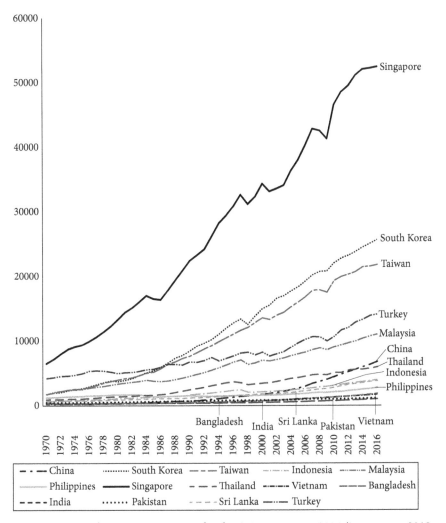

Figure 7.4 Trends in GDP per capita for the Asian-14: 1970–2016 (in constant 2010 US dollars)

Source: Author's calculations from UN National Accounts Statistics.

followed by Vietnam, Bangladesh, and Pakistan that brought up the rear. The widening gaps in per capita income levels among the Asian-14 are clear.

The gap between countries at the top and countries at the bottom in terms of per capita income levels in Asia was far wider than it was among the Asian-14. The ratio of GDP per capita in the richest country to GDP per capita in the poorest country in Asia, in current prices at market exchange rates, was 112:1 in 1970 and 102:1 in 2016.[12] This ratio fell slightly. Yet, it was more than 100:1 almost five decades later. The ratio of GDP per capita in the richest country to the poorest country in Asia, in 1990 international (Geary–Khamis) PPP dollars, was 61:1 in 1970 and 56:1 in 2016.[13] In PPP terms, the difference was less, but the gap was still enormous. It is only to be expected that the absolute differences between countries at the top and at the bottom in income per capita, expressed as multiples, diminish as the numeraire is changed from current dollars to PPP dollars. And end points in such a wide range make the difference seem that much larger. Even so, the enormous gap in levels, which are in fact arithmetic averages, is awesome.

There is another dimension to income inequality between countries. Inequality for all countries in Asia can be disaggregated into two components—inequality *between* countries and inequality *within* countries—by using the Theil index, which can be decomposed to separate the contribution of within-country and between-country inequality to overall inequality between countries.[14] It also has the useful property that the two components are perfectly additive so that there is no residual. Such an exercise in a study on Asia, during the period 1965–2014, shows that between-countries inequality dominated total inequality in Asia, which rose from 1965 to 2005 with dips during 1980–1985 and 1995–2000, to decline a little thereafter. This trend in inequality over time was almost completely driven by the between-countries component.[15] The same study estimated the Theil index, during 1965–2014, for three constituent sub-regions of Asia. It shows that sub-regional inequality was the highest in East Asia and was primarily attributable to the between-countries component, whereas sub-regional inequality, in South Asia (the lowest), and in Southeast Asia (the middle-range), was dominated by the within-countries component.[16] Clearly, much of the income inequality between countries in Asia was attributable to inequality *between*, rather than *within*, countries.

3. Inequality within countries

There are two dimensions of inequality within countries: income distribution between people and economic disparities between regions. This section will focus on the former, while the latter will be considered briefly.

It is exceedingly difficult to find systematic or complete evidence on changes in income distribution, particularly in developing countries. Asia is no exception. The problem lies partly in statistics at the national level, which makes international comparisons that much more difficult. Yet, it is important to sketch a picture, even if it is a rough approximation, of what happened to income inequality within countries in Asia. Table 7.1 puts together evidence on changes in income distribution, measured in terms of Gini coefficients,[17] in the Asian-14, for selected years during the period from 1970 to 2015. It needs to be said that the estimates for China, Malaysia, Singapore, South Korea, Taiwan, and Turkey are based on disposable income, while the estimates for Indonesia, Philippines, Thailand, Vietnam, India, Pakistan, Bangladesh, and Sri Lanka are based on

Table 7.1 Income distribution changes in the Asian-14: 1970–2015 (Gini Coefficients)

	c.1970	c.1980	c.1990	c.2000	c.2010	c.2015
China	27.9	31.0	34.9	43.8	48.1	46.2
South Korea	31.3	30.7	29.5	32.1	31.0	29.5
Taiwan	29.4	26.7	27.2	28.9	31.7	30.8
Indonesia	34.6	35.6	32.0	31.0	38.0	39.5
Malaysia	50.5	48.6	46.2	49.2	46.3	40.1
Philippines	46.0	41.0	43.8	42.8	41.8	40.1
Singapore	40.0	40.7	43.6	48.1	47.2	46.3
Thailand	42.6	45.2	45.3	42.8	39.4	37.9
Vietnam	–	–	35.7	37.0	39.3	34.8
Bangladesh	29.0	25.9	27.6	33.4	32.1	–
India	30.4	32.1	29.7	31.7	35.2	–
Pakistan	31.5	32.3	33.3	30.4	29.8	30.7
Sri Lanka	31.2	37.0	32.5	41.0	37.0	41.0
Turkey	56.8	51.0	44.1	46.0	40.2	39.7

Notes: See Appendix.

Source: UNU-WIDER World Income Inequality Database.

consumption expenditure. Consumption inequality is always lower than income inequality because the rich save and the poor do not, which is relevant for any interpretation of the data in the table.

It is possible to distinguish between the following sets of countries. In Malaysia, Philippines, and Thailand, income inequality was high until *circa* 2000 and diminished somewhat thereafter, while in Turkey income inequality, the highest in 1970, diminished steadily throughout. Yet, in these countries inequality was high even in 2015, when the Gini coefficient was around 40. In fact, in Philippines and Thailand, income inequality would have been higher than what these figures, based on consumption inequality, suggest. In Singapore, inequality was high to start with and increased further over time. China, Indonesia, India, Sri Lanka, and Bangladesh, were characterized by low or moderate income inequality in 1970. Inequality increased most rapidly in China, where the Gini coefficient rose from 28 in 1970 to 48 in 2010, even if it dropped a little to 46 in 2015. During this period, India, Indonesia, Bangladesh, and Sri Lanka experienced a significant increase in inequality, more than the data suggest because the Gini coefficients for these countries relate to the distribution of consumption rather than income. In South Korea and Taiwan, income inequality was relatively low and changed little during 1970–2015, partly because of land reforms that made the initial distribution more equal. In Pakistan, income inequality must have been higher than the moderate consumption inequality that remained unchanged, but its level is puzzling given the most unequal distribution of land. In Vietnam, even consumption inequality was not low, so that its income inequality was on the high side, despite its land reform and communist politics, which is surprising.

For another perspective on inequality within countries, using the same data sources, Table 7.2 traces the changes in the income shares of the top 10 per cent and bottom 50 per cent of the population in each of the Asian-14 for selected years during 1970–2015. Once again, these figures measure income inequality in six countries and consumption inequality in eight countries as specified above. In Malaysia, Philippines, Thailand, and Turkey, the share of the top 10 per cent was far more than the share of the poorest 50 per cent. It was probably the same in China, Indonesia, and Singapore, but the evidence is incomplete. For each of these three countries, there is only one observation during the entire period, which shows that the share of the top 10 per cent was significantly higher than that of the bottom 50 per cent, and the difference was large at 13 percentage points in China.

Table 7.2 Share of top 10 per cent and bottom 50 per cent in the income of the Asian-14

(in percentages)

	1970	1980	1990	2000	2010	2015
Top 10 per cent						
China	–	–	–	32.0	–	–
South Korea	23.0	–	25.7	24.1	24.3	23.8
Taiwan	22.4	24.3	24.2	24.9	25.9	25.2
Indonesia	–	–	–	–	–	31.9
Malaysia	39.8	38.5	36.4	38.4	34.6	–
Philippines	38.8	32.7	34.7	34.1	32.7	31.3
Singapore	–	33.2	–	–	28.0	–
Thailand	34.8	35.5	36.4	33.7	30.7	29.2
Vietnam	–	–	28.6	29.9	30.9	26.8
Bangladesh	–	21.9	24.6	27.9	26.9	26.8
India	–	–	–	28.9	25.8	29.8
Pakistan	–	33.6	27.1	28.5	25.8	26.1
Sri Lanka	–	26.4	27.5	33.2	29.9	32.9
Turkey	44.7	–	35.1	31.9	29.3	33.5
Bottom 50 per cent						
China	–	–	–	19.0	–	–
South Korea	29.5	–	26.7	28.2	27.9	28.4
Taiwan	30.5	29.8	29.8	29.0	27.6	28.8
Indonesia	–	–	–	–	–	24.2
Malaysia	18.1	18.8	20.1	18.2	19.3	–
Philippines	19.9	23.2	21.4	22.2	22.5	23.4
Singapore	–	–	–	–	23.6	–
Thailand	21.8	20.5	20.9	22.0	23.8	24.6
Vietnam	–	–	26.4	25.6	24.2	26.7
Bangladesh	–	32.5	30.8	28.1	28.8	28.6
India	–	–	–	26.1	30.4	27.3
Pakistan	–	23.1	27.9	28.6	30.4	29.8
Sri Lanka	–	28.3	28.8	23.5	26.3	24.4
Turkey	14.2	–	22.1	26.2	24.2	22.0

Note: See Appendix.

Source: UNU-WIDER World Income Inequality Database.

The shares were close together for Vietnam only in 2015 and for Sri Lanka until 2000, apart from which the share of the top 10 per cent exceeded that of the bottom 50 per cent. In India and Pakistan, the shares of the top 10 per cent and bottom 50 per cent were close for most of the years. It was only in South Korea, Taiwan, and Bangladesh that the share of the top 10 per cent was consistently less than the share of the bottom 50 per cent.

The two measures of inequality (Tables 7.1 and 7.2) reveal similar trends, reinforcing each other. There are, however, two points worth noting. In terms of the shares of the top 10 and bottom 50 per cent, Bangladesh was much the same as South Korea and Taiwan. This is misleading, because consumption distribution data underestimate the share of the top 10 per cent in income, who do much of the saving that is not included. In India and Pakistan as well, the roughly equal shares of the top 10 and bottom 50 per cent could be deceptive for the same reason.

It is reasonable to infer that, in most of the Asian-14, income inequality increased in many countries where it was low to start with, and remained at high levels in other countries even if it decreased from higher initial levels. The only exceptions were South Korea and Taiwan where inequality was low to begin with and remained almost unchanged over the entire period. It needs to be stressed that the Asian-14 were neither exceptions nor unusual in this era, as income inequality was driven up by markets and globalization across the world. In fact, there is an extensive literature on the subject which suggests that, even if inequality levels differ across countries, there is a global trend of rising income inequality among people almost everywhere.[18] In a study on income distribution in 135 countries, Palma (2011) finds that the share of the top 10 per cent in national income has risen and the share of the bottom 40 per cent has fallen, while the share of the middle 50 per cent is relatively stable. In a simple metaphor, the rich have become richer and the poor have become poorer.

Given the space constraint, a meaningful discussion on the underlying reasons is not possible here. Suffice it to suggest a few plausible hypotheses. In the earlier stages of development, rapid economic growth led to rising income inequalities. But there was more in this era of markets and globalization. As a consequence of privatization and deregulation, capital gained at the expense of labour everywhere as profit shares rose while wage shares fell. The mobility of capital and the immobility of labour changed the nature of the employment relationship. Structural reforms, which cut tax rates and brought flexibility to labour markets, reinforced this trend. The object of managing inflation was transformed into a near-obsession by the sensitivity of international financial markets, so that governments adopted deflationary macroeconomic policies that squeezed employment. Financial liberalization, which meant a rapid expansion of public as well as private debt, was associated with the mergence of a new rentier class. And the inevitable concentration in the ownership of financial assets probably contributed to a worsening of income distribution.[19]

The other manifestation of rising inequality within countries in Asia was the increase in economic disparities between regions. Economic theory suggests that increasing returns to scale and advantages associated with agglomeration of capital and knowledge could perpetuate, even increase, spatial inequalities.[20] This phenomenon is neither surprising nor altogether new. It is in the logic of markets, accentuated by economic liberalization, which tend to widen regional disparities because there is a cumulative causation that creates market driven virtuous circles or vicious circles. Regions that are better endowed with natural resources, physical infrastructure, skilled labour, or educated people, experience a rapid growth. Like magnets, they attract resources and people from elsewhere. In contrast, disadvantaged regions tend to lag behind and become even more disadvantaged. Over time, the gap widens through such cumulative causation.

This has happened in most countries that have experienced rapid growth. Asia is no exception. There are two dimensions of increasing spatial inequalities: the widening urban–rural income gap and the growing disparities between geographical regions within countries. Almost every country in Asia has experienced the former. Rapid economic growth has also been associated with rising inequality between regions or provinces, particularly in large countries such as China, India, and Indonesia, but also elsewhere. In China, as the focus of reforms shifted to the urban sector, regional inequality rose from the mid-1980s largely due to the widening urban–rural gap, while economic disparities between coastal China in the east and the hinterland in the west mounted from the mid-1990s, largely due to rapid industrialization in coastal areas, supported by government policies, driven by markets and globalization.[21] In India, the urban–rural gap has widened rapidly.[22] Economic reforms led to faster growth in states, mostly in the west and the south, whereas the poorer states in the eastern and central parts of India experienced slow growth.[23] The divide was mostly but not entirely regional. The ratio of per capita income, at constant prices, in the eleven richer states, in comparison with the remaining poorer states, increased from 160:100 in 1980–1981 to 231:100 in 2013–2014.[24] In Indonesia, the economic gap between Java and the other islands was always there. This gap has widened as manufacturing is concentrated around Jakarta and Surabaya in Java.[25] The other islands are still heavily dependent on production and exports of commodities, so that world commodity prices determine incomes.[26] These examples can be multiplied across other Asian countries, where rapid economic growth has been associated with rising regional disparities.

4. Absolute poverty in Asia

In the early post-colonial era, Asia was the poorest continent in the developing world. Even in 1970, its GDP per capita in current prices at market exchange rates was one-fourth that of Latin America and three-fifths that of Africa (Nayyar, 2013). It was also home to an overwhelming proportion of the world's poor outside Sub-Saharan Africa. During 1970–1990, the share of Asia in world GDP registered a modest increase and the divergence in per capita incomes came to an end. This process gathered momentum thereafter, as the share of Asia in world GDP increased rapidly and the beginnings of a modest convergence in per capita incomes became discernible. Did its remarkable economic transformation change the lives of poor people in Asia? The answer to this question is critical and depends upon whether absolute poverty in Asia was reduced significantly in this era of transformations.

It needs to be said that the measurement of poverty poses problems because there are conceptual alternatives, methodological difficulties, and data constraints (Atkinson, 1987). There are three conceptual alternatives.[27] The simplest is the headcount measure, which estimates the proportion of the population or the number of people below a specified poverty line defined in terms of critical minimum needs so that anyone below it lives in absolute poverty. The poverty gap index comes next, which estimates the mean distance below the poverty line as a proportion of the line, so that it determines the proportion of national income that would be needed to lift everyone out of absolute poverty. There is a set of more complex measures, such as the Sen P measure, which uses the Gini coefficient to measure inequality among those below the poverty line (Sen, 1976). Simply put, as the complexity of the poverty measure increases, the data constraints are more while the methodological difficulties are less. Needless to add, international comparisons make the task more difficult.[28]

The headcount measure is the most widely used because it is the simplest to estimate and to understand. Of course, the methodological difficulties associated with it are considerable, which range from choosing poverty lines, through finding appropriate price indices for adjusting poverty lines to inflation over time, to using sample data on household consumer expenditure or family incomes from surveys for estimates at a macro-level. Each is a source of endless debates. Such exercises, which count the poor, are either national estimates or World Bank estimates. There can be little doubt that national estimates are better and more robust in terms of their methodology and database although even these are often much debated on points of disagreement or controversy. World Bank estimates are simply not as good in terms of their methodology or statistical foundations. Some question their method of estimation (Pogge and Reddy, 2010). Others argue that the World Bank underestimates poverty (Kaplinsky, 2005). A few even argue that the World Bank overestimates poverty (Sala-i-Martin, 2006). Of the three arguments, the first is the most convincing, the second is perfectly plausible (as the weight assigned to food and necessities in the consumption basket needs to be larger), while the third is far-fetched.[29] However, World Bank estimates are the only possible source for inter-country comparisons over time and are used here to sketch the contours of a global picture. It must be stressed that the evidence needs to be interpreted with caution.[30]

The latest World Bank estimates use two poverty lines, which are $1.90 per person per day and $3.20 per person per day in 2011 PPP dollars. The first is the mean of the poverty lines in terms of consumption per capita in the poorest fifteen countries of the world, whereas the second is the median poverty line for thirty-two lower-middle-income countries.[31] The usual methodological difficulties that characterize national estimates are also present here. But the object of inter-national comparisons introduces another insofar as national poverty lines are first converted into a common currency using PPP exchange rates and then the international poverty line is converted into the national currency for measuring poverty using the same PPP exchange rates. This problem is accentuated because the changed methodology of World Bank PPP estimates has led to large, some-times inexplicable, increases in income for some countries.[32]

Table 7.3 presents estimates, in terms of the proportion of population and the number of people below the two poverty lines, for each of the Asian-14 as well as Asia, for three selected years 1984, 1996, and 2012, to keep the data within manageable limits. It shows that most of the poor in Asia lived in the Asian-14, and that absolute poverty was concentrated in countries with large populations—China, India, and Indonesia—although the numbers were also significant in Vietnam, Bangladesh, and Pakistan. There was virtually no absolute poverty in Singapore, South Korea, and Taiwan, while it was negligible in Turkey.

Between 1984 and 2012, the proportion of the population below the poverty line of PPP$1.90 per day declined sharply by 70 percentage points in China, 60 percentage points in Indonesia, 34 percentage points in India, and 50 percentage points in Vietnam and Pakistan. By 2012, this percentage was double-digit only in India, Bangladesh, Indonesia, and Philippines, while it was almost negligible in Thailand, Vietnam, and Sri Lanka. The progress was almost as impressive in terms of reducing the number of poor people. China reduced this number by 700 million and Indonesia by 85 million. India was the exception, even though it reduced this number by 140 million because, in 2012, as many as 268 million people were still below this poverty line. In 1984, of all the people in Asia below the poverty line of PPP$1.90 per day, one-half lived in China and one-fourth lived in India, whereas in 2012, one-fifth lived in China and more than one-half lived in India.

However, it is clear that progress was far slower in terms of reducing the proportion of population and the number of people living below the poverty line of PPP$3.20 per day. It is not as if these proportions and numbers did not drop. They did. Yet, in 2012, as much as 36 per cent of the population and 1.5 billion people in Asia lived below this higher poverty line. Of these, 1.14 billion people lived in China, India, and Indonesia. But progress in India was far slower than in China, as this number rose. In 1984, of all the people in Asia below the poverty line of PPP$3.20 per day, 45 per cent lived in China and 29 per cent

Table 7.3 Proportion and number of poor in the Asian-14: 1984–2012

	Below PPP $1.90 per day			Below PPP $3.20 per day		
	1984	1996	2012	1984	1996	2012
(percentage of population)						
China	75.8	42.1	6.5	96.4	73.1	20.2
Indonesia	71.4	47.4	11.7	91.7	79.8	43.5
Philippines	28.1	17.7	12.1	57.6	43.3	38.7
Thailand	19.6	2.3	0.1	43.1	15.2	1.5
Vietnam	52.9	35.5	2.8	80.0	71.2	13.4
Bangladesh	29.9	35.7	14.8	76.7	75.3	52.9
India	54.8	45.9	21.2	85.5	81.1	60.4
Pakistan	62.2	15.9	7.9	87.9	63.4	46.4
Sri Lanka	13.3	8.9	1.9	45.4	41.5	16.1
Turkey	1.7	2.6	0.3	10.9	10.7	3.4
Asia	58.4	37.9	11.4	82.4	68.8	36.2

	Below PPP $1.90 per day			Below PPP $3.20 per day		
	1984	1996	2012	1984	1996	2012
(in millions)						
China	785	512	87	1000	890	272
Indonesia	115	95	29	148	159	108
Philippines	15	13	12	31	32	38
Thailand	9	1	0	21	9	1
Vietnam	37	27	2	56	55	12
Bangladesh	27	43	24	70	91	86
India	409	432	268	638	764	763
Pakistan	61	20	14	86	80	82
Sri Lanka	2	2	0	7	8	3
Turkey	1	1	0	6	6	3
Asia	1563	1293	474	2205	2347	1504

Notes: The number and proportion of poor in South Korea, Singapore, and Malaysia are not included in the table as the estimates are either insignificant or zero. World Bank estimates of poverty do not include Taiwan.

Source: PovcalNet, World Bank, available at http://iresearch.worldbank.org/PovcalNet/.

lived in India, whereas in 2012, 18 per cent lived in China and 50 per cent lived in India.[33]

There is another dimension to this problem. Those who lived below the poverty line of PPP$1.90 per day were the perennial poor who were probably unable to reach the critical minimum even in terms of nutrition. Those who lived below the poverty line of PPP$3.20 per day were the vulnerable poor who might have been able to reach the critical minimum in terms of food and clothing plus some basic needs but not appropriate shelter or adequate healthcare and education. Clearly, the population between the two poverty lines was vulnerable, as any shock such as a bad harvest, high inflation, employment cuts, or an illness in the family, could have pushed them down further into poverty. In fact, this number of the vulnerable poor in Asia rose from 640 million in 1984 to 1030 million in 2012.

The reduction of absolute poverty in Asia in less than three decades is impressive by historical standards. It was fast growth that lifted people out of poverty.[34] Yet, it is striking that poverty persisted as much as it did in Asia despite its rapid economic growth and rising share of world income. Of the total number of people in Asia below both poverty lines, China and India, taken together, accounted for about four-fifths in 1984 and in 2012, even if the distribution of this number between the two Asian giants was reversed. This was despite unprecedented growth rates that were phenomenal in China and impressive in India.

There is a triangular relationship between growth, inequality and poverty, which could provide an explanation. The extent to which economic growth, for any given rate of growth, translates into poverty reduction depends upon what happens to economic inequality. If there is no change in economic inequality, increments in output or income accrue to different segments or fractile groups of the population in exactly the same proportion as the initial income distribution. Thus, a much larger proportion of the increment in income accrues to the rich who are a relatively small proportion of the population, while a much smaller proportion of the increment in income accrues to the poor who are a relatively large proportion of the population. It follows that economic growth translates into a less than proportionate poverty reduction. It is only if economic growth is associated with a reduction in economic inequality that it would translate into a more than proportionate poverty reduction; indeed, reduced inequality could also reduce poverty in the future if it stimulates growth. Of course, the reality was the opposite. Since higher rates of economic growth in Asia were associated with an increase in economic inequality, the poverty reduction must have been less than proportionate. This would explain the persistence of absolute poverty in Asia, although there were substantial reductions in proportions below both the poverty lines, despite the unprecedented rates of economic growth.

5. Well-being of people

The preceding discussion suggests that the remarkable transformation of Asia over the past fifty years led to a significant reduction in absolute poverty. It was also associated with rising economic inequality within countries, except in South Korea and Taiwan. In this context, the fundamental question that arises is whether economic development in countries meant social progress for their peoples. In searching for an answer, it must be recognized that economic growth, while necessary, is transformed into meaningful development if, and only if, it improves the well-being of people, which is both *constitutive* of, and *instrumental* in, development.[35]

The well-being of people is constitutive of development as an end in itself, because the welfare of humankind is the essence of development. The well-being of a person depends upon a livelihood that yields income opportunities to provide for food, clothing, and shelter, just as it depends upon good health and basic literacy, which are essential aspects of decent living conditions. This is not only about meeting basic human needs. It is also about the quality of life, which imparts a sense of dignity to people as individuals. Livelihoods yield an income to support private consumption. For the poor, such incomes might suffice for their necessities, but need to be supplemented by public provision of basic health and education services as social consumption.

The well-being of people is instrumental in development, because employment, healthcare, and education are crucial as means to the end. Employment creation can both mobilize and create resources for development. It mobilizes the most abundant yet underutilized resource, people, for development. It creates resources insofar as it increases the productivity of labour. The same people who constitute resources on the supply-side provide markets on the demand-side in the process of development since wages are incomes. This interactive causation is a potential source of economic growth.[36] Similarly, healthcare, which ensures the physical well-being of people, and education which creates capabilities in people, ensure that productivity of labour is higher than it would otherwise be, thus contributing to economic growth. It is for this reason that Myrdal (1968) emphasized health and education, described as 'investment in man', also characterized by some economists as human capital, as necessary means in the quest for development.[37] In fact, over fifty years, the spread of education in society and the provision of healthcare have been at the foundation of success at development in Asia.[38]

For the continent as a whole, its economic transformation was indeed associated with a social transformation. In Asia, between 1965 and 2016, the infant mortality rate dropped from 160 to twenty-three per 1000 live births, life expectancy at birth increased from forty-nine to seventy-two years, while literacy rates rose from 43 to 82 per cent. There were, of course, differences between constituent sub-regions, as these indicators of social progress improved the most in East Asia and the least in South Asia, with West Asia slightly better than Southeast Asia somewhere in between (Table 2.1). Given the diversity of Asia, however, it is necessary to consider such outcomes at the country level.

Table 7.4 presents compiled evidence on these social indicators of development for each of the Asian-14, in 1970, 1990, and 2016, along with their levels of GDP per capita in real terms for reference and comparison. In this context, it is essential to remember that income per capita is an arithmetic mean while social indicators are also statistical averages, so that neither captures the actual living conditions of people, particularly the vulnerable and the poor. All the same, the evidence in the table shows significant progress in terms of social development. Infant mortality rates plummeted in all countries, although the 2016 levels were still on the high

Table 7.4 Economic and social indicators of development for the Asian-14: 1970–2016

	GDP per capita (in constant 2010 USD)			Infant Mortality Rate (per 1000 live births)			Life Expectancy at Birth (in years)			Adult Literacy Rate (in percentages)		
	1970	1990	2016	1970	1990	2016	1970	1990	2016	1970	1990	2016[a]
China	226	705	6773	79	42	9	59	69	76	61	78	95
South Korea	1817	8454	25686	47	13	3	62	72	82	76	92	97
Taiwan	1775	7636	21803	27	5	4	69	74	79	76	91	98
Indonesia	659	1653	3974	113	62	22	55	63	69	55	82	95
Malaysia	1731	4535	11032	42	14	7	64	71	75	64	83	93
Philippines	1257	1526	2753	55	41	23	61	65	69	85	94	96
Singapore	6514	22430	52458	22	6	2	68	75	83	66	89	97
Thailand	923	2463	5963	71	30	9	59	70	75	75	93	93
Vietnam	266	424	1735	54	37	17	60	71	76	69	88	94
Bangladesh	402	389	1023	148	100	28	48	58	73	22	35	73
India	354	533	1855	142	89	34	48	58	69	34	48	69
Pakistan	465	729	1162	144	106	63	53	60	67	20	43	57
Sri Lanka	711	1128	3832	54	18	8	65	70	75	83	91	91
Turkey	4216	6750	14117	127	55	11	52	64	76	45	79	96

Sources and Notes: See Appendix. The figures on adult literacy rates in the column for 2016, which are the latest available for each of the countries, relate to different years during the period 2010–2015.

side in some. Life expectancy rose by 10–25 years, to reach a level of 70–80 years in most countries. Adult literacy rates increased by 30–50 percentage points, to a range of 90–95 per cent in all except three countries.

There are, inevitably, differences between economies. By 2016, in Singapore, South Korea, Taiwan, Turkey, Malaysia, and China (in descending order of real GDP per capita), infant mortality rates were single-digit, life expectancy was in the range of 75–83 years, and adult literacy rates were 95 per cent or more. Thailand and Sri Lanka came close to the best performers, despite lower income levels. Indonesia and Philippines, at similar income levels, did not make as much progress, except in adult literacy rates. Vietnam at a distinctly lower income level fared better. India, Bangladesh, and Pakistan were the laggards in terms of all three social indicators, with Pakistan doing the worst among the Asian-14. Income per capita levels were important underlying factors, but China, Sri Lanka, and Vietnam—as also Kerala in India—demonstrate that social development is possible even at lower income levels. Even so, there is a connection between the economic and social aspects of development, where the causation runs in both directions. Rising, or higher, per capita income levels are associated with improving, or better, social indicators, and *vice-versa*.

There is a cumulative causation in the interaction between human well-being and economic development, as the constitutive and the instrumental complement each other through positive feedback mechanisms. Improvements in the well-being of people and the process of economic development reinforce each other, dispensing with the need to mediate between economic growth and social development, creating a virtuous circle that makes for success at development. The opposite is also possible. If the process of economic development does not improve the well-being of people, it might create a vicious circle in which neither growth nor development are sustainable, because the feedback mechanisms between the constitutive and the instrumental are absent or negative. Unequal opportunities for people in terms of access to healthcare and education through public provision can only lead to unequal outcomes in terms of incomes and well-being. Such inequality of outcomes can, in turn, accentuate inequality of opportunities. A relative deprivation in the space of opportunities, and the capabilities that such opportunities create or foster, could lead to an absolute deprivation in the space of outcomes, whether employment, incomes, or assets. Similarly, a relative deprivation in the space of outcomes could also lead to an absolute deprivation in the space of opportunities, and hence the capabilities required for engaging with markets. It should be recognized that unequal opportunities and unequal outcomes could also accentuate each other over time across generations.

Conclusion

Rapid economic growth in Asia was associated with an unequal distribution of its benefits among countries and between people. Compared with industrialized countries, the convergence of per capita incomes was rapid in South Korea, Taiwan, Singapore, significant in China and Malaysia, somewhat less in Thailand and Sri Lanka, and negligible elsewhere. The experience of the Asian-14 does not validate the convergence hypothesis, as there was no consistent relationship between the initial level of per capita income and its subsequent rate of growth. There was, in fact, a widening gap in per capita income levels within the Asian-14, while the gap between the richest and poorest countries in Asia was awesome. Much of the income inequality between countries in Asia was attributable to inequality between, rather than within, countries.

Yet, there was also a significant increase in inequality between people within economies (except South Korea and Taiwan), just as there was a marked increase in inequality between regions within countries, both of which were more pronounced in countries that experienced rapid growth. The benefits accrued largely to people and regions that were already well endowed. Even so, rapid growth did lead to a substantial reduction in absolute poverty. During 1984–2012, the proportion of the population below the specified international poverty lines declined sharply everywhere in Asia, more for the lower than for the higher poverty line. However, the absolute number of people below both poverty lines remains large, while the number of people between the two poverty lines, who are vulnerable, rose sharply over this period. The scale of absolute poverty that persists, despite unprecedented growth, is just as striking as the sharp reduction therein. The poverty reduction could have been much greater, were it not for the rising inequality.

Among the Asian-14, rising per capita incomes and improving social indicators—life expectancy and literacy rates—were related and the causation ran in both directions. However, the well-being of people is crucial because it is both constitutive of, and instrumental in, development. Thus, social progress for people and economic development for countries, together, can reinforce each other in a virtuous circle. But unequal opportunities and unequal outcomes, together, can also accentuate each other over time, making matters worse both for the well-being of people and for the development of nations.

8

Asian development and the world economy

This book began with a historical perspective on Asia in the world economy, to set out the initial conditions for development that existed in Asian countries in the early post-colonial era. It then outlined the broad contours of the rise of Asia in the world economy during the past fifty years. Thereafter, it sought to focus on critical issues to analyse the economic transformation of Asia with reference to selected countries—the Asian-14—essentially because, given the enormous diversity of Asia, such an analysis of the development process is possible only at country-level.

It is time to return to the big picture for two reasons: the whole could be different from the sum total of its parts, and economics needs to be situated in the wider context of not just politics but also history and geography. The object of this chapter is to address three broad questions. What has engagement with the world economy meant for Asian development over the past five decades? What are the possible economic implications of this Asian development for the world economy in times to come? What does a transformed Asia imply for international institutions, multilateral rules and global governance? In doing so, it begins with a discussion on the evolution of the relationship between Asia and the world in retrospect, and ends with some reflections on how the present global economic and political conjuncture might shape the relationship between Asia and the world in prospect.

Section 1 considers the evolution of the relationship between Asia and the world during the post-colonial era, in which economics and politics were closely intertwined with geography and history. Section 2 highlights the profound change in the economic significance of Asia and its engagement with the world economy through international trade, investment, and finance to analyse its impact on Asian development. Section 3 examines the possible economic implications, both positive and negative, of rapid growth in Asia for the world economy, industrialized countries, and developing countries. Section 4 explores how the discernible shift in the balance of economic power towards Asia might, or might not, influence structures of governance in the global context. Section 5 touches upon the growing economic problems and mounting political challenges in a changing world that could affect the future prospects of Asian development.

Resurgent Asia: Diversity in Development. Deepak Nayyar, Oxford University Press (2019). © United Nations University World Institute for Development Economics Research. DOI: 10.1093/oso/9780198849513.001.0001

1. Asia and the world

The connections between Asia and the world outside the continent go back at least a millennium if not longer. For our purpose, it would suffice to focus on the historical evolution of this relationship during the period 1500–1950. This could be divided further into two periods: the pre-colonial era (1500–1850), and the colonial era (1850–1950). The earlier period is important as a point of reference and comparison for considering the post-colonial era, beginning *circa* 1950, which was characterized by change and continuity, during the second half of the twentieth century.

The pre-colonial era witnessed two phases.[1] In the first phase (1500–1650), there was a European intrusion into Asia, by Portugal, Holland, England, and France. The Voyages of Discovery—Christopher Columbus to America in 1492 and Vasco da Gama to India in 1498—so described from a European perspective, were a critical turning point. The colonization of the Americas was followed by the age of mercantilism in Europe that witnessed an expansion of trade. Old World trade and New World silver turned out to be powerful complements in stimulating trade flows as Europe paid for its imports of textiles, spices, porcelain, and silks from Asia by imports of silver obtained from America. It was not long before the Portuguese, Dutch, British, and French East India companies integrated Asia into global trade, slowly extending the geographical spread and economic profitability of their operations. Yet, until 1650, Mughal India, Qing China, and Tokugawa Japan were strong centralized states that exercised complete control within their borders. This changed slowly but surely over the next two centuries as the sea power of the European intruders exerted mounting pressure on the land-based Asian economic systems. The European trading companies, confined to the coastal peripheries and their trade to start with, made gradual political intrusions and succeeded in destabilizing the great Asian empires in India and China, threatening and eroding their sovereignty, while the American gunboats of Commodore Perry imposed free trade on an autarchic Tokugawa Japan.

By the mid-nineteenth century, European economic and political intrusions into Asia ultimately transformed a *de facto* colonization into a *de jure* colonial era. There were two sets of factors that drove this process. The first, which exercised a strong influence over the period 1800–1870, was made up of the Industrial Revolution in Britain which spread to Western Europe, the evolution of colonialism in Asia, rather different from that in the Americas earlier, facilitated by the revolution in transport and communication which shrank the world. The economics of colonialism might have begun with the object of extracting the resources for capital accumulation necessary to finance industrialization in Europe. But it was not long before Asia became a source of primary commodities and a market for manufactured goods. The second set, which exercised a strong influence over the period 1870–1914, was made up of the politics of imperialism and the economics of globalization, where the imposition of free trade was followed by a subordination of structures of production.[2] The influence of these factors possibly waned over the period 1914–1950, interspersed as it was by two World Wars and the Great Depression, but the inherent logic of colonialism and imperialism remained unchanged. In this era, there was intense competition among European countries—Britain, France, Holland, and Portugal—in their quest for empires in Asia. Ultimately, Britain captured most of the spoils, but the political rivalry between European powers continued. It extended to the conflicting interests of the British and Russian empires in Central Asia, manifest in 'The Great Game', throughout the nineteenth century.

The end of the Second World War was the beginning of the end for colonialism in Asia, as nationalist movements and revolutionary struggles brought independence to countries. But the economic interests of European countries in the erstwhile colonies—access to resources and markets—remained alive and strong in the post-colonial era, as their governments sought to protect European capital and firms in Asia. The British did not give up hope of superpower status until the Suez crisis of 1956. The French also had illusions until their empire in Africa was intact. However, the pretence was hollow. The outcome of the Second World War led to a recognition, followed by an acceptance, of United States leadership, as both Britain and France relied on its support to manage conflicts that arose in Asia. Apart from vested economic interests of its colonial past, Asia also became the main arena for contesting political ideologies—capitalism versus communism—in the Cold War between the US and the then USSR, as both sought to protect and extend their spheres of influence.

During the post-colonial era, the relationship between Asia and the world was thus shaped by a geopolitics in which economics and politics, juxtaposed with history and geography, were closely intertwined. This had two manifestations: the Cold War in East and Southeast Asia, and the strategic interests in West Asia driven by oil in the Middle East. The political contest between capitalism and communism coincided with the anti-imperialist sentiment of decolonization in Asia.[3] These two political undercurrents shaped each other in a dialectical manner. It evolved into a new relationship between imperialism and nationalism that worked almost in parallel across the ideological superpower divide, since it accommodated decolonization, multiculturalism, and nationalism as much as different shades of ideologies.[4] In this context, it is worth noting that the United States was somewhat different from its European partners, insofar as it had long practised imperialism without colonialism, except in the Philippines, perhaps because it was conscious of its own colonial past. But it was not new to imperialism, as it had created a network of client states in Central America and the Caribbean in the early twentieth century.

The Cold War era witnessed many conflicts and wars in Asia. It began with the war in the Korean peninsula, with support for North Korea from USSR and China and support for South Korea from the US cloaked as a United Nations force, which lasted three years, cost 2.5 million lives, and ended with an armistice that preserved the status quo with a marginally modified divide along the 38th parallel. The First Indochina War between the Viet Minh in the North supported by the USSR and the South supported by France backed by the US, stretched almost eight years, ending with the defeat of the French at Dien Bein Phu in 1954. The Second Indochina War, known as the Vietnam War, began soon after in late 1955, across Vietnam, Cambodia, and Laos, with the South supported by the US and the North supported by the USSR and China, spanned two decades and came to an end with the fall of Saigon in 1975, leading to the unification of Vietnam and the re-emergence of Cambodia and Laos. The First Malayan Emergency during 1948–1960, a war between Commonwealth, essentially British, forces and the Malayan Communist Party, lasted twelve years. A Second Malayan Emergency, an armed conflict between Malaysian federal security forces and the communists, which dragged on from 1968 to 1989, followed. In Indonesia, the largest non-ruling communist party in Asia (PKI), was simply wiped out in an anti-communist purge by the Sukarno government during 1965–1966.[5] Most of these political conflicts in Asian countries, which originated in their own histories of anti-imperialist movements, were driven and sustained by superpower rivalry between the US— supported by Europe, and the USSR—supported by China. The later USSR–China rift also had significant consequences. The Cold War era came to an end during the early 1990s, in politics with the collapse of communism in the USSR, and in economics with the ascendance of the Washington Consensus that led Asian countries to a much greater reliance on markets and openness, although the pace and sequence of economic liberalization differed across economies.

The strategic interests of the US, Britain, and France, driven by the massive oil reserves in the Middle East, shaped geopolitics in West Asia during the post-colonial era. This has been so for seven decades. In the early Cold War era, the US–Britain alliance with Turkey and Pakistan was part of the same geopolitics. Other than that, the old superpower rivalry surfaced only in Afghanistan. The turbulent relationship with Iran provides the most striking example. It began with the coup that overthrew Prime Minister Mossadegh in 1953, who had nationalized oil, and resumed after the Shah of Iran was exiled in 1979, leading the US to impose a trade embargo on Iran from 1995 to 2015, lifted in 2016 and reimposed in 2018. The reprisals against Iraq began with its invasion of Kuwait in 1990, as hostility mounted over time, culminating in the invasion of Iraq by the US, supported by Britain, in 2003, which led to the overthrow of Saddam Hussein who was executed in 2006, and the withdrawal of US forces in 2011, leaving Iraq in complete disarray. Both Iran and Iraq are essentially Shia-muslim countries, whereas Saudi Arabia, which has had strong and consistent support from the

US, is an overwhelmingly Sunni-muslim country. The Sunni–Shia muslim divide is at the core of political conflict in West Asia.

There are three ironies of history embedded in the Cold War era and the political engagement of the Western world with post-colonial Asia that are worth noting. First, while the US and its European allies waxed eloquent about democracy and freedom as their objectives, their patronage was extended mostly to dictators, oligarchies, monarchies, or military regimes, who were not only undemocratic but also neglected the rights, concerns, and aspirations of ordinary people. Second, in East and Southeast Asia, some economies on opposite sides of the ideological divide, which were a part of the conflict in the Cold War era— South Korea, Taiwan, and China—turned out to be star performers, while Malaysia and Vietnam also emerged as success stories in Asian development. But that is not all. The US détente with China in the 1970s began as a counterpoint to Soviet influence in Asia. Four decades later, as China aspires to superpower status, it is perceived as a threat by the US. Third, the strategic geopolitics of the US and its allies in West Asia, which led to interventions in, embargos on, or invasions of, sovereign countries, has ended up in a globalization of Islam, which questions Western hegemony.[6]

2. Asia's engagement with the world economy

The economic transformation of Asia in just fifty years, which is a short timespan in history, has been remarkable. Its growing engagement with the world economy has been an integral part of the process, while the dramatic increase in its relative importance for the world economy is an outcome of that process.

Table 8.1 sets out evidence on the rapidly changing economic significance of Asia in the world during the period 1970–2016, outlining broad contours to sketch the big picture. Its share in world population, always large, ranged between one-half and three-fifths throughout. But its share of world GDP in current prices at market exchange rates more than trebled from less than one-tenth to three-tenths. This increased share in world output was distributed across sectors. Between 1970 and 2016, the share of Asia in world value added in agriculture increased from 40 per cent to 55 per cent. The most striking change was in the sphere of industrialization, as Asia's share in world manufacturing value added, and in world exports of manufactured goods, multiplied tenfold from 4 per cent to 40 per cent.

The increasing relative importance of Asia is also reflected in its engagement with the world economy. Between 1970 and 2016, its share of world merchandise trade, exports, and imports, rose from one-twelfth to one-third. During 1980–2016, its share in world exports of services increased from one-tenth to one-fourth and in world imports of services from roughly one-sixth to three-tenths. In foreign direct investment, between 1990 and 2016, Asia's share in the world inward

Table 8.1 Economic significance of Asia in the world: 1970–2016 (as a percentage of total for the world economy)

	1970	1980	1990	2000	2010	2016
GDP	8.7	11.4	10.2	13.5	22.9	29.9
Population	53.7	55.4	56.8	58.6	58.4	58.0
Value added in agriculture	41.3	41.7	46.0	50.8	53.7	55.2
Manufacturing value added	3.6	5.8	8.3	10.9	32.8	40.8
Manufactured exports	4.0	6.3	15.1	23.8	35.5	39.0
Merchandise exports	8.4	18.0	17.0	24.0	33.0	36.0
Merchandise imports	8.4	13.3	15.9	20.9	30.0	31.9
Exports of services	–	10.3	11.6	16.8	20.8	24.5
Imports of services	–	17.8	14.3	19.7	26.0	28.6
FDI inward stock	–	–	15.5	14.1	14.2	17.2
FDI outward stock	–	–	3.0	8.0	11.8	19.0
Remittances	–	29.9	26.3	34.8	43.1	45.8
Foreign exchange reserves	11.2	21.8	17.5	32.9	54.9	53.9

Source: See Appendix.

stock remained almost unchanged around 15 per cent, while its share in the world outward stock increased from 3 per cent to 19 per cent. Asia's significance in the sphere of international investment was clearly far less than in international trade, and its relative importance increased only as a continent-of-origin but not as a continent-of-destination. The story of remittances was similar to other spheres, as Asia's share in world remittances rose from 30 per cent in 1980 to 45 per cent in 2016. For a continent that was traditionally foreign-exchange-scarce, the rise in Asia's share of world foreign exchange reserves from one-tenth in 1970 to more than one-half in 2016 is striking. Much of this accumulation occurred, as a strategic form of self-insurance, after the Asian financial crisis in 1997, because countries sought to reduce their vulnerability to international financial markets and dependence on multilateral financial institutions like the IMF.

In the past century, no country on the path to development has industrialized without manufacturing steel, cement, and automobiles. Table 8.2 presents evidence compiled from different sources on the top ten producing countries of motor vehicles, motorcycles, steel, and cement in the world in 2016. It shows the emergence of Asian countries as major producers in each of these sectors. In motor vehicles, China, India, and South Korea are among the top ten,[7] whereas in motorcycles nine among the top ten are Asian countries. In steel, China, India, South Korea, and Turkey are among the top ten. Japan (an industrialized country in Asia, hence not part of this study) is also among the top ten in motor vehicles, motorcycles, and steel. In cement, China, India, Iran, Turkey, Vietnam, Indonesia, and Saudi Arabia are among the top ten. Of course, large countries such as China and India have large markets. Yet, in 1970, it would have been difficult to imagine

Table 8.2 Top ten producing countries in the world for selected sectors, 2016

Rank	Motor Vehicles		Motorcycles		Steel		Cement	
	Country	Number Millions	Country	Number Millions	Country	Million Tons	Country	Million Tons
1.	China	28.1	India	18.8	China	787	China	2410
2	United States	12.2	China	16.6	Japan	105	India	290
3.	Japan	9.2	Indonesia	6.6	India	96	United States	86
4.	Germany	5.7	Thailand	2.4	United States	79	Iran	78
5.	India	4.5	Pakistan	1.4	Russia	71	Turkey	77
6.	South Korea	4.2	Brazil	1.3	South Korea	69	Vietnam	70
7.	Mexico	3.6	Taiwan *	1.1	Germany	42	Indonesia	63
8.	Spain	2.9	Philippines	0.8	Turkey	33	Saudi Arabia	61
9.	Brazil	2.2	Japan	0.5	Brazil	31	Brazil	60
10.	France	2.1	Malaysia	0.4	Italy	23	Russia	56

Sources: See Appendix.

* Taiwan, Province of China

that, in less than fifty years, so many Asian countries, even China and India, would be among the top ten producing countries of the world in these manufacturing sectors. This is another dimension of Asia's increasing relative importance in the world economy.

The earlier chapter on openness and industrialization has already analysed several aspects of Asia' engagement with the world economy. Therefore, to avoid repetition, the discussion that follows in this section will focus only on the aspects of international trade, international investment, and international finance not considered so far.

During 1970–2016, the increase in Asia's share of world merchandise trade, both exports and imports, was phenomenal. This was an outcome of increasing openness that was also conducive to industrialization and development wherever it was a part of co-ordinated trade policy and industrial policy that used openness in a strategic manner. Asia was always an importer of traditional services such as shipping, transport, and insurance, which were closely associated with merchandise trade, but there was an expansion in financial, communication, business, and technological services driven by the needs of industrialization and development. The quarter century starting 1990 witnessed the emergence of Asia as an exporter of services, in both traditional and non-traditional domains (particularly software and information technology but also business and financial services) as countries diversified structures of production. The same period witnessed an integration with global production networks that was reflected in trade flows.

However, it is seldom recognized that a significant proportion of merchandise exports and imports were trade within Asia rather than trade with the rest of the world. Table 8.3 disaggregates the merchandise exports and imports of Asia into primary products and manufactured goods, making a distinction between country-groups as destinations for exports and sources of imports, for three selected years: 1995, 2005, and 2016. It shows that, between 1995 and 2016, the share of intra-Asia trade rose from 45 per cent to 63 per cent in total exports of primary products and from 41 per cent to 50 per cent in total exports of manufactured goods, so that there was a corresponding decline in the share of trade with the rest of the world, which was the residual. Over the same period, the share of intra-Asia trade remained unchanged at 46–47 per cent in total imports of primary products, but rose from 36 per cent to 56 per cent in total imports of manufactured goods leading to a sharp decline in the corresponding share of the rest of the world which was the residual. A further disaggregation of the rest of the world into other Asia (made up of Japan and Israel, the industrialized countries in the region) and the non-Asian rest of the world is also revealing. It shows that during 1995–2016, the share of other Asia (essentially Japan) dropped from 37 per cent to 15 per cent in total exports of primary products and from 20 per cent to 11 per cent in total exports of manufactured goods. There was little change in the share of other Asia (essentially Japan) in total imports of primary products, but this

Table 8.3 International trade within developing Asia and with the rest of the world: 1995–2016 (in percentages)

	1995				2005				2016			
	Intra-Developing Asia Trade	Trade with the rest of the world	Of which, Other Asia	Total Trade	Intra-Developing Asia Trade	Trade with the rest of the world	Of which, Other Asia	Total Trade	Intra-Developing Asia Trade	Trade with the rest of the world	Of which, Other Asia	Total Trade
Merchandise Exports												
Primary products	44.8	55.2	37.3	100.0	51.2	48.8	28.1	100.0	63.4	36.6	15.4	100.0
Manufactured goods	41.4	58.6	19.8	100.0	44.5	55.5	15.8	100.0	50.0	50.0	11.2	100.0
Merchandise Imports												
Primary products	47.1	52.9	9.1	100.0	56.2	43.8	6.5	100.0	46.3	53.7	7.6	100.0
Manufactured goods	36.2	63.8	40.3	100.0	50.5	49.6	25.8	100.0	56.4	43.6	16.5	100.0

Note: Primary products are defined as SITC 1+2+3+4+68. Manufactured goods are defined as SITC 5+6+7+8 less 68. Other Asia is made up of Japan and Israel, the industrialized countries in Asia, which are included in the rest of the world.

Source: United Nations, UNCTAD Stat.

share dropped sharply from 40 per cent to 17 per cent in total imports of manufactured goods. It is clear that Japan was the hub for, and at the apex of, trade within the Asian continent in 1995. But its significance diminished rapidly over the next two decades. Table 8.3 also confirms that the decline in the share of the rest of the world in the trade of Asian developing countries was attributable to the contraction in the share of Japan. It would be reasonable to infer that China has replaced Japan as the hub of intra-Asian trade in the period from 1995 to 2016, while intra-Asia trade has become more significant. It is possible that intra-Asia trade is overestimated by the double-counting implicit in the assembly operations of global value chains, for which China is the important hub, as the final goods are exported from Asia largely to industrialized countries.[8]

It is not possible to distinguish between foreign direct investment that is intra-regional within developing Asia and outside with the rest of the world because statistics are unavailable. Foreign direct investment in Asia induced manufactured exports and supported industrialization, particularly in Southeast Asian countries and China, especially where there was integration into global production networks, but this was not so everywhere as it was shaped by the decisions of transnational corporations together with policies in host countries. In a few countries, such as Singapore, Malaysia, Thailand, and Vietnam—somewhat less in Indonesia and Philippines—this importance was reflected in magnitudes of the inward stocks of foreign direct investment as a proportion of GDP, and inward flows for foreign direct investment as a proportion of gross capital formation. In other Asian countries, the significance was more qualitative and quantitative. In any case, Asia's modest share of inward stocks of foreign direct investment in the world changed little during 1990–2016.

Foreign direct investment by Asia is the more interesting story. The outward stock of foreign direct investment by Asian countries rose from $67 billion in 1990 to $4960 billion in 2016, while average outflows rose from $45 billion per annum during 1991–2000 to $342 billion per annum during 2009–2016.[9] This was concentrated mostly in six economies—China, Singapore, South Korea, Taiwan, India, and Malaysia—in descending order of magnitudes of both stocks and flows. Taken together, the six accounted for about three-fifths of both the outward stock in 2016 and the average annual outflow during 2009–2016 for Asia.[10] It would seem that these countries created their own transnational corporations. Among the top 100 non-financial multinational enterprises from developing countries and transition economies ranked by value of financial assets, in 2016, as many as sixty-seven were from Asia, once again dominated by the aforesaid six.[11] Of these, the distribution was twenty-two from China, twelve from Hong Kong, eight from Singapore, six each from India, South Korea, and Taiwan, five from Malaysia, with one each from Philippines and Thailand. Among the top twenty, there were thirteen from Asia, of which the distribution was four from China, two each from India, South Korea, and Singapore, and one each from Taiwan, Hong Kong, and Malaysia.[12] In contrast, among the top 100 non-financial multinational enterprises from all economies in the world, in 2017, ranked by the value of their financial assets, there were only eight from Asia, of which four were from China, two from South Korea and one each from Taiwan and Hong Kong, but there were none in the top twenty while there were only four in the top fifty.[13]

The economic stimulus and strategic motive for the internationalization of firms from Asia were provided by a wide range of underlying factors driving the process, which differed across countries, sectors, and firms. There were two paths—foreign direct investment and acquisitions of firms—in host countries. The liberalization of economic policy regimes and a greater access to financial markets were enabling developments. But Asian firms could not have become international without the capacity and the ability to compete in the world market. The attributes of Asian firms that created these capabilities were embedded in their past and emerged over a much longer period of time while learning to industrialize. Traditional foreign direct investment was motivated either by sourcing for primary commodities or by seeking market access for manufactured exports. But the motives for mergers and acquisitions were different. The conventional literature argues that mergers or acquisitions are driven by the oligopolistic or monopolistic power of firms, which seek to source inputs or capture markets through ownership and control rather than trade. However, Asian firms often used this path not as a means of exploiting existing comparative advantage but as a means of realizing or augmenting potential comparative advantage. In fact, the objectives ranged from sourcing raw materials and market access for exports, to horizontal or vertical integration, delivery of services, capture of international brand names, and access to technology in the world of manufactured goods.[14] Such outward foreign investment has implications, both positive and negative, for firms at a micro-level, industries or sectors at a meso-level, and home countries at a macro-level.[15] There also exists a literature on transnational corporations from developing countries.[16] It would mean too much of a digression to enter into a discussion here. Yet, it is clear that outward foreign investment by Asia, which was concentrated in six countries, reflected their success in industrialization.

In contrast with international investment, however, Asia's engagement with the world economy, through international finance, did more harm than good and, on balance, its consequences for development were negative. Capital account liberalization meant an integration into international financial markets that was premature. Governments were tempted by the prospects of capital inflows in the form of portfolio investment, which could finance current account deficits and help accumulate foreign exchange reserves, or short-term and medium-term borrowing abroad by domestic firms, which could finance investment at low interest rates. But the fact that such capital flows could be withdrawn on demand, making them footloose and volatile, was just ignored, while the underlying macroeconomic dilemmas fraught with risk were simply not recognized. An economy needs a high interest rate with a strong exchange rate to sustain portfolio investment in terms of profitability and confidence. This erodes the competitiveness of exports over time and enlarges the trade deficit. Larger trade deficits and current account deficits require larger portfolio investment inflows, which beyond a point undermine confidence and create adverse expectations even if the government keeps the exchange rate pegged. But when a stifling of exports does ultimately force an exchange rate depreciation, confidence may simply collapse and lead to capital flight. This can precipitate a crisis leading to a run on domestic currencies.

The frequency and intensity of such crises in countries that are integrated into international financial markets has increased with the passage of time.[17] The Asian financial crisis in 1997–1998 had nasty consequences that imposed huge social costs on economies and people in East and Southeast Asian countries.[18] Its implications persisted long after the crisis. Capital account liberalization reduced degrees of freedom in the use of macroeconomic policies, which could not be deployed to maintain levels of output and employment. Expansionary fiscal and monetary policies, large government deficits to stimulate domestic demand, or low interest rates to stimulate investment, could no longer be used because of an overwhelming fear that such measures could lead to speculative capital flight and a run on the national currency. Thus, there were longer-term consequences too, as growth slowed down and investment levels slumped. In fact, Indonesia, Malaysia, Philippines, Thailand, success stories in Asian development until then, had not quite recovered even a decade later; to some extent, even South Korea, Taiwan, and Singapore lost their earlier momentum.[19]

3. Economic implications for the world

Asian development over the past fifty years is likely to have significant implications for the world in many spheres. The following discussion simply seeks to focus on the possible economic implications of rapid growth in Asia, if it is sustained, which is bound to exercise considerable influence—positive or negative—on future prospects for the world economy, industrialized countries, and developing countries.

Growth in lead economies drives growth elsewhere in the world by providing markets for exports, resources of investment, finances for development, and technologies for productivity. Britain in the nineteenth century and the United States in the twentieth century are classic examples of these transmission mechanisms that worked as engines of growth for the world economy. And, despite its diminished dominance, the United States continues to perform that role.[20]

It is simply not possible, at least not yet, to think of Asia as an engine of growth in the four dimensions mentioned above, except perhaps as a market for exports. Its economic size is not as large as its population suggests, since income levels are relatively low. The Asian giants—China and India—do have a potential. However, China cannot stimulate growth elsewhere even as a market for exports because of its big current account surplus and massive trade surplus, which have diminished now but are still in surplus. India cannot do so, despite it substantial current account deficit and large trade deficit, because its share of world GDP is much smaller than that of China.[21] For this reason, contrary to the belief of some who propagated the decoupling hypothesis, Asia could not drive world economic recovery in the aftermath of the global financial crisis despite the resilience of its larger economies. In fact, South Korea, Taiwan, Malaysia, Thailand, and Singapore witnessed a sharp slowdown in growth during the Great Recession in industrialized countries. Even so, in future, implications for the world economy could be positive if, as the old engine of growth slows down, Asia emerges as a supporting driver of growth. China, which supports but does not yet lead growth in the world economy,[22] obviously has the potential to stimulate growth.

The impact of rapid growth in Asia on the industrialized countries could be either positive or negative. The focus is often on the negative. But there is also the positive.

There are three reasons why the impact may be negative. First, rapid economic growth in Asia may worsen the terms of trade for industrialized countries. The burgeoning demand in China and India could drive up the prices of primary commodities in the world market. At the same time, rising wages in Asia could drive up prices of labour-intensive manufactured goods in the world market. Both could turn the terms of trade against industrialized countries. However, the consequences would be easy to absorb since the process would be spread over a long period of time.[23] Second, for the industrialized countries, Asian countries could emerge as potential locations to compete for investment. This may happen if firms from the industrialized countries, whether the United States or Europe, relocate production in Asia. But this is not likely to happen on a significant scale, for such investment is not a zero-sum game in an expanding world economy and technological change might even reverse the process. Third, the economic rise of Asia may lead to a downward pressure on employment levels and real wages in the industrialized countries. It needs to be said that this concern is somewhat exaggerated. It is important to recognize that the stagnation in real wages and the high levels of unemployment in the industrialized countries are attributable to the nature of technical progress, which has replaced several unskilled workers with a few skilled workers, the reduced bargaining power of workers (and trade unions) because of labour market deregulation, and the impact of macroeconomic policies which have sought to maintain price stability at the expense of full employment. The source of these problems lies within the industrialized countries and not in their trade with developing countries.[24] Moreover, in the long run, productivity increase in Asia would be followed, after a time, by a commensurate increase in real wages,[25] as it has in many of these countries.

It is just as important to recognize that rapid economic growth in Asia may have a positive impact on the industrialized countries.[26] First, starting from low levels of income per capita and high income elasticities of demand, higher incomes associated with rapid growth would create expanding markets for exports from industrialized countries. Second, Asian supplies of cheap manufactured goods could help reduce inflationary pressures in industrialized countries, thereby enabling them to maintain higher levels of output and employment than would otherwise be possible. Third, Asia could be a source of new technologies that could help extend production possibility frontiers and consumer possibility frontiers in the industrialized economies. In fact, this is already happening in mobile phones, solar panels, high-speed trains, and possibly in artificial intelligence and nano-technology.

Rapid economic growth in Asia could have a positive impact on developing countries elsewhere if it improves their terms of trade, provides appropriate technologies, and creates new sources of finance for development, whether investment or aid.

It is clear that, for some time to come, the positive impact on developing countries would be transmitted through an improvement in their terms of trade.[27] Rapid economic growth in China and India, is bound to boost the demand for primary commodities exported by developing countries. The reasons are simple enough. Both China and India have large populations. Further, in both countries, levels of consumption per capita in most primary commodities are low, while income elasticities of demand for most primary commodities are high. The commodities boom might have come to an end, for now, but this underlying factor remains. In the long run, such burgeoning demand will almost certainly raise prices of primary commodities in world markets and thereby improve the terms of trade for developing countries.

The positive impact of Asia on developing countries through the other potential channels of transmission is not as clear. In principle, it is possible that Asia would develop technologies that are more appropriate for the factor endowments and the economic needs of developing countries. But it is too early to come to a judgement on this matter. Similarly, some Asian countries—China, India, and South Korea—are already sources of finance for development. Their foreign aid programmes, particularly those of China and India in Africa, are significant but not without their problems.[28] Their contribution in terms of foreign direct investment in developing countries was, to begin with, limited mostly to strategic sourcing of oil and minerals, especially for China, but this is not so for South Korea and India.[29]

The emergence of Asia in the world economy could also have a negative impact on developing countries if it provides them with competition in markets for exports or as destinations for investment. At this juncture, China is clearly the largest supplier of labour-intensive manufactured goods in the world market. Other Asian economies also sell such manufactures, even if they are not as large as China. There can be little doubt that manufactured exports from Asia span almost the entire range, including resource-based manufactures, in which other developing countries could have a potential comparative advantage. Hence, it is plausible to argue, though impossible to prove that, on balance, Asia could possibly have a negative impact on manufactured exports from other developing countries, particularly in Africa, which have to compete with them for export markets in industrialized countries.[30] This can change if and when China, followed by India, Thailand, Indonesia, and Vietnam vacate their space in the international trade matrix, in much the same way as other latecomers to industrialization in Asia—South Korea, Taiwan, and Singapore—vacated their space in the market for simple labour-intensive manufactures for countries that followed in their footsteps. It is not likely, at least in the medium term, because these countries have large reservoirs of surplus labour at relatively low wages not only in the rural hinterlands but also in the urban informal sectors that might continue for some time to come.[31] Of course, this is no more than a plausible hypothesis about possible future developments, which cannot be tested. Given that Asian countries are now among the most attractive destinations for transnational firms seeking to locate production in the developing world, it is once again plausible to suggest, though impossible to prove, that foreign direct investment in these economies might be at the expense of developing countries elsewhere.

The less discernible but more significant negative impact of Asian development on developing countries lies in barriers to change in the traditional specialization in production reflected in the existing patterns of trade between industrializing Asia and the rest of the developing world that are dominated by an exchange of manufactured goods for primary commodities. This is, in fact, characteristic of China's pattern of trade with countries in Africa and Latin America, which are predominantly sources of primary commodities, or natural resources, and markets for manufactured goods, for China. Such traditional patterns of specialization might even have been a source of deindustrialization in Africa and Latin America.[32] Indeed, this could perpetuate the dependence of some African and Latin American countries on exports of primary commodities without creating possibilities of increasing value added before export or entering into manufacturing activities characterized by economies of scale. Such path-dependent specialization can only curb the possibilities of structural transformation.[33] Asia can support industrialization in developing countries only if there is a successful transition from a complementary to a competitive pattern of trade, so that inter-sectoral trade is gradually replaced by intra-sectoral or intra-industry trade.

4. The global context

It is necessary to recognize that the importance of Asia in the world would be shaped not only in the sphere of economics but also in the realm of politics. Its emerging significance in the world economy is attributable in part to its share in world population and world income and in part to its engagement with the world economy through international trade, international investment, inter-national finance, and international migration.[34] Even so, in the economic sphere, Asia's potential importance in the future far exceeds its actual importance at present. In the realm of politics, however, Asia's importance is more discern-ible at the present juncture, which is attributable in part to its size and in part to its rise.

The beginnings of a shift in the economic and political balance of power in the world are discernible. This is partly a consequence of the increasing significance of developing countries in the world economy, during the last quarter of the twen-tieth century, driven largely by the rise of Asia (Nayyar, 2013). The process gathered momentum in the early 1990s and reached a critical threshold in the early 2000s. And rapid economic growth in Asia continued to outpace that in industrialized countries. This might not have been enough for cognition of a changing reality. It was the conjuncture that made an enormous difference. The financial crisis that surfaced in the United States in late 2008, and the Great Recession that followed in its aftermath, was the deepest crisis in capitalism since the Great Depression. This eroded the triumphalism of capitalism that followed the collapse of communism in 1991, and reinforced the shift in the balance of power somewhat more towards the developing world.

The international economic and political architecture for the world was created seventy-five years ago at the end of the Second World War by the victors. It was led by the United States, with support from Britain. The UN was born in 1945. The IMF and the World Bank were established in 1944 by the West. The GATT (the General Agreement on Tariffs and Trade)—a treaty among countries that were contracting parties, rather than an institution—was created in 1948, after the US Congress did not ratify the Havana Charter that had proposed an Inter-national Trade Organization with a comprehensive mandate. At the time, most Asian countries were European colonies. Japan was under US occupation forces. Asia, the poorest yet most populous continent in the world, had no voice, let alone influence, in shaping the international institutions and multilateral rules that were created for global governance.[35]

It is no surprise that the system created then was born with a democratic deficit. In terms of representation, the principle of one-country-one-vote in the UN and the GATT was not the same as the principle of one-person-one-vote in a political democracy, but it was more representative than the principle of one-dollar-one-vote in the IMF and the World Bank. In terms of decision-making, the system was even less democratic. Where some countries had more votes than others, while some were not even represented, the system was obviously undemocratic. In a world of unequal partners, however, even one-country-one-vote cannot ensure a democratic mode of decisions. Much depends on how decisions are made. The right of veto in the UN Security Council is explicitly undemocratic. But decision-making by consensus, since voting is not the norm, as in the GATT, now the WTO, or the UN General Assembly, can also be undemocratic, if there is bilateral arm-twisting or if a consensus is hammered out among a small sub-set of powerful players, while most countries, often silent spectators, are in the end a part of the apparent consensus.[36]

The world has changed beyond recognition over seventy-five years. But these institutions are essentially the same apart from minor modifications or accommodations. In the UN, China alone is a permanent member of the Security Council with a right to veto. And it is also a member of the P-5. There is no such representation for any other country from the developing world, whether Asia, Africa, or Latin America, or even industrialized countries such as Japan and Germany. An expansion in the permanent membership of the UN Security Council, with or without a veto, is imperative. In the World Bank and the IMF, apart from Japan, only India and China from Asia are permanent members of their Executive Boards. The industrialized countries may be the principal shareholders but the developing countries are the principal stakeholders, interest payments from whom provide much of the income of the Bretton Woods twins. Of course, Europe was a stakeholder until around 1960, and became a stakeholder once again after the global financial crisis in 2008. The WTO, established in 1995, is better in terms of representation, but remains undemocratic in terms of decision-making.

Asia is home to almost 60 per cent of the people in the world and accounts for 30 per cent of world GDP. Of the 193 member countries in the UN, and 164 member countries in the WTO, excluding Japan, as many as thirty-six are from developing Asia, in addition to eight transition economies from Central Asia and West Asia that are also member countries. In the IMF and World Bank, developing countries from Asia have 21.6 per cent and 21.4 per cent, respectively, of the total voting rights. Of this, just four countries—China, India, South Korea, and Indonesia accounted for 10 per cent of the voting rights in the World Bank and 11.4 per cent of the voting rights in the IMF.[37] Yet, Asia's voice and influence in these international institutions is disproportionately small compared with its present economic or political significance in the world. This inequity is embedded in history, but the time has come to reform existing institutions so as to reduce their democratic deficits and make them more representative of the present rather than the past world.

But that is not all. The existing institutions cannot suffice for global governance in this changed world. There are emerging needs like co-ordinating global macroeconomic management, regulating international financial markets, governing transnational corporations, and creating a framework for cross-border movements of people. In addition, it has become essential to promote 'global public goods' such as a sustainable environment, and to control 'global public bads' such as international crime or trade in drugs, arms, people, or organs, and international tax evasion. The necessary institutions, rules, or practices that are missing will need to be put in place sooner rather than later. Asian countries will have to be proactive, and not just reactive, in international negotiations to reform existing institutions and create missing institutions in the global context.

The economic rise of Asia, and the associated increase in its political significance, suggest that its quest for its place in the world is now more plausible than it would have been even twenty-five years ago. However, it is by no means either automatic or assured. It would require collective action because a large group of countries with mutual interests is much more likely to be heard in terms of voice, and to be effective in terms of influence, than single countries by themselves. There will always be some conflict of interest, particularly in economic spheres, among developing Asian countries, but there will also be areas where it should be possible to find a common cause and accept trade-offs. In this context, it needs to be said that intra-regional economic co-operation already in place, as in ASEAN, or in ASEAN partnerships with China, India, and South Korea in the form of free trade agreements, or in bilateral trade agreements, are useful stepping stones. So is inter-continental co-operation among developing countries and transition economies. For example, institutions such as the New Development Bank, established by the BRICS, which are a source of potential competition for multilateral financial institutions, might force them to be less coercive towards smaller or poorer countries in terms of conditionality imposed, but cannot be a substitute for reforming existing institutions. Similarly, arrangements for regional co-operation in Asia that create practices, frameworks, or rules in domains where there are missing institutions could be valuable building blocks, but these cannot be a substitute for international collective action.

On the whole, it would seem that Asia has a considerable potential for articulating a collective voice in the world of multilateralism. Co-ordination and co-operation among Asian countries carries significant possibilities for exercising influence on multilateral institutions, which could reshape rules and create policy space for countries that are latecomers to development, and help create missing institutions. Such co-ordination and co-operation, which is in the realm of the possible, has not surfaced. There could be two reasons for the minimal co-ordination and co-operation so far. For one, in the early stages of change, these countries might not have recognized their potential for exercising collective influence. For another, their relationship with each other may be characterized more by rivalry, economic or political, and less by unity. There is a visible rivalry between the Asian giants, China, an aspiring superpower, and India, a large developing country. In addition, there are serious concerns among Asian countries about the phenomenal rise and growing power of an overwhelming China. It is obviously difficult to predict how reality might unfold in times to come. Even so, it is important to recognize that once large Asian countries become major players, which China already is, and India could join the league in times to come, there is a clear and present danger that they might opt for a seat at the high-table with industrialized countries, for the pursuit of national interest rather than the spirit of solidarity among developing countries or the logic of collective action. The way forward might be an Asian Union, a political formation that comes together for common political purpose in the global context, but does not engage with issues that could lead to a conflict of economic interests between countries. Of course, such a separation is easier said than done.

5. A changing world

As the second decade of the twenty-first century draws to a close, it is an awkward if not difficult economic and political conjuncture for the world, which makes the future uncertain. It provides a sharp contrast with the preceding twenty-five years, when the economic transformation of Asia gathered momentum. The world economy in that era of markets and globalization, which was conducive to, and supportive of development in Asia, was very different from what it seems now. And it is plausible to suggest that the unfolding realities discernible in the world are a consequence of seeds sown in the preceding era, which might be coming to an end.

Among countries, the benefits of prosperity created by markets and globalization accrued primarily to a small number of countries in the industrialized and developing worlds. In the former, it was the United States and a few countries in Western Europe, while Southern Europe and the transition economies in Eastern Europe lagged behind. In the latter, it was twelve from the Asian-14 that created the initial conditions, combined with institutions and policies. Even among this small group, some did better than others, while China was the star performer. Latin America stayed roughly where it was, but much of Africa experienced some regress. In countries that were winners, most of the benefits accrued to small proportions of their populations. Hence this era witnessed a marked increase in economic inequality between people within countries, and between the rich and the poor in the world. There was an alarming increase in the share of the super-rich (top 1 per cent) and the ultra-rich (top 0.1 per cent) in national income everywhere, as income distribution worsened across the world. It is no surprise that inequality in wealth was even more pronounced as the distribution of assets became far more unequal.[38] Such mounting inequalities, which are ethically unacceptable and politically unsustainable, are responsible for widespread discontents among people across the world.

The strains are beginning to surface as the world is confronted with increasing economic problems and political challenges. These have begun to disrupt the smooth sail of globalization. Economic growth has slowed down almost everywhere. Some exceptions apart, recovery from the global financial crisis and the Great Recession is slow, uneven and fragile. Unemployment levels in most industrialized countries are high, while there has been no significant increase in real wages for a large proportion of those employed. In many developing countries, poverty persists despite the reduction in absolute poverty, while economic inequality has been rising.

There is a political backlash. Economies might have become global. But politics remains national or local. Citizens want governments to be responsive to their concerns, instead of worrying about international financial markets or global economic obligations. And, in democracies, governments are accountable to their people. The most common manifestation of this political backlash is resurgent nationalisms riding on populist or chauvinist sentiments. Political processes and election outcomes across the world—United States, Europe, Latin America, and Asia—reflect this phenomenon. In industrialized countries, there is a growing disillusionment with mainstream political parties, challenged by populist anti-establishment movements, nationalist-populist political parties, or far-right xenophobic populist leaders, who exploit fears about openness in immigration and trade as a threat to jobs. The story is similar in developing countries as nationalist-populist political parties and leaders challenge or oust incumbent governments, exploiting religious beliefs, ethnic divides, or rampant corruption. Such political mobilization of economic discontents unleashes chauvinisms and nationalisms that seek to exclude the perceived other.

There is an irony in this situation. The political backlash in industrialized countries, in the perceptions of people excluded from prosperity, might be partly attributable to the rise of Asia in the world economy. It could be well among the factors underlying the mounting pressures for protectionism in trade and restrictions on immigration. The political backlash in Asia might also be partly attributable to the rising economic inequalities within and between countries. The future prospects of Asia in the world economy will be shaped, *inter alia*, by how this politics of discontents unfolds.

Conclusion

During the post-colonial era, the relationship between Asia and the world was shaped by a geopolitics in which economics and politics, juxtaposed with history and geography, were closely intertwined. East and Southeast Asia became the main arena for contesting political ideologies—capitalism versus communism—in the Cold War, while West Asia was the stage where strategic interests, driven by oil, played out. Both were associated with conflicts and wars that shaped trajectories of development.

Three specific aspects of Asia's emerging engagement with the world economy, with implications for development, deserve mention. More than one-half of Asia's merchandise trade is within developing Asia. Its relative importance increased over time, and after 1995 China replaced Japan as the hub for such trade. The share of Asia in the stock of outward foreign direct investment in the world, during 1990–2016, rose from one-thirtieth to one-fifth. This internationalization of Asian firms—concentrated in China, Singapore, South Korea, Taiwan, India, and Malaysia—is based on the acquisition of capabilities over a much longer period while learning to industrialize. However, capital account liberalization and premature integration into international financial markets has done more harm than good, with negative consequences for development.

Rapid economic growth in Asia has implications, both positive and negative, for the world, industrialized countries, and developing countries. It is not, at least yet, an engine of growth for the world economy. For industrialized countries, it might worsen their terms of trade, but it could provide them with expanding markets, cheap manufactured goods and new technologies. For developing countries, it could improve their terms of trade, provide finances and technologies for development, but it could also have an adverse impact on their industrialization prospects.

The international economic and political architecture for global governance was created around 1945. Asia had no voice in that process. The shifting balance of power provides Asia with an opportunity to influence the reform of existing institutions and the creation of missing institutions. However, co-ordination and co-operation among Asian countries, to exercise collective influence, has not surfaced yet, possibly because their relationship is characterized by rivalry—economic and political—rather than unity. At the same time, economic problems confronting the world have led to a political backlash in the form of resurgent nationalisms across countries, creating an international milieu very different from the preceding quarter century when the economic transformation of Asia gathered momentum. The uncertain future is a challenge.

9

Contemplating the future

The objective of this book is to analyse the phenomenal economic transformation of Asia, which would have been difficult to imagine, let alone predict, fifty years ago. In doing so, it provides an analytical narrative of this remarkable story of economic development, situated in historical perspective, and an economic analysis of the underlying factors, with a focus on critical issues in the process of, and outcomes in, development. Given the size and the diversity of the continent, the aggregate level is not always appropriate. Thus, the study disaggregates Asia into its four constituent sub-regions, and further into fourteen selected economies: China, South Korea, and Taiwan in East Asia; Indonesia, Malaysia, Philippines, Singapore, Thailand, and Vietnam in Southeast Asia; Bangladesh, India, Pakistan, and Sri Lanka in South Asia; and Turkey in West Asia. These economies, described as the Asian-14, account for more than four-fifths of the population and income of Asia.

This chapter concludes. Section 1 outlines the contours of change to recapitulate the essentials of the transformation in Asia, and highlights the major analytical conclusions that relate to the debates on development. Section 2 considers prospects, in terms of opportunities and challenges, for countries that have led the process so far and for those that might follow in their footsteps. Section 3 reflects on the future, with reference to the past, to speculate how the changed international context, and new challenges on the horizon, might shape, or be influenced by, development in Asia over the next twenty-five years.

1. Asian transformations: some lessons

The underdevelopment and development of Asia has its historical context. In 1820, two centuries ago, Asia accounted for two-thirds of world population and almost three-fifths of world income, where just two countries, China and India, accounted for one-half of world population and world income. The colonial era witnessed a precipitous decline in this economic significance. By 1962, the share of Asia in world population diminished to 50 per cent, while its share of world income plummeted to 15 per cent. For China and India, taken together, these shares plunged to 35 per cent and 8 per cent respectively. The outcome was the 'Great Divergence'. Income per capita in Asia, as a proportion of that in the West, dropped from one-half in 1820 to less than one-tenth in 1962. This was associated

Resurgent Asia: Diversity in Development. Deepak Nayyar, Oxford University Press (2019). © United Nations University World Institute for Development Economics Research. DOI: 10.1093/oso/9780198849513.001.0001

with the 'Great Specialization', which meant that Western Europe produced manufactured goods while Asia produced primary commodities. Consequently, the share of China and India in world manufacturing production collapsed from 47 per cent in 1830 to 5 per cent in 1963. The decline and fall of Asia was attributable to its integration with the world economy, through trade and investment, shaped by colonialism and driven by imperialism. The industrialization of Western Europe and the deindustrialization of Asia were, in fact, two sides of the same coin, which had a devastating impact on China and India.

The transformation of Asia over the past fifty years, reflected in its demographic transition, social progress, and economic development, has been phenomenal. In 1970, it was the poorest continent in the world, marginal except for its large population. By 2016, there was a striking change in its relative importance. Its share of world GDP rose from less than one-tenth to three-tenths, while its income per capita surpassed that of developing countries and converged towards the world average income level, although the convergence was at best modest compared with industrialized countries because the initial income gap was so enormous. Growth in GDP and GDP per capita in Asia was much higher than in the world economy, industrialized countries, and the developing world, both Africa and Latin America. Over this period, the share of Asia in world industrial production jumped from a miniscule 4 per cent to more than 40 per cent. Its share of world merchandise trade rose from one-twelfth to one-third. East Asia was the leader and South Asia was the laggard, with Southeast Asia in the middle, while progress in West Asia did not match its high income levels.

There were pronounced structural changes in the composition of output and employment, which led to a sharp decline in the share of agriculture, a significant increase in the share of the industrial sector, and a much greater increase in the share of the services sector everywhere. The increase in the share of the manufacturing sector was less than that of the industrial sector and not uniform across countries. Even so, industrialization was impressive. During 1970–2016, for Asia, and the Asian-14, the share of the manufacturing sector in GDP rose from one-tenth to one-fourth. There was also a marked increase in the degree of openness of economies in Asia, reflected in their growing engagement with the world economy through international trade, investment, and finance.

Rising per capita incomes were associated with a transformation in social indicators of development, as infant mortality rates fell sharply, while life expectancy and literacy rates rose sharply, everywhere. Rapid economic growth also led to a massive reduction in absolute poverty across countries in Asia. However, the absolute number of people below the specified international poverty lines remained large, while the number of people between the two poverty lines, who are vulnerable, rose to more than 1 billion. The scale of absolute poverty that persists, despite unprecedented growth, is just as striking as the sharp reduction therein. The poverty reduction could have been much greater but for the rising inequality. Inequality between people within economies rose everywhere, except for South Korea and Taiwan. Inequality between economies also rose. There was, in fact, a widening gap in per capita income levels within the Asian-14, while the gap between the richest and poorest countries in Asia was awesome.

Development outcomes were unequal not only for people but also for countries in Asia. Among the Asian-14, in just fifty years, South Korea, Taiwan, and Singapore joined the league of industrialized economies. China was a star performer throughout, making impressive strides in development from 1990. The economic dynamism of Indonesia, Malaysia, and Thailand waned after the Asian financial crisis. The growth performance of India, Bangladesh, and Vietnam was most impressive during the past quarter century, although the South Asian countries were laggards in poverty reduction and social indicators. In comparison, the performance of Sri Lanka was respectable, while that of Turkey was average, but that of Pakistan and Philippines was relatively poor.

This book suggests some important analytical conclusions that contribute not only to our understanding of development in Asia but also to the debate on development. A few are highlighted here.

It is, of course, necessary to recognize the diversity of Asia. There were marked differences between countries in geographical size, embedded histories, colonial legacies, nationalist movements, initial conditions, natural resource endowments, population size, income levels, and political systems. The reliance on markets and the degree of openness in economies varied greatly across space and over time. The politics, too, ranged widely from socialism through State capitalism to capitalism, from authoritarian regimes to political democracies, and from one-party states to multi-party systems. Outcomes in development, which differed not only between countries at any point in time but also within countries over time, were diverse. There were different paths to development, because there were no unique solutions, or magic wands. Hence, there were choices to be made, which were shaped by a complex mix of economic, social and political factors in the national context, where history mattered. Yet, despite such diversity, there are discernible patterns, pointing to substantive analytical lessons that emerge from the Asian development experience.

The economic transformation of Asia in the past fifty years provides a sharp contrast with the decline and fall of Asia in the colonial era during the preceding 150 years. Unlike Latin America and Africa, most Asian countries did have a long history of well-structured states and cultures, which were not entirely destroyed by colonialism. Thus, for Asian countries, political independence, which restored their economic autonomy and enabled them to pursue national development objectives, was an important underlying factor and driving motivation in their quest for catching up.

In a radical departure from the stagnation in colonial times, over the past fifty years, rates of economic growth in most of the Asian-14 were unprecedented in history. Investment and savings, which rose rapidly and were much higher than elsewhere in the developing world, were drivers of growth on the supply-side. The spread of education in society and the provision of healthcare for people, which contributed to human capital formation, along with the creation of a physical infrastructure, which eased constraints on the supply-side, were also sustained drivers of growth in countries that were success stories. On the demand-side, growth was primarily investment-led and private-consumption-expenditure-led. The interaction between the supply-side and the demand-side in the Asian-14 suggests that there was a virtuous circle of cumulative causation, where rapid investment growth coincided in time with rapid export growth, leading to rapid GDP growth. But this did not happen in countries where rapid investment growth and rapid export growth did not coincide, or where growth in both was slow.

It is clear that many of the Asian-14 did not follow orthodox prescriptions of balanced budgets and price stability for macroeconomic management. In fact, they were heterodox in their objectives and policies. Their primary macroeconomic objectives were economic growth and employment creation. Their macroeconomic policies were also much broader and more versatile in their use of policy instruments. Their success in maintaining high growth rates increased their degrees of freedom, which enabled them to finance government deficits and raise sustainable levels of government borrowing, while making higher inflation rates politically more acceptable, none of which would have been possible if economic growth was slow.

The transition from a situation, *circa* 1970, when the agricultural sector was dominant to a situation, in 2016, when the services sector was dominant, was far from uniform in the Asian-14. In earlier stages of development, such labour transfer between sectors was growth-promoting. In later stages of development, productivity increase within sectors was growth-promoting. The relative importance of these two drivers differed across countries, as well as sectors, and changed over time. However, apart from South Korea, Taiwan, Singapore, and perhaps, Malaysia, the process of structural transformation in the Asia-14 is uneven and incomplete. The share of agriculture in employment far exceeds that in output in most countries, while its productivity levels are much lower than those in non-agricultural sectors. There is a loss of dynamism in manufacturing for industrialization in some countries and premature deindustrialization in others. It is necessary to address the neglect of agriculture and renew the emphasis on manufacturing, just as it is essential to exploit the synergies and complementarities between manufacturing and services. Economic growth cannot be sustained and structural transformation cannot be completed even if one of three sectors is a weak link in the chain.

Economic openness has performed a critical supportive role in Asian development, wherever it has been in the form of strategic integration with, rather than passive insertion into, the world economy. However, analysis of the industrialization experience in the Asian-14 shows that openness, while necessary, was not sufficient. It was conducive to industrialization only when combined with industrial policy. Clearly, success at industrialization in Asia was driven by sensible industrial policy that was implemented by effective governments. In future, however, technological learning and technological capabilities are also essential to provide the foundations for sustaining industrialization.

Governments performed a critical role, ranging from leader to catalyst or supporter, in the economic transformation of Asia spanning half a century, while their willingness and ability to do so depended on the nature of the state, which in turn was shaped by politics. The state and the market are complements rather than substitutes and the two institutions must adapt to each other in a co-operative manner over time. Success at development in Asia was about managing this evolving relationship between states and markets, by finding the right balance in their respective roles, which also changed over time. Countries, where governments did not, or could not, perform this role, and were unable to evolve their role vis-à-vis markets, lagged behind in development. The Asian experience suggests that efficient markets and effective governments, in tandem, provided the way forward to development.

The developmental states in South Korea, Taiwan, and Singapore, for whom Japan was the role model, which could co-ordinate policies across sectors over time in pursuit of national development objectives using the carrot-and-stick to implement their agenda, led the economic transformation of these countries, enabling them to become industrialized nations in just fifty years. However, the nature of these states was an outcome of circumstances in history and conjuncture that were very specific to them. China emulated these developmental states, in an altogether different political context with much success, and Vietnam has followed, two decades later, on the same transition path, as both countries have strong, one-party communist governments, with clear objectives, that could co-ordinate and implement policies. It is not possible to replicate these states elsewhere in Asia. Even so, for the other countries in the Asian-14, where states were less effective in implementing their agenda, governments did manage to introduce economic policies and evolve institutional arrangements that were conducive to industrialization and development. In these countries, it is only institutionalized checks and balances that can make governments more development-oriented and people-friendly. There are possibilities within political processes. There are also non-state institutions, or state institutions other than governments, that can perform this role. This is obviously more feasible in democracies than in authoritarian regimes.

Among the Asian-14, rising per capita incomes and improving social indicators—life expectancy and literacy rates—were related and the causation ran in both directions. However, the well-being of people is crucial because it is both constitutive of, and instrumental in, development. Thus, social progress for people and economic development for countries, together, can reinforce each other in a virtuous circle. But unequal opportunities and unequal outcomes, together, can also accentuate each other over time, making matters worse both for the well-being of people and for the development of nations.

2. Opportunities and challenges

Is it, then, possible to speculate or hypothesize about the prospects of Asia in the world economy over the next twenty-five years? The past is relevant. And so is the present. But the future is not just about linear extrapolations. Yet, growth scenarios for the future are based on assumptions about growth rates, even if adjusted over time, based on the past. In attempting such projections, most exercises, at different levels of sophistication, are based on models of capital accumulation and productivity growth combined with demographic scenarios, allowing for inter-country differences in economic and institutional factors.[1]

Long-term macroeconomic forecasts of GDP at market exchange rates, by the Economist Intelligence Unit, suggest that the top ten economies in the world, in 2050, in descending order would be China, United States, India, Indonesia, Japan, Germany, Brazil, Mexico, Britain, and France. The same forecast estimates that, by 2050, the GDP at market exchange rates for each of the top three (China, United States, and India) will be larger than that of the next five (Indonesia, Germany, Japan, Brazil, and Mexico) put together. [2] Of course, GDP per capita in the Western countries will remain far higher than that in the Asian or Latin American countries.

There are long-term projections, by OECD, of GDP in constant 2010 PPP US dollars, for major countries, which show that the share of Asia (excluding Japan) in world GDP will be 50 per cent in 2030, 53 per cent in 2040 and 55 per cent in 2050.[3] This suggests that the share of Asia (excluding Japan) in world GDP in 2050 will return to its level in 1820 when it was 56 per cent.[4] The same OECD projections are available for China and India. The share of China in world GDP will be 27 per cent in 2030, returning to its level around 1850, as it was 33 per cent in 1820 and 17 per cent in 1870. The share of India in world GDP will be 16 per cent in 2040, returning to its level in 1820, when it was 16 per cent.

It might be instructive to extend such comparisons of the future with the past to per capita income levels in Asia. Maddison statistics provide information on the share of Asia in world GDP and world population during 1820–2008, while OECD projections provide statistics on the share of Asia in world GDP and UN projections provide statistics on the share of Asia in world population during 2030–2050. The share of Asia in world GDP divided by its share in world population, is the equivalent of the ratio of Asian GDP per capita to world GDP per capita. This ratio was 0.87 in 1820, 0.63 in 1870, 0.43 in 1913, 0.30 in 1950, where it stayed until 1973, rising to 0.54 in 2001 and 0.66 in 2008.[5] This ratio will rise to 0.88 in 2030, 0.98 in 2040, and 1.04 in 2050.[6] Therefore, in 2030, per capita income in Asia, relative to the world, will return to its level in 1820. By 2040, Asian per capita income would be the same as world per capita income, returning perhaps to the situation *circa* 1750.[7]

It is no surprise that such exercises project a much higher share for Asia, or China and India, in world GDP, in 2030, 2040, and 2050. Of course, these projections suggest broad orders of magnitude rather than precise predictions. Even so, such statistical exercises highlight the power of compound growth rates. Rates of growth do indeed matter. If GDP grows at 7 per cent per annum, national income doubles in ten years. If GDP per capita grows at 5 per cent per annum, per capita income doubles in fourteen years. In fact, growth rates have been in this range for many countries in the Asian-14 for the past twenty-five years. Even if somewhat lower growth rates are sustained, their cumulative impact over time can only accelerate the catch-up process. However, growth is not simply about arithmetic. Indeed, it is about more than economics. Therefore, in reflecting on the economic prospects of Asian countries in the next twenty-five years, it is necessary to consider the opportunities they could exploit and the challenges that they might face.

The economic determinants of potential growth suggest that several countries in Asia may be able to sustain high rates of economic growth for the next twenty-five years, perhaps longer, for the following reasons. Their large population size is expected to increase further, which makes labour a source of growth, and their income levels are low, which means that the possibilities of growth are greater. Their demographic characteristics, in particular the high proportion of young people in the population, which would mean an increase in their workforce and savings rates for some time to come, are conducive to growth, provided these countries can harness the demographic dividend through education that creates capabilities among people. Their wages are significantly lower than in the world outside, which is an important source of competitiveness for some time to come. Their social infrastructure for education and healthcare, as well as their physical infrastructure, remains less than developed despite the progress so far, so that further improvements are bound to reinforce the momentum of growth. However, these sources of growth will not be available for economies that have led the transformation of Asia, particularly South Korea, Taiwan, and Singapore. China might reach that stage soon. In fact, East Asia, including China, will witness a contraction in its labour force, so that growth will have to be sustained by a more efficient utilization of capital through technological progress based on investment in R&D. The potential for growth, in terms of the above-mentioned factors on the supply-side, will be greater in South Asia than in Southeast Asia or West Asia. Among the Asian-14, India, Indonesia, Vietnam, and Bangladesh could realize this potential. Turkey and Sri Lanka are at a much later stage in their demographic transition but are better endowed in terms of social indicators and human resource development. Malaysia and Thailand need to revive their economic dynamism, which has not recovered since the Asian financial crisis.

There is also an opportunity on the demand-side. Rising income levels and improving living standards in Asian countries, particularly those with relatively low per capita incomes, will drive domestic demand that could act as a stimulus to growth within these economies. At the same time, it would also create expanding markets for developing Asia as a whole. The economic integration of Asia over the past twenty-five years, through trade and investment fostered by global value chains, facilitated by the internationalization of Asian firms and institutional arrangements for trade liberalization, might enable the rest of the continent to benefit from such rising demand. This opportunity might be enhanced further if there is an economic recovery in the industrialized countries.

The opportunities are, however, juxtaposed with formidable challenges. The most important among these, perhaps, is the combination of persistent poverty, rising inequality, and jobless growth. Economic growth in Asia has led to a massive reduction in absolute poverty. During 1984–2012, the number of people below the poverty lines of PPP $1.90 per day and PPP $3.20 per day were reduced by 1.1 billion and 0.7 billion respectively. Yet, in 2012, there were 0.5 billion and 1.5 billion people, respectively, still below these poverty lines. Poverty reduction would have been much greater were it not for rising inequality between people within countries. The problem was accentuated by growing disparities between regions within countries. Employment that provides livelihoods is the only sustainable means of reducing absolute poverty. However, in the Asian-14, during 1991–2016 as compared with 1971–1990, both GDP growth and employment growth were significantly slower, while the relationship between them was weaker as productivity rose. Slower GDP growth was always associated with even slower employment growth, but rapid economic growth was not always associated with commensurate employment growth. Apart from the success stories—South Korea, Taiwan, and Singapore—the poverty–inequality–unemployment nexus persisted in many of the Asian-14. Of course, absolute poverty in Asia might be minimal by 2030. But the problems of rising economic inequality and inadequate employment opportunities, unless addressed, will mount. This challenge is not simply economic. It is also social and political. And, ultimately, economic growth can be sustained if it eradicates poverty, reduces inequality, and creates employment. Such inclusive growth is the only sustainable way forward for Asian countries lagging behind the leaders, because it would enable them to mobilize their most abundant resource, people, for the purpose of development, and reinforce the process of growth through cumulative causation.

There is another challenge that Asian countries might face in their continuing quest for development, which is the middle-income trap. It describes a situation where a country makes the transition from low-income to middle-income status but gets stuck there, unable to move from middle-income to high-income status.

The first stage in this transition is driven by abundant cheap labour and high investment rates. Growth slows down as these factors wane in their impact. And industrialization stops at labour-intensive goods as wages rise. The second stage in the transition requires higher productivity levels and a capacity to innovate. This, in turn, requires nurturing managerial and technological capabilities, fostering vertical diversification in production processes, encouraging technological-upgrading, inducing technological-learning, and creating R&D capacities. The attainment of these strategic long-term objectives depends on the quality of industrial policy and of human resources. Among the Asian-14, South Korea, Taiwan, and Singapore have already made this transition. China is on the way. Turkey has a potential. But Malaysia, Thailand, and Indonesia, success stories until the late 1990s, have not managed to move to the next stage yet. India, together with Vietnam and Bangladesh, in the low-income stage at present, which have the potential for continuing rapid economic growth, must begin to address this potential constraint now in a strategic long-term perspective.

3. An Asian century?

The whole is different from the sum total of the parts. The future prospects of Asia in the world economy are likely to be influenced by, just as they are likely to shape, the international context. Five questions arise. Do recent changes in the global political economy have any longer-term implications for Asia? What is the likely impact of the profound technological changes on the horizon for development in Asia? What are the possible environmental consequences of the rise of Asia? How would the leading industrialized countries respond or adjust to the erosion of their economic dominance and political hegemony? Is this going to be an Asian century? These are complex questions that could have important implications for how the future unfolds. But it is difficult to provide answers, let alone predict outcomes, in a world with so many uncertainties and imponderables. In any case, such a task is beyond the scope of this book. Even so, these are touched upon briefly if only to recognize their significance.

As the second decade of the twenty-first century draws to a close, it is an awkward if not difficult economic and political conjuncture for the world, which makes the future uncertain. It provides a sharp contrast with the preceding three decades, when the transformation of Asia gathered momentum. The world econ-omy in that era of markets and globalization, which was conducive to economic development in Asia, was very different from what it seems now. The strains are beginning to surface as the world is confronted with mounting economic prob-lems and political challenges. These have begun to disrupt the smooth sail of globalization. Economies might have become global. But politics remains national. There is a political backlash in the form of resurgent nationalisms riding on populist or chauvinist sentiments. In industrialized countries, nationalist-populist political parties, or far-right xenophobic populist leaders, exploit fears about openness in immigration and trade as a threat to jobs. In developing countries, nationalist-populist political parties or leaders, challenge or oust incumbent governments, exploiting religious beliefs, ethnic divides, or rampant corruption. Such toxic nationalisms are attempting to create identities with divides, whether insider–outsider or majority–minority, seeking to exclude the perceived other. This identity politics is often just a disguise for populist leaders or dominant groups seeking to capture or retain political power. It is no surprise that they also fuel protectionist sentiments. There is an irony in this situation. The political backlash in industrialized countries, in the perceptions of people excluded from prosperity, might be partly attributable to the rise of Asia in the world economy. The political backlash in Asia might be partly attributable to the rising economic inequalities within and between Asian countries. The future prospects of Asia in the world economy will be shaped, *inter alia*, by how this economics and politics of discontents unfolds. In this changed world, more of the same might be difficult, even unlikely, for Asia. The future, then, might not be shaped by the past. It will be shaped, in important part, by how Asia responds to these challenges.

There are technological changes, already on the anvil or on the horizon, which include advanced robotics, artificial intelligence, 3-D printing, and the Internet of Things, which could have far-reaching implications for the location of production, manufacturing-led development, the future of manufacturing, employment possibilities, especially for low-skilled labour, and the future of work. This could be particularly important for Asia in the next twenty-five years, as latecomers attempt to follow in the path of the early-birds hoping to use labour-intensive manufactured exports as a springboard for their industrialization and development. Global value chains that have engaged in offshoring production through assembly operations or component manufacture in Asia, could be partly replaced by a re-shoring or relocation of production in the United States or Western Europe. Thus, developing countries in Asia might lose employment either if activities are moved out or if labour is displaced by the adoption of new technologies. It is too early, and there is not enough evidence yet, for any systematic judgement. Recent research suggests that robots are likely to replace labour in the manufacturing or assembly of consumer electronics, computers, and automobiles, but are not likely to do so in traditional labour-intensive manufactured exports from Asia such as textiles, clothing and footwear, or resource-based manufactures.[8] The latter are a significant proportion of manufactured exports from Asia. It must also be recognized that such technological changes are nothing new, and have been part of the process of evolution of the world economy over the past two centuries. In the past, such game-changing technical progress, dubbed as industrial revolutions when they occurred, led to similar fears, but outcomes turned out to be much better than expected. The contraction of employment in some sectors was followed, with time lags, by an expansion of employment in other sectors. In the long run, technological progress extends both production-possibility frontiers and consumption-possibility frontiers. The appropriate response, then, is reskilling workers and rethinking goods. If some existing opportunities are lost because of technological change, Asia will need to create new opportunities in their place.

The environmental consequences of rapid growth in Asia are bound to be significant. This issue has not been discussed in the book. And there is a vast literature on the subject.[9] Given the complex issues, it would mean too much of a digression to enter into a discussion here. Yet, it is essential to recognize the problem. The energy needs of the two mega-economies, China and India, are enormous. This is not surprising, as levels of consumption per capita are low and income elasticities of demand are high. Much the same is true for Indonesia and the many medium-size countries in the Asian-14. The negative potential is obvious as CO_2 emissions rise, which could turn into a constraint on growth. But there is also a positive spin that is possible. Growing consciousness about environmental stress and climate change, among people and countries in Asia, could lower thresholds of tolerance on what are acceptable levels of pollution. It may also increase the availability of clean technologies. There could, then, be some shift from energy sources that use fossil fuels to those that reduce carbon emissions. Thus, the environmental constraint on growth may not turn out to be binding. Even so, the problem of developing sustainable non-carbon energy sources does present a major challenge to patterns of economic growth in the long term. History is not much help in thinking about this dilemma. The Industrial Revolution transformed production possibilities and social relations but it was based on a shift to fossil fuel energy sources.

The rise of Asia, beginning *circa* 1970, which gathered momentum after 1990, has slowly chipped away at the economic dominance and political hegemony of the United States and Western Europe. It was reinforced, for some time, following the collapse of communism in the USSR and Eastern Europe in 1991. But the triumph of the new unipolar world was diluted, if not shaken, in the aftermath of the global financial crisis. The shift from the G-7 (sometimes G-1) to the G-20, in 2008, even if symbolic, was an implicit recognition of change. Just one decade later, the geopolitics of the world has changed profoundly because of unexpected developments. Under President Donald Trump, it would seem that *Pax Americana* is in voluntary decline. Indeed, a withdrawal syndrome is discernible, as the Unites States appears to be relinquishing its leadership role in the world. This could, of course, change. At the same time, however, the decline of Western Europe, in a relative rather than absolute sense, is discernible. There is an irony in this emerging situation, juxtaposed as it is with the rise of Asia, when compared with the past of Western Europe and Asia in history over the past two centuries. But that is not all. The globalization of Islam is also seeking to challenge Western hegemony. There is an important lesson that emerges from history. Dominant powers are reluctant to cede economic or political space to newcomers. But the emergence of new centres of production in economics and new centres of power in politics does have a profound effect on hegemonic powers in terms of political economy. Such processes are always slow and the present conjuncture represents an interregnum because the resurgence of Asia, except for China, is not large enough to shift the hegemonic balance. Asian countries together could, even at this stage, exercise some collective influence through co-ordination and co-operation. For this purpose, however, China and India would need to set aside their rivalry and find ways to work together. Yet, the beginnings of change with some erosion of Western hegemony are visible. This is a complex phenomenon that will be played out over a long period of time. Both the duration and the outcome of this process are unpredictable.

The answer to the four questions posed above depends, in significant part, on how Asia responds to its challenges, which would also shape the answer to the fifth question. The past, and the present, both suggest that Asia will perform well in terms of economic growth over the next twenty-five years. Its share in world GDP will continue to rise, and its GDP per capita will converge to the world average, but the income gap in relation to industrialized countries will narrow slowly and persist much beyond 2050. Of course, this growth can be sustained for long only if it is inclusive, and its benefits accrue a much larger proportion of populations. In contemplating the future, we can learn from experience. In the late 1960s, pessimism about the development prospects for Asia was widespread. Yet, the past fifty years turned out to be so completely different from what was expected. Surely, then, the present conjuncture, difficult as it might seem, should not lead to the conclusion that the future for Asia, and the world, is dark. On the whole, there is more reason for optimism than for pessimism. If there is turbulence ahead, it will not go unchallenged. In fact, Asia is much better placed to confront challenges than it was fifty years ago. Its responses now, as much as then, will shape its future. In this process, the accountability of governments to their peoples will make a real difference. Political systems in Asian countries that are diverse do not often pass this litmus test. All the same, there are many more countries with democratic systems than there were fifty years ago. Democracies in Asia are flawed. Even so, they are democracies, with some institutionalized checks and balances that could function as self-correcting mechanisms. The growing political consciousness among people as citizens, together with their aspirations for better lives, empowered by digital technologies and demonstration effects, will make governments more accountable over time. In sum, even if the future is uncertain, the past and the present provide reason for optimism.

The answer to the fifth question needs to be contextualized in history. The early nineteenth century was a turning point in the world. It was the beginning of the end of Asia's overwhelming significance in the world economy. And it was the beginning of the rise of Europe, in particular Britain, to dominance in the world. The early twentieth century was the next turning point. It was the beginning of the end of Britain's dominance. And it was the beginning of the rise of the United States to dominance in the world. This process spanned half a century. The early twenty-first century perhaps represents a similar turning point. It could be the beginning of the end of the dominance of the United States in the world. The recent rise of Asia and the emergence of its powerhouse economies, which constitutes a striking transformation, has led to a belief, voiced by some, that this could be the Asian century.[10] The parallels drawn are with Britain in the nineteenth century, and the United States in the twentieth century, when the dominance of these countries in the world was reflected in politics, economics, and even culture. This belief is hyperbole.

There can be little doubt that, *circa* 2050, a century after the end of colonial rule, Asia will account for more than one-half of world income, and will be home to more than one-half the people on earth. It will, thus, have an economic and political significance in the world that would have been difficult to imagine fifty years ago, even if it was the reality in 1820. In terms of income per capita, however, it will be nowhere as rich as the United States or Europe. Thus, Asian countries would emerge as world powers, without the income levels of rich countries. China will be large and influential. And so might India. But, as a continent, Asia will not have the dominance that Britain had in the past or the United States has even now. The most likely scenario, in 2050, is a multipolar world, in which dominance might not be so striking. The United States and China will most probably be the leading countries with an economic and political significance in this world. But it is likely that this group will be larger, including India, Indonesia, and Japan from Asia, Brazil and Mexico from Latin America, with Germany, France, and possibly Britain from Europe. The presence of what are now developing countries in this group will depend, in large part, on whether they can transform themselves into inclusive societies where economic growth, human development, and social progress move in tandem. Even in such a multipolar world, a shift in the balance of power towards Asia is discernible. And the past of Asia could be a pointer to its future.

Statistical sources and notes

Chapter 1

Tables 1.1 to 1.3 and Figures 1.1a and 1.1b

These tables and figures are based on the historical statistics compiled by Maddison on GDP and population, which have been published in several monographs or books (1995, 2001, 2003, and 2007) but have been revised from time to time. The complete statistical series that incorporates revisions is available on the Maddison Database 2010, 'Historical Statistics of the World Economy: 1—2008 AD' (https://www.rug.nl/ggdc/histo ricaldevelopment/maddison/releases/maddison-database-2010). The statistics presented in the tables and used in the figures are based on the author's calculations from this online database. GDP and GDP per capita are measured, in PPP terms, in 1990 international Geary–Khamis dollars. The composition of the country-groups is as follows. Western Europe includes Andorra, Austria, Belgium, Cyprus, Denmark, Faeroe Islands, Finland, France, Germany, Gibraltar, Greece, Greenland, Guernsey, Iceland, Ireland, Isle of Man, Italy, Jersey, Liechtenstein, Luxembourg, Malta, Monaco, Netherlands, Norway, Portugal, San Marino, Spain, Sweden, Switzerland, and the United Kingdom. Western Offshoots includes United States, Canada, Australia, and New Zealand. Eastern Europe includes Albania, Bulgaria, Czechoslovakia, Hungary, Poland, Romania, and Yugoslavia. Former USSR includes Armenia, Azerbaijan, Belarus, Estonia, Georgia, Kazakhstan, Kyrgyzstan, Latvia, Lithuania, Moldova, Russian Federation, Tajikistan, Turkmenistan, Ukraine, and Uzbekistan. *The West* includes Western Europe, Western Offshoots, Eastern Europe, former USSR, and Japan. *The Rest* includes Africa, Asia (except Japan), and Latin America.

Table 1.1

For the year 1820: the coverage for Western Europe, Western Offshoots, Eastern Europe, and former USSR is as given above. In population estimates, there are fifty-five countries in Asia (including China, India, and Indonesia, where Indonesia includes Timor), six countries in Africa and forty-four countries in Latin America, with residual estimates for other countries in the regions. Asia excludes Japan (for which there is a separate estimate). In GDP estimates, there are forty-seven countries in Asia, six countries in Africa, and twenty-six countries in Latin America, with residual estimates for other countries in the regions.

For the years 1870 and 1913, for both population and GDP estimates in this table, the coverage, in terms of the number of countries in each of the regions is almost the same as in 1820. For Asia, Africa, and Latin America, it was smaller in 1900 and 1940, but larger in 1950 and 1962.

Table 1.2

For China, the figure for 1940 relates to 1938.

Table 1.3

The average annual growth rates in the table are calculated as point-to-point compound growth rates, since the data are available only for the selected years.

Table 1.5

For each of the four sub-regions of Asia, the constituent economies are as follows: East Asia includes China, South Korea, North Korea, Mongolia, Macao, Taiwan, and Hong Kong. South Asia includes Afghanistan, Bangladesh, Bhutan, India, Maldives, Nepal, Pakistan, and Sri Lanka. South East Asia includes Brunei, Cambodia, Indonesia, Laos Malaysia, Myanmar, Philippines, Singapore, Thailand, and Vietnam. West Asia includes Bahrain, Iran, Iraq, Jordan, Kuwait, Lebanon, Oman, Qatar, Saudi Arabia, Syria, Turkey, UAE, and Yemen.

The multiple sources for the data in the table and explanatory notes are set out below:

For demographic indicators, World Bank, *World Development Indicators*, online database. For population figures, UN Population Statistics. The figures for the sub-regions are population-weighted averages for the countries in the sub-region.

For social indicators, there are different sources. For life expectancy and infant mortality rates, World Bank, *World Development Indicators*, online database. On infant mortality rates, 1965 figures are not available for Bhutan, Brunei, Cambodia, Laos, Myanmar, Qatar, and Saudi Arabia. Data on infant mortality rates in East Asia relate to 1960 (not 1965), for China, South Korea, North Korea, and Mongolia, and are obtained from UNDP, *Human Development Report 1991*. For (adult) literacy rates (total, males and females), the Barro-Lee dataset (http://www.barro-lee.com). The figures on these social indicators for the sub-regions are population-weighted averages for the countries in the sub-region, excluding those for which information is not available.

For economic indicators on income, structure, openness, and investment, United Nations, UNCTAD Stat, based on UN National Accounts Statistics and International Trade Statistics. The figures are GDP-weighted averages for the countries in each sub-region, except for GDP, which is the total for the countries in each of the sub-regions.

Different sources are used for the two infrastructure indicators. For electricity consumption per capita, US Energy Information Administration (http://www.eia.gov/beta./international). The figures on electricity consumption per capita for 1970 relate to 1980, and there are no data on West Asia. Thus, the average for Asia does not include West Asia. Statistics are available for the following economies: China, Hong Kong, South Korea, Mongolia, and Taiwan in East Asia; Afghanistan, Bangladesh, Bhutan, India, Maldives, Nepal, Pakistan, and Sri Lanka in South Asia; Brunei, Cambodia, Indonesia, Laos, Malaysia, Philippines, Singapore, Thailand, and Vietnam in Southeast Asia. For each sub-region, the averages are population-weighted. For road kms per 100 sq metres of land area, International Roads Federation, *World Road Statistics*, various issues. Statistics are available for the following countries in 1970: Hong Kong and South Korea in East Asia; India and Sri Lanka in South Asia; Indonesia, Malaysia, Thailand, and Vietnam in Southeast Asia; Iran, Iraq, Lebanon, Saudi Arabia and Syria in West Asia. For each sub-region, the figures are simple averages of countries for which information is available.

For urban–rural population ratios, UN Population Statistics. The figures are population-weighted averages for countries in each sub-region.

Chapter 2

Table 2.1

The sources, and the explanatory notes, are the same as for Table 1.5 above. So are the figures for 1965 and 1970. This table also incorporates figures for 2016. The averages for each sub-region are either population-weighted or GDP-weighted, depending upon the indicator, as explained above. There are only two minor differences. The data on infant mortality rates for all countries is from World Bank, *World Development Indicators*, online database. For statistics on road kms per 100 sq kms of land area, the country coverage, for 2015, is more than it was in 1970. East Asia includes China, Hong Kong, Mongolia, and South Korea; South Asia includes Bhutan, India, Nepal, Pakistan, and Sri Lanka; Southeast Asia includes Brunei Darussalam, Indonesia, Laos, Malaysia, Myanmar, Singapore, Thailand, and Vietnam; West Asia includes Bahrain, Iran, Iraq, Jordan, Kuwait, Lebanon, Oman, Qatar, Saudi Arabia, State of Palestine, Syrian Arab Republic, and Turkey.

Tables 2.2 to 2.9

The constituent economies in each of these four sub-regions are: (a) East Asia: China, Hong Kong, Macao, Mongolia, North Korea, South Korea, and Taiwan; (b) Southeast Asia: Brunei Darussalam, Cambodia, Indonesia, Laos, Malaysia, Myanmar, Philippines, Singapore, Thailand, Timor-Leste, and Vietnam; (c) South Asia: Afghanistan, Bangladesh, Bhutan, India, Maldives, Nepal, Pakistan, and Sri Lanka; and (d) West Asia: Bahrain, Iran, Iraq, Jordan, Kuwait, Lebanon, Oman, Palestine, Qatar, Saudi Arabia, Syria, Turkey, United Arab Emirates, and Yemen.

The figures for the two major country-groups in these tables, Industrialized Countries and Developing Countries, do not add up to the total (or to 100 for percentage figures) because there is a third residual country-group in the world, made up of Eastern Europe and the former USSR (classified as transition economies in UN statistics). This residual group is not part of the analysis, and its significance in the world economy has diminished rapidly since late 1991.

Chapter 3

Table 3.8

The sources of data are specified in the two tables. GDP is measured in constant 2010 dollars. The average annual GDP growth rates for each of the periods have been calculated by fitting a semi-log linear regression equation $L_nY = a + bt$ and estimating the value of b. Employment is measured in number of persons. The average annual employment growth rate for each of the sub-sectors—agriculture, industry, and services—has been estimated separately, by fitting a semi-log linear regression equation $L_nE = a + bt$ and estimating the value of b. For industry and services, taken together, the employment figures for the two sectors were added, for each of the periods in each of the countries, and the average annual employment growth rate was estimated by fitting a semi-log linear regression equation $L_nE = a + bt$ and estimating the value of b. For the period

1971–1990, the GGDC online database provides complete time-series data on employment for each of the countries, except Malaysia, which is available for 1975–1990. For the period 1991–2016, ILO STAT, which are based on national employment statistics, do not provide complete time-series data for every country as some observations are missing for some countries. For the missing values, ILO Model Statistics provide estimates, which have been used in this table to complete the time-series so as to estimate average annual growth rates.

Table A.3.1

The incremental capital output ratio (ICOR) in an economy is the share of investment in GDP divided by the real GDP growth rate. This follows from ICOR = dK/dY, where K is capital stock and Y is GDP. In other words, ICOR = (dK/Y) ÷ (dY/Y), which is I/Y ÷ GDP growth rate, where I is investment. In the table, GDP is measured in constant 2010 US dollars, while the share of investment in GDP is measured at current prices. ICORs have been estimated as a three-year average centred around the benchmark year specified in the table, with the exception of 1971 where the average is for 1971, 1972, and 1973. In estimating the ICORs, the occasional outlier value (due to a negative or very low GDP growth rate) has been omitted.

Table A.3.1 Incremental capital output ratios

	1971	1980	1990	2000	2010	2015
China	6.06	5.34	7.19	4.31	4.83	6.32
South Korea	2.39	4.47	4.44	4.47	6.94	9.82
Taiwan	2.08	4.10	3.51	4.09	4.28	9.76
Indonesia	1.80	2.85	3.25	7.63	5.81	6.92
Malaysia	1.74	4.07	3.60	3.34	3.76	5.10
Philippines	3.83	7.39	6.49	5.99	4.14	3.45
Singapore	3.28	4.39	3.99	4.64	3.11	11.52
Thailand	4.79	5.62	3.88	5.39	3.37	6.34
Vietnam	5.59	2.32	2.82	4.89	5.74	4.30
Bangladesh	1.29	5.10	4.84	4.27	4.72	4.43
India	9.80	4.07	4.87	5.18	4.80	4.34
Pakistan	6.77	2.60	3.70	5.00	7.06	3.02
Sri Lanka	4.97	5.50	6.91	5.73	5.13	6.52
Turkey	3.70	4.43	2.60	3.58	3.00	6.38

Source: Author's calculations from United Nations, National Accounts Statistics.

Figure 3.1

The decomposition of aggregate demand into its principal components requires calculating the share of Private Consumption Expenditure (PCE), Government Final Consumption Expenditure (GFCE), Gross Capital Formation (GCF) and Net Exports (NE), all in real terms (at constant prices), in the annual incremental change in real GDP for successive years over the period 1971–2016. Since different deflators are used for the different components of aggregate demand to obtain their respective values in real terms in the national accounting framework, the total of the different components of aggregate demand in real terms is not necessarily equal to the incremental real change in GDP. This difference is adjusted across all the components of aggregate demand so that, taken together, the share of the components adds up to 100 per cent. The adjusted shares are then averaged for the indicated periods, namely 1971–1980, 1981–1990, 1991–2000, 2001–2008 and 2009–2016. In calculating the period average, observations for some years have been dropped on account of incomplete data, outlier values, or a significant negative change over successive years in some components of aggregate demand. On an average, out of 46 data points covering the period 1971–2016 no more than 5–6 data points have been dropped for most economies spread across the different sub-periods, with the exception of Taiwan, Bangladesh, and Sri Lanka, where ten data points were omitted in estimating the averages for the different periods. Table A.3.2 presents the data used in plotting the bar charts in Figure 3.1 in Chapter 3 of this book.

Table A.3.2 Decomposition of aggregate demand into its principal components for the Asian-14 (percentages)

	PCE	GFCE	GCF	NE		PCE	GFCE	GCF	NE
China					**Thailand**				
1971–1980	38.9	18.1	51.2	−8.2	1971–1980	49.0	13.3	24.6	13.2
1981–1990	48.3	10.9	33.4	7.4	1981–1990	46.2	10.4	41.3	2.1
1991–2000	39.4	16.7	35.5	8.4	1991–2000	57.9	11.8	49.8	−19.5
2001–2008	31.6	11.3	50.0	7.1	2001–2008	49.5	15.6	47.5	−12.7
2009–2016	38.9	14.2	52.6	−5.7	2009–2016	47.7	24.2	52.2	−24.1
South Korea					**Vietnam**				
1971–1980	56.0	16.6	34.8	−7.5	1971–1980	85.4	5.5	9.8	−0.7
1981–1990	53.0	12.2	39.2	−4.4	1981–1990	82.5	7.2	10.3	−0.1
1991–2000	60.0	8.8	43.0	−11.8	1991–2000	61.2	5.1	32.1	1.6
2001–2008	52.7	17.1	19.5	10.8	2001–2008	61.6	5.5	38.3	−5.4
2009–2016	37.6	15.7	39.1	7.5	2009–2016	65.5	7.7	27.5	−0.8
Taiwan					**Bangladesh**				
1971–1980	51.7	19.6	38.2	−9.5	1971–1980	62.7	8.3	35.7	−6.6
1981–1990	59.9	21.3	33.2	−14.4	1981–1990	92.5	4.7	7.8	−5.0
1991–2000	66.5	14.9	42.8	−24.2	1991–2000	47.1	3.8	29.3	19.8
2001–2008	40.3	1.9	24.5	33.4	2001–2008	66.4	7.2	34.8	−8.4
2009–2016	52.0	10.4	36.8	0.7	2009–2016	55.8	5.7	39.0	−0.6
Indonesia					**India**				
1971–1980	53.2	42.6	11.2	−6.9	1971–1980	33.0	3.4	63.1	0.5
1981–1990	39.3	57.2	5.6	−2.0	1981–1990	53.8	18.2	26.4	1.6
1991–2000	51.3	47.3	4.2	−2.9	1991–2000	43.7	17.6	61.9	−23.2
2001–2008	42.4	52.3	11.5	−6.3	2001–2008	46.5	5.2	50.0	−1.8
2009–2016	36.2	53.5	7.5	2.7	2009–2016	55.8	10.1	29.5	4.6
Malaysia					**Pakistan**				
1971–1980	50.7	14.3	39.6	−4.6	1971–1980	111.0	12.0	37.3	−60.4
1981–1990	35.3	8.6	65.8	−9.8	1981–1990	65.9	17.0	22.3	−5.3
1991–2000	33.8	8.5	60.3	−2.6	1991–2000	85.2	1.3	10.7	2.7
2001–2008	58.8	15.4	15.4	10.4	2001–2008	72.7	12.6	27.2	−12.4
2009–2016	64.9	13.5	36.9	−15.3	2009–2016	76.9	16.0	−6.4	13.5

Continued

Table A.3.2 Continued

	PCE	GFCE	GCF	NE		PCE	GFCE	GCF	NE
Philippines					Sri Lanka				
1971–1980	51.5	15.7	33.8	–1.0	1971–1980	–2.7	–4.4	58.7	48.5
1981–1990	44.0	8.2	65.5	–17.7	1981–1990	78.7	5.5	2.9	12.9
1991–2000	68.6	12.9	36.5	–18.0	1991–2000	64.7	7.4	25.1	2.8
2001–2008	73.9	4.7	21.8	–0.4	2001–2008	48.9	8.5	64.7	–22.1
2009–2016	73.5	18.0	19.6	–11.2	2009–2016	65.6	10.5	43.7	–19.8
Singapore					Turkey				
1971–1980	43.5	9.2	38.3	9.1	1971–1980	66.9	21.4	17.8	–6.1
1981–1990	38.8	6.4	40.5	14.3	1981–1990	42.5	21.8	28.2	7.5
1991–2000	39.0	6.3	64.4	–9.7	1991–2000	46.2	10.6	52.7	–9.5
2001–2008	26.0	7.0	24.3	42.7	2001–2008	58.5	13.3	52.0	–23.8
2009–2016	32.6	12.3	9.2	45.9	2009–2016	54.9	7.8	51.2	–13.8

Source: Author's calculations from UN National Accounts Statistics.

Chapter 4

Table 4.4

For each of the three sectors—agriculture, industry, and services—GDP is measured in constant 2010 US dollars, while employment is measured in number of persons. ILO STAT, based on national employment statistics, do not provide complete time-series data for every country because, for some years in some countries, actual employment figures are not available. For such missing values, ILO Model Statistics provide estimates, which have been used in this table to complete the time-series for each country. Output per worker has been calculated, dividing the GDP in constant prices by total employment, respectively, for each sector in each country. The average annual growth rates for output, employment, and output per worker, for each of the three sectors in each of the fourteen countries, are estimated by fitting a semi-log linear regression equation $Log_n X = a + bt$ and estimating the value of b.

Chapter 5

Table 5.4

Concessional Development Assistance (CDA) has two components: Official Development Assistance (ODA) from donor countries and Other Official Financing (OOF) from multilateral institutions. The data relate to gross inflows. CDA figures are available for Bangladesh from 1971 and for China from 1979. There is no CDA reported for Singapore after 1996, for Taiwan after 1997, and for South Korea after 2000, so that annual averages cover the years for which data are available. UN National Accounts Statistics are available only from 1970, so that gross capital formation data for 1961–1970 are obtained from the World Bank *World Development Indicators*. However, the World Bank does not provide gross capital formation statistics for Taiwan and Vietnam during 1961–1970, so the percentages could not be calculated.

Chapter 7

Table 7.1

The headings for columns in this table are $c.1970$, $c.1980$, $c.1990$, $c.2000$, $c.2010$, and $c.2015$, because data on Gini coefficients in the specified years are not necessarily available for all countries in the Asian-14, so the figures are for the closest possible year. In the column $c.1970$, the figure on Turkey is for 1968, on Bangladesh and Thailand for 1969, on Pakistan, Philippines, and Hong Kong for 1971, and on Singapore for 1972. In the column $c.1980$, the figure on India is for 1977, on Turkey for 1978, on Pakistan for 1979, on Thailand, China, and Taiwan for 1981, on Sri Lanka for 1982, on Bangladesh for 1983, on Malaysia for 1984, and on Philippines for 1985. In the column $c.1990$, the figure on Turkey is for 1987, on Malaysia for 1989, on Bangladesh, Philippines and Taiwan for 1991, and on Vietnam for 1992. In the column $c.2000$, the figure on Malaysia is for 1997, on India and Indonesia for 1999, on Pakistan for 2001, and on Sri Lanka, Vietnam, and Turkey for 2002. In the column $c.2010$, the figure on Philippines and Malaysia is for 2009, and on India for 2011. In the column $c.2015$, the figure on Pakistan, Indonesia, Thailand, and Taiwan is for 2013, on Vietnam and Malaysia for 2014, and on Sri Lanka for 2016.

The Gini coefficients in the table are based on nationally representative household surveys. The Gini coefficients for Malaysia, China, and Singapore are based on per capita disposable income, while the Gini coefficients for South Korea, Taiwan, and Turkey are based on equivalized disposable income. The Gini coefficients for Bangladesh, Pakistan, Sri Lanka, India, Indonesia, Philippines, Thailand, and Vietnam are based on per capita consumption expenditure.

Table 7.2

The figures in this table are for the same years, and based on the same surveys, as in Table 7.1. The only exception is South Korea, for which the figure in the column $c.2000$ is for 2006 and the figure in the column $c.2015$ is for 2012.

Table 7.3

The World Bank poverty estimates, for the proportion of the population and the number of people below the two specified poverty lines, are based on national surveys, reporting the distribution of consumption or income, except in the case of estimates for China, India, and Indonesia, where the national estimates have been derived from the respective rural and urban distributions. The estimates for China in 1984 and Philippines in 2012 are based on income distributions. The rest are all based on consumption distributions. The choice of 1984, 1996, and 2012, the years for which the poverty estimates are presented, has been guided by the consideration that estimates are available for those years, or years close to those years, for the maximum number of countries. Thus, for most countries, the poverty estimates for 1984, are during 1983–1985, except for Thailand in 1981, Turkey in 1986, and Vietnam in 1992. Similarly, for most countries, the poverty estimates for 1996 are during 1994–1997, except for Vietnam in 1999. The poverty estimates for 2012, too, are during 2011–2012 for most countries, except for Bangladesh in 2016. The poverty estimates for Asia as a whole, and its constituent sub-regions, are based on estimates for forty countries. These include South Korea (2006) and Malaysia (2012), where estimates are based on income distributions.

Table 7.4

The sources of data for this table are as follows. For GDP per capita, UN National Accounts Statistics. For infant mortality rates, life expectancy at birth and adult literacy rates, in 1990 and 2016, World Bank, *World Development Indicators* online database (https://data.wor ldbank.org/indicator). For adult literacy rates in 1970 for all the Asian-14, and in South Korea and Taiwan for all years, the Barro–Lee dataset accessed at http://www.barrolee.com. For Taiwan, data on infant mortality rates and life expectancy at birth are from UN Population Division, World Population Prospects.

The data on adult literacy rates in 1970, derived from Barro-Lee dataset, is not strictly comparable with the WDI dataset for 1990 and 2016. However, for the overlapping years, the figures in the two datasets are close to each other, which makes them roughly comparable. In the case of the WDI dataset, the adult literacy data for all countries are not necessarily available for the same year. Therefore, data for the closest available year have been used. For the year 1990, the adult literacy rate for Malaysia, Bangladesh, and India is for 1991, Vietnam for 1989, Pakistan for 1998, Thailand for 2000, and Sri Lanka for 2001. For the year 2016, the adult literacy rate for Vietnam is for 2009, China, South Korea, Taiwan, Malaysia, and Sri Lanka for 2010, India for 2011, Philippines for 2013, Pakistan for 2014, and Thailand and Turkey for 2015.

The infant mortality rate is the number of infants who die before reaching one year of age, per 1000 live births, in any given year. Life expectancy at birth indicates the number of years a newborn infant would live, if prevailing patterns of mortality at the time of its birth were to stay the same throughout its life. The adult literacy rate is the percentage of people aged fifteen and above, who can both read and write, understanding a short simple statement about their everyday life.

Figures 7.1 and 7.2

The source for data on GDP per capita in 1990 International Geary–Khamis dollars, is the Maddison Project Database, Version 2018, 1990$ benchmark (www.ggdc.net/maddison).

GDP per capita of each of the Asian-14, provided in the database, was calculated as a percentage of GDP per capita of industrialized countries to create a time-series for the ratio during the period 1970–2016. Industrialized countries include twenty developed economies (Australia, Austria, Belgium, Canada, Denmark, Finland, France, Germany, Greece, Ireland, Italy, Netherlands, New Zealand, Norway, Portugal, Spain, Sweden, Switzerland, the United Kingdom, and the United States), for each of which GDP was calculated by multiplying its GDP per capita by its population. Thereafter, for each year, the sum total of their GDP was divided by the total population of the twenty countries to obtain a time-series on GDP per capita for industrialized countries from 1970 to 2016.

Chapter 8

Table 8.1

The sources for this table were as follows: for GDP and population, Table 2.1. For value added in agriculture, UNCTAD Stat based on UN National Accounts Statistics. For manufacturing value added, Table 2.5. For manufactured exports, Table 5.8. For merchandise exports and imports, Table 2.7. For exports and imports of services, Table 5.3 (as comparable data are not available after 2013, the figures reported for 2016 relate to 2013). For FDI inward and outward stocks, UNCTAD Foreign Direct Investment Online database. For remittances, Table 2.9. For foreign exchange reserves, IMF Balance of Payments Statistics.

Table 8.2

For motor vehicles, OICA, International Organization of Motor Vehicle Manufacturers (motor vehicles include passenger cars, light commercial vehicles, minibuses, trucks, buses, and coaches). For motorcycles, Automotive Industry Portal, Mark Lines. For steel, World Steel Association, www.worldsteel.org. For Cement, US Geological Survey, Mineral Commodity Summaries.

Endnotes

Chapter 1

1. For a discussion, see Myrdal (1968, volume I, chapter 4, pp. 129–74).
2. For an even longer-term perspective, spanning several millennia, on human history in the context of the world economy, see Morris (2010).
3. See Maddison (1995, 2001, and 2003).
4. Maddison adopts the Geary–Khamis approach, which is appropriate for comparisons across a large number of countries over long periods of time. The method is 'multilateral' rather than 'binary' and it assigns a weight to countries corresponding to the size of their GDP, which makes comparisons transitive and imparts other desirable properties. This approach was also adopted by Kravis, Heston, and Summers (1978). The Maddison exercise uses 1990 as the benchmark year to provide the inter-spatial and inter-temporal anchor for GDP estimates. Thus, the numeraire is termed '1990 international Geary–Khamis dollars'. For a more detailed discussion, see Maddison (2003).
5. See, for example, Clark (2009).
6. In this context, it is worth noting that the sharp decline in the share of Asia in world GDP, which was attributable mostly to China and India, was relative rather than absolute. It was a consequence of stagnation or much slower growth compared with the rest of the world. See Table 1.3.
7. This was possibly attributable to the end of colonialism in Latin America, where independence came to most countries in the early nineteenth century, which may have facilitated the adoption of policies that enabled them to perform better than Asia. For a lucid analysis of economic development in Latin America since independence, see Bertola and Ocampo (2012).
8. For a more detailed discussion of the debate on this issue, see Nayyar (2013).
9. Such a comparison, with supporting evidence, is made by Pomeranz (2000), Findlay and O'Rourke (2007), and Parthasarathi (2011).
10. The large 'white-settler' population in many African colonies meant that the living standards of natives were even lower than what the GDP per capita suggests.
11. See Williamson (2002), Nayyar (2006), and Williamson (2006).
12. For evidence on tariff rates, see Bairoch (1993) and Maddison (1989).
13. Evidence on the size and composition of trade between Europe and Asia, Africa, or Latin America during this era is limited and sparse. See Nayyar (2013, pp. 27–8).
14. While mines were dependent on natural resource endowments, crops from elsewhere were brought to plantations in colonies, for example, tea in India, rubber in Malaya, coffee in Indonesia, sugar in the Caribbean, and so on.

15. These proportions have been calculated from Bairoch (1982, table 10, p. 296 and table 13, p. 304).

16. These ratios are calculated from Bairoch (1982, p. 294 and p. 302), who estimates per capita industrialization levels for country-groups and countries, based on triennial averages, as index numbers with the UK in 1900 as 100.

17. For an analysis of the Industrial Revolution in Britain, see Allen (2009).

18. For an analysis of this set of issues, see Bairoch (1981), Pomeranz (2000), Nayyar (2006), Williamson (2006), Findlay and O'Rourke (2007), Maddison (2007), Parthasarathi (2011), and Nayyar (2013).

19. For Japan, this was so only until 1911. But Japan imposed an unequal treaty on Korea in 1876, even when it was subject to unequal treaties with the West.

20. The idea of cumulative causation and vicious circles created by negative feedback effects is developed at some length by Myrdal (1968, volume III, appendix 2, pp. 1843–78). In such situations, the challenge of development is to transform this process of cumulative causation into virtuous circles through positive feedbacks and spread effects.

21. Myrdal (1968) devoted a whole chapter to this discussion on differences in initial conditions (volume I, chapter 14, pp. 673–405).

22. This what Veblen (1915) described as 'penalty of taking the lead' and what Gerschenkron (1962) described as 'advantages of relative economic backwardness'. For a more detailed discussion, see Chapter 7. See also Nayyar (2013).

23. This figure understates the relative importance of the primary sector in Asia. It was attributable to West Asia where the share of the primary sector in GDP was only 9 per cent but the sub-region accounted for 44 per cent of Asia's GDP in 1970. For East Asia, Southeast Asia and South Asia, taken together, the share of the primary sector in GDP was much higher at 42 per cent.

24. For a detailed discussion on how European colonialisms differed from each other, in Asian countries, see Myrdal (1968, volume I, chapter 4, pp. 129–74) and Maddison (2007, chapter 3, pp. 111–82).

25. In 1945, there were more than 1 million Japanese civilians in Manchuria (Maddison, 2007, p. 153). In sharp contrast, in 1805, there were only 31,000 British people in India, of whom 22,000 were in the army and 2,000 in civilian government. In 1931, there were 168,000, of whom 60,000 were in the army and police, 4,000 in civilian government, and 26,000 in the private sector, while 78,000 were family dependents (Maddison, 2007, p. 119).

26. In India in 1951, three years after independence, the literacy rate was just 18 per cent of the population (Nayyar, 2006a).

Chapter 2

1. The disaggregation of sub-regions in the text above lists forty countries. However, in the United Nations classification of countries, Hong Kong and Macao are listed as Special Administrative Regions of China while Taiwan is listed as a Province of China.

2. These islands include: Cook Islands, Fiji, Kiribati, Marshall Islands, Micronesia, Nauru, Palau, Papua New Guinea, Samoa, Solomon Islands, Tonga, Tuvalu, and Vanuatu. Timor-Leste is included in Southeast Asia only because it was a province of Indonesia until 2002.

3. This description is illustrated by a map of South Asia in Myrdal (1968), which includes all the selected countries (volume I, pp. 4–5). The scope and coverage of the study is also set out in the text (volume I, pp. 39–41). Among the country-specific chapters, there were separate chapters on India and Pakistan, but there was just one chapter on the rest in which there were three separate sections on: (i) Ceylon, (ii) Burma and Indonesia, and (iii) the remaining countries in Southeast Asia mentioned above (volume I, chapters 7, 8, and 9).

4. For an elaboration of these ideas, see Myrdal (1968, volume III, appendix 2, pp. 1843–78). For a critical evaluation, see Stewart (2019) and Nayyar (2019b).

5. There is a detailed assessment of possibilities and constraints for the countries studied: India (volume I, chapter 7; Pakistan (volume I, chapter 8); Ceylon and Southeast Asia (volume I, chapter 9). For each country, there is also a summary of the prospects: India (pp. 300–3), Pakistan (pp. 338–41), Ceylon (pp. 356–8), Burma and Indonesia (pp. 373–81), Malaysia (pp. 384–6), Philippines (pp. 389–90), Thailand (pp. 393–4), Cambodia (pp. 396–7), Laos (pp. 397–8) and Vietnam (pp. 398–409, although this thinking was strongly influenced by the wars that spanned decades: the first with France during 1945–1954 and the second, in effect, with the United States during 1954–1975).

6. This marked difference in comparison with Asia as a whole was attributable to West Asia where, in 1970, the share of the primary sector in GDP was only 9 per cent but the sub-region accounted for 44 per cent of Asia's GDP.

7. See Maddison Project Database, Version 2018, 1990 international $ benchmark (www.ggdc.net/maddison). This database provides GDP per capita in 1990 international dollars, updating the Maddison set up to 2016. GDP per capita figures for 2016 are available for 166 countries. This series was multiplied by population (using data from Maddison Project Database, Version 2018) to obtain GDP figures (in 1990$) for each country. The share of Asia in world GDP is the total GDP of thirty-five Asian countries (excluding Japan) expressed as a percentage of world GDP (total GDP of 166 countries).

8. Author's calculations from www.ggdc.net/maddison. GDP per capita for the country-groups has been calculated by estimating the total GDP in 1990$ for the country-group and dividing that figure by the total population of all the countries in the group.

9. Once again, a comparison with the past is instructive. The difference between East Asia and South Asia is mirrored in the difference between China and India. In terms of Maddison PPP statistics, in 1990 international (Geary–Khamis) dollars, in 2016, the share of China in world GDP was 20.2 per cent while that of India was 8.7 per cent. For China, its share of world GDP was 33 per cent in 1820 and 17.1 per cent in 1870. For India, its share of world GDP was 8.6 per cent in 1900. In 2016, GDP per capita as a proportion of that in Western Europe and Western Offshoots was 37.4 per cent for China and 17.4 per cent for India. For China, this GDP per capita ratio was 25.9 per cent in 1870 and 50.2 per cent in 1820. For India, this GDP per capita ratio was 18.8 per cent in 1900. Therefore, it is plausible to suggest that in terms of their shares in world GDP and GDP per capita ratios compared with industrialized countries, in 2016, China was roughly where it was in the mid-nineteenth century, whereas India was roughly where it was at the end of the nineteenth century. The figures for 2016 are calculated from www. ggdc.net/maddison while the figures for the past are from Tables 1.1 and 1.2.

10. In 1830, the share of Latin America, Africa, and Asia, together, in world manufacturing production was 60.5 per cent, while that of China and India, together, was 47.4 per cent (Table 1.4). In 1860, the share of Latin America, Africa, and Asia, together, was 36.6 per cent, while that of China and India, together, was 28.3 per cent. If one-third these differences of 13.1 per cent and 8.3 per cent respectively were attributable to other Asian countries, the share of Asia as a whole would have been around 51.7 per cent in 1830 and 39.4 per cent in 1860.

11. The focus here is on merchandise trade and on the dimensions of such trade. However, trade in services became more significant over time. The composition of merchandise exports and imports also changed significantly over time. Both these aspects are considered in Chapter 5.

12. International migration and economic development has been analysed at length elsewhere by the author (Nayyar, 2008c and 2013).

Chapter 3

1. See, for example, World Bank (1993), Amsden (2001), Akyuz et al. (1998), Singh (1998), and World Bank (2008).

2. The national income accounting identity $Y = C + I + X - M$ (income equals consumption plus investment plus exports minus imports), can be rewritten as $(I - S) = (M - X)$, given that $Y - C = S$, where S is saving.

3. Unfortunately, UN national accounts statistics, which do not make a distinction between public investment and private investment, are on total investment. If this information were available, it would almost certainly show that public investment was a major driver of investment in the Asian-14, particularly in the earlier stages.

4. For a more detailed discussion, which argues that public investment and private investment are complements rather than substitutes, see Nayyar (1997 and 2013).

5. For an analysis of the role of development banks in driving private investment, see Amsden (2001), Nayyar (2017), and Griffith-Jones and Ocampo (2018).

6. This argument is developed, at some length, by Akyuz et al. (1998) with reference to the experience of East Asian development. But it can also be extended to some other countries in the Asian-14, including some in Southeast Asia and South Asia, at least during some periods.

7. The critical role of strategic industrial policy and trade policy in East Asian industrialization is analysed by Amsden (1989), Wade (1990), and Chang (1996). For a discussion in the wider Asian context, see Lall (1997) and Nayyar (1997). On industrial policy and technological learning, see Noman and Stiglitz (2017).

8. This is an estimate of savings as a residual derived from the difference between gross domestic product and final consumption expenditure in the economy. The difference between gross national (disposable) income and final consumption expenditure would provide a better estimate. In an ideal world, of course, components of domestic savings—household savings, corporate savings, and government savings—are estimated directly, as in national accounts statistics. Therefore, these estimates of gross domestic savings as a percentage of GDP are not comparable with the figures on gross capital formation as a percentage of GDP in Table 3.4.

9. See World Bank, *World Development Report 1980*, pp. 118–19.

10. The seminal contribution to this literature is that of Solow (1956). For an analysis of the East Asian growth experience, in this framework, see Young (1995).

11. See Romer (1990) and Grossman and Helpman (1991).

12. This argument was first set out by Schultz (1964) and stressed by Myrdal (1968). It was subsequently confirmed in research relating to different parts of the developing world. See also Timmer (2014). On the Asian experience over the past fifty years, see Vos (2019).

13. The importance of education was emphasized by Myrdal (1968), who devoted Volume III of his study to education and health, which he described as 'investment in man'. On the importance and contribution of education to economic development in Asia over the past fifty years, see Mundle (2019).

14. For a short explanation of the methodology used in this decomposition exercise, see Appendix on statistical sources and notes. See also Table A.3.2 in the Appendix.

15. For a detailed discussion on the macroeconomics of the external sector, see Nayyar (1997). See also Nayyar (2013).

16. In the academic literature, for an early exposition of the orthodox view, see Little (1982). The two influential World Bank publications were the *East Asian Miracle* (1993) and the Report of the Commission on Growth and Development (2008). For a critical evaluation of this perspective, see Singh (1995), Amsden (1989), Chang (2003), Stiglitz et al. (2006), and Nayyar (2007 and 2013).

17. The remaining four in the thirteen were Brazil, Botswana, Malta, and Oman.

18. See, for example, Stiglitz et al. (2006), and Taylor (1983 and 2004), Bhaduri (1986), and Nayyar (2007 and 2008).

19. In addition, the use of three-year averages smoothens out short-term year-to-year fluctuations. It is also based on fifteen observations, rather than just five for the benchmark years, over a period of thirty-two years.

20. For evidence on Malaysia and Thailand, see World Bank (1993, pp. 107–9) and on India, see Nayyar (1996).

21. For a discussion on the macroeconomic crises in South Asian countries, see Mahmud (2001). On India, see Nayyar (1996) and Bhaduri and Nayyar (1996). On Bangladesh, Pakistan, and Sri Lanka, see Osmani (2019).

22. For a discussion on the causes and consequences of the East Asian financial crisis that surfaced in 1997, see Palma (1998), Chang (2000), Jomo (2001), Chang et al. (2001), and Ocampo and Stiglitz (2008).

23. The stock of internal public debt of central governments, during 1990–2016 on an average, was in the range of 30 per cent for South Korea and Indonesia, 50 per cent for Malaysia, Philippines and India, 25 per cent for Thailand and Turkey, while it was more than 75 per cent for Pakistan and Sri Lanka, and 100 per cent for Singapore (calculated from IMF *Government Finance Statistics Yearbook* and World Bank, *World Development Indicators*).

24. The contrast is even more striking earlier. During the three decades 1961–1991, the average annual rate of inflation, in consumer prices, was 7.5 per cent in the East Asian Tigers and the Southeast Asian NICs, and about the same at 8 per cent in South Asia, while it was 20 per cent in Sub-Saharan Africa and 192 per cent in Latin America and the Caribbean (World Bank, 1993, p. 110).

25. For a detailed discussion, see Amsden (1989), Wade (1990), and Chang (1996). See also Lall (1990) and Nayyar (2013).

26. During the decade 1981–1990, the average annual current account deficit was in the range of 3–4 per cent for Indonesia, Malaysia, Philippines, and Thailand, 5.5 per cent in Sri Lanka, about 2.5 per cent in Bangladesh and Pakistan, and 1.7 per cent in India. Singapore and Taiwan had current account surpluses. These current account deficits could have been higher in the 1970s because of the successive hikes in oil prices but cross-country data are only available starting 1980 (calculated from UNCTAD Stat).

27. It is worth noting that the foreign debt of South Korea in 1980 was the fourth largest in the world, while Indonesia's foreign debt tripled during the 1980s (World Bank, 1993, p. 107).

28. Between end-1990 and end-2016, the stock of long-term external debt of the public sector, as a proportion of GDP, diminished from 13 per cent to 1 per cent in China, from 45 per cent to 19 per cent in Indonesia, from 26 per cent to 21 per cent in Malaysia, from 53 per cent to 11 per cent in Philippines, from 15 per cent to 6 per cent in Thailand, from 36 per cent to 13 per cent in Bangladesh, from 22 per cent to 7 per cent in India, from 41 per cent to 19 per cent in Pakistan, from 61 per cent to 36 per cent in Sri Lanka, and from 26 per cent to 12 per cent in Turkey (calculated from World Bank *International Debt Statistics*). South Korea, Taiwan, and Singapore had no external debt in this period.

29. For a discussion on the use of capital controls and heterodox interventions in foreign exchange management, see Jomo (2001) and Ocampo and Stiglitz (2008). The Chiang Mai Initiative is a multilateral currency swap arrangement among the ASEAN countries plus China, Japan, and South Korea, established in 2010 with a pool of $120 billion that has since then doubled to $240 billion, which has not been used so far.

30. It is worth noting that foreign exchange reserves of the Asian-14, as a proportion of total foreign exchange reserves in the world, rose from 18 per cent in 1990 to 33 per cent in 2000 and 55 per cent in 2010 (see Table 8.1).

31. For an exposition of, and discussion on, the hypothesis set out here briefly, see Nayyar (2012 and 2014). It must also be recognized that the time horizons for creating jobs immediately and the ability to create jobs through industrialization are often very different, creating political compulsions.

Chapter 4

1. There is some absorption of surplus labour in services, even in the first stage, particularly in services that are complementary to manufacturing.

2. See, for example, Schumpeter (1942), Hirschman (1958), Chenery (1960), Ocampo et al. (2009), McMillan and Rodrik (2011), and Nayyar (2013).

3. Surplus labour in the agricultural sector earns a subsistence wage. If workers move to the urban sector, they need to earn a subsistence-plus wage that would compensate them for the cost of moving and the higher cost of living.

4. For a detailed discussion on this issue, situated in the wider context of the role of the services sector in the process of development, see Gaurav Nayyar (2012).

5. In a seminal contribution, Coase (1937) argued that the size of a firm is determined by finding an optimal balance between contractual relations that are 'internal' to the firm

and 'external' to the firm, as the entrepreneurial function is characterized by decreasing returns attributable to rising overhead costs and the propensity to make mistakes.

6. See Nayyar et al. (2018).

7. For a more detailed discussion, see Gaurav Nayyar (2012).

8. The evidence cited in this paragraph is from Nayyar (2013), which also provides a more detailed discussion of the issue, with supporting evidence on differences in structural change and economic growth between the three continents in the developing world.

9. McMillan and Rodrik (2011). They extend this argument further to argue that, during the period 1990–2005, in some Latin American and Sub-Saharan African countries, structural change was growth-reducing because the large share of primary products in exports limited the scope for productivity-enhancing structural change.

10. In a similar study, using evidence on structural change in sixty-seven developing countries and twenty-one advanced economies during 1950–2005, Szirmai (2012) shows that there was a clear relationship between rising industrial shares and economic growth in developing countries, but that was not so for manufacturing, which was important but was not an engine of growth.

11. In this study, Africa includes Botswana, Ethiopia, Ghana, Kenya, Malawi, Mauritius, Nigeria, Senegal, South Africa, Tanzania, and Zambia, while Latin America includes Argentina, Bolivia, Brazil, Chile, Colombia, Costa Rica, Mexico, Peru, and Venezuela, whereas Asia includes essentially India. China is no more than a point of reference. This selection of countries is determined primarily by the availability of statistics on the GGDC database. In addition, there is a short discussion on four low-income Asian countries—Bangladesh, Cambodia, Laos, and Vietnam—based on other sources.

12. UN national accounts statistics start only from 1970. If evidence were available for the preceding two decades, it would show that the drop in the GDP share of agriculture was far greater. Available evidence from national sources suggests that, *circa* 1950, the GDP share of agriculture was in the range of one-half to three-fifths, in most of the Asian-14 (Chang and Zach, 2019).

13. For China, UN national accounts statistics provide data on manufacturing value added starting only in 2004. Thus, 1970 and 1990 figures for China are not available.

14. The ILO database provides statistics on employment in all the fourteen countries starting from 1991 in agriculture, industry, and services but not separately for manufacturing. For earlier years, employment statistics are available on the GGDC database only for nine countries in the Asian-14; however, the starting and ending years differ so that information on all nine countries is available only for the period 1975–2010.

15. Author's calculations from the GGDC database.

16. See, for example, Singh and Dasgupta (2007) and Rodrik (2016).

17. Evidence from twenty-five countries in Africa, Latin America, and Asia also provides support for this proposition (Diao et al., 2017).

18. This argument is developed, at some length, elsewhere by the author (Nayyar, 2019a). For an analysis of the services sector in the development process, with special reference to India, see Gaurav Nayyar (2012).

19. On the critical role of agriculture in structural transformations, where these issues are discussed at length, see Timmer (2014).

20. The discussion in this paragraph draws upon the analysis, with supporting evidence and arguments, in Vos (2019). See also Montes (2019), Tarp (2019), and Osmani (2019) in the companion volume, Nayyar (2019).

21. For a more detailed discussion on industrialization in Asia, which is also situated in the context of structural change, see Chang and Zach (2019).

22. Szirmai and Verspagen (2015) examine the role of the manufacturing sector as a driver of growth in developing countries during 1950–2005 and find that it had a moderate positive impact, which appears to have waned since 1990, but it was definitely not an engine of growth.

23. This simple distinction, based on Nayyar (2019a), is useful for analytical purposes. However, the heterogeneity of the services sector, which can be explored in terms of analytical distinctions, production characteristics, or employment attributes, is far more complex. For a detailed discussion, see Gaurav Nayyar (2012).

24. It would mean too much of a digression to enter into a further discussion on this issue here. There is a literature on this subject that is limited but there is some research. See, for example, Rakshit (2007), Eichengreen and Gupta (2011), Nayyar (2012). See also Nayyar (2019a).

25. See McMillan and Rodrik (2011), Nayyar (2013), and ADB (2013).

26. See Nayyar et al. (2018).

27. For an analysis, with supporting evidence, see Hallward-Driemeier and Nayyar (2017) and Nayyar et al. (2018).

Chapter 5

1. See Myrdal (1968, volume II, chapter 13).

2. In this context, it is worth noting that the rise in Asia's export–GDP ratio in 1980, as also in 2000, was attributable to the spike in world oil prices, since its import–GDP ratio and its share of world imports in both 1980 and 2000 was much lower.

3. This is reflected in the peaks in Indonesia's export–GDP ratios, as well as its share of world exports, in 1980 and 2000, while its import–GDP ratio, and its share of world imports, in those years was far lower.

4. World trade is defined as the merchandise exports plus merchandise imports and these shares of countries have been calculated from US dollar values in current prices at market exchange rates.

5. It is worth noting that a significant proportion of Asia's merchandise trade was trade within Asia. For an analysis of intra-Asia trade, see Chapter 8.

6. For a detailed discussion on the factors underlying the much-enhanced possibilities of international trade in services, see Nayyar (1988).

7. During 1961–1970, this proportion would have been much higher in Taiwan, and just as high in Vietnam, but data on gross capital formation are not available. In that decade, the average annual gross aid inflow was $104 million to Taiwan and $321 million to Vietnam, compared with $316 million to South Korea and $219 million to Indonesia.

8. For a discussion on the emergence of large international firms from Asian countries, see Chapter 8.

9. For an analysis of the economic implications and consequences of such portfolio investment flows to Asian countries, see Chapter 8.

10. See Myrdal (1968), volume II, chapter 24.

11. The discussion on industrialization in this chapter treats it as synonymous with manufacturing, so that it excludes mining, construction, and utilities, which are a part of the industrial sector in national accounts statistics.

12. It should be noted that the peak levels reported here are based on statistics for the selected benchmark years in Table 5.7. Time-series data might yield different peak levels and peak years.

13. These percentage shares have been calculated from UN *National Accounts Statistics.*

14. Between 2000 and 2016, the share of the United States, the European Union, and Japan, taken together, in world manufacturing value added dropped by 22.5 per cent, while the share of China rose by 19.5 per cent and that of other Asian countries rose by 11 per cent.

15. For an analysis of the industrial slowdown in Southeast Asian countries, see Chang and Zach (2019).

16. These peak levels are based on data for selected benchmark years in Table 5.8. Peak levels and peak years might be different with time-series data.

17. In fact, the import content of such manufactured exports (particularly in computer, electronic, and optical equipment) was very high (Table 5.9). Thus, in 2016, the share of medium- and high-technology manufactures in the total imports of these three countries was also rather high at 55–60 per cent.

18. This earliest phase is analysed by Helleiner (1973) and Nayyar (1978).

19. See Helleiner (1973), Sharpston (1975), and Nayyar (1978).

20. The location decision of transnational corporations was strongly influenced by perceptions of political stability and labour docility (Nayyar, 1978).

21. There is a growing literature on this subject. See, for example, Feenstra (1998), Humphrey and Schmitz (2002), Kaplinsky (2005), and Gereffi et al. (2005), Milberg and Winkler (2013), UNCTAD (2013), Gereffi (2018), and Nathan et al. (2018).

22. Calculated from the OECD–WTO TIVA database, which also provides statistics on the dollar values of exports. For the eleven countries in Table 5.9, in 1995, the gross value of total exports from these three sectors was $259 billion while the gross value of total manufactured exports was $512 billion. In 2011, these figures were $1,349 billion and $3,246 billion respectively. In the eleven economies, the percentage shares of the three sectors, taken together, in the gross value of total manufactured exports in 1995 and 2011 respectively were: China (46 and 48), South Korea (56 and 41), Taiwan (47 and 51), Indonesia (34 and 22), Malaysia (44 and 41), Philippines (69 and 51), Singapore (58 and 36), Thailand (39 and 29), Vietnam (54 and 36), India (37 and 18) and Turkey (45 and 33); these percentages have been calculated from statistics in dollar values reported in the OECD–WTO TIVA database. There was a decline everywhere except for China and Taiwan. While these changes over time might just reflect a change in the composition of manufactured exports, the different levels across countries probably reflect differences in the degree of engagement with global value chains.

23. For an analysis of the rising domestic content in China's manufactured exports, using firm-level and customs transaction-level data, see Kee and Tang (2016). It is plausible

to suggest, though impossible to establish, that the rising domestic value added in China may have been a factor underlying the slowdown in such world trade.

24. Interestingly, North Korea was far more industrialized, and richer, than South Korea, as industrialization under Japanese colonialism was concentrated in the former.

25. The significance of past manufacturing experience is emphasized by Amsden (2001). But this is an overstated hypothesis. For a discussion, see Nayyar (2013).

26. For an analysis of major policy shifts over time in Turkey, starting 1950, see Önis and Senses (2007).

27. See, for example, Little et al. (1970), Bhagwati (1978), and Krueger (1978).

28. For a more detailed discussion, see Nayyar (2013). See also Helleiner (1992) and Nayyar (1997).

29. For a critical evaluation, see Diaz-Alejandro (1975), Krugman (1987), and Nayyar (1996).

30. See Amsden (1989), Wade (1990), (Lim, 1995), and Chang (1996) who provide systematic evidence on the proactive role of the state in these countries.

31. In this context, it is important to note that much the same can be said about industrialized countries, where industrial protection and state intervention were just as important, at earlier stages of their development when they were latecomers to industrialization (Chang, 2002; Reinert, 2007).

32. For an analysis, with supporting evidence, see the companion volume (Nayyar, 2019). See, in particular, Chang and Zach (2019), Kozul-Wright and Poon (2019), Wade (2019), Khan (2019), Nayyar (2019b), Lin (2019), and Montes (2019).

33. There is a vast literature on industrial policy. See, for example, Reich (1982), Pinder (1982), Johnson (1984), Lindbeck (1981), Landesmann (1992), Chang (1996), and Noman and Stiglitz (2017).

34. For an analysis, with supporting arguments and evidence, see Chang and Zach (2019) and Wade (2019). See also Amsden (1989), Wade (1990), Ranis (1992), Lim (1995), Chang (1996), Lall (1997), Chang (2004), and Nayyar (2013 and 2017).

35. For a detailed discussion on strategies and policies for industrialization in China, see Lin (2012 and 2019), Kozul-Wright and Poon (2019) and Chang and Zach (2019).

36. See Tarp (2019).

37. Industrialization and development in these countries is analysed at some length in Montes (2019). It is also discussed in Chang and Zach (2019). See also Jomo (2001a) and Coxhead (2015). There are, in addition, several studies on country experiences: Indonesia (Hill, 1996; Booth, 1998), Malaysia (Jomo, 1993; Rasiah, 1995), and Thailand (Lall, 1998).

38. For a discussion on economic development in South Asia in the companion volume, see Basu (2019) on India, and Osmani (2019) on Pakistan, Bangladesh, and Sri Lanka. On India, see also Chaudhuri (2002), and Nagaraj (2003, 2016).

39. For an analytical narrative, see Khan (2019), who cites this as an example of a 'political settlement' in which Daewoo had a credible assurance of potential *ex post* rent if it could deliver on its commitment to impart export capabilities in garments to its partner firm Desh.

40. For a more detailed discussion, see Nayyar (2017b).

41. For a narrative of, and discussion on, developments in these sectors, see Chaudhuri (2005) on pharmaceuticals, Bhargava (2013) on automobiles, and Balakrishnan (2006) and Karnik (2012) on software.

42. To begin with, the ratio of equity held by the government and Suzuki was 74:26. Suzuki had the option to increase its equity to 40 per cent after five years (on meeting the condition), which was exercised in 1987. The company was listed in stock exchanges in 1992 with equity shares at 50:50. Suzuki became a majority owner in 2002 with 54 per cent equity. In 2007, the government sold its equity in the market.

43. Statistics published by the Society of Indian Automobile Manufacturers (www. siamindia.com). Passenger vehicles produced and exported were 3.8 million and 0.8 million respectively, while the rest were commercial vehicles.

44. Statistics published by the National Association of Software and Services Companies (NASSCOM) and the Ministry of Commerce.

45. For this reason, the heterodox literature places the acquisition and development of technological capabilities centre-stage in the story of success at industrialization. See, for example, Pack and Westphal (1986), Lall (1987), Dahlman et al. (1987), Amsden (1989), Lall (1990), and Bell and Pavit (1993).

46. The literature on this subject is limited. For a perceptive analysis of learning, situated in a wider context, see Stiglitz and Greenwald (2014).

47. These figures are from the OECD online database on R&D expenditure. In 2015, the highest R&D–GDP ratio in the world was in Israel at 4.25 per cent, while averages for the OECD and for the EU-28 were 2.34 per cent and 1.96 per cent respectively.

Chapter 6

1. Williamson (1994) was perhaps the first to use the term 'Washington Consensus' to describe this set of policies, which were advocated by the World Bank and the IMF. These institutions were based in Washington, DC. And such policies were prescribed as conditions in their lending to developing countries.

2. See, for example, Amsden et al. (1994), Stiglitz (1998), and Easterly (2001).

3. For an exposition of this view, see Rodrik (2005), Taylor (2007), and Nayyar (2008d).

4. For a more detailed discussion, see Nayyar (2013).

5. There is an extensive literature on the subject. For a succinct analysis of market failures in development, see Stiglitz (1989). For a critical analysis of government failures in development, from the perspective of orthodox economics, see Krueger (1990). For a simple exposition of both sets of failures, see Bhaduri and Nayyar (1996).

6. For a discussion, see Nayyar (1997) and Lall (1997).

7. See, for instance, Polanyi (1944) who examined the complex interaction between state regulation and the growth of the market as an institution.

8. The argument developed here draws upon the earlier work of the author. See Nayyar (1997, 2003, and 2007). See also Bhaduri and Nayyar (1996).

9. There is an extensive literature on the subject. See, for example, Amsden (1989), Stiglitz (1989), Shapiro and Taylor (1990), Wade (1990), Bhaduri and Nayyar (1996), Chang (1996), and Amsden (2001).

10. The role of the state in the public provision of education in Asia is examined at length in Mundle (2019).
11. For a discussion in the context of agrarian transformations in Asia, see Vos (2019).
12. Cf. Amsden (2001) and Nayyar (2017).
13. For a more detailed discussion, see Lall (1990), Amsden (2001), Chang (2007), and Nayyar (2013).
14. See, for example, North (1990), North and Weingast (2000), and Besley and Persson (2011).
15. See Lall (1992, 1997) and Amsden (2001).
16. For an analysis of states that followed in the footsteps of Japan, see Amsden (1989) and Chang (1996) on South Korea, Wade (1990) on Taiwan, and Lim (1995) on Singapore.
17. This idea of the developmental state, in the smaller East Asian countries, was developed further by (Amsden, 1989), Wade (1990), Evans (1995), and Kohli (2004). It is discussed further in the companion volume by Wade (2019), and by Evans and Heller (2019) who also include China and Vietnam in the same category.
18. For an analytical narrative, see Khan (2019).
19. There is an extensive literature of economic reforms in Asia, which are also discussed in the country-studies and sub-region studies of the companion volume (Nayyar, 2019). See, for example, Lin (2019) on China, Montes (2019) on Malaysia, Philippines, Thailand, and Cambodia, Tarp (2019) on Vietnam, and Osmani (2019) on Bangladesh, Pakistan, and Sri Lanka. On India, there is a voluminous literature. See, for example, Nayyar (1996a), Bhaduri and Nayyar (1996), Nayyar (2017b) and Basu (2019).
20. For a discussion on why China introduced economic reforms in 1978, see Lin (2019).
21. This has now come to be recognized widely with the work of Amsden (1989), Wade (1990), Lim (1995), and Chang (1996), which provided systematic evidence based on careful research that contradicted the orthodox neoclassical interpretation of the East Asian Miracle.
22. This proposition is borne out by studies in the companion volume (Nayyar, 2019). See Evans and Heller (2019), Kozul-Wright and Poon (2019), Chang and Zach (2019), Vos (2019), Lin (2019), Wade (2019), Montes (2019), and Nayyar (2019b).
23. Cf. Amsden (2001) and Nayyar (2013).
24. For a detailed discussion on the importance of learning to unlearn from development, see Nayyar (2008d).
25. The influence of colonial legacies, nationalist movements and revolutionary struggles on the nature of governments and politics in post-colonial Asia is analysed in Duara (2019).
26. There are differences among authors of this school of thought in terms of emphasis, or nuances, but their thinking has much in common. See, for example, North and Weingast (2000), Besley and Persson (2011), and Acemoglu and Robinson (2012). For a lucid and critical survey of this literature, see Bardhan (2016).
27. Duara (2019), Wade (2019), and Khan (2019) stress the importance of the Japanese colonial legacy, and the implications of the early Cold War era, for the state and development in South Korea and Taiwan. See also Amsden (1989) on South Korea and Lim (1995) on Singapore.
28. The idea of embedded autonomy in East Asian developmental states is developed at length by Evans (1995). See also Kohli (2004) and Evans and Heller (2019).

29. It might be tempting to infer that sunset clauses were more difficult to implement in political democracies that were unable to cut the umbilical cord. However, authoritarian regimes fared no better in scaling-down or phasing-out infant industry protection. Developmental states were the exception.

30. This distinction is developed in Nayyar (1996a) and Bhaduri and Nayyar (1996).

31. The Liberal Democratic Party in Japan is an example of such intra-party consultations. So was the Congress Party in India in the era until 1977, when it ran the national government and ruled most of the states. In a very different context, it has been suggested that there are such consultations within the Communist Party in Vietnam that extend beyond leaders to members of the party (Tarp, 2019).

32. For a discussion on federalism and decentralization in considering the role of the state in development, see Bardhan (2016). There is a possibility that decentralization is prone to capture by local elites. Yet, its potential benefits are much greater.

33. The much-cited success stories of micro-credit in Bangladesh are Grameen Bank and BRAC. For an account of the former, see Yunus (2007).

34. The classic statements of liberalism are to be found in the writings of Adam Smith, Jean Jacques Rousseau and, in particular, John Stuart Mill. More recent contributions, representing different views, are Berlin (1969), Sen (1970), and Rawls (1971).

35. This literature began life in the era of classical political economy. The most important contributions were those of Smith (1776) and Mill (1848). See also Hayek (1960).

36. The principle that the will of the majority should always prevail in a democracy has been a matter of debate for a long time. John Stuart Mill, for example, argued that 'the government of the whole by a mere majority of the people', the principle of majority rule, is undemocratic. This was, then, developed into an argument for proportional representation (Mill, 1946).

37. This paragraph draws upon earlier work of the author (Nayyar, 2003).

38. For an extensive discussion on the importance of political democracy in market economies, see Sen (1999), who recognizes that markets have obvious instrumental virtues. And he goes on to suggest that, if the extension of a choice set is good, a market economy may also have some intrinsic virtues. For a survey of the literature on democracy and development, see Bardhan (2016).

39. See, for example, de Toqueville (1835). A novel by Gore Vidal, *1876*, Random House, New York, 1976, also provides a fascinating historical narrative of the United States 100 years after independence.

40. See Slater (2012) and Slater and Wong (2013).

41. It is also not clear how the future might unfold in South Korea, Taiwan, and Singapore, as these developmental states will have to evolve in a different incarnation in a changed context (Wade, 2019). In China and Vietnam, much will depend on how their political systems evolve in the future.

Chapter 7

1. For an analysis of the share of Asia in world GDP and its GDP per capita as a proportion of that in industrialized countries, during 1970–2016, see Chapter 2.

2. See Okhawa and Rosovsky (1973).

3. The central Gerschenkron idea was also formalized in several models. See, for example, Nelson and Phelps (1966), Gomulka (1970), and Findlay (1976).

4. See, for example, De Long (1988). There is, however, a study by Rodrik (2013) which finds unconditional convergence when the sample is restricted to the manufacturing sector.

5. There are empirical studies, for selected countries, which focus on this period to suggest that growth in GDP per capita is negatively related to the initial level of GDP per capita. See, for instance, Barro (1991) and Islam (1995). However, these results depend partly on the choice of countries and of periods.

6. Blanchard (2011) provides a detailed discussion.

7. See De Long (1988) and Pritchett (1997).

8. For average annual rates of growth of GDP per capita, during 1970–2016, see Table 3.2, and for the distinction between high (more than 5 per cent), medium (3.5 to 5 per cent) and low (less than 3.5 per cent) growth rates, see Table 3.3. For initial levels of GDP per capita, see Table 7.4.

9. For an analysis of changes in the distribution of Asia's GDP between each of it constituent sub-regions, and their respective GDP per capita as a proportion of that in industrialized countries, during 1970–2016, see Chapter 2.

10. The West Asian oil-exporting countries are Bahrain, Iran, Iraq, Kuwait, Oman, Qatar, Saudi Arabia, and United Arab Emirates. The LDCs are Afghanistan, Bangladesh, Bhutan, Cambodia, Laos, Myanmar, Nepal, and Timore-Leste. The group of other Asian developing countries includes Brunei Darussalam, Maldives, Mongolia, North Korea, Jordan, Lebanon, Palestine, and Syria. The Central Asian countries— Kazakhstan, Kyrgyzstan, Tajikistan, Turkmenistan, and Uzbekistan—are not included in this residual group because national accounts statistics for these countries are available starting only in 1992.

11. It is worth noting that Bangladesh is among the group of Least Developed Countries in Asia. However, it is also included in the Asian-14. If Bangladesh were excluded from the LDCs country-group, the divergence experienced by LDCs would be even greater.

12. In terms of GDP per capita, for 1970 and 2016 both, the richest country was Qatar (US$4,921 and US$59,324), while the poorest countries were Laos (US$44) and Afghanistan (US$584), respectively. See UN National Accounts Statistics.

13. In 1970, the richest and poorest countries were Qatar (PPP$32,573) and Laos (PPP$533) respectively. In 2016, the richest and poorest countries were Singapore (PPP$32,708) and Afghanistan (PPP$585). See GGDC Maddison online database.

14. The Theil index is a measure of inequality based on information theory. If all countries in a continent (or in the world) have exactly the same per capita income, the Theil coefficient would have a value of zero. If all the income in a continent (or in the world) accrues to just one country, the Theil coefficient would have a value of log N where N is the number of countries.

15. For an analysis, with supporting evidence, see Wan and Wang (2019).

16. For a discussion on trends over time in these sub-regions, see Wan and Wang (2019).

17. The Gini coefficient is a measure of inequality that is used by economists. It is best explained with a simple example. If all persons in an economy have the same, equal,

income, it has a value of zero. If all the income in an economy accrues to just one person, it has a value of 100.

18. See, for example, Bourguignon and Morrisson (2002), Cornia (2004), Milanovic (2005), Atkinson and Piketty (2010), Atkinson et al. (2010), Milanovic (2011), Palma (2011), Piketty (2014), Atkinson (2015), and Bourguignon (2015).

19. For a more detailed discussion, see Nayyar (2006 and 2013).

20. This is highlighted in the literature on endogenous growth theory and new economic geography. See, for example, Romer (1986) and Krugman and Venables (1995).

21. For an analysis, with supporting evidence, see Wan (2007) and Wan et al. (2007).

22. Between 1992–1993 and 2012–2013, GDP per capita in the agricultural sector as a proportion of GDP per capita in the non-agricultural sector dropped from 14 per cent to 10 per cent (calculated from national accounts statistics and population statistics of India). See also Nayyar (2019a).

23. On economic growth and regional inequality in India, see Cherodian and Thirlwall (2015) and Lolayekar and Mukhopadhyay (2017). On the widening gap between the north and the south, see Paul and Sridhar (2015).

24. The eleven richer states were Andhra Pradesh, Karnataka, Kerala, and Tamil Nadu from the south, Gujarat, Maharashtra and Goa from the west, and Delhi, Haryana, Himachal Pradesh, and Punjab from the north. The poorer states (the rest), included Assam, Bihar, Jammu and Kashmir, Madhya Pradesh, Odisha, Rajasthan, Uttar Pradesh, and West Bengal, plus the smaller states in the north-east and a few union territories. The states of Chhattisgarh, Telangana, and Uttarakhand, which were created after 1980–1981, are included in the group of their erstwhile state. For the richer states taken together, their per capita income, as compared to that of India was 114:100 in 1980–1981 and 147:100 in 2013–2014. For the poorer states, these ratios were 71:100 and 64:100 respectively. Per capita income refers to per capita GDP at factor cost in 2004–2005 prices. Author's calculations from EPWRF *India Time Series*, www.epwrfits.in, based on India's national accounts statistics.

25. For an analysis of regional economic inequality in Indonesia, during 1983–2004, see Akita et al. (2011), who show that as the share of mining has decreased the spatial distribution of manufacturing has played a more important role in shaping regional inequality, while the primacy of Jakarta with its urbanization economies, facilitated by globalization and trade, has determined much of overall regional inequality in Indonesia.

26. These are petroleum, coal, and palm oil from Kalimantan, copper, coffee, and cocoa from Sulawesi and agricultural commodities, including timber from Sumatra. But the poor on these islands do not benefit from booms in commodity prices.

27. For a detailed discussion, see Rohini Nayyar (1991).

28. On the complexity of international comparisons, see Atkinson and Bourguignon (2001) and Deaton (2005).

29. This issue is discussed at greater length in Nayyar (2013).

30. It might be worthwhile for the interested reader to compare World Bank estimates of poverty with another set of estimates of absolute poverty in Asia that adopt the same poverty lines, for the period 1965–2014, using data on household consumption from the Penn World Tables and statistics on inequality from the UNU-WIDER World

Income Inequality Database, for its constituent sub-regions and selected countries. See Wan and Wang (2019) in the companion volume.

31. The database is provided by 1600 surveys for thirty-six countries in Asia.

32. For a critical evaluation, see Chang (2010).

33. Using the same poverty lines of PPP$1.90 per day and PPP$3.20 per day, Wan and Wang (2019) show that there was a similar rapid decline in absolute poverty in Asia as well as these selected countries. However, the proportion of the population, and the number of the poor, below both poverty lines is significantly higher in the World Bank estimates than in the Wan and Wang estimates.

34. For a systematic analysis of the factors underlying the reduction of absolute poverty in Asia, in which rapid growth was the most important, see Wan and Wang (2019).

35. Sen (1999) develops a similar idea in a different context to argue that freedoms are both constitutive of, and instrumental in, development.

36. For an analysis of, and discussion on, why employment should be the primary objective of macroeconomic policies for development, see Nayyar (2014).

37. In fact, Part Seven of *Asian Drama*, Volume III, titled 'Population Quality' sought to focus on education and health (pp. 1533–1828).

38. For a systematic analysis of education and health in the context of economic development in Asia during the past fifty years, see Mundle (2019).

Chapter 8

1. For a lucid analysis of the European intrusion into Asia during this era, see Findlay (2019).

2. This era of globalization created winners and losers, unleashing conflicts and rivalries, which brought it to an end in 1914. See Hobsbawm (1987), Rodrik (1997), Williamson (2002), Nayyar (2006 and 2013).

3. On the intersections between imperialism and nationalism, and the dialectical relationship with decolonization, with a discussion on how it differed across regions and countries, see Duara (2004).

4. This hypothesis is developed, at some length, in a perceptive analysis of the Cold War as a historical period in Asia, and elsewhere, by Duara (2011).

5. Estimates of the number of people who were killed in this purge range from 0.5 to 2 million.

6. This argument, that the globalization of Islam has emerged a counter-hegemonic force outside the Western world, is developed by Duara (2011).

7. In addition, four other Asian countries—Thailand (12), Turkey (14), Indonesia (16) and Iran (18)—were among the top twenty producers of motor vehicles in the world.

8. For a discussion on manufacturing in Asia as a part of global production networks, see Baldwin and Forslid (2014).

9. See UNCTAD Foreign Direct Investment online database.

10. Calculated from UNCTAD Foreign Direct Investment online database US dollar values of stocks and flows.

11. See UNCTAD (2018, annex tables).

12. These thirteen firms, with their ranks, and industry where necessary, in brackets, were: China Shipping Corporation (COSCO, 2), China National Offshore Oil Corporation (CNOOC, 4), China MinMetals Corporation (CMC, 17), and China State Construction and Engineering Company (CSCES, 20) from China; Tata Motors (12) and Oil and Natural Gas Corporation (ONGC, 14) from India; Samsung Electronics (4) Hanwha Corporation (wholesale trade, 13) from South Korea; Broadcom Ltd (electronic components, 6) and Singapore Telecommunications (15) from Singapore; Hon Hai Precision Industries (electronic components, 3) from Taiwan; Petronas (oil, 8) from Malaysia; and C.K. Hutchison Holdings (retail trade, 1) from Hong Kong. See UNCTAD (2018, annex tables).

13. See UNCTAD (2018, annex tables). The four in the top fifty (economy and rank in brackets) were Hutchison (Hong Kong, 21), Hon Hai (Taiwan, 31), Samsung (South Korea, 39) and COSCO (China, 47).

14. For an analysis of different underlying factors, with examples, see Nayyar (2008a).

15. For a detailed discussion on possible economic implications, see Nayyar (2008a).

16. See, for example, Lecraw (1977), Lall (1983), Wells (1983), Dunning et al. (1998), Mathews (2006), UNCTAD (2006), Kumar (2007), and Nayyar (2008a).

17. For a macroeconomic analysis, see Nayyar (2003) and Ocampo and Stiglitz (2008).

18. For a discussion on the Asian financial crisis, see Palma (1998) Chang (2000), Jomo (2001), Chang et al. (2001), and Ocampo and Stiglitz (2008).

19. This slowdown is discussed at some length in Chapters 3 and 5. See also Chang and Zach (2019).

20. For a more detailed discussion, see Nayyar (2010 and 2011a).

21. This argument is developed elsewhere by the author (Nayyar, 2011a).

22. See United Nations (2006).

23. For a discussion, see Rowthorn (2008) and (Nayyar, 2010).

24. For an elaboration of this argument, see Nayyar (1996 and 2014). Trade-effects on employment are, however, also beginning to surface. In an analysis of US labour markets during 1980–2007, Autor et al. (2015) attempt to untangle the effects of import competition from China, and of technology, on employment. They find that the impact of trade on employment rises in the 2000s as imports accelerate, while the effect of technology appears to shift from automation of production activities in manufacturing towards computerization of information-processing tasks in manufacturing.

25. This proposition is validated by economic history (Krugman, 1994).

26. See Singh (2007), Rowthorn (2008), and Nayyar (2008b).

27. See Kaplinsky (2006), Singh (2007), Rowthorn (2008), and (Nayyar, 2008b).

28. For an evaluation, see Toye (2008), Cheru and Obi (2010), and Nayyar (2012a). In fact, Chinese over-lending is becoming a problem for some countries in Asia, Africa, and Latin America (Venezuela and, to some extent, Ecuador). Difficulties have also begun to surface with China's Belt-and-Road Initiative in many host countries.

29. The examples from South Korea are Hyundai and Kia in automobiles, with Samsung and LG in electronics, and Posco in steel. Indian firms in developing countries are in pharmaceuticals, steel, information technology, mobile phone networks, and financial services.

30. Kaplinsky and Morris (2008) analyse the negative implications of Asian manufactured exports on the prospects of industrialization in Sub-Saharan Africa. See also Nayyar (2010).
31. The increasing use of robots in China could also adversely affect labour-intensive manufactured exports from Africa. See Hallward-Driemeier and Nayyar (2017).
32. See Kaplinsky and Morris (2008), Jenkins et al. (2008) and Nayyar (2012a).
33. For a more detailed discussion, see Nayyar (2010 and 2012a).
34. The important issue of international migration is not touched upon in this chapter, nor is it addressed in this book, because of the space constraint. But it has been analysed by the author elsewhere in earlier work. See Nayyar (2002b, 2008c, and 2013).
35. There is an extensive literature on the subject of global governance. See, for example, United Nations (1995), Nayyar (2002), Nayyar (2002a), Stiglitz (2002), Held and McGrew (2002), ILO (2004), and Stiglitz (2006). On reform of the international trading system, see Nayyar (2002a) and Stiglitz and Charlton (2005). On reform of the international monetary system, see Ocampo (2017).
36. This range of issues is analysed, at some length, in Nayyar (2002a).
37. The figures cited in this paragraph on the number, or share, of developing countries from Asia (which does include the Pacific Islands), are obtained from the UN, WTO, IMF, and World Bank websites.
38. On the share of the top 1 and 0.1 per cent in national income, see Atkinson and Piketty (2010). On rising economic inequality, see Atkinson (2015) and Bourguignon (2015). On wealth inequality, see Piketty (2014). On social and political consequences of inequality, see Stiglitz (2012).

Chapter 9

1. Among the earliest was the frequently cited Goldman Sachs study (O'Neill et al. 2004) that attempted to project GDP and GDP per capita for Brazil, Russia, India, and China (BRICS) in 2050. There were more sophisticated exercises that used simple convergence equations to make projections about GDP and GDP per capita for China and India in PPP terms and at market exchange rates (Rowthorn, 2008).
2. Of these, in 2014, China—ranked second, Brazil—ranked seventh, and India—ranked ninth were among the top ten, whereas Italy—ranked eighth and Russia—ranked tenth lose their place to Indonesia and Mexico in 2050. See Economist Intelligence Unit (2015).
3. See OECD Stats, *Long-term Baseline Projections*, Economic Outlook Number 103, July 2018 (https://stats.oecd.org). These projections are available for thirty-five OECD member-countries (which include Japan, South Korea, and Turkey) and eleven non-OECD countries (which include China, India, Indonesia, and Saudi Arabia). Taken together, these forty-six countries account for more than 80 per cent of world GDP. Thus, the share of Asia would be correspondingly lower if such projections were available for all countries. Even so, these shares represent reasonable approximations.
4. For the shares of Asia, China, and India in world GDP, see Table 1.1. Of course, Maddison PPP statistics are not strictly comparable with OECD projections, although

both are similar insofar as their country-coverage is not complete. However, they do provide a plausible basis for a rough comparison over a period that spans more than two centuries.

5. These ratios have been calculated from the shares of Asia in world GDP and world population in Table 1.1.

6. UN population projections for the share of Asia (excluding Japan) in world population are 56.4 per cent in 2030, 54.7 per cent in 2040, and 52.7 per cent in 2050. See *World Population Prospects: 2017 Revision*, Population Division, United Nations. The OECD projections for the share of Asia (excluding Japan) in world GDP, cited above, are 49.7, 53.0, and 54.6 per cent respectively.

7. There are no reliable estimates of per capita income prior to 1820. In comparing per capita incomes of Asia and Western Europe *circa* 1750, Kuznets (1971) suggests that Asia was clearly lower, while Bairoch (1981) suggests that Asia was slightly higher. But differences in per capita income between different parts of the world were not large then (for a discussion, see Nayyar, 2013). Therefore, it is plausible to suggest that, around 1750, per capita incomes in Asia and the world were roughly the same.

8. For an analysis, with supporting evidence, see Hallward-Driemeier and Nayyar (2017).

9. See, for example, Stern (2007), Foley (2009), Heal (2009), Khor (2010), United Nations (2011), and Lucas and Semmler (2014).

10. See, for example, Kohli et al. (2011), Lee (2018), and Khanna (2019).

References

Abramovitz, Moses (1986). 'Catching Up, Forging Ahead and Falling Behind', *Journal of Economic History*, 46: 385–406.

Acemoglu, Daron and James Robinson (2012). *Why Nations Fail: The Origins of Power, Prosperity and Poverty*, New York: Crown Business, Random House.

Akita, T., P.A. Kurniawan, and S.M. Yata (2011). 'Structural Changes and Regional Income Inequality in Asia', *Asian Economic Journal*, 25: 55–77.

Akyuz, Y., Ha-Joon Chang and Richard Kozul-Wright (1998). 'New Perspectives on East Asian Development', *Journal of Development Studies*, 34: 4–36.

Allen, Robert C. (2009). *The British Industrial Revolution in Global Perspective*, Cambridge: Cambridge University Press.

Amsden, Alice H. (1989). *Asia's Next Giant: South Korea and Late Industrialization*, New York: Oxford University Press.

Amsden, Alice H. (2001). *The Rise of the Rest: Challenges to the West from Late Industrializing Economies*, New York: Oxford University Press.

Amsden, Alice H. (2007). *Escape from Empire: The Developing World's Journey through Heaven and Hell*, Cambridge, MA: The MIT Press.

Amsden, Alice H., J. Kochanowicz and Lance Taylor (eds.) (1994). *The Market Meets its Match: Restructuring the Economies of Eastern Europe*, Cambridge, MA: Harvard University Press.

Arrow, Kenneth J. (1962). 'The Economic Implications of Learning by Doing', *Review of Economic Studies*, 29: 155–73.

Asian Development Bank (ADB) (2013). 'Asia's Economic Transformation: Where to, How and How Far?', in *Key Indicators for Asia and the Pacific 2013*, Manila: Asian Development Bank.

Atkinson, A.B (1987). 'On the Measurement of Poverty', *Econometrica*, 55: 749–64.

Atkinson, A.B. (2015). *Inequality: What can be Done?* Cambridge, MA: Harvard University Press.

Atkinson, A.B. and Francois Bourguignon (2001). 'Poverty and Inclusion from a World Perspective', in Joseph E. Stiglitz and Pierre-Alain Muet (eds.) *Governance, Equity and Global Markets*, Oxford: Oxford University Press.

Atkinson, A.B. and T. Piketty (eds.) (2010). *Top Incomes: A Global Perspective*, Oxford: Oxford University Press.

Atkinson, A.B., T. Piketty and E. Saez (2010). 'Top Incomes in the Long Run of History', in A.B. Atkinson and T. Piketty (eds.) *Top Incomes: A Global Perspective*, Oxford: Oxford University Press.

Atkinson, A.B. and Joseph E. Stiglitz (1969). 'A New View of Technological Change', *Economic Journal*, 79: 573–8.

Autor, D., D. Dorn and G. Hanson (2015). 'Untangling Trade and Technology: Evidence from US Labour Markets', *Economic Journal*, 125: 621–46.

Bairoch, Paul (1981). 'The Main Trends in National Income Disparities since the Industrial Revolution', in P. Bairoch and M. Levy-Laboyer (eds.) *Disparities in Economic Development since the Industrial Revolution*, Basingstoke: Macmillan.

Bairoch, Paul (1982). International Industrialization Levels from 1750 to 1980, *Journal of European Economic History*, 11: 269–333.

Bairoch, Paul (1983). 'A Comparison of Levels of GDP per capita in Developed and Developing Countries: 1700–1980', *Journal of Economic History*, 43: 27–41.

Bairoch, Paul (1993). *Economics and World History: Myths and Paradoxes*, Chicago: Chicago University Press.

Balakrishnan, P. (2006). 'Benign Neglect or Strategic Intent: Contested Lineage of Indian Software Industry', *Economic and Political Weekly*, 41: 3865–72.

Baldwin, R. and R. Forslid (2014). 'The Development and Future of Factory Asia', in B. Ferranini and D. Hummels (eds.) *Asia and Global Production Networks*, Cheltenham: Edward Elgar.

Bardhan, Pranab (2016). 'State and Development: The Need for a Reappraisal of the Current Literature', *Journal of Economic Literature*, 54: 862–92.

Barro, R.J. (1991). 'Economic Growth in a Cross-Section of Countries', *Quarterly Journal of Economics*, 106: 407–43.

Basu, Kaushik (2019). 'India', in Deepak Nayyar (ed.) *Asian Transformations: An Inquiry into the Development of Nations*, Oxford: Oxford University Press.

Baumol, W.J. (1967). 'Macroeconomics of Unbalanced Growth: The Anatomy of Urban Crisis', *American Economic Review*, 57: 415–26.

Baumol, W.J. (1986). 'Productivity Growth, Convergence and Welfare: What the Long-Run Data Show', *American Economic Review*, 76: 1072–85.

Bell, M. and K. Pavitt (1993). 'Accumulating Technological Capability in Developing Countries', *Proceedings of the World Bank Annual Conference on Development Economics*, 1992: 257–81.

Berlin, I. (1969). *Four Essays on Liberty*, Oxford: Clarendon Press.

Bertola, Luis and Jose Antonio Ocampo (2012). *The Economic Development of Latin America since Independence*, Oxford: Oxford University Press.

Besley, T. and T. Persson (2011). *Pillars of Prosperity: The Political Economy of Development Clusters*, Princeton, NJ: Princeton University Press.

Bhaduri, Amit (1986). *Macroeconomics: The Dynamics of Commodity Production*, London: Macmillan.

Bhaduri, Amit (2019). 'Macroeconomic Perspective on Development', in Deepak Nayyar (ed.) *Asian Transformations: An Inquiry into the Development of Nations*, Oxford: Oxford University Press.

Bhaduri, Amit and Deepak Nayyar (1996). *The Intelligent Person's Guide to Liberalization*, New Delhi: Penguin Books.

Bhagwati, Jagdish (1978). *Foreign Trade Regimes and Economic Development: Anatomy and Consequences of Exchange Control*, Cambridge, MA: Ballinger.

Bhargava, R.C. (2013). *The Maruti Story*, New Delhi: Collins Business.

Blanchard, Olivier (2011). *Macroeconomics*, New York: Prentice Hall.

Booth, A. (1998). *The Indonesian Economy in the Nineteenth and Twentieth Centuries: A History of Missed Opportunities*, New York: St. Martin's Press.

Bourguignon, Francois (2015). *The Globalization of Inequality*, Princeton, NJ: Princeton University Press.

Bourguignon, Francois and Christian Morrisson (2002). 'The Size Distribution of Income among World Citizens: 1820–1992', *American Economic Review*, 92: 727–44.

Chang, Ha-Joon (1996). *The Political Economy of Industrial Policy*, London: Macmillan.

Chang, Ha-Joon (2000). 'The Hazard of Moral Hazard: Untangling the Asian Crisis', *World Development*, 28: 775–88.

Chang, Ha-Joon (2002). *Kicking Away the Ladder: Development Strategy in Historical Perspective*, London: Anthem Press.

Chang, Ha-Joon (2003). 'East Asian Industrialization', in H.J. Chang (ed.) *Rethinking Development Economics*, London: Anthem Press.

Chang, Ha-Joon (2007). *Institutional Change and Economic Development*, Tokyo: UNU Press and London: Anthem Press.

Chang, Ha-Joon (2010). *23 Things They Don't Tell You About Capitalism, Change and Economic Development*, New York: Bloomsbury.

Chang, Ha-Joon and Kiryl Zach (2019). 'Industrialization and Development', in Deepak Nayyar (ed.) *Asian Transformations: An Inquiry into the Development of Nations*, Oxford: Oxford University Press.

Chang, Ha-Joon, G. Palma, and D.H. Whittaker (eds.) (2001). *Financial Liberalization and the Asian Crisis*, Basingstoke and New York: Palgrave.

Chaudhuri, Sudip (2002). 'Economic Reforms and Industrial Structure in India', *Economic and Political Weekly*, 37: 155–62.

Chaudhuri, Sudip (2005). *The WTO and India's Pharmaceuticals Industry: Patent Protection, TRIPS, and Developing Countries*, New Delhi: Oxford University Press.

Chenery, Hollis B. (1960). 'Patterns of Industrial Growth', *American Economic Review*, 50: 624–54.

Cherodian, R. and A.P. Thirlwall (2015). 'Regional Disparities in Per Capita Income in India', *Journal of Post-Keynesian Economics*, 37: 384–407.

Cheru, Fantu and C. Obi (eds.) (2010). *The Rise of China and India in Africa*, London: Zed Books.

Clark, Colin (1940). *The Conditions of Economic Progress*, London: Macmillan.

Clark, Gregory (2009). 'Review of Angus Maddison, Contours of the World Economy: 1–2030 AD', *Journal of Economic History*, 69: 1156–61.

Clemens, Michael A. and Jeffrey G. Williamson (2002). 'Close Jaguar Open Dragon: Comparing Tariffs in Latin America and Asia before World War II', NBER Working Paper Number w9401, Cambridge, MA: National Bureau of Economic Research.

Coase, R.H. (1937). 'The Nature of the Firm', *Economica*, 4: 386–405.

Cornia, G. Andrea (ed.) (2004). *Inequality, Growth and Poverty in an Era of Liberalization and Globalization*, Oxford: Oxford University Press.

Coxhead, I. (ed.) (2015). *Routledge Handbook of Southeast Asian Economies*, London: Routledge.

Dahlman, Carl, B. Ross-Larson and Larry Westphal (1987). Managing Technological Development: Lessons from Newly Industrializing Countries, *World Development*, 15: 759–75.

Dasgupta, Sukti and Ajit Singh (2007). 'Manufacturing, Services and Premature De-industrialization in Developing Countries', in G. Mavrotas and A. Shorrocks (eds.) *Advancing Development: Core Themes in Global Economics*, London: Palgrave Macmillan.

Deaton, Angus (2005). 'Measuring Poverty in a Growing World (or Measuring Growth in a Poor World)', *Review of Economics and Statistics*, 87: 353–78.

De Long, Bradford (1988). 'Productivity Growth, Convergence and Welfare: Comment', *American Economic Review*, 78: 1138–54.

De Toqueville, A. (1835). *Democracy in America* (2002 edition), New York: Bantam Dell, Random House.

Diao, X., Margaret McMillan and Dani Rodrik (2017). 'The Recent Growth Boom in Developing Countries: A Structural Change Perspective', NBER Working Paper 23132, Cambridge, MA: National Bureau of Economic Research.

Diaz-Alejandro, Carlos F. (1975). 'Trade Policies and Economic Development', in P.B. Kenen (ed.) *International Trade and Finance: Frontiers for Research*, Cambridge: Cambridge University Press.

Duara, Prasenjit (2004). *Decolonization: Perspectives from Now and Then*, London: Routledge.

Duara, Prasenjit (2011). 'The Cold War as a Historical Period: An Interpretative Essay', *Journal of Global History*, 6: 457–80.

Duara, Prasenjit (2019). 'Nationalism and Development', in Deepak Nayyar (ed.) *Asian Transformations: An Inquiry into the Development of Nations*, Oxford: Oxford University Press.

Dunning, John H. (1983). 'Changes in the Level and Structure of International Production', in Mark Casson (ed.) *The Growth of International Business*, London: Allen and Unwin.

Dunning, J.H., R. van Hoesel and R. Narula (1998). 'Third World Multinationals Revisited: New Developments and Theoretical Implications', in J.H. Dunning (ed.) *Globalization, Trade and Foreign Direct Investment*, Oxford and New York: Pergamon Press.

Easterly, William (2001). *The Elusive Quest for Growth*, Cambridge, MA: The MIT Press.

Economist Intelligence Unit (2015). *Long-term Macroeconomic Forecasts: Key Trends to 2050*, London: The Economist.

Eichengreen, Barry and P. Gupta (2011). 'The Service Sector in India's Road to Economic Growth', NBER Working Paper 16757, Cambridge, MA: National Bureau of Economic Research.

Eichengreen, Barry and P. Gupta (2013). 'The Two Waves of Services Sector Growth', *Oxford Economic Papers*, 65: 96–123.

Evans, Peter (1995). *Embedded Autonomy: States and Industrial Transformation*, Princeton, NJ: Princeton University Press.

Evans, Peter and Patrick Heller (2019). 'The State and Development', in Deepak Nayyar (ed.) *Asian Transformations: An Inquiry into the Development of Nations*, Oxford: Oxford University Press.

Feenstra, R. (1998). 'Integration of Trade and Disintegration of Production in the Global Economy', *Journal of Economic Perspectives*, 12: 31–50.

Findlay, Ronald (1976). 'Relative Backwardness, Direct Foreign Investment and the Transfer of Technology: A Simple Dynamic Model', *Quarterly Journal of Economics*, 92: 1–16.

Findlay, Ronald (2019). 'Asia and the World Economy in Historical Perspective', in Deepak Nayyar (ed.) *Asian Transformations: An Inquiry into the Development of Nations*, Oxford: Oxford University Press.

Findlay, Ronald and Kevin H. O'Rourke (2007). *Power and Plenty: Trade, War and the World Economy in the Second Millennium*, Princeton, NJ: Princeton University Press.

Fisher, A.G.B (1935). *The Clash of Progress and Security*, London: Macmillan.

Foley, Duncan (2009). 'Economic Fundamentals of Global Warming', in J.M. Harris and N. R. Goodwin (eds.) *Twenty-First Century Macroeconomics: Responding to the Climate Challenge*, Cheltenham: Edward Elgar.

Foreman-Peck, James (1983). *A History of the World Economy: International Economic Relations since 1850*, Brighton: Wheatsheaf Books.

Friedman, Milton (1957). 'The Permanent Income Hypothesis', in M. Friedman (ed.) *A Theory of the Consumption Function*, Princeton, NJ: Princeton University Press.

Gereffi, G. (2018). *Global Value Chains and Development*, New York: Cambridge University Press.

Gereffi, G., J. Humphrey and Timothy Sturgeon (2005). 'The Governance of Global Value Chains', *Review of International Political Economy*, 12: 78–104.

Gerschenkron, Alexander (1962). *Economic Backwardness in Historical Perspective*, Cambridge, MA: Harvard University Press.

Gomulka, Stanislaw (1970). 'Extensions of the Golden Rule of Research of Phelps', *Review of Economic Studies*, 37: 73–93.

Griffith-Jones, Stephany and Jose Antonio Ocampo (eds.) (2018). *The Future of National Development Banks*, Oxford: Oxford University Press, 2018.

Grossman, G. and Helpman, E. (1991). *Innovation and Growth in the Global Economy*, Cambridge, MA: MIT Press.

Hallward-Driemeier, Mary and Gaurav Nayyar (2017). *Trouble in the Making: The Future of Manufacturing-Led Development*, Washington, DC: World Bank.

Hayek, F.A. (1960). *Constitution of Liberty*, London: Routledge and Kegan Paul.

Heal, Geoffrey (2009). 'The Economics of Climate Change: A Post-Stern Perspective', *Climate Change*, 96: 275–97.

Held, D. and A. McGrew (2002). *Governing Globalization: Power, Authority and Global Governance*, Cambridge: Polity Press.

Helleiner, Gerald K. (1973). 'Manufactured Exports from Less Developed Countries and Multinational Firms', *Economic Journal*, 83: 21–47.

Helleiner, Gerald K. (ed.) (1992). *Trade Policy, Industrialization and Development*, Oxford: Clarendon Press.

Hicks, John R. (1937). 'Mr. Keynes and the Classics', *Economica*, 5: 147–59.

Hill, H. (1996). *The Indonesian Economy Since 1966*, Cambridge: Cambridge University Press.

Hirschman, Albert O. (1958). *The Strategy of Economic Development*, New Haven, CT: Yale University Press.

Hobsbawm, Eric (1987). *The Age of Empire*, London: Weidenfeld and Nicolson.

Humphrey, J. and Hubert Schmitz (2002). 'How Does Insertion in Global Value Chains Affect Upgrading in Industrial Clusters', *Regional Studies*, 36: 1017–27.

ILO (2004). 'A Fair Globalization: Creating Opportunities for All', Report of the World Commission on the Social Dimension of Globalization, Geneva: ILO.

Islam, N. (1995). 'Growth Empirics: A Panel Data Approach', *Quarterly Journal of Economics*, 110: 1127–70.

Jenkins, R., E.D. Peters and M.M. Moreira (2008). 'The Impact of China on Latin America and the Caribbean', *World Development*, 36: 235–53.

Johnson, C. (1982). *MITI and the Japanese Miracle: The Growth of Industrial Policy, 1925–1975*, Stanford, CA: Stanford University Press.

Johnson, C. (1984). 'The Idea of Industrial Policy', in C. Johnson (ed.) *The Industrial Policy Debate*, San Francisco, CA: Institute of Contemporary Studies.

Jomo, K.S. (1993). *Industrializing Malaysia: Policy, Performance, Prospects*, London: Routledge.

Jomo, K.S. (ed.) (2001). *Malaysian Eclipse: Economic Crisis and Recovery*, London: Zed Books.

Jomo, K.S. (ed.) (2001a). *Southeast Asia's Industrialization: Industrial Policy, Capabilities, and Sustainability*, New York: Palgrave.

Kaldor, Nicholas (1962). 'Comment on Economic Implications of Learning by Doing', *Review of Economic Studies*, 29: 246–50.

Kaldor, Nicholas (1966). *Causes of Slow Rate of Growth in the United Kingdom*, Cambridge: Cambridge University Press.

Kanbur, Ravi (2019). 'Gunnar Myrdal and Asian Drama in Context', in Deepak Nayyar (ed.) *Asian Transformations: An Inquiry into the Development of Nations*, Oxford: Oxford University Press.

Kaplinsky, Raphael (2005). *Globalization, Poverty and Inequality*, Cambridge: Polity Press.

Kaplinsky, Raphael (ed.) (2006). 'Asian Drivers: Opportunities and Threats', *IDS Bulletin*, 37: 107–14.

Kaplinsky, Raphael and M. Morris (2008). 'Do the Asian Drivers Undermine Export-Oriented Industrialization in SSA?', *World Development*, 36: 254–73.

Karnik, K. (2012). *The Collection of Competitors: The Study of Nasscom and the IT Industry*, New Delhi: Harper Collins.

Kee, H.L. and H. Tang (2016). 'Domestic Value Added in Export: Theory and Firm Evidence from China', *American Economic Review*, 106: 1402–36.

Keynes, J.M. (1936). *The General Theory of Employment, Interest and Money*, London: Palgrave Macmillan.

Khan, Mushtaq H. (2019). 'Institutions and Development', in Deepak Nayyar (ed.) *Asian Transformations: An Inquiry into the Development of Nations*, Oxford: Oxford University Press.

Khanna, P. (2019). *The Future is Asian: Commerce, Culture and Conflict in the Twenty-first Century*, New York: Simon and Schuster.

Khor, Martin (2010). 'The Equitable Sharing of Atmospheric and Development Space', *Research Paper 33*, Geneva: South Centre.

Kohli, Atul (2004). *State-Directed Development, Political Power and Industrialization in the Global Periphery*, New York: Cambridge University Press.

Kohli, H.S., A. Sharma and A. Sood (2011). *Asia 2050: Realizing the Asian Century*, New Delhi: Sage Publications.

Kozul-Wright, Richard and Daniel Poon (2019). 'Economic Openness and Development', in Deepak Nayyar (ed.) *Asian Transformations: An Inquiry into the Development of Nations*, Oxford: Oxford University Press.

Kravis, I.B., A. Heston, and R. Summers (1978). *International Comparisons of Real Product and Purchasing Power*, Baltimore, MD: The Johns Hopkins University Press.

Krueger, A.O. (1978). *Foreign Trade Regimes and Economic Development: Liberalization Attempts and Consequences*, New York: National Bureau of Economic Research.

Krueger, A.O. (1990). 'Government Failures in Development', *Journal of Economic Perspectives*, 4: 9–23.

Krugman, Paul (1987). 'Is Free Trade Passe?', *Journal of Economic Perspectives*, 1: 131–44.

Krugman, Paul (1994). 'Competitiveness: A Dangerous Obsession', *Foreign Affairs*, 73: 28–44.

Krugman, P. and A.J. Venables (1995). 'Globalization and the Inequality of Nations', *Quarterly Journal of Economics*, 110: 857–80.

Kumar, Nagesh (2007). 'Emerging TNCs: Trends, Patterns and Determinants of Outward FDI by Indian Enterprises', *Transnational Corporations*, 16: 1–26.

Kuznets, Simon (1966). *Modern Economic Growth: Rate, Structure and Spread*, New Haven, CT: Yale University Press.

Kuznets, Simon (1971). *Economic Growth of Nations*, Cambridge, MA: Harvard University Press.

Lall, Sanjaya (1983). *The New Multinationals: The Spread of Third World Enterprises*, New York: John Wiley.

Lall, Sanjaya (1987). *Learning to Industrialize: The Acquisition of Technological Capability in India*, Basingstoke: Macmillan.

Lall, Sanjaya (1990). *Building Industrial Competitiveness in Developing Countries*, Paris: OECD Development Centre.

Lall, Sanjaya (1991). 'Explaining Industrial Success in the Developing World', in V. N. Balasubramanyam and S. Lall (eds.) *Current Issues in Development Economics*, London: Macmillan.

Lall, Sanjaya (1992). 'Technological Capabilities and Industrialization', *World Development*, 20: 165–86.

Lall, Sanjaya (1997). 'Imperfect Markets and Fallible Governments: The Role of the State in Industrial Development', in Deepak Nayyar (ed.) *Trade and Industrialization*, Delhi: Oxford University Press.

Lall, Sanjaya (1998). 'Thailand's Manufacturing Competitiveness: An Overview', in J. Witte and S. Koeberle (eds.) *Competitiveness and Sustainable Economic Recovery in Thailand*, Bangkok: National Economic and Social Development Board.

Lall, Sanjaya (2000). 'The Technological Structure and Performance of Developing Country Exports', *Oxford Development Studies*, 28: 337–69.

Landes, David S. (1969). *The Unbound Prometheus: Technological Change and Industrial Development in Western Europe since 1750 to the Present*, Cambridge: Cambridge University Press.

Landesmann, Michael (1992). 'Industrial Policies and Social Corporation', in J. Pekkarenin, M. Pohjola and R. Rowthorn (eds.) *Social Corporatism*, Oxford: Clarendon Press.

Lecraw, D.T. (1977). 'Direct Investment by Firms from Less Developed Countries', *Oxford Economic Papers*, 29: 442–57.

Lee, J.W. (2018). *Is this the Asian Century?* Singapore: World Scientific Publishers.

Lewis, W. Arthur (1954). 'Economic Development with Unlimited Supplies of Labour', *The Manchester School*, 22: 139–91.

Lewis, W. Arthur (1978). *The Evolution of the International Economic Order*, Princeton, NJ: Princeton University Press.

Lim, Linda (1995). 'Foreign Investment, The State and Industrial Policy in Singapore', in Howard Stein (ed.) *Asian Industrialization and Africa*, London: St Martin's Press.

Lin, Justin, Y. (2012). *Demystifying the Chinese Economy*, Cambridge: Cambridge University Press.

Lin, Justin Y. (2019). 'China', in Deepak Nayyar (ed.) *Asian Transformations: An Inquiry into the Development of Nations*, Oxford: Oxford University Press.

Lindbeck, A. (1981). 'Industrial Policy as an Issue of the Economic Environment', *The World Economy*, 4: 391–406.

Little, I.M.D.(1982). *Economic Development*, New York: Basic Books.

Little, I.M.D., T. Scitovsky and M. Scott (1970). *Industry and Trade in Some Developing Countries A Comparative Study*, London: Oxford University Press.

Lolayekar, A. and P. Mukhopadhyay (2017). 'Growth Convergence and Regional Inequality in India', *Journal of Quantitative Economics*, 15: 307–28.

Lucas, B. and W. Semmler (2014). *The Oxford Handbook of the Macroeconomics of Global Warming*, Oxford: Oxford University Press.

Lucas, Robert E. (2000). 'Some Macroeconomics for the 21st Century', *Journal of Economic Perspectives*, 14: 159–68.

Maddison, Angus (1983). 'A Comparison of Levels of GDP per capita in Developed and Developing Countries, 1700–1980', *Journal of Economic History*, 43: 27–41.

Maddison, Angus (1989). *The World Economy in the Twentieth Century*, Paris: OECD Development Centre.

Maddison, Angus (1995). *Monitoring the World Economy: 1820–1992*, Paris: OECD Development Centre.

Maddison, Angus (2001). *The World Economy: A Millennial Perspective*, Paris: OECD Development Centre.

Maddison, Angus (2003). *The World Economy: Historical Statistics*, Paris: OECD.

Maddison, Angus (2007). *Contours of the World Economy, 1–2030 AD: Essays in Macroeconomic History*, Oxford: Oxford University Press.

Mahmud, Wahiduddin (2001). *Adjustment and Beyond: The Reform Experience in South Asia*, Basingstoke: Palgrave.

Mathews, J.A. (2006). 'Dragon Multinationals: New Players in 21st Century Globalization', *Asian Pacific Journal of Management*, 23: 5–27.

McMillan, Margaret and Dani Rodrik (2011). 'Globalization, Structural Change and Productivity Growth', in M. Bacchetta and M. Jansen (eds.) *Making Globalization Socially Sustainable*, Geneva: ILO-WTO.

Milanovic, Branko (2005). *Worlds Apart: Measuring International and Global Inequality*, Princeton, NJ: Princeton University Press.

Milanovic, Branko (2011). *The Haves and the Have-Nots: A Brief and Idiosyncratic History of Global Inequality*, New York: Basic Books.

Milberg, Will and D. Winkler (2013). *Outsourcing Economics: Global Value Chains in Capitalist Development*, Cambridge: Cambridge University Press.

Mill, J.S. (1848). *Principles of Political Economy*, with an Introduction by W.J. Ashley, London: Longmans.

Mill, J.S. (1946). *On Liberty (1859)* and *Considerations on Representative Government (1861)*, with an Introduction by R.D. McCallum, Oxford: Oxford University Press.

Modigliani, F. (1970). 'The Life-Cycle Hypothesis and Inter-Country Differences in the Savings Ratio', in W. Eltis, M.F.G. Scott, and J.N. Wolfe (eds.) *Induction, Growth and Trade: Essays in Honour of Roy Harrod*, Oxford: Oxford University Press.

Modigliani, F. (1976). 'Life-Cycle, Individual Thrift and the Wealth of Nations', *American Economic Review*, 76: 297–313.

Montes, Manuel F. (2019). 'Southeast Asia', in Deepak Nayyar (ed.) *Asian Transformations: An Inquiry into the Development of Nations*, Oxford: Oxford University Press.

Morris, Ian (2010). *Why The West Rules—For Now: The Patterns of History and What They Reveal About the Future*, New York: Farrar, Straus and Giraux, Picador.

Mundle, Sudipto (2019). 'Education and Health', in Deepak Nayyar (ed.) *Asian Transformations: An Inquiry into the Development of Nations*, Oxford: Oxford University Press.

Myrdal, Gunnar (1968). *Asian Drama: An Inquiry into the Poverty of Nations, Volumes I, II, and III*, London: Allen Lane, The Penguin Press.

Nagaraj, R. (2003). 'Industrial Policy and Performance since 1980', *Economic and Political Weekly*, 38: 3707–15.

Nagaraj, R. (2017). 'Economic Reforms and Manufacturing Sector Growth', *Economic and Political Weekly*, 52: 61–8.

Nathan, Dev., M. Tiwari, and S. Sarkar (2018). *Development with Global Value Chains: Upgrading and Innovation in Asia*, New Delhi: Cambridge University Press.

Nayyar, Deepak (1978). 'Transnational Corporations and Manufactured Exports from Poor Countries', *Economic Journal*, 88: 59–84.

Nayyar, Deepak (1988). 'Political Economy of International Trade in Services', *Cambridge Journal of Economics*, 12: 279–98.

Nayyar, Deepak (1994). 'International Labour Movements, Trade Flows and Migration Transitions', *Asia and Pacific Migration Journal*, 3: 31–48.

Nayyar, Deepak (1996). 'Free Trade: Why, When and for Whom?', *Banca Nazionale del Lavoro, Quarterly Review*, 49: 330–50.

Nayyar, Deepak (1996a). *Economic Liberalization in India: Analytics, Experience and Lessons*, Calcutta: Orient Longman.

Nayyar, Deepak (1997). 'Themes in Trade and Industrialization', in Deepak Nayyar (ed.) *Trade and Industrialization*, Delhi: Oxford University Press.

Nayyar, Deepak (1998). 'International Trade and Factor Mobility: Economic Theory and Political Reality', in Deepak Nayyar (ed.) *Economics as Ideology and Experience*, London: Frank Cass.

Nayyar, Deepak (ed.) (2002). *Governing Globalization: Issues and Institutions*, Oxford: Oxford University Press.

Nayyar, Deepak (2002a). 'The Existing System and the Missing Institutions', in Deepak Nayyar (ed.) *Governing Globalization: Issues and Institutions*, Oxford: Oxford University Press.

Nayyar, Deepak (2002b). 'Cross-Border Movements of People', in Deepak Nayyar (ed.) *Governing Globalization: Issues and Institutions*, Oxford: Oxford University Press.

Nayyar, Deepak (2003). 'Globalization and Development Strategies', in John Toye (ed.) *Trade and Development: Directions for the Twenty-first Century*, Cheltenham: Edward Elgar.

Nayyar, Deepak (2006). 'Globalization, History and Development: A Tale of Two Centuries', *Cambridge Journal of Economics*, 30: 137–59.

Nayyar, Deepak (2006a). 'India's Unfinished Journey: Transforming Growth into Development', *Modern Asian Studies*, 40: 797–832.

Nayyar, Deepak (2007). 'Development through Globalization?', in George Mavrotas and Anthony Shorrocks (eds.) *Advancing Development: Core Themes in Global Economics*, Basingstoke: Palgrave Macmillan.

Nayyar, Deepak (2008). 'Macroeconomics of Structural Adjustment and Public Finances in Developing Countries: A Heterodox Perspective', *International Journal of Development Issues*, 7: 4–28.

Nayyar, Deepak (2008a). 'The Internationalization of Firms from India: Mergers and Acquisitions', *Oxford Development Studies*, 36: 111–31.

Nayyar, Deepak (2008b). 'The Rise of China and India: Implications for Developing Countries', in Philip Arestis and John Eatwell (eds.) *Issues in Economic Development and Globalization*, London: Palgrave Macmillan.

Nayyar, Deepak (2008c). 'International Migration and Economic Development', in Narcis Serra and Joseph Stiglitz (eds.) *The Washington Consensus Reconsidered: Towards a New Global Governance*, Oxford: Oxford University Press.

Nayyar, Deepak (2008d). 'Learning to Unlearn from Development', *Oxford Development Studies*, 36: 259–80.

Nayyar, Deepak (2010). 'China, India, Brazil and South Africa in the World Economy: Engines of Growth?', in Amelia Santos-Paulino and Guanghua Wan (eds.) *Southern Engines of Global Growth*, Oxford: Oxford University Press.

Nayyar, Deepak (2011). 'Economic Growth and Technological Capabilities in Emerging Economies', *Journal of Innovation and Development*, 1: 245–58.

Nayyar, Deepak (2011a), 'The Financial Crisis, the Great Recession and the Developing World', *Global Policy*, 2: 20–32.

Nayyar, Deepak (2012). 'Macroeconomics and Human Development', *Journal of Human Development and Capabilities*, 12: 7–30.

Nayyar, Deepak (2012a). 'The Emerging Asian Giants and Economic Development in Africa', in Akbar Noman, Kwesi Botchwey, Howard Stein and Joseph Stiglitz (eds.) *Good Governance and Growth in Africa*, Oxford: Oxford University Press.

Nayyar, Deepak (2013). *Catch Up: Developing Countries in the World Economy*, Oxford: Oxford University Press.

Nayyar, Deepak (2014). 'Why Employment Matters: Reviving Growth and Reducing Inequality', *International Labour Review*, 153: 351–64.

Nayyar, Deepak (2017). 'Development Banks and Industrial Finance', in Akbar Noman and Joseph Stiglitz (eds.) *Efficiency, Finance and Varieties of Industrial Policy*, New York: Columbia University Press.

Nayyar, Deepak (2017a). 'Can Catch Up Reduce Inequality?', in P.A.G. van Bergeijk and R. van der Hoeven (eds.) *Sustainable Development Goals and Income Inequality*, Cheltenham: Edward Elgar.

Nayyar, Deepak (2017b). 'Economic Liberalization in India: Then and Now', *Economic and Political Weekly*, 52: 41–8.

Nayyar, Deepak (ed.) (2019). *Asian Transformations: An Inquiry into the Development of Nations*, Oxford: Oxford University Press.

Nayyar, Deepak (2019a). 'India's Path to Structural Transformation: An Exception and the Rule', in Celistin Monga and Justin Lin (eds.) *The Oxford Handbook of Structural Transformation*, Oxford: Oxford University Press.

Nayyar, Deepak (2019b). 'Rethinking Asian Drama: Fifty Years Later', in Deepak Nayyar (ed.) *Asian Transformations: An Inquiry into the Development of Nations*, Oxford: Oxford University Press.

Nayyar, Gaurav (2012). *The Service Sector in India's Economic Development*, New York: Cambridge University Press.

Nayyar, Gaurav and M. Jose (2018). 'Developing Countries and Services in the New Industrial Paradigm', Policy Research Working Paper WPS 8659, Washington, DC: World Bank.

Nayyar, Gaurav, M. Cruz, and L. Zhu (2018). 'Does Premature Industrialization Matter? The Role of Manufacturing versus Services in Development', Policy Research Working Paper No: 8596, Washington, DC: World Bank.

Nayyar, Rohini (1991). *Rural Poverty in India: An Analysis of Inter-State Differences*, Delhi: Oxford University Press.

Nelson, Richard and Phelps, E.S. (1966). 'Investment in Humans, Technological Diffusion and Economic Growth', *American Economic Review*, 56: 69–75.

Nelson, Richard and S.J. Winter (1982). *An Evolutionary Theory of Economic Change*, Cambridge: Cambridge University Press.

Noman, Akbar and Joseph E. Stiglitz (eds.) (2017). *Efficiency, Finance and Varieties of Industrial Policy*, New York: Columbia University Press.

North, Douglass C. (1990). *Institutions, Institutional Change and Economic Performance*, Cambridge: Cambridge University Press.

North, Douglass C. and B.R. Weingast (2000). 'Institutional Analysis and Economic History', *Journal of Economic History*, 49: 803–32.

Ocampo, Jose Antonio (2017). *Resetting the International Monetary (Non) System*, Oxford: Oxford University Press.

Ocampo, Jose Antonio, and Joseph Stiglitz (eds.) (2008). *Capital Market Liberalization and Development*, Oxford: Oxford University Press.

Ocampo, Jose Antonio, Codrina Rada, and Lance Taylor (2009). *Economic Structure, Policy and Growth in Developing Countries*, New York: Columbia University Press.

Okhawa, K. and H. Rosovsky (1973). *Japanese Economic Growth: Trend Acceleration in the Twentieth Century*, Stanford, CA: Stanford University Press.

O'Neill, J., S. Lawson, D. Wilson, et al. (2004). *Growth and Development: The Path to 2050*, London: Goldman Sachs.

Önis, Z. and Senses, F. (2007). 'Global Dynamics, Domestic Coalitions and Reactive State: Major Policy Shifts in Post-War Turkish Economic Development', METU Economic Research Centre, Working Paper No. 20636.

Osmani, S.R. (2019). 'South Asia', in Deepak Nayyar (ed.) *Asian Transformations: An Inquiry into the Development of Nations*, Oxford: Oxford University Press.

Pack, H. and L. Westphal (1986). 'Industrial Strategy and Technological Change: Theory and Reality', *World Development*, 12: 87–128.

Palma, Gabriel (1998). 'Three and a Half Cycles of Mania, Panic and (Asymmetric) Crash: East Asian and Latin America Compared', *Cambridge Journal of Economics*, 22: 789–808.

Palma, Gabriel (2003). 'The Three Routes to Financial Crises', in Ha-Joon Chang (ed.) *Rethinking Development Economics*, London: Anthem Press.

Palma, Gabriel (2011). 'Homogeneous Middles vs. Heterogeneous Tails, and the End of the Inverted-U: It's All About the Share of the Rich', *Development and Change*, 42: 87–153.

Parthasarathi, Prasannan (2011). *Why Europe Grew Rich and Asia Did Not: Global Economic Divergence, 1600–1850*, Cambridge: Cambridge University Press.

Paul, S. and K.S. Sridhar (2015). *The Paradox of India's North–South Divide: Lessons from the States and Regions*, New Delhi: Sage.

Piketty, Thomas (2014). *Capital in the Twenty-First Century*, Cambridge, MA: Harvard University Press.

Pinder, J. (1982). 'Causes and Kinds of Industrial Policy', in J. Pinder (ed.) *National Industrial Strategies in the World Economy*, London: Croom Helm.

Pogge, Thomas and Sanjay Reddy (2010). 'How Not to Count the Poor', in Joseph E. Stiglitz, Sudhir Anand and Paul Segal (eds.) *Debates in the Measurement of Poverty*, Oxford: Oxford University Press.

Polanyi, Karl (1944). *The Great Transformation: The Political and Economic Origins of Our Times*, Boston, MA: Beacon Press.

Pomeranz, Kenneth (2000). *The Great Divergence: China, Europe and the Making of the Modern World Economy*, Princeton, NJ: Princeton University Press.

Pritchett, Lant (1997). 'Divergence, Big Time', *Journal of Economic Perspectives*, 11: 3–17.

Pritchett, Lant, Kunal Sen, and Eric Werker (eds.) (2018). *Deals and Development: The Political Dynamics of Growth Episodes*, Oxford: Oxford University Press.

Rakshit, Mihir (2007). 'Services-Led Growth: The Indian Experience', *Money and Finance*, ICRA Bulletin, 165–204.

Ranis, Gustav (ed.) (1992). *Taiwan: From Developing to Mature Economy*, Boulder, CO: Westview Press.

Rasiah, R. (1995). *Foreign Capital and Industrialization in Malaysia*, London: Macmillan.

Rawls, J. (1971). *A Theory of Justice*, Oxford: Clarendon Press.

Reich, R. (1982). 'Why the U.S. Needs an Industrial Policy', January–February, https://hbr.org/1982/01/why-the-us-needs-an-industrial-policy.

Reinert, E.S. (2007). *How Rich Countries Got Rich and Why Poor Countries Stay Poor*, New York: Carroll and Graf.

Robertson, D.H. (1938). 'The Future of International Trade', *Economic Journal*, 48: 1–14.

Rodrik, Dani (1997). *Has Globalization Gone Too Far?* Washington, DC: Institute for International Economics.

Rodrik, Dani (2005). 'Rethinking Growth Strategies', *WIDER Annual Lecture 8*, Helsinki: UNU-WIDER.

Rodrik, Dani (2013). 'Unconditional Convergence in Manufacturing', *Quarterly Journal of Economics*, 128: 165–204.

Rodrik, Dani (2016). 'Premature Deindustrialization', *Journal of Economic Growth*, 20: 1–33.

Romer, P. (1986). 'Increasing Returns and Long-Run Growth', *Journal of Political Economy*, 94: 1002–37.

Romer, P. (1990). 'Endogenous Technological Change', *Journal of Political Economy*, 98: S71–102.

Rosenberg, N. (1994). *Exploring the Black Box: Technology, Economics, and History*, Cambridge: Cambridge University Press.

Rowthorn, Robert E. (2008). 'The Renaissance of China and India', in Philip Arestis and John Eatwell (eds.) *Issues in Economic Development and Globalization: Essays in Honour of Ajit Singh*, London: Palgrave.

Rowthorn, Robert E. and John R. Wells (1987). *De-Industrialization and Foreign Trade*, Cambridge: Cambridge University Press.

Sala-i-Martin, X. (2006). 'The World Distribution of Income', *Quarterly Journal of Economics*, 121: 351–97.

Schultz, T.W. (1964). *Transforming Traditional Agriculture*, New Haven, CT: Yale University Press.

Schumpeter, Joseph A. (1942). 'The Creative Response in Economic History', *Journal of Economic History*, 7: 149–59.

Sen, Amartya (1970). *Collective Choice and Social Welfare*, Amsterdam: North-Holland.

Sen, Amartya (1976). 'Poverty: An Ordinal Approach to Measurement', *Econometrica*, 44: 219–31.

Sen, Amartya (1999). *Development as Freedom*, New York: Alfred E. Knopf.

Shapiro, Helen and Lance Taylor (1990). 'The State and Industrial Strategy', *World Development*, 18: 861–78.

Sharpston, M. (1975). 'International Subcontracting', *Oxford Economic Papers*, 27: 94–135.

Singh, Ajit (1995). 'The Causes of Fast Economic Growth in East Asia', *UNCTAD Review*, pp. 91–127.

Singh, Ajit (1998). 'Savings, Investment and the Corporation in the East Asian Miracle', *Journal of Development Studies*, 34: 112–37.

Singh, Ajit (2007). 'Globalization, Industrial Revolutions in India and China and Labour Markets in Advanced Countries: Implications for National and International Economic Policy', ILO Working Paper 81, Geneva: ILO.

Slater, D. (2012). 'Strong-State Democratization in Malaysia and Singapore', *Journal of Democracy*, 23: 19–33.

Slater, D. and J. Wong (2013). 'The Strength to Concede: Ruling Parties and Democratization in Developmental Asia', *Perspectives on Politics*, 11: 717–33.

Smith, Adam (1776). *The Wealth of Nations*, with an Introduction by Andrew Skinner (1970), Harmondsworth: Pelican Books.

Solow, Robert M. (1956). 'A Contribution to the Theory of Economic Growth', *Quarterly Journal of Economics*, 70: 65–94.

Stern, Nicholas (2007). *The Economics of Climate Change*, Cambridge: Cambridge University Press.

Stewart, Frances (2019), 'Gunnar Myrdal's Methodology and Approach Revisited', in Deepak Nayyar (ed.) *Asian Transformations: An Inquiry into the Development of Nations*, Oxford: Oxford University Press.

Stiglitz, Joseph E. (1989). 'On the Economic Role of the State', in A. Heertje (ed.) *The Economic Role of the State*, Oxford: Basil Blackwell.

Stiglitz, Joseph E. (1998). 'More Instruments and Broader Goals: Moving Toward the Post-Washington Consensus', *WIDER Annual Lecture 2*, Helsinki: UNU-WIDER.

Stiglitz, Joseph, E. (2002). *Globalization and its Discontents*, London: Penguin, Allen Lane.

Stiglitz, Joseph, E. (2006). *Making Globalization Work*, London: Penguin, Allen Lane.

Stiglitz, Joseph, E. (2012). *The Price of Inequality*, New York: W.W. Norton.

Stiglitz, Joseph, E. and A. Charlton (2005). *Fair Trade For All*, Oxford: Oxford University Press.

Stiglitz, Joseph, E. and Bruce Greenwald (2014). *Creating a Learning Society: A New Approach to Growth, Development and Social Progress*, New York: Columbia University Press.

Stiglitz, Joseph, E., Jose Antonio Ocampo, Shari Spiegel, Ricardo Ffrench-Davis and Deepak Nayyar. (2006). *Stability with Growth: Macroeconomics, Liberalization and Development*, Oxford: Oxford University Press.

Szirmai, A. (2012). 'Industrialization as an Engine of Growth in Developing Countries', *Structural Change and Economic Dynamics*, 23: 406–20.

Szirmai, A. and B. Verspagen (2015). 'Manufacturing and Economic Growth in Developing Countries: 1950–2005', *Structural Change and Economic Dynamics*, 34: 46–59.

Tarp, Finn (2019), 'Vietnam', in Deepak Nayyar (ed.) *Asian Transformations: An Inquiry into the Development of Nations*, Oxford: Oxford University Press.

Taylor, Lance (1983). *Structuralist Macroeconomics*, New York: Basic Books.

Taylor, Lance (2004). *Reconstructing Macroeconomics*, Cambridge, MA: Harvard University Press.

Taylor, Lance (2007). 'Development Questions for 25 Years', in G. Mavrotas and A. Shorrocks (eds.) *Advancing Development: Core Themes in Global Economics*, London: Palgrave.

Timmer, C. Peter (2014). *Managing Structural Transformation*, WIDER Annual Lecture 18, Helsinki: UNU-WIDER.

Timmer, C. Peter (2019). 'Indonesia', in Deepak Nayyar (ed.) *Asian Transformations: An Inquiry into the Development of Nations*, Oxford: Oxford University Press.

Tinker, H. (1974). *A New System of Slavery: The Export of Indian Labour Overseas: 1830–1920*, Oxford: Oxford University Press.

Toye, John (2008). 'China's Impact on Sub-Saharan Economic Development: Trade, Aid and Policies', in Philip Arestis and John Eatwell (eds.) *Issues in Economic Development and Globalization: Essays in Honour of Ajit Singh*, London: Palgrave.

UNCTAD (1994). *World Investment Report 1994*, Geneva: United Nations.

UNCTAD (2006). *World Investment Report: FDI from Developing Countries and Transition Economies: Implications for Development*, New York and Geneva: United Nations.

UNCTAD (2013). *World Investment Report 2013*, Geneva and New York: United Nations.

UNCTAD (2018). *World Investment Report 2018: Investment and New Industrial Policies*, New York and Geneva: United Nations.

United Nations (1995). *Our Global Neighbourhood: Report of the Commission on Global Governance*, New York: Oxford University Press.

United Nations (2006). *Diverging Growth and Development*, World Economic and Social Survey 2006, New York: United Nations.

United Nations (2011). *The Great Green Technological Transformation*, World Economic and Social Survey 2011, New York: United Nations.

van der Hoeven, Rolph (2019). 'Unemployment, Employment, and Development', in Deepak Nayyar (ed.) *Asian Transformations: An Inquiry into the Development of Nations*, Oxford: Oxford University Press.

Veblen, Thorstein (1915). *Imperial Germany and the Industrial Revolution*, London: Macmillan.

Vos, Rob (2019). 'Agricultural and Rural Transformations in Development', in Deepak Nayyar (ed.) *Asian Transformations: An Inquiry into the Development of Nations*, Oxford: Oxford University Press.

Wade, Robert (1990). *Governing the Market: Economic Theory and the Role of Government in East Asian Industrialization*, Princeton, NJ: Princeton University Press.

Wade, Robert H. (2019). 'East Asia', in Deepak Nayyar (ed.) *Asian Transformations: An Inquiry into the Development of Nations*, Oxford: Oxford University Press.

Wan, Guanghua (2007). 'Understanding Regional Poverty and Inequality Trends in China: Methodological and Empirical Issues', *Review of Income and Wealth*, 53: 28–34.

Wan Guanghua and Chen Wang (2019). 'Poverty and Inequality', in Deepak Nayyar (ed.) *Asian Transformations: An Inquiry into the Development of Nations*, Oxford: Oxford University Press.

Wan, Guanghua, M. Lu, and Z. Chen (2007). 'Globalization and Regional Inequality in China', *Review of Income and Wealth*, 53: 35–59.

Wells, L.T. (1983). *Third World Multinationals: The Rise of Foreign Investment from Developing Countries*, Cambridge, MA: The MIT Press.

Williamson, Jeffrey G. (1996). 'Globalization, Convergence and History', *Journal of Economic History*, 56: 277–306.

Williamson, Jeffrey G. (2002). *Winners and Losers over Two Centuries of Globalization*, WIDER Annual Lecture 6, Helsinki: UNU-WIDER.

Williamson, Jeffrey G. (2006). *Globalization and the Poor Periphery Before 1950*, Cambridge, MA: The MIT Press.

Williamson, John (1994). *The Political Economy of Policy Reform*, Washington, DC: Institute of International Economics.

World Bank (1993). *The East Asian Miracle*, New York: Oxford University Press.

World Bank (2008). *The Growth Report: Strategies for Sustained Growth and Inclusive Development*, Washington, DC: World Bank.

Young, Alwyn (1995). 'The Tyranny of Numbers: Confronting the Statistical Realities of the East Asian Growth Experience', *Quarterly Journal of Economics*, 110: 641–80.

Yunus, Muhamad (2007). *Banker to the Poor: Micro-Lending and the Battle against World Poverty*, New York: Public Affairs, Perseus Books.

Index

Note: Tables and figures are indicated by an italic '*t*' and '*f*' following the page number. References to tables and figures also cover the explanatory text in the Appendix. Endnotes are indicated by an 'n' following the page number. They are cited in the index where they contain information that is additional, rather than supplementary, to the content of the main text.

For the benefit of digital users, table entries that span two pages (e.g., 52–53) may, on occasion, appear on only one of those pages.